Environmental Risks and the Media

Edited by
Stuart Allan, Barbara Adam
and Cynthia Carter

London and New York

First published 2000 by Routledge
11 New Fetter Lane, London EC4P 4EE

Simultaneously published in the USA and Canada
by Routledge Inc
29 West 35th Street, New York, NY 10001

Routledge is an imprint of the Taylor & Francis Group

© 2000 Stuart Allan, Barbara Adam and Cynthia Carter
for selection and editorial matter. Individual chapters
© contributors

Typeset in Garamond by
J&L Composition Ltd, Filey, North Yorkshire
Printed and bound in Great Britain by Biddles Ltd., Guildford
and Kings Lynn

British Library Cataloguing in Publication Data
A catalogue record for this book is available
from the British Library

Library of Congress Cataloging in Publication Data
A catalogue record for this book has been requested

ISBN 0–415–21447–5 (Pbk)
ISBN 0–415–21446–7 (Hbk)

Environmental Risks and the Media

'The cr⸴ ew
categor; ng
about c⸴ of
occurrⁱ⸴ in
terms ⸴ ⸴an
genetic⸴ to

⸴ck

Envi⸴ ⸴ts
and hazar⸴ ⸴p-
ular concep⸴ ⸴r-
feres are bei⸴. to
think about en ge
– are becoming ⸴

Examining bot⸴ ⸴n-
sider the tensions b⸴ ⸴n-
ment. How do the ⸴ of
environmental risk? W⸴ ⸴o-
warriors' and 'green guer⸴ a's
emphasis on spectacular ϵ⸴ he
public tendency to overestⁱ⸴ g-
term ones?

LIBREX —

Contributors: Barbara Adam, Stuart Allan, Alison Anderson, Cynthia Carter, Simon Cottle, Justine Coupland, Nikolas Coupland, Peter Glasner, Anders Hansen, Susan Hutson, Mark Liddiard, M. Mark Miller, Suzanne Moffatt, Peter Phillimore, Bonnie Parnell Riechert, Elizabeth Stanko, Bronislaw Szerszynski, Mark Toogood, John Tulloch, Joost van Loon, C. Kay Weaver, Kris M. Wilson, Maggie Wykes.

With a foreword by **Ulrich Beck**

Stuart Allan is Senior Lecturer in Media and Cultural Studies at the University of the West of England, Bristol. **Barbara Adam** is Reader in the School of Social Science at Cardiff University. **Cynthia Carter** is Lecturer in the School of Journalism, Media and Cultural Studies at Cardiff University.

Contents

Figures and tables

Figures

Tables

Contributors

Barbara Adam is Professor in Social Theory at Cardiff University, Wales. She is the founder and consulting editor of *Time and Society* and during 1994–6 held an Economic and Social Research Council (ESRC) Fellowship under the Global Environmental Change Initiative. She has published extensively on the theme of social time. Her most recent monograph is *Timescapes of Modernity: The Environment and Invisible Hazards* (Routledge 1998).

Stuart Allan is Senior Lecturer in Cultural and Media Studies at the University of the West of England, Bristol. He has written widely on the media, and has a special interest in news coverage of nuclear issues. His books include *News Culture* (Open University Press 1999) and the co-edited collections *Theorizing Culture* (UCL Press/NYU Press 1995) and *News, Gender and Power* (Routledge 1998).

Alison Anderson is Senior Lecturer in Sociology at the University of Plymouth. Among her current research interests is the media coverage of the genetically modified food debate. She has written a number of articles on the media representation of environmental issues and a sole-authored book, *Media, Culture and the Environment* (UCL Press 1997).

Cynthia Carter is Lecturer in the School of Journalism, Media and Cultural Studies at Cardiff University, Wales. She is a co-editor of *News, Gender and Power* (Routledge 1998) and is joint editor (with Lisa McLaughlin) of the forthcoming journal *Feminist Media Studies* (Routledge). She is currently writing a book with C. Kay Weaver on violence and the media (Open University Press).

Simon Cottle is Professor of Media Communication at Bath Spa University College, England. He is the author of *TV News, Urban Conflict and the Inner City* (Leicester University Press 1993), *Television and Ethnic Minorities: Producers' Perspectives* (Avebury 1997) and, with A. Hansen, R. Negrine and C. Newbold, *Mass Communication Research Methods* (Macmillan 1998). He is currently editing *Ethnic Minorities and the Media: Changing Cultural Boundaries* (Open University Press 2000) and writing *Communicating Conflict*.

Justine Coupland is Senior Lecturer at the Centre for Language and Communication Reasearch, Cardiff University, Wales. She has published widely in the area of social interaction, particulary in relation to identity and relational issues, discourse and the lifespan, and talk in medical contexts. She is currently editing a book *Small Talk* (Addison Wesley Longman 2000)

Nikolas Coupland is Professor and Director of the Centre for Language and Communication Research, Cardiff University, Wales, and co-editor (with Allan Bell) of the *Journal of Sociolinguistics*. He has published eleven books on various aspects of sociolinguistics and discourse analysis. He is currently co-editing *The Discourse Reader* (Routledge 1999) and *Sociolinguistics and Social Theory* (Addison Wesley Longman 2000).

Peter Glasner is Research Professor in Sociology in the Centre for Social and Economic Research at the University of the West of England, Bristol. He has published widely in the area of the new genetic technologies, and is joint editor of *New Genetics and Society* (Carfax). His books include *The Politics of Uncertainty. Regulating rDNA Research in Britain* (co-author, Routledge and Kegan Paul 1986), *Genetic Imaginations: Ethical, Legal and Social Issues in Human Genome Research* (co-editor, Ashgate 1998) and *The Social Management of Genetic Engineering* (co-editor, Ashgate 1998).

Anders Hansen is MA Course Director and Lecturer in Mass Communications at the Centre for Mass Communication Research, University of Leicester. His main research interests focus on journalistic practices and media roles in relation to health and medicine, science, and environmental issues. He edited *The Mass Media and Environmental Issues* (Leicester University Press 1993) and is a co-author with S. Cottle, R. Negrine and C. Newbold of *Mass Communication Research Methods* (Macmillan 1998).

Susan Hutson is Senior Lecturer in Sociology at the University of Glamorgan, Wales. She has held research contracts with the ESRC, Rowntree Foundation, Welsh Office and other statutory and volunteer bodies. Her main publications include, with Mark Liddiard, *Youth Homelessness: The Construction of a Social Issue* (Macmillan 1994) and, with David Clapham, *Homelessness: Public Policies and Private Troubles* (Cassell 1999).

Mark Liddiard is Lecturer in Social Policy at the University of Kent, Canterbury. He undertook research on runaways and young homeless people in Wales over the period 1988–91, and has since written on the media coverage of youth homelessness and its impact on both public attitudes and policy making. His most recent work is focusing on museums and the heritage industy, and he is currently working on a book, *Making Histories of Sexuality and Gender* (Cassell).

M. Mark Miller is Professor in the School of Journalism at the University of Tennessee, Knoxville, USA. He is a former newspaper reporter and editor and holds a doctorate in communication from Michigan State University. His research interests include public opinion and policy formation processes, environmental risk communication and computerised content analysis, and quantitative research methodology.

Suzanne Moffatt is Lecturer in Social Epidemiology in the Department of Epidemiology and Public Health at the University of Newcastle upon Tyne. She did her PhD in sociolinguistics at Newcastle University on the development of English among young Punjabi-speaking children. Since then, her research has centred around studies of industrial pollution and health in north-east England. She has published a number of articles on public views about pollution and health risks.

Peter Phillimore lectures in Social Anthropology in the Department of Social Policy, Newcastle upon Tyne University. He has a PhD from Durham University, based on fieldwork in north India. Since then his research has been centred on north-east England, in studies of health inequalities, air pollution and health, and most recently the politics of environmental health. He is co-author (with Peter Townsend and Alastair Beattie) of *Health and Deprivation: Inequality and the North* (Routledge 1988) and a number of articles.

Bonnie Parnell Riechert, a former newspaper journalist, is co-ordinator of communications for the University of Tennessee Agricultural Experiment Station, USA. She holds a PhD in Communications from the University of Tennessee, and has research interests in environmental and political communication, risk communication, computer assisted content analysis and policy agenda building. She is an adjunct faculty member in the Marketing Department at the University of Tennessee.

Elizabeth Stanko is Professor of Criminology in the Law Department, Brunel University. She is the author of *Intimate Intrusions* (Routledge 1985), *Everyday Violence* (Pandora 1990) and numerous articles exploring gender, safety and fear of crime. She is currently the Director of the ESRC's Programme on Violence.

Bronislaw Szerszynski is Lecturer in Environment and Culture at the Centre for the Study of Environmental Change (CSEC), Lancaster University, England. His research interests include risk, environment, social movements, religion and the mass media. He is co-editor of *Risk, Environment and Modernity* (Sage 1996).

Mark Toogood is Research Fellow at CSEC, where he also lectures on the MA in Environment, Society and Culture. His research interests have been broadly concerned with questions of nature/culture and ecological representation. He has written on ecology and national identity, on the phenome-nology of abstract art, and is currently writing an archaeology of ecological knowledge and institutions and their place in western cultural history.

John Tulloch is Professor of Media Communication at Cardiff Universtiy, Wales. Previously he was Professor of Cultural Studies, Director of the Centre for Cultural Risk Research, and Director of Research in the Arts Faculty, Charles Sturt University, New South Wales, Australia. He has pub-lished eleven books in the area of film, television and literary theory. His recent books include *Television, Risk and AIDS* (with Deborah Lupton, Allen and Unwin 1997); currently he is writing *Performing Culture* (Sage) and *Watching Television Audiences* (Edward Arnold).

Joost van Loon obtained a PhD in Sociology from Lancaster University in 1996. He now works as a Senior Lecturer in Social Theory at the Nottingham Trent University and is closely associated with the Theory, Culture and Society Centre, He has published extensively on issues of risk, technology and culture. He is currently working on epidemiology and newly emerging viruses.

C. Kay Weaver lectures in the Department of Management Communication at the University of Waikato, New Zealand. She is co-author of *Cameras in the Commons* (Hansard Society 1990) and *Women Viewing Violence* (British Film Institute 1992). She is an associate editor of the forthcoming journal *Feminist Media Studies*, and is currently working on a book on violence and the media with Cynthia Carter (Open University Press).

Kris M. Wilson is Assistant Professor of Journalism at the University of Texas at Austin, USA. He spent nearly a decade in television news as a reporter, producer, anchor and news director. He earned an MA in environmental journalism, and a doctorate in geography, specialising in the science of cli-mate change and communicating science through the media. In this posi-tion as both scientist and journalist, his research focuses on strengthening science journalism.

Maggie Wykes is Lecturer in the Department of Journalism Studies, University of Sheffield. She teaches media history, products and analysis. Her research interests are discourse, gender and deviance in print, broadcast and recently Net media. She is currently writing a book on news, crime and culture (Pluto Press).

Foreword

Ulrich Beck

Over the course of the centuries, humanity has learnt to deal with self-generated uncertainties. The crucial category here is that of risk. This concept refers to those practices and methods by which the future consequences of individual and institutional decisions are controlled in the present. In this respect, risks are a form of institutionalised reflexivity and they are fundamentally ambivalent. On the one hand, they give expression to the adventure principle; on the other, risks raise the question as to who will take responsibility for the consequences, and whether or not the measures and methods of precaution and of controlling manufacuted uncertainty in the dimensions of space, time, money, knowledge/non-knowledge and so forth are adequate and appropriate.

The category of risk becomes central at the point where the apparent boundaries of nature and tradition dissolve into decisions. Both in terms of conceptual history as well as in their triumphal march through the institutions, risks are a modern phenomenon. They are an invention of civilisation which is being ever further perfected (using probability theory and mathematical methods, for example) as modern society and its balance between uncertainty and self-control develops. At the same time, this invention is being applied to more and more fields of action – technology, the labour market, health, ecology, biography.

The crucial point about the risk society now, however, is that modern society has brought forth a new category of risk in the second half of the twentieth century: namely, risks which cannot be controlled. We are no longer talking about comets crashing to earth or accidents with a greater or lesser degree of probability of occurring. Rather, what is at issue are rapid advances of modernisation that are *successful* in terms of their degree of impact and range of consequences – the triumphs of human genetics, for example – but which generate radical uncertainty because no one is able to assess their consequences.

These risks, involving low probability of occurrence and unforeseeable consequences, open up a gulf between knowledge and decision, between the chain of rational arguments and the course of action which attemps to resolve the dilemma. This is where the moral and political dynamic of the risk society emerges. Although no one, with good reason, can say what the consequences of a decision will be and how these are to be evaluated – in other words, the situation is undecidable as far as knowledge is concerned – we have to make decisions. In some ways, this situation already applies to the First Modernity. In the case of the Second Modernity the situation is radically new, inasmuch as the consequences of decisions disable the institutionalised rationality of risk control in both spatial and temporal respects. This may be because no one can demonstrate the systematic knowledge based on experience that is needed for assessing the consequences, or it may also be that the decision concerns human-ity's survival. Thus, in the Second Modernity, in 'risk modernity', we have to make decisions – for example, regarding human genetics, cloning or geneti-cally modified food – which will affect our survival, without an adequate foun-dation of knowledge. Contemporary society thus finds itself in a risk trap. When deciding for (or against) a particular course of action, it can no longer rely upon a rational assessment of the risk potential. Advertising campaigns on the part of industry, goverment experts, ethics committees; all that any of these can do is paper over this radical openness and uncertainty. But they cannot overcome it.

The typical script which institutions in the risk society follow when dealing with this situation of making crucial decisions under conditions of lack of knowledge goes according to the maxim: cover it up and engage in self-deception. First, risks are usuallly uncovered not within, but *outside* the insti-tutions that bear responsibility in the economy, science and politics. Second, the mass media play a decisive role in this, with their portrayal of conflicting definitions of risk, that is, their representation, or construction, of risks and uncertainties. As the uncovering of risks and uncertainties usually involves complex arguments, and because risks are not perceptible by the senses in every-day life, the public eye of the media takes on a key significance in the risk soci-ety. Third, when risks have been made public, the institutions that bear responsibility react with a *politics of denial*. Fourth, this is then complemented by so-called salami tactics: admit only to what has already been made known and is irrevocable. Fifth, there is ultimately always just one explanation: *human error*. This chess move, usually concealed under the guise of 'operational error', deflects questions about the fundamental gap between decision and knowledge and about systemic errors. Sixth, time-consuming studies are subsequently undertaken which place their hopes in the rapid fall-off of media interest in risk conflicts, with good reason, for even in the case of potential or current catas-trophes, the time-span involved in maintaining the public reporting of risks in the media amount to only a few days or a few weeks. Seventh, the result is always the same: *no one is really made liable*. But the enormous costs, loss of cred-ibility, and threat to material existence associated with the public debate about risks – because whole markets and industrial sectors collapse (think of the BSE crisis) – affect, finally, the weak especially (in the case of BSE, farmers) and the taxpayer.

This book underlines the key significance of the mass media in the risk soci-ety. This is something I have addressed again and again, if only with bold theories – as Simon Cottle (1998a), as well as the editors in their introduction to this volume, have so convincingly shown. This is clearly not sufficient given the significance of the subject and is to be attributed to my limitations alone. For the risk society can be grasped theoretically, empirically and politically only if one starts from the premise that it is always also a knowledge, media and information society at the same time – or, often enough as well, a society of non-knowledge and disinformation. These, then, are some of the issues which undergo further elucidation in the contributions to this timely and important book.

translated by Kathleen Cross

Acknowledgements

We are delighted to acknowledge a number of people who have made important contributions to the realisation of this project.

Our first word of appreciation goes to our contributors, all of whom have been a pleasure to work with over the past year or so. While putting together an edited collection is always hard work, it is also great fun sharing ideas with people who have similar research interests.

Several of the chapters presented here found their initial basis at the Media, Risk and the Environment symposium held in Cardiff in 1997. A special thank you to two people who helped us to co-organise this event, Louise Godley and Ian Welsh. We are similarly pleased to acknowledge the role of the Tom Hopkinson Centre for Media Research (Cardiff University), the School of Social Science (Cardiff University), and the School of Humanities and Social Sciences (University of Glamorgan) in providing institutional support. A word of gratitude, as well, to both the Higher Education Funding Council of Wales (HEFCW) and the British Council in Wales for additional financial assistance. And, of course, an appreciative thank you to everyone who participated in the symposium's debates.

This book began its life with UCL Press, and we would like to thank Caroline Wintersgill and her team for commissioning it for publication. At Routledge, we are grateful to Rebecca Barden, Christopher Cudmore and colleagues for their enthusiastic commitment to seeing this project through to a successful conclusion.

Stuart Allan, Barbara Adam and Cynthia Carter

Introduction

The media politics of environmental risk

Stuart Allan, Barbara Adam and Cynthia Carter

> The environment story is one of the most complicated and pressing stories of our time. It involves abstract and probabilistic science, labyrinthine laws, grandstanding politicians, speculative economics, and the complex interplay of individuals and societies. Most agree that it concerns the very future of life as we know it on the planet. Perhaps more than most stories, it needs careful, longer-than-bite-sized reporting and analysis, now.
>
> (Stocking and Leonard 1990: 42)

> ... there is a big difference between those who take risks and those who are victimised by risks others take.
>
> (Beck 1998a: 10)

In choosing the title *Environmental Risks and the Media* for this book, we wanted to signal from the outset our commitment to establishing a fresh analytical basis for rethinking some of the more familiar assumptions associated with research in this area of inquiry. We recognise, of course, that each of the component terms conjoined by our title, namely 'environment', 'risk' and 'media', exists in a state of conceptual tension. That is to say, the boundaries which delimit their respective meanings are the subject of intense discursive conflict, and as such are constantly being drawn and redrawn in relation to the social hierarchies of time, space and place.

It is our sense that academic debates over precisely what constitutes 'the environment' have never been more openly contested than they are today. Configurations of the environment as a purely natural realm, one existing outside of the social dynamics of human activity, are increasingly being subjected to challenges from across the breadth of the humanities and social sciences. Recurrently called into question is the very definition of the 'natural' as being somehow reducible to the observable 'raw materials' of the world. Indeed, at a time when growing numbers of public commentators are engaged in disputes over the potential dissolution of 'the actual' into 'the virtual', the language of environmentalism – in the eyes of many researchers – is fast becoming anachronistic in its appeal to 'nature' to sustain its convictions. A range of contradictory characteristics typically projected upon 'nature' are aptly described by Soper (1995) in her book *What is Nature?*, where she observes that in popular imagery:

> Nature is both machine and organism, passive matter and vitalist agency. It is represented as both savage and noble, polluted and wholesome, lewd and innocent, carnal and pure, chaotic and ordered. Conceived as a feminine principle, nature is equally lover, mother and virago: a source of sensual delight, a nurturing bosom, a site of treacherous and vindictive forces bent on retribution for her human violation. Sublime and pastoral, indifferent to human purposes and willing servant of them, nature awes as she consoles, strikes terror as she pacifies, presents herself as both the best of friends and the worst of foes.
>
> (Soper 1995: 71)

Of particular significance for our purposes here, however, are the ways in which these ideological tensions around 'nature' are negotiated across the field of the mass media. Nature, as Alexander Wilson (1992: 12) writes, 'is filmed, pictured, written, and talked about everywhere', leading him to maintain that there are in fact many different natures being re-articulated via media discourses. Here, though, he makes the crucial point that the current crisis around 'the natural' is not only 'out there in the environment'. Rather, he argues, it is also a 'crisis of culture', one which 'suffuses our households, our conversations, our economies' (A. Wilson 1992: 12).

This insight throws into sharp relief a series of questions about the extent to which media representations of nature serve to reaffirm as 'common-sense' references to 'the environment' as a stable, totalised entity against which 'the human' is to be measured. Accordingly, we begin by highlighting the emergence and ensuing development of a number of analytical approaches committed to examining how the mass media portray the environment as a social problem. In appraising the formative influence of these early investigations, we attempt to show that much of this work succeeded in securing a range of vital insights into how media accounts construct certain preferred definitions of environmental realities.[1] The broad lines of this discussion are then developed further through an assessment of the conceptual turn to issues of 'risk', especially as envisaged in the work of Ulrich Beck. This focus on risk, we suggest, has helped to initiate an important break from these earlier approaches in several decisive ways. Identified as being particularly consequential, for example, are the 'relations of definition' underpinning media discourses which condition what can and should be said about environmental risks, threats and hazards by 'experts' and 'counter-experts', as well as by members of the 'lay public'. Following this sketch of several of the more prominent contours of the research terrain, then, the last section of this chapter echoes the larger structure of the book by offering an overview of the respective contributions.

Media discourses about 'the environment'

It is something of a truism for many researchers interested in the circumstances surrounding the emergence of public discourses of 'the environment' in places such as Europe and North America that everything changed in 1969. That was the year startling images of planet Earth were relayed from the surface of the moon, the impact of which – many have maintained since – fundamentally recast the environmental perceptions of what was for a fleeting instant a near-global citizenry.[2]

These images evidently contributed to what may be appropriately described as an 'epistemological break' at the level of media representation; never again would claims about the relative effects of human societies on 'the natural world' fit quite so comfortably into 'traditional' categories. 'By conquering the frontier of outer space,' Schoenfeld *et al.* (1979: 43) write of the response in the USA, 'Americans seemingly discovered another frontier, the search for a state of harmony between humankind and the only earth we have; and reporters and editors watched – and responded.' The enhancement of media attention directed to conservation issues around this time (*Time* magazine, for example, introduced an 'Environment' section in its 1 August 1969 edition) was also attributable to other events, such as the disastrous break-up of a super-tanker off the coast of Cornwall, south-west England, in 1967 and, in the USA, the 1969 Santa Barbara Channel Union Oil leak. These events engendered sustained debate among interested claims-makers, such as government agencies, industry spokespeople, scientists, citizen action pressure groups, consumer organisations and academics, thereby ensuring that a range of what were often acrimonious disputes featured prominently on the news agenda. That said, however, it quickly became apparent to many reporters seeking to translate the complex language routinely employed by these claims-makers that it would be necessary, in turn, to develop a distinct vocabulary to interpret the environment as 'news' for the benefit of audiences anxious to understand the long-term implications of these events for their own lives.

Critical examinations of the pertinent types of news coverage produced during this period indicate that the preferred terms of 'conservation' were gradually being supplanted by new, or at least sharply redefined, ecological concepts explicitly associated with 'the environment' as a social problem (A. Anderson 1997; Hannigan 1995; Lowe and Morrison 1984; Neuzil and Kovarik 1996; Schoenfeld 1980). Emergent forms of environmental discourse typically stretched notions of conservation beyond the earlier emphasis on natural resources so as to encompass the human species as an organism in need of protection in the face of possible extinction. This shift in the rhetorical strategies of claims-makers posed an acute challenge to the seemingly 'commonsensical' division between 'nature' and 'humanity' that had been a recurrent – if largely tacit – feature of news reportage and, as a result, much public debate. More specifically, it was becoming increasingly evident from one news organisation to the next that to the extent a 'classic environmental story' could be identified, it was in practice more accurately described – to quote one reporter – as a 'business-medical-scientific-economic-political-social-pollution story' (cited in Schoenfeld *et al.* 1979: 52). This growing awareness that 'the environment' defied institutional routinisation *vis-à-vis* existing news beats (in contrast with, for example, the courts, city hall, health, education, sports, finance and so forth) led to the invention and widespread implementation of 'environment beats' in order to generate the right types of 'newsworthy' items.

The ensuing 'information explosion' about 'the environment' underpinned its transformation into a 'hot news story'. In the USA, according to Sachsman (1976), events like the Santa Barbara oil spill had 'caused print and broadcast editors to begin taking seriously their own local problems of air and water pollution, overcrowding, and the loss of natural resources' (D.B. Sachsman 1976: 54; see also Molotch and Lester 1974). Significantly, however, the steady rise in environmental awareness during the 1970s in countries like those in North America (Earth Day 1970, for instance, received extended news coverage in the USA) and Europe sparked a corresponding intensification of efforts among corporate public relations agencies. If throughout the 1960s the consequences of industrial pollution, to take one example, had been largely accepted by both journalists and members of the public as simply an inevitable price to be paid for enjoying the benefits of modern society, this was largely attributable to the concerted promotional campaigns mobilised by public relations (PR) practitioners (see also Beder 1997; A. Wilson 1992).[3] At stake, in their view, was the need to regulate the parameters of public debate to advantage, an objective which became increasingly difficult in the 1970s as journalists began to look further afield for their sources of information. Also during this period, and in conjunction with the ascent of environmental beats or bureaux, news organisations were recognising the need to hire specialist personnel who were better able to critically appraise the scientific and technical claims being made by special interest groups.

Nevertheless, according to many commentators at the time, as the mid-1970s approached there occurred a marked decline in the level of public interest in environmental issues. Investigating the situation in Canada, for example, Parlour and Schatzow (1978) contend that an explanation for this decline can be linked to the following factors:

1   The decline in interest was initiated by the mass media through the sudden displacement of environmental issues by other issues, such as energy, unemployment and inflation.
2   The surficial impact of mass media coverage of environmental issues on public attitudes and behaviour led to a very rapid decline in public concern once the reinforcing and sustaining influence of the mass media disappeared.
3   The institutionalisation of concern within the political system after 1970

undoubtedly led to the feeling that the problems were being 'solved'; not an unexpected response given the ease with which the public were able to justify the transfer of responsibility for these problems from the individual to the institutional level.

(Parlour and Schatzow 1978: 15)

Reaffirmed throughout their study of the media's environmental coverage from 1960 up to 1972 (the year of the UN Conference on the Environment) is the assumption that public awareness and concern for environmental issues correlates with the relative amount of coverage being generated by the news organisations. Moreover, media attention is held to be a key determinant in the legitimisation of the environment as a major political issue, one in need of continuous monitoring by the state at a structural level (in the USA, for example, ecological concerns were institutionalised in government agencies such as the Environmental Protection Agency and the Council on Environmental Quality in the 1970s, both of which were regularly treated by journalists as authoritative news sources). Perhaps most significant of all, however, is Parlour and Schatzow's (1978) conviction that the institutionalisation of environmental concerns by the state virtually ensures that they will be ultimately rendered subordinate to the priorities of economic growth and performance, and that news organisations are inclined to do very little to challenge this outcome (see also A. Anderson 1997; Chapman *et al*; 1997, A. Hansen 1993b; Howenstine 1987; Linné 1991).

A range of critical analyses of how the media routinely engaged with different environmental issues, events and crises during the latter part of the 1970s and into the 1980s provide further evidence to support this line of argument. Evidently, it is only by the start of the 1980s that something resembling an 'ecological conscience' finally began to penetrate the typical newsroom in countries such Britain and the USA in a serious way. Drawing on data collected via his interviews with environmental reporters in the USA, Schoenfeld (1980) cites the words of one of them which neatly pinpoints a crucial question at the heart of environmental journalism at the time:

> Do you give readers what they should know or something they will read? The challenge of the environmental beat is to convey a sense of immediacy and pertinence, usually by telling the story in human terms . . . I try to find the human element while writing about an increasingly complex world of bewildering facts and figures. Every beat needs that, but this beat demands it.
>
> (cited in Schoenfeld 1980: 462)

This prioritisation of the 'human element', and with it the corresponding emphasis on the *extraordinary* at the expense of the *ordinary*, decisively shapes what gets reported and how. A focal point for several research inquiries during this period concerned the ways in which news coverage typically places a priority on spectacular (and, in the case of television, visually sensational) events. Reporting about natural disasters, such as earthquakes, hurricanes, drought or floods (see W. C. Adams 1986; Gaddy and Tanjong 1986; Krug 1993; Major and Atwood 1997; Simon 1997; Singer and Endreny 1987; Sood et al. 1987), is shown to be consistently preferred by news organisations over and above 'everyday' hazards, ranging from pesticide-dependent farming, exposure to asbestos dust, lead in petrol or sunbathing. Greenberg et al. (1989a), in their analysis of US network television reporting on environmental risk in the mid-1980s, concluded that 'the disproportionate coverage – from the scientific perspective on risk – of chemical incidents, earthquakes, and aeroplane accidents probably reinforces the public's well-documented tendency to overestimate sudden and violent risks and underestimate chronic ones' (Greenberg et al. 1989a: 276).

Several of the imperatives underlying the more salient 'news values' associated with 'extraordinary' environmental risks at the time were made all too apparent following the catastrophic events at Chernobyl in the Ukraine. 'The Chernobyl era', as it has since been described by Russian commentators, began in the early morning of 26 April 1986 when a nuclear reactor overheated and exploded. Two people were killed instantly (with twenty-nine more to follow in the next year), massive fires broke out across the reactor complex and fissionable isotopes were released into the environment. The particular weather conditions helped to send a radioactive plume of gas and particles over 1,500 metres into the atmosphere (Bunyard 1988: 35), promptly diffusing its radiation across the whole of Europe and beyond in the form of nuclear rain. For European countries, the first sign that something was wrong occurred two days later when workers at a nuclear reactor in northern Sweden registered abnormally high levels of radiation emanating from a source they could not immediately determine.

Official news of the accident was very slow to emerge from Tass, the Soviet news agency in Moscow. It was nearly seventy-two hours after the disaster before the first reference to it appeared, and even then it contained little by way of information (local radio announcements, in contrast, had been made at the start of the evacuation of Pripyat after about thirty-six hours). The afternoon edition of Izvestia on 29 April reproduced the official announcement:

> An accident has taken place at the Chernobyl power station, and one of the reactors was damaged. Measures are being taken to eliminate the consequences of the accident. Those affected by it are being given assistance. A government commission has been set up.
>
> (cited in McNair 1988: 140)

Many Soviet officials were quick to discredit western news agencies for exaggerating the scale of the problem, insisting that they were deliberately distorting the facts in the interest of promoting anti-Soviet propaganda. It is indeed fair to say that much of the western news coverage was anything but 'journalistically balanced' in its appraisal of the situation. In the USA, the three main televisual networks and several major newspapers reported that over 2,000 people had died. The *New York Post* went even further, publishing the head-line: 'MASS GRAVE – 15,000 reported buried in Nuke Disposal Site'. Dominant themes identified in the coverage included representations of Soviet officials as having scant regard for human life, being committed to concealing the truth about the accident and being hopelessly reliant on backward, primi-tive nuclear technology (Friedman *et al*. 1987; Luke 1987; McNair 1988; Nohrstedt 1993; Rubin 1987; Wilkins and Patterson 1987).

In retrospect, a more significant issue emerges than the one signalled by jour-nalists engaging in Cold War politics. Specifically, to the extent that the resul-tant news coverage framed the crisis at Chernobyl as a 'freak accident', a 'one in a million technical blunder', it was contributing to the implicit *naturalisa-tion* of nuclear power as a safe source of energy. These types of news accounts, as Luke (1987: 153) argues, served to 'stress the strengths of the status quo, glossing over the accident that has torn only a small, temporary hole in the conventional order'. This framing of the crisis was made easier to sustain, in part, because previous nuclear accidents had transpired under conditions of secrecy, including those at Chalk River, Canada (1952), Windscale in the UK (1957), Kyshtym in the Ural mountains (1957), as well as in Idaho (1961) and just outside Detroit (1966) in the USA (see Gamson and Modigliani 1989; Irwin 2000; Luke 1987; Spinardi 1997; Welsh 2000). For many reporters cov-ering the Chernobyl crisis, then, the only point of reference was the partial meltdown which took place at the Three Mile Island nuclear power plant in the USA in March 1979 (for discussions of the news coverage of that event, see Cunningham 1986; Friedman 1981; Mazur 1981; Rubin 1987; Sandman and Paden 1979; Stephens and Edison 1982). The similarities between how the two nuclear accidents were covered are striking, leading Rubin (1987: 42–3) to point out, for example, that officials in charge 'were quick to put the best face on developments and reluctant to confirm bad news. This demeanour dimin-ished their credibility and reduced the number of potentially trustworthy sources with firsthand knowledge of the accident to few, or even none.' Moreover, he adds, 'certain kinds of information – particularly the amount of radiation released beyond the confines of the plant – were simply never pro-vided or were provided too late to assist a worried public' (Rubin 1987: 43). Indeed, as Giddens (1998: 28–9) observed following the tenth anniversary of the Chernobyl disaster: 'No one knows whether it is hundreds – or millions – of people who have been affected by the Chernobyl fall-out.'

Many of the deficiencies indicative of western news coverage of post-Chernobyl developments in nuclear energy are attributable to the journalistic search for the novel and the unusual, for dramatically compelling 'news pegs' confinable within episodic narratives. This is not to suggest that British or

North American journalists, for example, are failing to report on various problems associated with nuclear power technologies. Typical of this coverage, however, is an emphasis on specific events, such as accidental 'leaks' or 'spills', to the detriment of a thorough accounting of the embodied risks for the public over a period of time longer than yesterday's headline. The parameters of public debate over nuclear power are now largely defined by disputes among 'experts' regarding how best to 'administer' and 'regulate' these technologies. The news audience is regularly asked to accept that nuclear power is 'clean', 'efficient' and 'harmless'. Indeed, a careful consideration of the competing discourses of nuclear risk being articulated across the public sphere can reveal how definitions of 'environmental friendliness', particularly when coupled with those of 'cost effectiveness', recurrently displace arguments for alternative, non-nuclear technologies as being both 'impractical' and 'uneconomical'. The main consequence of this displacement is that the scientific, political and economic rationales being mobilised to legitimise the continued production of nuclear technologies appear to be evermore firmly entrenched in a 'common sense' of nuclearism endorsed on the pages of most newspapers or televisual newscasts (for discussions of nuclearism as it pertains to nuclear weapons, see also Allan 1995, 2000; Boyer 1985; Cohn 1987; Ruthven 1993; Sullivan 1998; Weart 1988).

The tendency for the news media to represent an environmental crisis as a specific event-oriented catastrophe, as opposed to recognising that it is an outcome of bureaucratic calculations and decisions, has been well documented by researchers. As Wilkins and Patterson (1990) maintain:

> While risk analysis indicates that not all risks are alike, news media coverage of a variety of hazards and disasters tends to follow predictable patterns. Neither the unpredictability nor the high degree of complexity of hazards fits neatly into a newsgathering process that places a high priority on meeting deadlines. Therefore, news about hazards often is moulded to the medium. A day-long debate about the location of a toxic dump is reduced to 30-second 'sound bites' from each side and footage about angry demonstrators staging 'pseudo-events' for the benefit of the cameras. In the end, the audience is *entertained* by the hazard without being *informed about it*.
>
> (Wilkins and Patterson 1990: 13)

These types of factors have been discernible in a variety of instances of news coverage concerned with other environmental disasters during the mid-1980s and since, including the 1984 chemical leak at the Union Carbide pesticide plant in Bhopal, India, which reportedly killed over 2,500 people in a matter of days (Salomone *et al.* 1990; Wilkins and Patterson 1987). A further instance is the oil spill of the *Exxon Valdez* in the Alaskan waters of Prince William Sound in 1989, at the time the largest spill in US history. In their critique of the 'disaster narrative' which emerged in the reports of some newspaper journalists, Daley and O'Neill (1991) maintain that it 'naturalised the spill, effectively withdrawing from discursive consideration both the marine transport system and the prospective pursuit of alternative energy sources.' As a result, they contend, attendant environmental issues were directed 'away from the political arena and into the politically inaccessible realm of technological inevitability', thereby reproducing 'the political and corporate hegemony of Big Oil' (Daley and O'Neill 1991: 53; see also C. Smith 1992).

Public concern about environmental issues in countries like Britain reached new levels in the latter part of the 1980s, although it had arguably peaked by the early 1990s judging from the vantage point of today. This perception has been based on studies of news coverage (A. Hansen 1991, 1993a), as well as by considering such factors as opinion poll surveys, membership figures for environmental organisations and the advent of 'green' consumerism with the launch of new 'environmentally friendly' products in shops (Gauntlett 1996; see also Darier 1999; Harré et al. 1999). These same kinds of factors currently suggest that popular interest in environmental issues is on the wane, a dilemma which defies a straightforward solution. At least part of an explanation may be found in the growing recognition of the intricate ways in which environmental risks are seen to impinge upon everyday life in 'first world' countries, as Lacey and Longman (1997) maintain:

> As the debate has matured it has become apparent that the problems are more complex and involve 'us' as well as 'them'. The destruction of the tropical rainforests involves poverty, exploitation, international debt and the demand for tropical hardwoods from Western nations. The problem of global warming involves the vast consumption of fossil fuels by Western nations for heating, transport and manufacture. There are no easy solutions to these problems.
>
> (C. Lacey and Longman 1997: 115)

Studies of environmental reporting during this period have discerned an array of environmental concerns which did not receive sustained high-level news coverage despite being long-term threats, in part due to their non-event-oriented characteristics. That is to say, these lines of inquiry have pinpointed the extent to which this coverage is event-centred as opposed to issue-sensitive, the main result being that those potential sources capable of placing the event in question into a larger context are regularly ignored, trivialised or marginalised (see also A. Anderson 1991; Nelkin 1995; Ostman and Parker 1986; Wiegman et al. 1989). Those sources able to address long-term environmental consequences, or speak to issues of mitigation and prevention, are shown to be routinely displaced from journalistic 'hierarchies of credibility' (Becker 1967) or else made to adapt their message to the discursive rules of inclusion and exclusion in operation (see also Allan 1999; Dunwoody and Scott 1982; Moore and Singletary 1985; Sibbison 1988).

Specific analyses of media reports have focused on the coverage of, for example, acid rain, ozone depletion, global warming or the loss of tropical rainforests (Badri 1991; Bell 1994a, 1994b; Burgess 1990; C. Lacey and Longman 1993; Liebler and Bendix 1996; Shanahan and McComas 1997), hazardous wastes, toxic chemicals and radioactivity (Aziz 1995; Corner *et al.* 1990; Freudenburg *et al.* 1996; Greenberg *et al.* 1989a, 1989b; Rossow and Dunwoody 1991; Singer and Endreny 1987) or even naturally occurring environmental hazards, such as geological radon (Sandman *et al.* 1987; Stocking and Leonard 1990). Similarly investigated have been a host of related 'food scares' (salmonella in eggs, *E. coli* in meat, phthalates in baby milk and so forth), many of which underscored – if only briefly – the environmental risks associated with food production (Fowler 1991; D. Miller and Reilly 1995). In Britain, for example, the identification of Bovine Spongiform Encephalopathy (BSE) or 'mad cow disease' in the country's cattle sparked a 'beef crisis' which led to a sharp, if temporary, drop in meat consumption (Adam 1998; R. Brookes and Holbrook 1998; Kitzinger and Reilly 1997; Macnaghten and Urry 1998; Moeller 1999; Powell and Leiss 1997). In their analysis of the reasons why BSE did not receive adequate media coverage until the then Conservative government officials finally admitted that the disease may be linked to the fatal new variant of Creutzfeldt Jacob's Disease (nvCJD) in humans, Kitzinger and Reilly (1997: 344) cite an all too telling remark made by one of the journalists they interviewed: 'We needed dead people, well, we've got them now.'

In order to elucidate further the complex ways in which the media help to shape public perceptions of contending 'expert' assessments of environmental risks, our attention turns in the next section to Beck's (1992a) conception of the 'risk society'. As will be shown, his conceptual intervention brings to the fore a number of consequential issues associated with the media politics of environmental risks which otherwise tend to be obscured in related types of inquiries.

'The jungle of interpretations and jurisdictions'

'Today,' writes Ulrich Beck, 'if we talk about nature we talk about culture and if we talk about culture we talk about nature' (1998a: 10–11). As he proceeds to elaborate, any conception of modern society which is sensitive to issues of 'risk' needs to recognise that the world is much more open and contingent than was typically postulated via the old theoretical distinction nature/culture:

> When we think of global warming, the hole in the ozone layer, pollution or food scares, nature is inescapably contaminated by human activity. This common danger has a levelling effect that whittles away some of the carefully erected boundaries between classes, nations, humans and the rest of nature, between creators of culture and creatures of instinct, or to use an

earlier distinction, between beings with and those without a soul. . . . In risk society, modern society becomes reflexive, that is, becomes both an issue and a problem for itself.

(Beck 1998a: 11)

To clarify, Beck designates contemporary societies as *risk societies*, social formations where large-scale environmental risks, dangers and hazards have become a central structuring feature (just as the logic of wealth creation and distribution dominated industrial society, see also Goldblatt 1996; Hannigan 1995; Rutherford 1999). The known threat of catastrophes, it follows, is always everywhere present; processes of environmental degradation are no longer calculable and predictable since their latent impacts are unbounded with reference to time, space and place.

Accordingly, the 'risk society' produces and seeks to legitimise the very hazards which are beyond the control of its institutions, such as those of science, politics, industries, markets and capital. As Beck (1996a) explains:

The entry into risk society occurs at the moment when the hazards which are now decided and consequently produced by society *undermine and/or cancel the established safety systems of the provident state's existing risk calculations*. In contrast to early industrial risks, nuclear, chemical, ecological and genetic engineering risks a) can be limited in terms of neither time nor place, b) are not accountable according to the established rules of causality, blame and liability, and c) cannot be compensated or insured against. Or, to express it by reference to a single example: the injured of Chernobyl are today, years after the catastrophe, not even all *born* yet.

(Beck 1996a: 31, original emphasis)

The indeterminacies associated with contemporary environmental hazards are thus of an ontological-structural and epistemological-cosmological nature. Their reach into modern societies' knowledge bases is far deeper and their permeation of that social fabric much more extensive than notions of 'uncertainty' or 'unintended consequences' would otherwise lead us to believe (see also J. Franklin 1998; Lash *et al.* 1996; Robertson *et al.* 1996). Closely linked, then, is Beck's suggestion that through the threat to people, animals, plants and the elements that sustain life, modern societies such as those in Europe and North America are re-experiencing their interdependence and oneness with nature. They are encountering forms of knowledge that have been progressively eroding the organising tenets of earlier 'meta-narratives' held to be consistent with the 'traditions' of their intellectual heritage.

The driving forces of global modernisation impress upon many of us living in modern societies the realisation of interconnectedness. Levels of what Beck (1992a: 74) calls a 'human consciousness of nature' are both 'wounded and awakened' in the awareness of hazards:

people have the experience that they breathe like the plants, and live *from* water as the fish live *in* water. The toxic threat makes them sense that they participate with their bodies in things – 'a metabolic process with consciousness and morality' – and consequently, that they can be eroded like the stones and the trees in the acid rain. A community among Earth, plant, animal and human being becomes visible, a *solidarity of living things*, that affects everyone and everything equally in the threat.

(Beck 1992a: 74, original emphases)

This dissolution of the culture/nature dichotomy is the historical product of industrial society's activities which impose on an earth community of living and inanimate beings the unintended consequences of environmental risks. As Beck suggests with regard to examples such as nuclear or chemical contamination, 'we experience "the end of the other", the end of all our carefully cultivated opportunities for distancing ourselves and retreating behind this category' (Beck 1992b: 109). The 'social explosiveness of hazard' brings about in its wake the implosion of industrial notions of risk perception.

Scientists, as many of them are quick to acknowledge, tend to frame issues of risk in terms of probabilities which are little more than confident expressions of uncertainty (J. Adams 1995). Confronted by scientific uncertainty, the lay public is likely to turn to the mass media for a greater understanding of what is at stake. Journalists, in particular, are charged with the responsibility of imposing meaning upon uncertainties, that is, it is expected that they will render intelligible the underlying significance of uncertainties for their audience's everyday experiences of modern life. More often than not, news accounts will offer the assurance that a potential environmental risk will remain uncertain only until further research and scientific investigation are able to provide the expected clarity and certitude. The notion of risk, as Beck (1992a) contends, implies the potential for decisions and calculation. This relies, in turn, on the presupposition that the past is a reliable guide to possible future states (the idea of risk, as Giddens (1998: 27) observes, 'is bound up with the aspiration of control and particularly with the idea of controlling the future'). In contrast to these more conventional conceptions associated with future unknowns, then, Beck's (1992a) formulation of 'risk society' underlines the point that irreducible indeterminacy is a condition that has to be encompassed and embraced in personal and public responses to environmental hazards.

If the status of the media in 'risk society' has been left relatively undertheorised in Beck's writings to date, this is not to suggest that he fails to appreciate their structurating significance in the formation of public opinions about risk (for an insightful assessment of his work on the media, see Cottle 1998a). Indeed, Beck (1995) accords to the media a crucial role in the organisation and dissemination of knowledge about economic decision-making and political control *vis-à-vis* the uncertainties associated with environmental risks:

The system of institutionally heightened expectations forms the social
background in front of which – under the close scrutiny of the mass media
and the murmurs of the tensely attentive public – the institutions of industrial society present the dance of the veiling of hazards. The hazards, which
are not merely projected onto the world stage, but really threaten, are illu-
minated under the mass media spotlight.

(Beck 1995: 101)

Important questions thus arise as to who in the media wields this spotlight,
under what circumstances and, moreover, where it is (and is not) directed and
why. It follows that it is of the utmost significance how issues of proof, accountability and compensation are represented in and by media discourses. Risks, as
Beck writes, can 'be changed, magnified, dramatised or minimised within
knowledge, and to that extent they are particularly *open to social definition and
construction*' (Beck 1992a: 23, original emphasis). The ways in which the media
help to demarcate the limits of risk, as always both in conjunction with and
opposition to other institutions across society, consequently need to be carefully unravelled for purposes of analysis.

When examining environmental risks it is immediately apparent that there
are no times, spaces or places outside of 'nature', just as there are no positions
from which the journalist may 'objectively' observe. Everyone, every being,
every thing, present and future, is implicated, if in exceedingly uneven positions of power. Nature, as Beck suggests, 'is *neither* given *nor* ascribed' (Beck
1992a: 80, original emphasis). Nevertheless, one media-contested dispute
between 'experts' after another is more than likely to reaffirm as 'common sense'
the assumption that scientific knowledge must be 'harnessed' so that nature
can be 'controlled' or 'managed' in the interest of promoting economic expansion and capital accumulation. This assumption has become *naturalised*, to varying degrees, as a largely unquestioned feature of 'media debate', thereby
foreclosing potential options and choices for trans/actions more appropriate to
the conditions Beck (1992a) deems to be characteristic of the 'ecological field
of conflict'. Here we hasten to add, however, that it is not our intention to suggest that there is a 'reality out there' that is being falsified (consciously or not)
by journalists or other media practitioners. What we do want to argue, however, is that environmental knowledge is always mediated in and through contending discourses organised to advance certain truth-claims over and above
alternative ones. This capacity to define potential risks and hazards is broadly
aligned with the distribution of power among 'credible', 'authoritative' and
'legitimate' definers of 'reality' across the media field.

This process of mediation is, of course, fraught with uncertainty, ambiguity
and contradiction. The preferred 'models' of the scientist, for example, do not
'translate' easily into the reportorial strategies of the journalist anxious to convey their meaning to the intended audience. 'Risk societies', writes Beck, 'are
currently trapped in a vocabulary that lends itself to an interrogation of the

risks and hazards through the relations of definition of simple, classic, first modernity' (Beck 1998a: 19). As a result, he continues, this vocabulary is 'singularly inappropriate not only for modern catastrophes, but also for the challenges of manufactured uncertainties' (Beck 1998a: 19). In the case of scientific perspectives, then, they must therefore undergo a process of journalistic narrativisation before they are likely to 'make sense' to a public facing unknown and barely calculable risks. 'Dispassionate facts' must be marshalled into a 'news story', ideally one with a distinct beginning, middle and end, as well as with easily identifiable 'good' versus 'evil' conflicts. This struggle to narrativise the scientific world necessarily situates journalists at the point where, as Beck (1992a) observes, the antagonisms between those who produce risk definitions and those who consume them are at their most apparent. Daily newspaper reading, as he notes, becomes 'an exercise in technology critique.'

Far from simply 'reflecting' the reality of environmental risks, it follows, media discourses effectively provide contingently codified (rule-bound) definitions of what should count as the reality of environmental risks. This constant, always dynamic process of mediation is accomplished primarily in ideological terms, but not simply at the level of the media text *per se*. Instead, the fluidly complex conditions under which these texts are both produced and consumed or 'read' will need to be accounted for via critical modes of inquiry. As Beck (1995) writes:

> All this gives the mass media a leading role in sounding the social alarm – so long as they dispose of the institutionally guaranteed right to select their own topics. What eludes sensory perception becomes socially available to 'experience' in media practices and reports. Pictures of tree skeletons, worm-infested fish, dead seals (whose living images have been engraved on human hearts) condense and concretise what is otherwise ungraspable in everyday life.
>
> (Beck 1995: 100)

Indeed, it is our contention that in modern societies it is virtually impossible even to begin to think through the following 'relations of definition' identified by Beck (1998a: 18) without recognising the centrality of the media to these processes:

1   Who is to determine the harmfulness of products or the danger of risks? Is the responsibility with those who generate those risks, with those who benefit from them, or with public agencies?
2   What kind of knowledge or non-knowledge about the causes, dimensions, actors, etc., is involved? To whom does that 'proof' have to be submitted?
3   What is to count as sufficient proof in a world in which we necessarily deal with contested knowledge and probabilities?
4   If there are dangers and damages, who is to decide on compensation for

the afflicted and on appropriate forms of future control and regulation?

(Beck 1998a: 18)

Underlying these and related types of questions is the recognition that we are inescapably dependent on the media to comprehend the 'world out there' beyond our immediate experience. It is these complex processes of mediation which work to turn environmental risks into a 'reality' to be represented on the pages of our newspapers or on our televisual screens. Consequently, then, we have to disrupt or 'de-normalise' the very familiarity of journalistic conventions, especially where they are inscribed in accordance with 'common-sense' commitments to privileging scientific rationalities as the most authoritative where issues of environmental degradation are concerned.

The contributors to this book share a commitment to questioning anew the media politics of environmental risks. A sense of urgency informs this intervention as across Europe and in North America the specific ways in which the media encourage their audiences to think about environmental risks are increasingly becoming the subject of public controversy. As Leiss and Chociolko (1994) maintain:

> Charges of media bias or sensationalism, of distorted or selective use of information by advocates, of hidden agendas or irrational standpoints, and of the inability or unwillingness of regulatory agencies to communicate vital information in a language the public can understand, are common. Such charges are traded frequently at public hearings, judicial proceedings, and conferences, expressing the general and pervasive sense of mistrust felt by many participants towards others.
>
> (Leiss and Chociolko 1994: 35–6)

There is, of course, some room for optimism. 'The mounting reliance of everyone in modern society on the judgements of "experts"', as Grove-White observes, 'is paralleled by the growing ability of many of us, reinforced by modern media, to deconstruct political reassurance couched as scientific or technical "fact"' (Grove-White 1998: 50–1). Public demands for the news media to improve their coverage do appear to be gaining ground, not least because 'the environment' is perceived to be the sort of 'soft' news story which attracts particular attention among women and young people (who, in turn, are highly sought after given the general state of decline in news audience figures). Moreover, it is similarly important to keep in mind that at the same time the media are playing a crucial role in sustaining the imperatives of 'expert' risk assessment, they are also creating spaces, albeit under severe constraints, for counter-definitions to emerge. 'The consequence for politics', as Beck points out, 'is that reports on discoveries of toxins in refuse dumps, if catapulted overnight into the headlines, change the political agenda. The established public opinion that the forests are dying compels new priorities' (Beck 1992a: 197–8).

This is to suggest, then, that the identification of the slips, fissures, silences and gaps in media reporting needs to be simultaneously accompanied by a search for alternatives, for ways to enhance the forms and practices of environmental journalism in a manner consistent with today's moral and ethical responsibilities for tomorrow. Many of the pressing issues discussed in this book relate to the 'monitoring' and 'surveillance' functions that Beck attributes to the media as privileged sites for larger definitional struggles over the scale, degree and urgency of environmental risks. In seeking to denaturalise the ways in which the media process certain 'expert' voices as being self-evidently 'authoritative' while simultaneously framing oppositional voices as lacking 'credibility', it is this very self-evidentness which needs to be recognised as a terrain of discursive struggle. 'In the case of risk conflicts', Beck declares, 'bureaucracies are suddenly unmasked and the alarmed public becomes aware of what they really are: *forms of organised irresponsibility*' (Beck 1998a: 15, original emphasis). Media institutions are very much implicated in these 'forms of organised irresponsibility'; their representations of the ideological contests being waged over the right to characterise the consequences of environmental risks are typically anything but 'balanced' or 'objective'. Regardless of what some journalists might insist, facts do not 'speak for themselves'. Moreover, those voices seeking to call into question scientific rationalities (as well as the values associated with 'progress' and 'economic growth') are not, by definition, 'irrational', 'biased' or 'misinformed'. News of environmental risks which reduces them to isolated events or incidents devoid of adequate context, where 'personalities' engaged in disputes are made to stand in for larger economic, political and cultural factors, fails to make the necessary connections at a social structural level.

This book is all about making these types of connections. A key point of departure for its contributors is this recognition that the taken-for-granted, 'commonsensical' assumptions underpinning the media's preferred 'relations of definition' are pivotal to the way we as members of the public negotiate the realities of environmental risks around us. The need to carefully deconstruct what Beck aptly calls 'the jungle of interpretations and jurisdictions', signalled only in a preliminary manner in this introductory chapter, thus serves as a guiding principle to be addressed throughout the chapters to follow.

Overview of the book's sections

In the spirit of a collective intervention, *Environmental Risks and the Media* is organised to extend and elaborate upon these lines of debate in new and, it is hoped, strategically important ways. It brings together the work of researchers actively exploring the dynamics by which environmental risks, threats and hazards are represented, transformed and contested across the discursive field of the mass media. Such an agenda necessarily entails the adoption of an extended definition of what constitutes 'the environment' in order to embrace the lived, embodied experience of risk perception as it is inflected in and through the media discourses circulating in societies like those in Europe and North America. Interwoven throughout this collection of chapters, then, is a shared commitment to reaching beyond the confines of a single discipline or method-ological strategy in order to attend to the mediation of environmental risks in all of their attendant complexities.

Mapping environmental risks

Like so many of the contributions to this book, Simon Cottle's 'TV news, lay voices and the visualisation of environmental risks' (Chapter 1) takes its cue from Ulrich Beck's discussion of 'risk society'. In particular, this chapter inves-tigates the extent to which Beck's conception of the 'voices of the "side effects"' – that is, ordinary people confronting environmental risks – feature within and across television news. Cottle explores the possibility that lay people being accessed into television news may be contributing to a form of 'social ration-ality' in contrast to, or even in opposition to, forms of institutionalised 'sci-entific rationality'. On closer examination, however, television's representation of environmental risks is found to be a good deal more complex than such ratio-nalistic ideas tend to suggest. Culturally there is much more going on than simply the imposition of dominant definitions, the play of rational arguments and/or processes of claims-making.

As Cottle proceeds to demonstrate, a culturally embedded 'environmental sensibility' appears routinely to inform television news and its visualisation of the environment as under threat. Lay voices, far from advancing claims couched in terms of 'social rationality', are generally positioned to play a symbolic role only. It is therefore his contention that although television news culturally res-onates with deep-seated feelings about 'nature' and the 'environment' and, as such, helps to constitute this widespread 'environmental sensibility', lay view-points and emergent forms of 'social rationality' find precious few opportuni-ties for public elaboration and discursive engagement. Environmental news access remains a prize worth struggling for, albeit one which is all too elusive for those voices positioned outside of the ideological boundaries of 'legitimate' discussion and debate.

Evidently, then, the ways in which the news media map or, more specifically, 'frame' certain preferred discourses of environmental risk raise significant ques-tions about access to public debate. M. Mark Miller and Bonnie Parnell Riechert's 'Interest group strategies and journalistic norms: news media fram-ing of environmental issues' (Chapter 2) extends this discussion by engaging with competing conceptions of the role the news media play in policy forma-tion on environmental issues. Journalists, they argue, not only provide infor-mation to the public, but also serve as a conduit between stakeholder groups and policy-makers. It follows, then, that socially responsible journalists must at all times seek to be 'neutral, factual, and objective' in their reporting. That said, however, facts do not exist in isolation; instead, they must be put into some sort of interpretive context or 'frame'.

Such frames, according to Miller and Riechert, may give an appearance of 'objectivity' and meet journalistic standards of factuality and yet be still guiding policy in a specific direction. Environmental stakeholders, their analysis suggests, try to articulate their positions to accommodate journalistic norms while focusing on frames congruent with their interests. Journalists are vulnerable in this regard because they rely on norms that emphasise an appeal to 'neutrality', focus on breaking news events and depend on 'credible' sources. Consequently, an inquiry into the selective ways in which journalists negotiate the definitions on offer by stakeholders competing for attention provides important insights into how limits are placed on what constitutes 'newsworthy' information about the environment.

The framing strategies employed by journalists to 'make sense' of environmental risks are similarly rendered problematic in Anders Hansen's 'Claims-making and framing in British newspaper coverage of the "Brent Spar" controversy' (Chapter 3). Here Hansen offers an analysis of British newspaper coverage of the controversy in 1995 between the environmental pressure group Greenpeace and the oil company Shell over the disposal of a redundant North Sea oil installation, the Brent Spar. Drawing on a constructionist and risk communication framework, he examines the claims-making processes at play in the elevation and development of the Brent Spar as a social problem. Of particular concern is the extent to which Greenpeace succeeded in commanding media attention, as Hansen demonstrates how the claims of the main players involved were inflected and framed very differently by various newspapers.

This exploration of the contending discourses mobilised via the claims-making process, especially those of science and risk assessment, effectively illuminates the types of framing strategies being deployed to secure or contest the credibility and legitimacy of key actors and their arguments. Hansen's analysis pinpoints the considerable ideological 'work' done by the newspapers themselves (rather than by the principal claims-makers), showing how their preferred ideological positions were in place from the outset and changed relatively little in the course of the controversy. While Greenpeace clearly succeeded in drawing media and public attention to a particular problem, Hansen contends that its success in terms of securing 'credibility' and 'legitimacy' for its claims was much less clear cut.

Important questions regarding the news media's framing of 'the environment' as a political issue similarly inform Maggie Wykes's 'The burrowers: news about bodies, tunnels and green guerrillas' (Chapter 4). She begins with the observation that youth culture in Britain is often enacted and depicted as 'different' to the extent that it borders the 'illegal' or the 'deviant'. This insight underpins her examination of the activities of new age travellers and environmental protesters, in particular those who have become 'tree-dwellers' and 'human moles' in protest at transport schemes to provide new roads and airport runways at sites across the UK. Figuring prominently among the voices of dissent are individuals such as 'Swampy' and 'Animal', several of whom are quickly established as 'media celebrities' in their own right.

In the course of analysing how the news media have followed and reported on the actions of the 'eco-warriors', Wykes places a particular emphasis on the discursive politics shaping journalistic accounts. More specifically, she privileges for critique the ways in which news reports focus on the names, biographies, bodies and habitats of the protesters, and in so doing engender a certain personalisation of resistance. The main result of this personalisation process, in turn, is a hierarchical projection of the individual 'private' body in a survival struggle over and above the collective 'public' body in struggle with political and economic culture. From this perspective, Wykes provides a critical commentary of several pertinent issues raised by this analysis in relation to recent developments in media theory concerned with cultural discourses of the environment.

De-naturalising risk politics

Part II opens with Alison Anderson's 'Environmental pressure politics and the "risk society"' (Chapter 5). Turning in the first instance to the writings of theorists such as Beck, Melucci and Castells on the 'information society', she proceeds to examine the role of new social movements in relation to recent examples of grassroots action directed at environmental risks. Particular consideration is given to symbolic politics, media packaging and issues of time and space.

Drawing, in part, upon findings from a study involving semi-structured interviews with environmental campaigners and policy-makers in Devon, southwest England, Anderson is interested in exploring the growth of grassroots environmental networks. Of particular relevance here are the contradictions inherent within the forces that shape discourses of identity, symbolic politics and strategically oriented action. That is to say, in her view new sources of identity have clearly emerged through the growth of non-party-based networks and community groups which often tend to be concerned with localised environmental issues. These dynamics offer the opportunity for shared emotional release, and tend to be non-hierarchical with a relatively rapid turnover of people. However, as she points out, explanations of the rise of environmentalism which focus solely upon identity and general value shifts among the population run the risk of divorcing expressions of environmental concern from real world events. While in her view there is some evidence which suggests that a large-scale shift has occurred in relation to the cultural politics of risk, dangers arise when treating social movements alone as carriers of a new form of society. In particular, Anderson argues, the emphasis upon identity and symbolic politics is not entirely novel and masks important ambivalences and contradictions.

In Chapter 6, Peter Phillimore and Suzanne Moffatt's '"Industry causes lung cancer": would you be happy with that headline? Environmental health and local politics' similarly engages with the cultural politics of environmental risks at the level of the local. Environmental pollution, they point out, has long been a sensitive public issue in Teesside (a conurbation of over 400,000 people in north-east England), one of western Europe's main centres of steel and chemical production. Industry and local government alike have made strenuous efforts, however, to constrain and guide public debate about air pollution and its implications for human health.

Against this backdrop, Phillimore and Moffatt elect to examine a range of events surrounding the publication in 1995 of an epidemiological investigation into the potential effects of industrial air pollution in Teesside. Although attention is devoted to the activities of the local media in reporting what is a complex environmental health story, their inquiry assumes as its principal focus the official efforts to 'manage' news reports of the research. In their view, the oft-repeated comment that 'we don't want any more bad news' symbolised a wider effort in local government and industry to play down inconvenient evidence and to reassure the public that concerns about health and pollution were not well founded. Phillimore and Moffatt thus place official representations of this epidemiological evidence in the context of a long history of such efforts to manage the portrayal of pollution in ways consistent with official renderings of 'the public interest'.

Several interesting parallels are apparent in Barbara Adam's 'The media timescapes of BSE news' (Chapter 7), which centres for purposes of critique on the ways in which British newspapers have represented the BSE beef crisis. She begins with the observation that BSE, more commonly known as 'mad cow disease', is a risk issue *par excellence* and yet it does not fall neatly within the conventional bounds of risks. Its probabilities, she points out, are unknown; indeed, ignorance and uncertainty surround questions about its causes, its consequences and its remedies. This poses problems for risk assessments where experts are expected to calculate the probabilities of particular risks occurring. Accordingly, Adam focuses on BSE and the posited link to the fatal new variant of Creutzfeldt Jacob's Disease in humans in order to explore the media–risk–environment triad with an eye to its temporal inflection on the pages of the 'quality' broadsheet press.

In considering the challenge posed by BSE for 'objective' news reporting, Adam analyses some of the coping strategies of newsworkers with reference to the complexities, ambiguities and uncertainties associated with this contemporary issue of environmental risk. It is her conviction that neither the politicians and their advisers, nor the news media, have successfully risen to the challenge of their public responsibilities. Instead, they are largely carrying on with their respective businesses 'as usual', which has meant that an intangible future-based health hazard is being translated into a quantifiable economic issue and a 'matter of national pride'. The main result of this, in her view, is the

effective silencing of those voices which are positioned so as to call into q
tion the public's trust in scientific assessments of risk.

A complementary perspective concerning the media's imposition of cultural
significance on environmental complexities, ambiguities and uncertainties is
developed by Peter Glasner's 'Reporting risks: problematising public participation and the Human Genome Project' (Chapter 8). Mapping and sequencing the human genome, that is, the genetic material of an individual as an
organism, is unlike many of the new technologies in that it directly affects all
of us at a very personal level. According to Glasner, it poses a threat to the
boundary between ourselves and the world in a way quite different from, for
example, the virtual realities of the new electronic technologies (which only
temporarily liberate individuals from their particular social and biological
characteristics, such as gender, class, ethnicity, age and so forth). In geno-
technologies, he points out, the connections are obscured, as are the boundaries
of risk being defined by (predominantly) scientific and medical experts.

Glasner moves first to situate his inquiry in relation to a range of social and
ethical issues associated with 'risk society', in general, and the ongoing attempt
to identify the genetic pairs which constitute the human genome, in particular. He then goes on to relate this discussion to the changing role of scientific
expertise, especially its relationship to lay knowledge, as it is recurrently framed
by different media outlets. At issue is the extent to which opportunities for
public debate on the future development of geno-technologies are being made
available across the terrain of the media. It is Glasner's contention that relatively little progress can be made until it is first recognised that the normative
limits defining what is a 'socially acceptable' application of these technologies
are embedded in hierarchical relations of discursive power.

Bodies, risks and public environments

Justine Coupland and Nikolas Coupland's 'Selling control: ideological dilemmas of sun, tanning, risk and leisure' (Chapter 9) investigates issues of environmental risk in relation to advertising texts promoting sunscreens and
tanning agents. Bodily exposure to the sun, they point out, entails a biomedical health risk, aggravated by ozone depletion in the upper atmosphere. It also
entails a threat to personal and social standing, through what is often referred
to as 'premature ageing'. Still, the late-modern project of the body asserts competing priorities, investing the exposed body, and often the tanned body, with
meanings of youthfulness, attractiveness and a form of relational power.
Consumerised and technologised 'solutions' to these and other ideological
dilemmas are offered by sunscreens and tanning agents as part of a vast industry of sun use.

Coupland and Coupland provide a critical interpretation of the semantics of
sun use embedded in skin-care product advertisements, drawn from recent
high-circulation magazines targeted at women. Their analysis focuses on how

such advertisements variably characterise agency and instrumentality as semantic roles in relation to the activities of tanning and bodily exposure. Such a line of inquiry shows, for example, how various forms of risk (to people as victims or 'affected objects') are edited and reconstituted as forms of control (by people as agents using technological instruments). Moreover, it displays how popular appreciation of specific clusters of risk phenomena is encouraged through media texts, but also how this appreciation is refashioned ideologically. On this basis, then, Coupland and Coupland discuss the differential strategies used by advertisers to target women in their roles as mothers (*vis-à-vis* 'self-protection') and as non-mothers, with responsibility for protection of children from risk of sun damage.

The theme of bodies, risks and public environments is addressed from a different vantage point in Susan Hutson and Mark Liddiard's 'Exclusionary environments: the media career of youth homelessness' (Chapter 10). Here attention turns to how the media represent the problem of homelessness as it pertains to young people living under often dangerous conditions in urban environments. An analysis is offered of the circumstances surrounding the emergence of youth homelessness as a media issue in Britain in 1989, and how it was subsequently treated by the newspaper press before its eventual displacement as an exigent matter of public concern years later.

The particular 'media career' of youth homelessness, that is, the varied pattern of the topic's progression across the media field, is linked with the activity of voluntary agencies committed to improving the situation. A host of factors are identified which underpin the relative media prominence of youth homelessness and, moreover, its preferred inflection as a 'charity issue'. Questions regarding the potential impact of the corresponding image politics on public perceptions of youth homelessness are similarly explored; in particular, the emphasis on city centre rough sleeping which overlooks, for example, the more common experience of young people sleeping on friends' floors in their own local area. As Hutson and Liddiard proceed to argue, there has been a marked shift in media images away from homeless young people as victims at risk to increasingly more typical representations of them as aggressive beggars and troublesome tenants whose very existence poses a threat to 'ordinary', 'decent' citizens like 'us' living in urban environments.

C. Kay Weaver, Cynthia Carter and Elizabeth Stanko's 'The female body at risk: media, sexual violence and the gendering of public environments' (Chapter 11) presents a range of related insights. Elaborating, in part, upon arguments derived from the recent work of several feminist cultural geographers, it is their contention that the news media help to construct public spaces as environments that pose considerable risk to women's physical safety and sexual reputation. As they seek to demonstrate, media reporting tends to concentrate on the risks of sexual attack by male strangers, therefore reinforcing an ideology of a woman's place being in the home, and the public environment being the domain of men.

This line of argument is empirically substantiated, first, by way of research into women's responses to a televisual crime reconstruction of the sexual assault and murder of a young female hitchhiker. Weaver, Carter and Stanko then discuss how journalists typically frame stories of sexual violence according to a patriarchal, consensual worldview. Routine framing strategies, they argue, contribute to cultural perceptions of the female body as a form which is at risk of violation and which therefore requires (patriarchal) 'protection'. From there they consider how women's fear of crime and perceptions of risk motivate them to adopt particular behavioural strategies on a day-to-day basis in an effort to better ensure their personal safety in public environments. Thus in examining how women are socialised to expect danger from men (particularly strangers), and to accept the supposed 'naturalness' of their subordination, the role of the media comes to the fore. Hence the need, in their view, to assess critically the extent to which media representations promote certain 'common sensical' constructions of the female body as a site of risk.

Many of these themes resound in John Tulloch's '"Landscapes of fear": public places, fear of crime and the media' (Chapter 12) to advantage. Adopting a 'situated' perspective, he offers a critical exploration of an array of different discourses of fear concerning crime in public environments. A qualitative analysis of local 'stories' of fear in these places, as he proceeds to show, facilitates the development of a new approach to media and risk via an examination of 'lay' micro-narratives. In this way a crucial emphasis is placed on how people negotiate local and mediated senses of control in the face of their fears about crime in the course of their daily lives.

To develop this mode of critique, Tulloch focuses on older people's use of media and other circuits of communication in their everyday encounters with certain public environments. If analysts of postmodern media are right that criminality and risk have become metaphors for the condition of postmodern fragmentation itself, he argues, it is important to remember the many (experientially *situated*) micro-narratives in and through which people actively negotiate this condition. On the one hand, he maintains, these local narratives add to postmodern fragmentation; but on the other, they remind us as 'experts' to return to a consideration of the effects of the media at the social level of lay understandings in 'lived culture'. It is Tulloch's contention that these 'lay knowledges' (affiliated to age, gender, class and so forth), as much as the single issue 'pragmatic alliances' that Beck emphasises, continue to be central to people's self-understandings and sense of control in the face of public 'landscapes of fear'.

Globalising environments at risk

Shifting from the local to the global, the final part of the book begins with Kris M. Wilson's 'Communicating climate change through the media: predictions, politics and perceptions of risk' (Chapter 13). Global climate change is a complex environmental topic, one with the potential – most would agree – to affect all life on Earth. It follows, then, that it is the media's responsibility to inform the public about scientific discoveries related to potential climate change. A consistent feature of the media coverage in the USA, however, has been an almost exclusive focus on the charged scientific debate and possible consequences of global warming, thereby providing little by way of a context in which to frame the potential environmental risks.

Wilson's discussion begins with an overview of the current science of climate change, before considering several key journalistic factors which influence press coverage of science. Next, he reports on data drawn from two opinion surveys, the first of which suggests that climate change knowledge is correlated with the source of knowledge. That is to say, those who relied primarily on television had a skewed view of climate change, with a poor understanding of risk and inflated perceptions of the scientific debate. A second study found reporter knowledge about climate change also to be lacking in many significant areas. Reporters who primarily relied on scientists as sources were much more knowledgeable about climate change. Most reporters, however, indicated that they prefer to use the news 'food chain', relying on previous media articles about climate change, thereby often exacerbating erroneous information. Given that a well-informed public is essential to formulate public policy on climate change (a view endorsed by the Intergovernmental Panel on Climate Change in the USA), Wilson proceeds to make several recommendations to improve climate change reporting and public learning about this complex and crucial environmental topic.

A further engagement with current debates about environmental risk and the media at the level of the global is advanced by Bronislaw Szerszynski and Mark Toogood's 'Global citizenship, the environment and the mass media' (Chapter 14). At issue, they contend, is the need to defend an expanded, culturalist conception of the role that the media might be playing in the creation of a critical global environmental citizenship *vis-à-vis* environmental risks. In their view, dominant notions of citizenship present an overly rationalistic picture of human deliberation, hence the need to develop a more hermeneutic conception of citizenship as always involving a particular kind of cultural self-interpretation. More specifically, Szerszynski and Toogood suggest that the media's role in an emergent global civil society has to be conceived not only in terms of the circulation of information and points of view, but also as providing cultural resources for non-local framings of the self as belonging to a global community of responsibility and care.

Having detailed this position, Szerszynski and Toogood then go on to argue that this approach implies that genres of media beyond news and documentary may be playing an important role in the generation of global citizenship, and that how any genre actually plays that role needs to be reconceived. At stake, in both conceptual and methodological terms, is the conviction that such a move also requires researchers and campaigners to broaden their attention from a concern with specific messages in the media. This means that researchers also need to take into account the role that the very form of the televisual experience itself might be playing in the creation of a global, cosmopolitan sensibility where environmental risks are concerned.

Finally, the book draws to a close with Joost van Loon's 'Mediating the risks of virtual environments' (Chapter 15). The principal aim here is to render problematic the concepts of environment and media in an attempt to extend Beck's (1992a) risk society thesis to the virtual world of information and communication technologies. Van Loon argues that apart from a critique of media representations of environmental risks, sociocultural theory also needs to undertake a thorough re-problematisation of risk itself. Accordingly, he invokes the concept of 'cyberrisk' to open up the scope of analysis to the material-informational technological processing of risks that comes before their discursive realisation in signifying practices.

The concept of cyberrisk, van Loon suggests, shows that what is often generically referred to as 'the environment' is in itself a technologically and discursively engineered process that challenges any conception of pre-symbolic valorisation. Moreover, cyberrisks also undermine the often implicitly invoked assumption that media representations operate solely on the symbolic planes of either the conscious or the unconscious realms of subjectivity. Instead of reinvoking a realist–constructionist dualism, then, he attempts to provide a radically different understanding of the mediation of environmental risk, one that ultimately forces us to question not only the world in which we live, now and in the future, but also what our being in the world actually entails. Using the example of computer viruses as an illustration, van Loon contends that we may have already entered into an irreversible stage at which the notion of an integral human being is being rapidly dissolved by the twin processes of information processing and telecommunications. This exploratory critique of the possibilities implied by a potential dissolution of 'the environment' thus constitutes a suitably provocative note on which to bring the discussion to a close.

In conclusion, then, it is our view that the relationship between research approaches seeking to prioritise environmental risks, on the one hand, and those which investigate media forms, practices, institutions and audiences, on the other, is in urgent need of substantive formalisation (after all, as Grove-White (1998: 50) points out, 'further environmental time-bombs are ticking away in the undergrowth'). Our hope is that *Environmental Risks and the Media* will be recognised as contributing to such a process of formalisation by identifying key areas of shared concern between highly varied disciplinary engagements with the media–environment nexus. Working together with our authors, we have sought to provide a book which discerns several important ways in which critical research can help facilitate interdisciplinary understandings of what are truly exigent issues and, in so doing, encourage new forms of dialogue, debate and intervention.

Notes

1 Although an emphasis is placed on the news media in this introductory chapter, as
   well as in the book overall, it is important to acknowledge the ways in which 'factual' representations of environmental risks interconnect with 'fictional' ones across
   the mediasphere. For discussions of genres other than news, such as they are found
   in areas like 'infotainment', weather reports, nature documentaries, televisual
   drama, children's programmes, advertising, museums, theme parks or cyberspace,
   see Berland 1993; Bousé 1998; Boyd-Bowman 1984; Dovey 1996b; Gauntlett
   1996; Irwin and Wynne 1996; Jagtenberg and McKie 1997; Langer 1998;
   Macnaghten and Urry 1998; Myers 1994; Shanahan 1993; Shields 1991; Thrift
   1996; A. Wilson 1992.
2 British environmental journalist, Richard D. North (1998), recalled this event with
   a certain degree of passion: 'Remember that image of the planet earth floating alone
   in the universe? The USA astronauts beamed it back to us. That's the image that
   spoiled it all. That's when we started talking nonsense about the world. Suddenly
   the world's happy materialists, and its happy consumers, were turned into guilt-
   ridden 'greens'. They saw the spaceman's view of the planet and they thought they
   saw something which was a fragile, static set of natural communities. Actually,
   nature is, of course, robust, and it's in constant tension. It's dynamic and it is
   absolutely full of opportunism. . . . What's more, nature's very nasty and it's
   extremely violent' (North 1998: 85).
3 'In 1961,' according to Powell and Leiss (1997), 'the USA federal government had
   1,164 people working as writers/editors and public affairs specialists. By 1990 the
   number in public information jobs was nearly five thousand, making the federal
   government the nation's largest singly employer of public information officers.' As
   they proceed to point out, those 'sources that are best organised to provide technical
   information to journalists in an efficiently packaged form have a great deal of control over what ultimately appears as news' (Powell and Leiss 1997: 231).

Part I

Mapping environmental risks

TV news, lay voices and the visualisation of environmental risks

Simon Cottle

The world of television news enacts tight editorial controls, controls that do not normally permit generous conditions of access to ordinary or lay voices and viewpoints. Of course, as we shall see, 'ordinary voices' are routinely accessed into TV news items but rarely are they granted an opportunity to develop their arguments or points of view at length, much less directly confront and challenge political and expert authorities. The following, then, represents a rare moment in the news mediation of environmental risks and, for that matter, TV news broadcasts more generally. In the excerpt below from BBC2's *Newsnight* programme, Frances Hall (the mother of Peter Hall, one of the first victims to die from Creutzfeldt-Jakob Disease, the human equivalent of Bovine Spongiform Encephalopathy) is ceded a degree of editorial control and narrates her own film report before participating in a live studio debate.

> Our son Peter was ill for more than a year. During that time I wrote to request that someone from the government would come and sit with me at his bedside and see what this devastating illness was doing to our strong, handsome young man. No one came. . . . Given the mounting evidence of a possible link between BSE and CJD can anyone offer me a logical explanation of how my son contracted this disease other than by eating BSE infected meat? Since Peter died I've taken a job in a local café; I see people confused about what's safe to eat. We've been told consistently that British beef is safe and that the most infected parts have been removed, but even if the red meat carries no infection we still see evidence of incorrectly butchered cattle with possibly infected parts still attached entering the human food chain, and offal being recycled into animal feed. Surely as Health Secretary, Stephen Dorrell, your only duty is to the nation's health? Can you assure me that no one else will be exposed to the dangers of BSE? Are precautions being enforced and will this really protect the public? Mr Dorrell I want you to watch the pictures of my son growing up, do they look much different to the pictures you have of your children? Does Peter show any signs of the tragically short span that he would have? I hold the government responsible for his death and their total incompetence and

mismanagement of a manmade disease. . . . Will the government now accept that the scientific advice it chose to follow, namely, that there was no conceivable risk from eating British beef, was wrong? Are the experts still the same? Is the government still being selective on the advice that it takes on behalf of the nation or is it now willing to err on the side of caution? These past months have been, and continue to be, a living night-mare for my family. We have been unable to come to terms with Peter's death because we know that if BSE had been treated with sufficient cau-tion he and many others would not have suffered this terrible illness.

(BBC2 *Newsnight* 20 June 1996)

The words spoken present an anguished plea and articulate challenge to the government Health Secretary of the day, Stephen Dorrell MP, requesting both information about and an acceptance of responsibility for the (mis)management of the BSE crisis in the UK, and her son's death. By tragic force of circum-stance an ordinary person has won a rare opportunity to convey her feelings, develop her argument and directly confront the 'responsible' Secretary of State, sitting (uncomfortably) in the *Newsnight* studio. The opportunity, I think, was not wasted. Her intervention into the world of public discourse, a world gen-erally framed in the impersonal terms and analytical rhetoric of officials, pro-fessionals and experts, is arguably all the more forceful for being grounded, in part at least, in the private realm of lived experience, familial relationships and emotions, and everyday concerns.

More theoretically, Frances Hall represents what Ulrich Beck in *Risk Society* (1992a) has termed 'the voices of the "side effects"'. Her tragic experience of the consequences of an invisible risk leads her to articulate a form of 'social rationality' (in contrast to 'scientific rationality') and confront the administra-tive failure of politicians to manage hazards as well as the technocratic failures of scientists to 'know' and therefore to be able to quantify, predict and control 'risks' – Beck's so-called 'manufactured uncertainties'.

What scientists call 'latent side effects' and 'unproven connections' are for them their 'coughing children' who turn blue in the foggy weather and gasp for air, with a rattle in their throat. On their side of the fence, 'side effects' have *voices, faces, ears* and *tears*. . . . Therefore people them-selves become small, private alternative experts in risks of modernization. . . . The parents begin to collect data and arguments. The 'blank spots' of modernization risks, which remain 'unseen' and 'unproven' for the experts, very quickly take form under their cognitive approach.

(Beck 1992a: 61, original emphasis).

Modern environmental risks (radioactivity, biogenetic releases, toxic chemicals, industrial pollution), according to Beck, are historically unprecedented in so far as they are manufactured, often invisible and potentially catastrophic in terms of their spatial and temporal reach – capable of circumnavigating the globe and wreaking havoc across generations. No wonder, then, that risks produce contested claims and deepen our dependency upon scientists and experts, even when those same scientists and experts cannot agree on the nature, extent and probable consequences of the risks produced by the science and technologies of modern civilisation.

> The growing awareness of risks must be reconstructed as a struggle among rationality claims, some competing and some overlapping. One cannot impute a hierarchy of credibility and rationality, but must ask how, in the example of risk perception, 'rationality' *arises socially*.
>
> (Beck 1992a: 59)

The mass media provide an important public arena where '"rationality" *arises socially*', since it is in and through the mass media that risks are 'defined and evaluated socially' (Beck 1992a: 112).

Ulrich Beck, then, has helped to raise important questions about the social evaluation of environmental risks, the nature of competing rationality claims and the part played in all this by the mass media (for a detailed critique see Cottle 1998a). With respect to his ideas on competing social and scientific rationalities, and especially his comments on 'the voices of the "side effects"', however, we need to know more about the actual representations of the mass media. We need to empirically map, for example, the extent and forms of lay access and how, if at all, the news media condition the public elaboration of 'social rationality' and the engagement with technocratic and scientific claims of scientists, politicians and experts. In the example above, Frances Hall helps to problematise the category of the 'expert' and 'expertise' and redefines both in more socially proximate ways. But to what extent and in what sense, exactly, have lay voices in television news been able to do likewise? Do the news media help to sustain forms of emergent 'social rationality' through the accessing of lay voices in the field of environmental risks?

This chapter sets out to explore such questions. With the help of findings from a systematic examination of news access, we can first chart the extent and nature of lay or ordinary involvement within and across TV news about the environment and environmental risks. Based on these findings, however, it soon becomes apparent that if we are to better understand the patterns and forms of lay access we need to go beneath the 'rational' veneer of news access. Often positioned by the news media to symbolise the 'human face' and consequences of a widespread perception of nature and the environment as 'under threat', these voices in fact rarely find an opportunity to advance rational claims – whether 'social' or 'scientific'. Television news positions ordinary people to symbolise or (literally) 'stand for' ordinary feelings and responses to the consequences of environmental risks, not to articulate a form of 'social rationality' much less discursively challenge 'scientific rationality'. With too few exceptions the discursive play of difference and contending rational accounts is preserved for other, non-ordinary, voices. Television news does, however, routinely help to visualise a deep-seated cultural sensibility towards the environment widely felt to be under threat from advancing industrialism and despoliation.[1] The roots of this environmental sensibility, of course, are historically long and culturally deep. They go back to the period of Romanticism if not earlier, and resonate with the change from traditional to modern, rural to urban societies and the pessimism towards industrialism that this spawned – a sensibility often premised upon a romanticised image of a rural idyll and a more communal and less alienated way of life. This environmental sensibility continues to surface across a number of cultural representations and practices. Urry, for example, observes how a 'romantic tourist gaze' continues to position physical landscapes as a site of visual consumption and concern (Urry 1992). The news media also trade in cultural views, and through selection and juxtaposition of scenes *visualise* the environment and environmental risks often in *spectacular* ways – ways, that is, which help to culturally position us as spectators viewing/sensing both the 'wonders' of nature as well as the awesome nature of environmental threats.

News visualisation of the environment, therefore, reflects much more than the inherent tele*visual* nature of the television medium and its appetite for 'good' background pictures, or even the genre conventions of TV news proclaiming *immediacy*, *factuality* and *objectivity* supported through the *authenticating* power of visuals (Brunsdon and Morley 1978; Fiske 1987; Graddol 1994). On closer examination, TV news scenes both *symbolise* and *aestheticise* cultural *views* of nature. As with accessed lay voices, in so far as these scenes 'work' representationally at a symbolic, aesthetic and affective level so they are not best captured within the formalised ideas of 'social rationality' and/or competing 'rationality claims'. To assume that they are is arguably to operate with an overly rationalist, language-based and/or discursive approach to mediated communication, and to underestimate its more imagistic, symbolic and ritualistic dimension and appeals (Carey 1989; Dayan and Katz 1992; Liebes and Curran 1998).

The focus of this chapter, then, is more on the *cultural politics* of TV news representation, and the role played in this by the journalistic positioning and packaging of news actors and the symbolic visualisation of the environment and environmental risks, rather than with the *strategic politics* of environmental sources struggling for media entry and their battling claims for public acceptance and legitimacy waged via the media stage. Of course both these senses of the 'political' inform the mediated play of environmental risks, but arguably the contribution of the former has so far received insufficient recognition and study. This chapter presents findings and arguments that suggest that the 'cultural politics' embedded within the forms and appeals of news presentation must now be given their due in our efforts to better understand the media politics of environmental risk.

TV news and 'the voices of the "side effects"'

It has become something of an orthodoxy in media studies and mass communication research that the media, and the news media especially, are structurally oriented to the institutions and centres of political, economic and social power, granting access as of right to the elites of society (Hall *et al.* 1978). A combination of bureaucratic expediency and the professional journalistic subscription to ideas of 'objectivity' results, it is said, in the privileging of 'authoritative' voices, that is, 'authority voices' who thereby secure definitional advantage and become the nation's 'primary definers'. A number of empirical case studies provide supporting evidence for this view. During the 1990s theoretical and empirical work, however, though not discounting the weighting towards sources of institutional power by the mass media, suggests that this blanket thesis tends to cover over a number of important qualifications, complexities and contingencies (P. Schlesinger 1990; A. Anderson 1991; D. Miller 1993; Deacon and Golding 1994; Kitzinger and Reilly 1997). The strategic politics enacted by competing news sources on the ground can contribute to a more dynamic, differentiated and contingent cast of news actors than often allowed for by the blanket idea of social dominance and news closure. Also, the news media (TV news is no exception) are richly differentiated by market share and cultural appeals and this too informs the 'cultural politics' of news representation and helps shape the cast of news actors gaining entry (Cottle 2000).[2] In so far as some social actors are routinely sought out, positioned and packaged by news producers within the conventionalised formats of news presentation to embody or symbolise a form of social experience so they do not, strictly speaking, play a definitional or claims-making role at all (Cottle 1993a, 1994). If this is so, then the complexities of news access are not exhausted with reference to definitional or claims-making activity – important though this is.

To help get a fix on all this in the context of our concern with news of the environment and environmental risk, it is useful to refer to a sub-sample of environmental TV news actors derived from a wider study of news access.[3] As Table 1.1 indicates, accessed 'ordinary voices', that is, the voices of the institutionally, organisationally and professionally non-aligned, secure (surprisingly perhaps) the highest percentage of news involvement.

These basic findings indicate that considerable lay involvement informs environmental news. Attending to the forms of entry characterising environmental news access (Table 1.2), we can also note how these structure TV news access and variously (and self-evidently) constrain or enable the opportunities of news access – hence their designation as 'restrictive', 'limited', 'extended' or 'expansive'.

Table 1.3 now charts the forms of entry gained by 'ordinary voices', environmental 'pressure groups' and, for ease of comparison, combined 'professionals/experts', 'scientists' and 'regulatory' authorities, as well as combined 'government/politicians' and 'regional/local administration'. Though 'ordinary

Table 1.1 TV news environmental actors

Actors		N	%
Ordinary voices		243	37.04
Pressure groups		57	8.69
	Sub-total	300	45.73
Government/politicians		61	9.30
Foreign government/country		89	13.57
Regional/local administration		30	4.57
	Sub-total	180	27.44
Professionals/experts		100	15.24
Regulatory bodies		10	1.52
Scientists		5	0.76
	Sub-total	115	17.52
Business/industry		47	7.16
Royalty/celebrity		14	2.43
	Total	656	100.00

Table 1.2 Environmental news: forms of actor entry

Form of entry		N	%
Restricted			
News visual		55	8.38
News reference		339	51.68
News actor reference		34	5.18
News attributed statement		18	2.74
	Sub-total	446	67.98
Limited			
News quotation		17	2.59
Filmed public speech		6	0.91
ENG (video) interview[a]		176	26.83
	Sub-total	199	30.33
Extended			
ENG group interview		1	0.15
Live interview		4	0.61
Live group interview		4	0.61
	Sub-total	9	1.37
Expansive			
Editorial control		2	0.30
	Total	656	100.00

Note a ENG is electronic newsgathering

voices' are statistically prominent, it is clear that they also feature most often within 'restricted' forms of news entry. Pressures groups fare slightly better in terms of their forms of entry as do 'professionals/regulatory bodies', while 'government and politicians' are both frequently referenced by the news media and

Table 1.3 Forms of entry and TV news environmental actors

N Column %	Total	Ordinary voices	Pressure groups	UK government/ local administration	Professional regulatory/ scientists
Total	656 100%	243 100%	57 100%	91 100%	115 100%
Restricted	446 67.98%	177 72.83%	22 38.59%	64 70.33%	69 60.00%
Limited	199 30.33%	65 26.74%	31 54.38%	25 27.47%	43 37.39%
Extended	9 1.37%	1 0.41%	4 7.01%	2 2.19%	1 0.86%
Expansive	2 0.30%	0 0%	0 0%	0 0%	2 1.74%

also involved in ENG ('electronic newsgathering' – video edited) interviews in over a quarter of all news entries.

As suggested at the outset, we can now see that what has been termed 'extensive' and 'expansive' forms of entry are indeed a rarity in television news, with less than one-third of 1 per cent of all news actors granted the form of opportunity secured by Frances Hall above. Is it the case, however, notwithstanding the 'restricted' and 'limited' forms of accessed presentation, that ordinary voices perhaps contribute a different form of knowledge to environmental news when compared to other social groups, as anticipated from the preceding discussion?

One way of approaching this is to examine the nature of accessed voices across the two dimensions of 'public–private', 'analytic–experiential'. Accessed news speech can be identified as 'public' if explicitly addressing the world of public affairs and/or collective concerns; 'private', if explicitly addressing an individual's own circumstances or familial world of home and/or personal relationships. Speech can also be characterised as 'analytic' if advancing a rationally engaged form of argument or point of view; 'experiential', if based on an account of experience or response that is emotionally charged. A few examples help illustrate these basic differences of accessed news speech. In a BBC2 *Newsnight* item about a proposal by UK motor manufacturers that the government should subsidise the purchase of new cars as a means of cutting back harmful emissions from the UK's 7 million cars over ten years old, three voices were accessed into the news presenter's filmed report.

> Sooner we get to having more new cars on the road, the better it is. The RAC have calculated that 50% of the emissions come from around 10% of the vehicles and there are 7 million vehicles on the road that don't meet

the emission standards, in fact this is quite a lot of the emissions and the sooner they are off the road the better.

(Chairman and managing director, Ford UK, BBC2 *Newsnight*)

I wouldn't be free without it; and I think that is the main thing. I wouldn't be able to do my degree, I wouldn't be able to go into work. It's just totally important to me and I do love it as well. It's not just the practical side of it. I love having a car. This car will probably go twenty years and all the resources, if it was scrapped, would be completely wasted.

(Music student/car driver, BBC2 *Newsnight*)

There are much better ways of spending that money, if what is really wanted is to cut pollution. That money could be used to provide incentives so that people didn't use their cars as much – maybe through tax breaks for employers, green commuter schemes. It could be used to encourage community car schemes so that people didn't even need to own a car in the first place.

(Environmentalist, BBC2 *Newsnight*)

As we can see, the first voice seeks to advance a public argument based upon a particular analysis of the current situation of car ownership within the UK, and presents a public-analytic statement. The second voice principally reflects upon her private experience of and personal feelings towards her own car, providing a form of private-experiential statement. The third voice returns the debate to the wider public assessment and analysis of the nature of the problem, and succinctly proposes a set of 'rational' responses clearly articulated in public-analytic terms. Less frequently, accessed voices can also advance a form of private-analytic, in contrast to private-experiential, form of speech promoting a more self-conscious and reasoned (and less experiential and descriptive) account of personal actions and/or circumstances. A local resident and supporter of the Brightlingsea campaign to stop the export of live calves to continental Europe, for example, was interviewed for BBC *Breakfast News*. Evidently aware of the ways in which the news media often stigmatise and delegitimise both protesters and their aims, she was keen to stress her lay status and 'respectability', that is, her 'ordinariness' measured in terms of political and organisational non-affiliation. In so doing, she advances a private-analytic form of news voice.

I can say I'm not an agitator; I'm not sitting here looking for a cause to go out and fight for. And you know, you do tend to deal with things at home and this is how I've got involved with it. It's happened at home, it's happened on our doorstep and it's made me see what's happening and you know you can only fight for what you are aware of at the time. I'm not looking for campaigns to fight for, I have got much better things to do with my life.

(Local resident/supporter, BBC *Breakfast News*)

Finally, voices that reference shared circumstances or conditions and draw attention to the collective nature of this experience, provide a form of public-experiential voice. The following office worker based on an industrial estate experiencing chemical pollution, for example, gives voice to the shared experience of her colleagues and fellow workers.

> The dust is an increasing problem particularly of late, we have noticed a lot more dust around. But it isn't just the dust, it's the atmosphere that is the worry as to what exactly we are breathing, and what is in the air. Sometimes we come in the morning and the smells are quite bad.
>
> (Office worker, BBC *Newswest*)

Now turning to a systematic examination of the 'nature of voice' exhibited/performed in interviews across all the environmental groups noted above, we find the information as shown in Table 1.4.

Clearly, as indicated in Table 1.4, the nature of accessed voices can vary considerably in terms of public–private, analytic–experiential involvement. When considering ordinary voices we find that over 83 per cent of all cases in fact give voice to experiential, in contrast to analytical, accounts. With nearly half of all such voices also positioned in relation to the private sphere of self and home, ordinary voices appear, therefore, to be routinely accessed by the news media to symbolically embody and 'represent' lay experience and do not, it needs to be said, give voice to an analytical point of view. Rather, accessed 'ordinary voices' *embody* and *symbolise* a subjectivist epistemology, an *experiential way of knowing, feeling, sensing* or *'being'* in the world. Often they literally 'stand for' the 'human side', or provide the 'human face' of environmental news stories. The personal reminiscence, the lived experience, the declared consumer preference, the witness to, or the victim of environmental risks and their consequences are all journalistically sought out and positioned to play a symbolic

Table 1.4 Environmental news actors: nature of voice

N Column %	Total	Ordinary voices	Pressure groups	UK government/ administration	Professional/ regulatory/ scientists
Total responses	196	72	39	34	51
Analytic/ public	93 47.44%	10 13.88%	19 48.71%	26 76.47%	38 74.50%
Analytic/ private	5 2.55%	2 2.77%	1 2.56%	1 2.94%	1 1.96%
Experimental/ public	61 31.12%	25 34.72%	18 38.46%	7 20.58%	11 21.56%
Experimental/ private	37 18.87%	35 48.61%	1 2.56%	0 0%	1 1.96%

role, not to elaborate discursively a form of 'social rationality'. No doubt their presence can be accounted for by an increasingly competitive news strategy to build audiences by addressing the 'common-denominator' interests and life-world circumstances of their imagined audiences, and in so doing 'humanise' the basis of their programme appeals. Not that this feature is confined to the more 'tabloid' variants of TV news; rather 'ordinary involvement' and an associated subjectivist epistemology can be found across the TV news spectrum, including those 'prestige' programmes often taken to present the world through an objectivist epistemology of proclaimed *neutrality*, *facticity* and *expert analysis* (Cottle 1993a, 1993b; Langer 1998). Though lay involvement may at first promise, then, to provide a different evaluation of and response to the management and consequences of environmental hazards when compared to the authorities and experts officially charged with their responsibility – in practice, as we have seen, this remains presentationally disempowered. The opportunities to advance perspectives grounded in forms of 'social rationality' are tightly controlled.

Interestingly, though beyond the immediate focus of our interest in lay access, Table 1.4 also indicates how environmental pressure groups (that is organised 'voices of the "side effects"') also appear to deploy 'experiential/public', as well as 'analytic/public', forms of address when accessed by the news media. Perhaps this tells us something about the green agenda and its deliberate framing within, and appeal to a more personalised, localised and 'human-scale' of political action (from Schumacher's earlier 'small is beautiful' to Greenpeace's more recent, 'think global, act local'). In other words, the evolving green agenda may well benefit from an 'elective affinity' with the news media's own evolving and professionally inscribed epistemological appeals – though to what extent this is so deserves thorough examination.

Clearly, space permitting, there is much more that could be examined and said about the nature and forms of accessed voices – both 'ordinary' and 'non-ordinary' – within environmental TV news. Enough has been indicated, none the less, that lay opinion and views of the environment are severely constrained by their forms of news entry, as well as a seeming professional practice that packages and positions ordinary voices to symbolise and embody the world of everyday experience. This subjectivist/experiential epistemology informs the presentation of environmental TV news and contributes to the accessing of ordinary people but it does not generally permit *direct* opportunities to confront or challenge the objectivist claims of experts, politicians and scientists involved in the management of risks – the opening example from *Newsnight* remains, then, a remarkable exception. Paradoxically, ordinary environmental news 'subjects' and their 'subjectivities' become objectified when positioned to symbolise and representationally embody, but are not permitted to argue for and elaborate upon, a locally grounded, culturally contingent and humanly or socially evaluated response to environmental risks or their political and scientific management.[4]

TV news visualising environmental risks

Above it was suggested that an approach to environmental news that confines its analytical sights on the discursive play of rationalities, whether scientific or social or even the interpenetration of the two, is likely to overlook the cultural resonance and symbolism routinely structured into news visualisation. Though not necessarily explicitly aligned to the changing discourses and formalised positions of environmental politics, such scenes can none the less contribute to a more culturally resonate if politically indistinct 'environmental sensibility'. Urry and Macnaghten have traced the historical emergence of, and cultural meanings attached to, 'nature' – including nature approached as landscape, as object of scientific study, as threatened and in need of protection, as providing resources for life, as source of spiritual renewal and communion, and, more generally, as 'the environment' (Urry 1992; Macnaghten and Urry 1998). A detailed study of TV news visualisation of 'nature' and the 'environment' would undoubtedly find considerable support for most if not all of these contemporary 'views' across the TV news landscape.[5] Just from the samples of news items collected for this study, it is apparent that alongside images of nature visualised or consumed in 'terms' of spectacle and landscape, TV news also routinely visualises the environment as under threat. Sometimes such scenes are explicitly anchored by the words and substantive framing of the news story concerned, sometimes by a more culturally resonate 'relay' of juxtaposed images.[6] Consider, for example, the news report below.

BBC1 *News* 27 April 1998 Lead Story (News presenter to camera) Environmental groups are increasingly concerned about the impact of poisonous flood water near Europe's biggest national park	Visuals News presenter: in studio. Still: dead fish, belly up.
in southern Spain. Toxic waste escaped on Saturday from an industrial reservoir near the Corton Donana national park in Southern Spain threatening to destroy plants and wildlife.	Still: map of Spain/location of national park.
The surrounding farmland has been devastated. Local farmers say that it could cost them up to £8 million.	Still: dead fish, belly up.
(Correspondent voice-over) This is the aftermath of the toxic spill, it has choked everything in its path.	Video: close-up of boot turning over dead animal lying in mud.

For Jose Antonio Deluna and his wife Carmen, these are days of despair.

Video: pull-back from dead animal to couple walking in front of mud-devastated fields.

Much of their thirty hectare farm is now under a sea of mud. Jose Antonio should have started harvesting his peach crop this week, now he's afraid that he may never be able to work his land again.

Video: three panning distance shots of mud stretching into tree lined distance.

(Voice of Jose Antonio with translator's voice-over)
For us this is total ruin, this is our business and our home. We don't even know whether we will be able to stay living here because we won't be able to farm.

Video: couple interviewed in front of muddied fields.

(Correspondent voice-over)
These pictures from the environ-mental group Greenpeace show how far the tide of toxic material has spread. They say it is a disaster for land and for health. The full effects won't be known for five or six years.

Video: aerial panning scenes of industrial reservoir and burst banks, following 'sea' of mud across devastated landscapes.

(Eva Hernandez: Greenpeace representative)
Heavy metals are now in this place, in the water, in the ground and only in a few years will we be able to know what is happening to the bird population, the fish population.

Video: Interview of Greenpeace representative in front of lush green vegetation.

(Correspondent voice-over)
The cost of this toxic spill is high and rising.

Video: mid-shot to close-up shot of dead fish, belly up.

Voladin Apearsa, the Swedish mining company involved, are bringing in senior executives as a government inquiry begins.

Video: distance to mid-shots of birds circling to land on mud-covered fields.

(Correspondent direct to camera)
The problems here are just beginning. The toxic waste is continuing to seep into the soil.

Video: correspondent standing in front of mud-devastated fields.

Hour after hour it is causing greater
contamination. Local people say it's
not only livelihoods that have been
destroyed here, but lives too.

Orla Guerin, BBC News, Seville.

Visually the news story above has been choreographed to 'underwrite' or help
authenticate the words, and deploys a crafted succession of iconic and symbolic
images. The informational value of most of the scenes, however, with the exception of the locating map of Spain, can be considered limited. Together such
scenes none the less help symbolise something of the scale, impact and future
consequences of the toxic pollution upon both wildlife and humans. The
repeated still image of the dead fish, belly up, for instance, helps frame the
item at the outset and is returned to later on in the video film report from
which it originates. We can also note how once again ordinary voices, even at
this considerable distance, are deliberately sought out and positioned to symbolise the human effects of this disaster. This particular visualisation of environmental catastrophe, then, is relatively straightforward, though we may want
to note the lush green visual backdrop accompanying the interviewed
Greenpeace representative which serves to heighten, through juxtaposition, the
contaminated and muddied scenes that predominate throughout the rest of the
report. Such scenes make use of a recognisable and now almost standardised
visual 'lexicon' deployed in the representation of environmental disaster stories
– scenes that is, which connect with an 'environmental sensibility' emotionally stirred by images of nature as industrially defiled and under threat. Given
its deep-seated cultural resonance, this visualisation of 'nature' as under threat
can also assume a more independent existence from the verbal narratives of
news. Consider the following for example.

HTV *News* 25 June 1997	Visuals
(Newscaster voice-over)	
An investigation's been launched after fire broke out at a controversial chemical plant in Wiltshire today.	Video: pan from fire-engines in tree-lined street to factory perimeter fence and visible tall chemical containers inside.
Workers were evacuated from Premier Environmental Waste in Westbury	Video: scenes of assembled workers outside.
as a precaution but no one was hurt.	Video: two yellow-suited, hooded fire-fighters walking towards camera down street with hoses.

Fire crews wearing chemical suits were called in to make the area safe.	Video: steam rising up into sky from opening in blackened metal tanks.
It's thought flames took hold when chemicals were accidentally mixed.	Video shot: rusty metal factory gates and stacked drums inside.
Today's blaze is the latest in a string of fires and chemical leaks at the factory.	Video shot: chemical drums, different colours and conditions stacked in yard.
The Environment Agency is looking into the cause of today's incident.	Video: middle-distance shot of fire-engines in tree-lined street.
	Video: scene of fire-fighters near fire-engines.

This 20-second news report includes seven different visual scenes. Though each purports to establish, iconically, the factual accuracy of the news narrative, when examined in sequence and juxtaposition these same images also serve to 'relay' a further set of overlaid meanings. Situated within an otherwise 'normal' tree-lined street, and set against the summer green of vegetation, the opening scene and panning shot help connote something of the environmental threat posed by the adjacent chemical factory – a scene that resonates, in other words, with the tensions of a cultural opposition between 'nature' and the risks posed by industrial technology. The sense of the 'abnormal' is visually reinforced, as is the accompanying sense of invisible manufactured threat, with the dramatic image of the two fire-fighters wearing, from head to foot, bright yellow suits with spacesuit-like hoods and blackened visors. When appearing with the voice-over declaring 'as a precaution, but no one was hurt', the drama of this visual image perhaps relays a different, less comforting, meaning. When followed by the scene of smoke (or could it be something more sinister?) wafting up into the blue sky from blackened metal tanks, the sense of threat from chemical emissions finds further symbolic confirmation. Following this, scenes of industrial infrastructure and their intrusion into an otherwise 'clean' and 'safe' environment also work symbolically to reinforce the cultural sense of threat – images of chained and rusting metal gates, dented and paint-peeling drums, chemical containers stacked in untidy precarious heaps. In such ways, then, even a 20-second ('restricted') news item can pack in a succession of culturally dense images – scenes that both resonate with and relay an environmental sensibility toward nature as under threat.

Such visualisations routinely inform news representations – watch any TV news programme over the course of a week and you will undoubtedly come across many similar *spectacular views*. The item above, for example, was immediately followed by an equally condensed news report about the bankruptcy of a man convicted for polluting a local river – replete with a rapid succession of environmental images juxtaposed alongside equally symbolic images of industrial and chemical despoliation. This, in turn, was followed by a lengthier news item about a local protest against the cutting down of ancient hedgerows by McAlpine, a major building contractor – again choreographed with numerous scenes structured around the oppositions of urban development and rural quietude, diggers and concrete and country lanes, bricks and mortar and the scattered chopped remains of former hedges. In other words, visual images that resonate with an environmental sensibility not only inform individual news items but also now flow across countless news stories, TV news programmes and schedules as a matter of course.

Conclusion

The principal finding here, then, is that TV news trades both commercially and symbolically in an environmental sensibility that resonates with cultural views of nature and environmental hazards. Given the competitive and commercial underpinning to the news media as well as their constitutive role within popular culture, perhaps this is not so surprising. What still needs further clarification, however, is the extent to which TV news serves as a barometer registering (and giving voice to) the recent explosion in environmental consciousness and discourses, or simply relies upon and activates an historically longer-serving set of cultural motifs, symbols and feelings. From the findings of this discussion there are grounds to suggest that often the latter is at play. The news media routinely visualise 'nature' and the environment in terms of deeply felt cultural oppositions that resonate with and help constitute an environmental sensibility – one where 'nature' and the 'environment' are now widely *felt* to be under threat. This 'spectacular' visualisation of the environment', by definition, however, cannot substitute for the necessary public elaboration and engagement of contending environmental perspectives and discourses, though it may well contribute a powerful undercurrent of feelings. Beck's (1992a) 'voices of the "side effects"' when accessed on to the televisual news stage can also contribute symbolically to this environmental sensibility though, as we have seen, they have precious few opportunities to elaborate a form of 'social rationality', much less directly engage the discourses of institutional authorities charged with the management of environmental risks. Paradoxically, as we have seen, Beck's 'voices of the "side effects"' are all too often rendered socially silent, notwithstanding their statistical and symbolic news presence, and they remain the discursive prisoners of tightly controlled forms of news entry and representation. To end, perhaps we should return to the rare 'example' of Frances Hall to remind ourselves of what exactly news access can mean when an 'ordinary person' manages to escape the cultural conventions of news sentiment, symbolic positioning and stunted presentational formats to elaborate a form of 'social rationality' in engaged public discussion. Environmental news access remains a prize worth struggling for.

Acknowledgements

I would like to thank Liza Bonthuys for helping to locate some of the news reports discussed in this chapter, Craig Bonnett who acted as research assistant on the three-year *News Access UK* research programme from which some of the quantitative data discussed here originates, and also Bath Spa University College for funding this same research.

Notes

1   Previous work on the mediating influences of a particular news form (regional TV news) on the representation of the 'inner city' (Cottle 1993a, 1994), as well as on the shaping impact of different UK TV news forms on environmental representation (Cottle 1993b), suggests that TV news is, in important respects, both culturally differentiated and mediates social issues according to these distinctive conventions and appeals.

2   Some of the most promising work to date that has begun to recognise the symbolic nature of environmental representation is Corner *et al.* (1990), Gamson and Modigliani (1989), A. Hansen (1993b) and Lowe and Morrison (1984).

3   This environmental sub-sample is derived from the three-year research programme *News Access UK* with data drawn from a two-week sample of forty news programmes across eight TV news outlets, generating a sample of 117 environmental related news items (representing 11.07 per cent of all TV news items) and a cast of 656 environmental news actors. Sample weeks began on 23 January 1995 and 5 June 1995. Additional, more recent, news items broadcast at the time of writing were also selected for qualitative discussion.

4   In these respects, lay knowledge as elaborated upon by Wynne (1996a) does not really find a voice within environmental news at all.

5   Earlier research into regional TV news, for example, found a routine preponderance of news items across the ten-year sample period that variously and visually endorsed a nostalgic view of past traditions, rural way of life and the passing of folk crafts; that featured unusual and sick animals inviting an affective response; that celebrated local/regional 'beauty spots' and surrounding 'scenic' countryside; and that reported on 'outdoors' leisure pursuits, activities and 'characters' situated within countryside settings. All this in addition to the more obviously 'environmental' news items focused through protests and demonstrations, accidents and pollution, published research reports, planning developments, and news reports on various environmental hazards (Cottle 1990). These findings endorse earlier research findings (Cottle 1993b).

6   For more on 'anchorage' and 'relay' see Barthes (1972) and different visual methodologies deployed in news research see Cottle (1998b).

Chapter 2

Interest group strategies and journalistic norms

News media framing of environmental issues

M. Mark Miller and Bonnie Parnell Riechert

The discursive context in which issues are presented has an important impact on public opinion and policy-making processes. It makes a difference if the issue of endangered species, for example, is discussed in terms of economic development, biodiversity or aesthetics. In fact, debate about environmental issues usually is more about how to look at issues than about the facts or values involved.

In this chapter we examine the concept of news media framing in the context of contentious issues. We also argue that opposing stakeholders try to gain public and policy-maker support for their positions not by offering new facts or by changing evaluations of the facts, but by altering the frames or interpretive dimensions for evaluating the facts. If this is the case, there is much to be learned by studying situations in which contentious stakeholders send competing frames on a collision course.

Conceptualising framing

The concept of framing can be traced to Gregory Bateson's paper (1955), 'A theory of play and phantasy', which was reprinted in his monograph *Steps to an Ecology of Mind* in 1972. Goffman credits Bateson with the idea in his book, *Frame Analysis: An Essay on the Organization of Experience* (Goffman 1974), which popularised it.

Communication researchers were quick to apply Goffman's insights into investigations of news. In her classic study of media sociology, Tuchman (1976: 1066) noted that 'framing implies identifying some items as facts, not others'. Similarly in a study of news coverage of Students for Democratic Society, Gitlin (1980: 6–7) observed that frames 'are the principles of selection, emphasis, and presentation composed of tacit little theories about what exists, what happens, and what matters.' These statements emphasise selection and emphasis of facts. Framing allows journalists to focus on facts and still shape discourse – either consciously or unconsciously.

Building on the pioneering framing studies of the 1970s and 1980s, researchers have given increasing focus on framing relating to news since the early 1990s. In fact, it served as the theme for a conference on 'Framing the

New Media Landscape' at the University of South Carolina in October 1997, which included more than sixty papers and presentations.[1] Many researchers have investigated how news media frame issues (see for example, Davis 1995; Entman 1991; Fine 1992; Hornig 1992). They usually think of framing as being driven by unifying ideologies that shape all content on a topic into a specific, dominant interpretation consistent with the interests of social elites. Hallin (1986, 1987), for example, argues that the 'Cold War' provided the frame for news coverage of international diplomacy for decades (see also Gitlin 1980; Gamson 1989; Vincent *et al*. 1989).

It may indeed require qualitative approaches to ascertain news frames when they are conceived as unifying ideological mechanisms. Under such a conception, frames are usually tacit although they can exert a powerful influence on what is seen. As Reese (1997) suggests, frames can even generate coverage blackouts in which some views are not included in news accounts and therefore are not available for analysis.

Analysing text via quantitative research emphasises variables or differences among observations. As such, it is not well suited to the task of discovering invariant themes in news, in ascertaining extra-textual meanings, or in discerning what facts and perspectives have been omitted. We argue, however, that invariance is not essential to the definition of frames and that when variance in presentation is admitted, quantitative techniques can be a powerful means for investigating the phenomenon. In particular these techniques apply when contentious stakeholders attempt to win public and policy-maker support for their points of view. Such situations are as common as they are revealing.

We think of framing as an ongoing process by which ideological interpretive mechanisms are derived from competing stakeholder positions. In this discussion the word 'stakeholders' is used to refer to the multiple groups in the policy-making process that 'stand to win or lose as a result of policy decisions' (W. Lyons *et al*. 1995: 497). In any contentious policy issue, different populations segments will have specific and competing concerns at stake. The selective nature of framing suggests that in their discussion of the complex issues these stakeholders will discuss those policy implications more salient to them, while ignoring other implications. For example, in press releases discussing environmental policies regulating wetlands conservationists focus on such things as wildlife habitat while property owners emphasise such things as property rights and compensation (Riechert 1996).

The term 'claims-maker' is equally appropriate in referencing the stakeholder groups. People who are involved as stakeholders in a policy issue engage in related discussions, both private and public. Members of these competing stakeholder groups become claims-makers when they articulate their perspective. As people speak from their perspective, they make claims and frame issues by emphasising certain aspects and ignoring others. Whether consciously or unconsciously, involved stakeholders will exclude competing or contradictory viewpoints in their discussion.

The selective nature of framing in this way limits public policy debates by stakeholders. This, in turn, limits news media discourse on contentious issues. As journalists report on complex issues they depend on available sources (officials, experts, eyewitnesses and so forth). While information in news articles is attributed to their source, it will be just as limited in scope and focus as the selective nature of comments by any particular set of stakeholders or claims-makers on whom journalists depend for information and quotable comments.

The more a particular stakeholder group is quoted in news articles, relative to competing stakeholder groups, the more prominently the selective issue definition is represented in news coverage, relative to competing frames. Studies by the authors and others demonstrate evidence of this stakeholder influence on media content. Riechert (1996) observed this in a computer-assisted content analysis of Associated Press news stories on wetlands from 1984 to 1995. She found that stories prominently quoting conservation spokespersons reflected a conservation frame far more than stories prominently quoting property-owner spokespersons. She found the obverse with regard to the property-owner frame. In this process, therefore, news media content is dependent on the comments and claims of stakeholders who are external to the news organisation but central to the issue debate (see Shoemaker and Reese 1996).

Stakeholders compete to win public opinion and establish their positions as official policy by promoting their own views of issues and events. If one such group triggers a process like the 'Spiral of Silence' described by Noelle-Neumann (1984), then it might establish its position as the only legitimate one. At the end of such a process it could be said that hegemony has been established (and qualitative techniques would be required for their investigation).

Schon and Rein (1994) in their monograph, *Frame Reflection: Toward the Resolution of Intractable Policy Controversies*, focus on issues such as abortion policy, environment and public housing, which have defied policy resolution. Such controversies persist, they argue, precisely because stakeholders marshall different facts and different interpretations of the facts. In a word, they 'frame' things differently. This leads to 'a remarkable ability . . . to dismiss evidence adduced by our antagonists' (Schon and Rein 1994: 5). 'When policy controversies are enduring and invulnerable to evidence, what tends to result is institutionalised political contention leading either to stalemate or to pendulum swings from one extreme position to another' (Schon and Rein 1994: 8). In such situations in which interest groups vie for support, frames become amenable to quantitative analysis.

Reporting Environmental Risk

News values

As Sachsman (1993), Wilkins and Patterson (1987) and others have noted, journalists do not report environmental risk; they report news. When journalists scrutinise the world looking for news, they evaluate what they see according to news values. These values are criteria for deciding what to report and how much emphasis to provide. Nearly all introductory reporting textbooks contain lists of news values which include such things as consequence, timeliness, proximity, prominence and human interest.

Environmental risk, in our view, is an abstraction about the possibility of damage and, by itself, does not possess any news value. Rather, it enters news by association with such things as newsworthy events (for example human-made or natural disasters) or conflict over policy by contending stakeholders, or the activities and afflictions of celebrities. Journalists operate according to business imperatives and the norms of their profession. The fundamentals here are that news must be factual and must attract an audience. Adherence to the facts assures continued access to officials, celebrities and other newsmakers, while adherence to news values such as proximity, timeliness and interest assures attractiveness to audiences.

As the American political commentator and philosopher Lippmann (1922) said of news: 'There must be manifestation. The course of events must assume a certain definable shape, and until it is in a phase where some aspect is an accomplished fact, news does not separate itself from the ocean of possible truth' (Lippmann 1922: 340). Schramm (1949: 288) in his classic essay, 'The Nature of News', observed that news is not the event but is the report of the event.

Environmental issues often are associated with risk or the probability that damaging events will occur. As noted above, environmental risk is not of itself sufficient to serve as the basis for news. To become news it must be associated with sufficient levels of one or more news values. News exists not because there is a significant risk, but because there is some triggering event such as an explosion, or an injury, or fight between government officials and their charges, or conflict among stakeholders.

The focus on events as the basis of news assures journalists of the timeliness of their reports. Perhaps more important, it allows them to eliminate a substantial number of situations from consideration. If journalists were to report on all situations in proportions to their importance measured in terms of potential impact, they would be overwhelmed. Stories on such topics as global warming would be endless, repetitive and boring.

Events can be conceived of as being both planned and unplanned. Planned events, many of which are designed to be covered by news media, are discussed under the topic 'Source selection' (pp. 51–3). With regard to unplanned events, including human-made and natural disasters, researchers have noted specific patterns in the time sequence of media coverage. In a study of television coverage of airline crashes, Vincent *et al.* (1989) noted that three narrative themes emerge as phases: first, disruption of normalcy, second, investigation of mystery, and third, restoration of normalcy. These authors assert that this pattern serves to perpetuate naïve beliefs and provide assurance that elites can be trusted. The Vincent *et al.* (1989) conclusions clearly apply in environmental disasters such as oil or toxic spills.

In covering a disaster, journalists need differing kinds of information in different phases. During the disruption of normalcy phase, journalists seek to establish the facts. Preferred sources are eyewitnesses. Private parties such as company spokespersons are listened to, but their statements are treated with scepticism. If the event is an ongoing danger such as an oil spill, then opinions of experts are sought to assess the risk. During the investigation phase, preferred sources are government investigators who are to establish the facts and experts who can put the facts in context and offer interesting conjectures as to why the disaster occurred. For some disasters this period may be over in a matter of days; for others it takes years. During the restoration phase, officials attempt to explain how the disaster occurred, offer assurance that the probability or recurrence has been minimised, and that justice has been served. If these objectives are not satisfied, then the disaster itself will slip into the background and news coverage will be driven by conflict among stakeholders at which time government officials, stakeholder spokespersons, and the general public become the principal sources of news. Of course, it is possible for a new, similar disaster to pre-empt the original event.

Conflict among stakeholders (which is discussed below) is a driving force for sustaining environmental news, but the environment seldom becomes news without such an event. The problems of global warming did not garner significant news coverage until the drought of 1988 brought the 'greenhouse effect' to the public consciousness, although it remains unclear that this drought was a manifestation of the problem. M. Miller *et al.* (1992) noted that the number of news stories containing the terms 'greenhouse effect' or 'global warming' increased dramatically in the summer of 1988. They attributed the surge to either of two events, a serious drought and a speech before the USA Congress by NASA scientist James Hansen. They were not, however, able to disentangle the impact of each event. Similarly, depletion of the ozone layer made little news until reports of 'an ozone hole' over Antarctica. Interestingly, ozone depletion generated little policy conflict or media attention and international policies to control chlorofluorocarbons were implemented with little news or public discussion.

Objectivity

Journalistic norms stress 'objectivity' and 'fairness' and preclude journalists from overtly taking sides on a controversial issue. But these norms do not prevent journalists from accepting the 'facts' as provided by stakeholders or from reporting the 'fact' that stakeholder spokespersons have articulated some opinion. Such things are the foundations of most news (see Singer and Endreny 1993: 127–8). News does not exist in a vacuum, of course, and journalistic norms do not prevent reporters from accepting the factual context offered by a source. Thus, the ways that news media frame issues can come directly from stakeholders with vested interests. Because news often comes from unexpected events, generally the first journalists who cover them have little expertise and little time to gather background information. They are, therefore, reliant on their sources to provide initial briefings and set expectations. Because reporters have the human tendency to see what they expect to see, these briefings can have a powerful effect on the frames set in early news coverage. This situation is exacerbated because later reporters use their colleagues' work as briefing materials and have their expectations reinforced.

Stakeholders articulate their positions to accommodate journalistic norms and seek to win public approval. Contentious stakeholders, needless to say, have to compete for media attention. Journalists select from the range of material presented according to the rules of the profession. This often leads journalists to present issues differently from how news sources want them to be portrayed. For example, Dyer *et al.* (1991) compared Associated Press coverage of Exxon Corporation with the company's press releases before and after the *Exxon Valdez* ran aground. They found that corporate news releases focused on environmental concerns while Associated Press (AP) coverage focused on legal ones. Further, the coverage of environmental and legal issues occurred together in AP stories far more often following the disaster. Dyer *et al.* (1991) say this pattern indicates that news media do not merely reflect the company line, they play an adversarial role. That is, the news media, in this case, rejected the company position that the disaster should be framed primarily as an environmental concern and insisted on framing it in terms of legal responsibility.

Objectivity is often viewed solely as an ethical imperative for journalists. However, as Tuchman (1976) observed, objectivity functions as a 'strategic ritual' designed to achieve self-serving goals for journalists. These include maintenance of diverse audiences, access to contentious news sources, and ease of reporting. Moreover, reporters need the protection offered by appeals to objectivity because they work under intense deadline pressures. As Swisher and Reese (1992: 989) put it, 'Reporters, seldom having the time or expertise to verify the truth, rely on an appearance of impartiality to fend off criticism. Objectivity becomes a routine, often manifest in balancing stories.' Appreciating the point requires an understanding of journalists' definition of facts. For journalists, facts are non-controversial occurrences. Attribution to sources offers a mechanism for preserving the factuality of non-verifiable assertion. Thus, journalists can report the 'fact' that an assertion was made without concern for the veracity of the assertion itself.[2]

Journalists can accept factual contexts provided by stakeholders without violating the cannon of objectivity. For example, casting the issue of preservation of old growth forest as an issue of jobs and economic stability is acceptable because such factors are associated with it. Objectivity obliges reporters to report facts, but it does not assure that they are getting the right facts.

Source selection

One of the best documented findings in news research is that journalists rely heavily on governmental sources. Sigal (1973) in his benchmark content analysis of the *New York Times* and the *Washington Post* found that a majority of news sources are governmental. The finding has been replicated across a variety of contexts and media. With regard to environmental concerns, Gamson and Modigliani (1989) and Nimmo (1985) found that official sources dominated coverage of the Three Mile Island nuclear shutdown. There are several reasons for the preponderance of government sources in news, including first, such sources are readily available and built into journalistic routines, second, they are generally thought to be credible, and third, in cases where there is great public danger such as nuclear disasters, toxic spills, and military manoeuvres, sources have complete control over access to physical locations and informed personnel. Riechert and Miller (1997b) found evidence of the impact of official positions on the framing of environmental news in a study of Associated Press coverage of wetlands during the terms of three US Presidents.[3] They found that during the Reagan years the issue was framed as an habitat restoration, during the Bush administration, as an economic issue, and during the Clinton presidency as a regulatory concern.

Because environmental risk often enters news via disaster or protest, journalists' preferences for official sources have particularly strong impact. The events driving environmental news occur in specific locations where local journalists provide initial coverage. These journalists turn to local government and corporate sources with whom they are familiar to obtain the grist for the first news stories. Thus these sources, upon whom journalists continually depend, have a strong influence on the initial framing of breaking environmental news. Because reporters from more distant locations are likely to examine initial reports before they get on the scene, initial framing is likely to be amplified.

The position of official sources contrasts sharply with that of environmental sources, who are likely to be unorganised residents, ad-hoc citizen groups or representatives of environment groups based in distant locations. Because of these characteristics, environmental sources are not likely to be credible, familiar or readily available to news sources. Perhaps more important, journalists are not likely to see them as ongoing sources of information and therefore see no reason to defer to them in maintaining steady sources of news. The differences in journalists' relationships with different kinds of sources offer at least a partial explanation for the frequent journalistic delegitimisation of environmental advocates. (This phenomenon is discussed more on pp. 52–3.)

Conflict among competing interests is a principal driving force of news. Usual discussions of news values note that situations involving conflict provide the drama needed to attract audiences and that the level of conflict is indicative of the passions participants feel and therefore the importance of the story to them. Perhaps more important, conflict motivates stakeholders to increase their efforts to influence the public policy-makers. Capturing news media attention and shaping its content are key means of meeting these goals.

Stakeholders make substantial efforts to have the points of view reflected in news media. The notion of 'information subsidy' described by Gandy (1982) and extended by Turk (1986, 1988) reveals the approach of public relations practitioners and the extent to which they go to accommodate journalistic demands. The notion of information subsidy encompasses a wide variety of activities that sources support to help journalists. Researching and writing the news release remain the primary public relations vehicle, but such things as providing interviews, tours, transportation and event tickets all count as information subsidies. The concept recognises that while it is a violation of journalistic ethics to accept direct payment for publishing materials, it is acceptable for journalists to accept assistance (subsidies) for gathering materials.

While the practices accepted under information subsidy leave the final judgement of what to present and how to present it to the journalists, it is clear that such subsidies affect the news. Objectivity is not an adequate constraint to prevent information subsidies from being effective. As Swisher and Reese (1992: 989) said, 'Public relations workers are well aware of the [journalists'] needs and exploit the objectivity routine by being highly quotable and accessible.'

Public relations practitioners stage events or at least design them with news media in mind. The practice is so common that the term 'pseudo-event' used to describe it has entered the popular lexicon. The term was invented by Boorstin (1971) to describe a practice which has significantly increased since then. Pseudo-events are not, however, a sure-fire means of capturing media attention. As Gitlin (1980) noted, groups can be delegitimised to such a degree that their efforts to gain media attention are either ignored or denigrated. While Gitlin based his conclusions about delegitimisation on research on Vietnam War protesters, it is clear that his ideas apply to at least some environmental activists. Gitlin observed that media essentially force protesters to choose between making reasoned arguments and being ignored, attracting media attention via dramatic or illegal activities and being delegitimised, or muting their positions so that they could be covered as routine news.

Hallin (1986) essentially agrees with Gitlin and describes three spheres of political discourse:

- The Sphere of Consensus where issues are agreed upon by the vast majority and journalists feel free to champion certain values;
- The Sphere of Legitimate Controversy in which major parties and players debate and are covered with balance and objectivity,
- The Sphere of Deviance in which points of view outside of the mainstream are expressed and journalists feel free to delegitimise the groups articulating them.

Although little research has applied Hallin's categories to environmental issues, it is interesting to note how they apply to mainstream groups such as the Boy Scouts, which generally espouses non-controversial environmental positions like harmony with nature; advocacy groups like Ducks Unlimited, which debate land-use issues with other interests, and more strident groups such as Greenpeace and EarthFirst!, which occasionally defy laws to make their points.

Conclusion

Frame-mapping analysis makes it possible to investigate the framing process with rigour and convenience. In particular, propositions concerning the strategies and circumstances that cause one frame to dominate the discourse need investigation. Thus, when news and policy processes are seen in the context of frames in collision, important propositions are open to investigation. Developments in computer-assisted content analysis allow numerous new opportunities for rigorous analysis comparing the relative prominence of distinct frames in text. In particular, the VBPro computer programs described here offer new possibilities for precise measurement of frames, and shifts over time in frame prominence, in news coverage.

Concept-mapping and frame-mapping methods devised by the authors have been used to illustrate how the dynamics of selective framing by stakeholders and media content operated in environmental risk issues such as pesticides, timber salvage and wetlands protection and regulation (M. Miller and Riechert 1994; Miller 1997; Riechert and Miller 1997a, 1997b). The methods referenced here may be used to investigate framing and media content related to any complex issue (Miller *et al.* 1998). Studies by these and other authors demonstrate the tendency of environmental risk issues to support numerous possible foci of emphasis by stakeholders. These frames compete as self-nominating directives for policy.

The conceptualisation of news media framing of issues as a process in which journalists and contending stakeholders interact has substantial implications for research on the media politics of environmental risk. Clearly environmental risk abounds in contemporary society, but generally lies dormant until some event drives it onto the public agenda. Whether the triggering event is a natural or human-made disaster, or is due to a stakeholder initiative, it activates contending stakeholders who seek to win public and policy-maker support. They do this by promoting their own interpretation of the issue, what we call framing. News media participate in the process by accepting and modifying the frames presented to them.

The keys to understanding this process lie in the examination of the imperatives under which journalists operate. Stakeholders attempt to exploit these imperatives, and in turn, journalists capitalise on conflict between stakeholders. This conflict motivates stakeholders or claims-makers to provide journalists with the grist for producing news in a manner that is economical and convenient for reporters.

Journalists' acceptance of materials from sources are manifest in news content. The multiple frames represented can be ascertained through frame-mapping analysis of texts unambiguously attributable to stakeholder groups (Riechert 1996; M. Miller 1997; Riechert and Miller 1997a). Such analysis reveals the terms that each stakeholder group uses to articulate its frame. The frequency of occurrences of each group's frame terms in news stories is indicative of the degree to which that group has captured media attention.

Shoemaker and Reese (1996) note the need for further research attention to be directed to news media content and its influences. They propose a hier-archical model of influences on media content, ranging from the individual level and the media routines level, to the organisation level, extramedia level and finally the ideological level representing hegemony. The ability of stake-holders in environmental risk issues to articulate their perspective to jour-nalists and (through journalists, in news media) to the public represents an influence on media content at the extramedia level. These processes merit increased attention by researchers.

Who frames the news? To whose views do the media give voice? Research comparing stakeholder frames in news media coverage can address these ques-tions and illuminate understanding of framing, media content, and environ-mental risk policy. Dearing and Rogers (1996) call for focused analyses of news coverage over time of single issues. Environmental risk issues are per-fectly suited for these kinds of investigations, in our view namely because they involve multiple stakeholders including competing advocacy groups, government officials, and private industries.

Notes

1 Papers from this conference (held at the Center for Mass Communications Research, University of South Carolina at Columbia, 12–14 October 1997) are being revised and edited for a forthcoming book *Framing in the New Media Landscape*, edited by Stephen D. Reese, August Grant and Oscar Gandy.

2 Our examinations of the relative frequencies of words in news copy indicate that 'said' is always among the ten most common, and in news copy there are numerous other forms of attribution. Usually no substantive nouns or non-auxiliary verbs are among the top twenty most common.

3 Miller and Riechert investigate media framing via a set of computer programs (VBPro) and techniques that they have invented. Essentially their approach uses computerised content analysis, multidimensional scaling, and cluster analysis to ascertain lists of words that tend to be used exclusively by one or another stake-holder in texts articulating their positions such as press releases. These lists of 'frame terms' are then used in subsequent content analysis of news texts such as Associated Press stories. The techniques are described in Riechert (1996), Miller (1997) and Miller and Riechert (forthcoming). The VBPro computer programs are copyrighted but are available without charge on the WorldWideWeb at:
http://excellent.com.utk.edu/~mmmiller/vbpro.html

Claims-making and framing in British newspaper coverage of the 'Brent Spar' controversy

Anders Hansen

Environmental issues and risks do not ordinarily present themselves for public concern or political action. Like other social problems (such as poverty, crime and drug-abuse) they need to be identified and defined as such, and made visible in the public sphere or in public arenas before they can acquire the status of 'social problems' that the public should be concerned about, and toward which politicians and other decision-makers should direct attention, legislation and resources. The identification and construction of social problems depend crucially on claims-makers; indeed in the now classic articulation of a constructionist perspective on social problems, Spector and Kitsuse (1987: 75) define 'social problems as the activities of individuals or groups making assertions of grievances and claims with respect to some putative conditions'.

If the construction of social problems depends on successful public claims-making, then the mass media constitute a key public arena in which the voices, definitions and claims of claims-makers (notably representatives of government, public authorities, formal political institutions, professional communities and associations, pressure groups and so on) are put on public display and compete with each other for legitimacy. However, the media are not merely a convenient public arena or window. Through the organisational and professional arrangements of news-making, they play an active role in the construction, inflection and framing of both issues and claims-makers. Gaining media coverage may often seem the most immediate task for claims-makers, but as Ryan (1991) states in her book on media strategies for grass-roots: 'gaining attention alone is not what a social movement wants; the real battle is over whose interpretation, whose framing of reality, gets the floor' (C. Ryan 1991: 53).

'Framing' in media coverage hinges on two dimensions: first, the selection/accessing of sources/claims-makers, and second, the presentation/evaluation of arguments/actors. As Entman (1993) argues:

> Framing essentially involves selection and salience. To frame is to select some aspects of a perceived reality and make them more salient in a

communicating text, in such a way as to promote a particular problem definition, causal interpretation, moral evaluation and/or treatment recommendation for the item described.

(Entman 1993: 52)

It is reasonable to expect a fair degree of 'fit' between who is quoted in media coverage and how issues are framed or defined. Indeed, in a study of US news coverage of climate change, Trumbo (1996) found a strong association between the types of claims-makers (scientists, politicians and interest groups) accessed by the media and the types and prominence of different frames, leading him to conclude 'that changes occurring in the life-course of this issue [climate change] apparently involved shifts linked to who was getting their message into the media rather than how the media was choosing to present the information' (Trumbo 1996: 281).

While analysis may confirm an association between the types of claims-makers accessed in environmental news reporting and the relative prominence of general thematic clusters or frames in media coverage, such an analysis does not go far enough. Crucially, it does not show us how different sources and their testimonies or claims are framed by the media, or how, through the framing and definitional work engaged in by the media themselves, sources and their claims may achieve legitimacy and credibility through media coverage, or alternatively, may be systematically undermined by such coverage.

Several problems arise in relation to claims-making about environmental risk. First, many environmental risks are relatively invisible and may not develop into future threats or disasters. Second, their development cycle tends to be ill fitted to the twenty-four-hour cycle of news production (Schoenfeld *et al.* 1979). Third, their causal or other connection to putative future outcomes is often shrouded in scientific uncertainty and in a language of probability and likelihoods. The scientific uncertainty which is inherent to much claims-making about environmental risks runs directly counter to conventional news values, yet in order to support and legitimise their claims, those who make claims about environmental risks must argue their case principally on scientific grounds.

Applying the notion of framing, the analysis undertaken in this chapter examines how a particular environmental issue (deep-sea dumping of redundant North Sea oil installations) and its principal promoter, the environmental pressure group Greenpeace, were covered by a sample of British national newspapers. The analysis demonstrates the considerable ideological work engaged in by newspapers in their variable coverage, inflection, contextualisation and elaboration of the claims made by key claims-makers in relation to a controversial issue, highlighting the gulf between commanding attention for an issue and securing legitimacy.

The Brent Spar coverage/analysis

On 30 April 1995 representatives from Greenpeace boarded and occupied a redundant oil terminal in the North Sea, the Brent Spar. Starting with this event, the pressure group succeeded, during the months of May and June 1995, in drawing the attention of the media and the public to an issue which had hitherto commanded very little media and public interest, the decommissioning and removal of redundant oil installations in the North Sea (see Figures 3.1 and 3.2).

More specifically, Greenpeace sought to highlight the plans of the multinational oil company Royal Dutch/Shell to tow the large redundant oil storage installation, the Brent Spar, from its position in the Brent field of the North Sea to the Atlantic Ocean where it would be sunk in waters of considerable depth. Exploiting the publicity generated around its Brent Spar occupation, its later eviction by Shell security personnel and its reoccupation of the Brent Spar during the months of May and June 1995, Greenpeace succeeded in stirring up sufficient media, political, and public interest (including the orchestration of widespread consumer boycotts in Germany and several other European countries) to eventually force Shell to suspend its dumping plans.

Contrary to its own scientific evidence and to the British government's permission and support for deep-sea disposal, but bowing to international consumer boycotts and international political pressure, Shell, on 20 June 1995, announced its decision to put on hold its plans to dispose of the Brent Spar in the Atlantic. The installation was subsequently towed to a Norwegian fiord

Figure 3.1 Greenpeace inflatable at Brent Spar: water cannon used by MV *Rembas* and MV *Torbas* at base of platform to prevent boarding
Source: © Greenpeace and David Sims June 1995

Figure 3.2 Greenpeace and Shell activity around the Brent Spar
Source: © Greenpeace June 1995

to await a decision about the manner of its decommissioning. In early September 1995, Greenpeace announced, by way of a letter of apology to Shell, that some of its initial claims about the amount of toxic material and pollutants on the Brent Spar had been based on erroneous measurements, but maintained that its fight against deep-sea dumping had nevertheless been justified and right.

The analysis which follows examines the coverage of the Brent Spar controversy in large circulation British national newspapers, with one from each of the three traditional format/style divisions of the national press: the *Daily Telegraph* (DTL) – quality/high-brow newspaper; *Daily Mail* (DML) – tabloid/middle-brow; and *Daily Mirror* (DMR) – tabloid/low-brow. Although nominally separate, the Sunday editions of these three newspapers are also included in the analysis: *Sunday Telegraph* (STL), *Mail on Sunday* (MOS) and *Sunday Mirror* (SMR).

Using the full-text electronic database FT-Profile, the body of text examined here consists of all newspaper articles from the three selected daily and Sunday newspapers containing the words 'Brent Spar' in the period January to October 1995. Throughout this analysis the dates of newspaper quotes refer to 1995.

Commanding attention

As Solesbury (1976) has pointed out, the first task in the process of success-fully elevating an issue to the status of 'social problem' is that of command-ing attention. In terms of 'commanding attention', putting an issue or problem into the public arena of the mass media and drawing public atten-tion to it, Greenpeace's Brent Spar action was in general terms highly suc-cessful. The proposed deep-sea dumping of the derelict North Sea Brent Spar oil terminal was, until Greenpeace's action, a non-issue as far as the British news media were concerned. There had been only a single article in each of the daily newspapers mentioning or referring to the Brent Spar in the months prior to Greenpeace's action, and of these only two (DTL 17 February and DML 2 March) made reference to the government's decision to allow deep-sea dumping.

Greenpeace's action on 30 April 1995 received prompt coverage in the *Mirror* and the *Mail*, but initially no mention in the *Telegraph*. The first reference to the Brent Spar occupation did not appear in the *Telegraph* until 12 May (PETERBOROUGH: CROSS LINE) and then only to emphasise a theme which would recur in much of the *Telegraph*'s subsequent coverage, namely that Greenpeace's campaigning priorities were wrong.

The *Telegraph*'s initial reluctance in covering Greenpeace's action signalled a major difference between it and the other papers in the framing of Greenpeace in particular and of the controversy more generally. The difference was already clear in the relatively small number of headlines during the first month of the controversy, May 1995. The *Mail* and the *Mirror* lent some credibility to Greenpeace's action both by emphasising the legitimacy of its actions and by quoting Greenpeace's allegations about the Brent Spar posing a hazardous pol-lution threat to marine life:

MURDER AT SEA: SCANDAL OF DUMPED RIGS THAT MAY WIPE OUT MARINE LIFE: Greenpeace seize oil rig to highlight danger of leav-ing deserted rigs to rot at sea.

(DMR 1 May)

PROTESTERS TAKE OVER 'DANGEROUS' OIL PLATFORM: Disused North Sea terminal contains poisons and radioactive waste, warns Greenpeace.

(DML 1 May)

PROTESTERS DIG IN FOR LONG STAY ON OIL PLATFORM: Greenpeace and Shell stand firm on Brent Spar future.

(DML 2 May)

IT WAS A WALKOVER, SAYS MAN WHO LED THE OIL RIG INVADERS

(DML 4 May)

GREENPEACE 'BLOWING A RASPBERRY' AT SCOTS LAW
(DML 19 May)

By contrast, the *Telegraph* reported criticism that Greenpeace's campaigning priorities were wrong (DTL 12 May), focused its headlines on Greenpeace losing its action (DTL 25 May), and included two letters to the editor arguing that 'Science' recommends dumping as the best solution (DTL 31 May) and 'OLD RIGS COULD SAVE FISH STOCKS' (DTL 26 May).

While the Greenpeace publicity stunt of occupying the derelict Brent Spar platform was the action which initially helped secure media attention and coverage, it is unlikely that this action in itself would have been sufficient for moving the issue along either in terms of continued media coverage or in terms of 'invoking action' (the third task in Solesbury's (1976) model of social problem construction). Apart from the obvious media event focus on the occupation of the Brent Spar and Shell's legal response putting an end to the occupation, reoccupation by Greenpeace and so on, it was Greenpeace's simultaneous promotion of the issue through other key news-forums which helped secure continued news coverage. As Eyerman and Jamison (1989) have rightly pointed out, Greenpeace's influence as a claims-maker hinges primarily on its gathering and strategic dissemination of information:

> Without strategic information, its campaigns would be merely media shows and they would long ago have stopped making news. It is the selective gathering of campaign-related facts, the selective dissemination of arguments to the media and other public fora, the selective testimony at hearings and conferences and international meetings that gives Greenpeace its enormous influence.
>
> (Eyerman and Jamison 1989: 14)

The Brent Spar action, carefully timed to coincide with or slightly precede intergovernmental discussions at the North Sea Conference in early June 1995, gave Greenpeace the means to influence and frame the agenda and emphasis of issues discussed in this key political news forum. Together with demonstrations and the orchestration of consumer boycotts of Shell petrol stations, particularly in Germany and other European countries, the Brent Spar action helped influence the claims-making and framing not just in the political forum of the North Sea Conference, but in the British Parliament as well as in another prime political news forum, the G7 Summit held in Halifax, Nova Scotia in mid-June 1995. The significance of moving the issue along through claims-making and framing in these other forums – distinguished by being themselves prime news foci – was reflected in the sheer amount of newspaper coverage. The volume of reporting only began to gather pace around the North Sea conference of early June and later peaks in the amount of coverage coincided with significant political events, such as the G7 Summit.

Framing civil protest

The *Telegraph*'s negative framing of Greenpeace, already signalled in its initial coverage and contrasting sharply with the more neutral framing in the *Mail* and its distinctly positive framing in the *Mirror*, continued throughout the period studied here and was significantly anchored in a wider discourse, unique to the *Telegraph*, on civil protest. This discourse in turn drew on and articulated a number of broader discourses, including those of 'law and order', a 'democracy' and 'nationalism'.

In early June, when the other papers were covering Greenpeace's attempt to reoccupy the Brent Spar after having been evicted in late May, the *Telegraph* instead published a feature-length discussion of what it described as the increasing resort to illegal means of protest by environmental and other protest groups. The article served a function, well known from both linguistic theory (Fowler 1991; Fairclough 1989) and from the constructionist literature, namely that of linking together and interpreting a series of vaguely related events or activities as symptoms of a deeper problem or social malaise.

> CIVIL DISOBEDIENCE: Protesters take law into own hands – campaigns have targeted poll tax, animal exports and new motorways/more and more demonstrators are willing to act illegally to further their various causes.
>
> (DTL 5 June)

From an early stage of its coverage, the *Telegraph* anchored the Greenpeace action within a larger discourse concerned with protest movements and groups generally, and a view in which such protest was seen as undemocratic, misguided, anti-business, un-accountable to processes of democratic decision-making and unnecessary in the sense that these kinds of protest are costly, a symptom of immaturity and a 'nuisance'. The *Telegraph* was thus the only newspaper to use the word 'nuisance' in any description related to Greenpeace or the Brent Spar.

From a paternalistic stance of describing Greenpeace and other protest groups as annoying but essentially inevitable adjuncts of a free democratic society, a more hostile frame was advanced and elaborated which identified pressure groups generally and Greenpeace in particular as threats to normal, law-abiding, democratic society. Significantly, the *Telegraph* was the only newspaper to discuss Greenpeace in terms of a direct threat to democracy and 'proper democratic' processes:

> like so many single-issue groups, and particularly those concerned with animal rights and environmental issues, Greenpeace feels little obligation to stay within the bounds of normal political behaviour, or indeed the law.
>
> (DTL 21 June)

> SILENCE THAT COST SHELL THE BATTLE – Hugo Gurdon, Industry Editor, says pressure groups threaten not just business but democracy.

... What are companies supposed to do to satisfy, or defeat, the environmental jihad? How can decent law-abiding companies give single-issue pressure groups what they want or get away with refusing their illiberal demands?

... Single-issue pressure groups, operating outside the normal channels of political debate and often illegally, are a threat not just to business but also to liberal democratic society.

(DTL 24 June)

GREENPEACE'S DIRECT ACTION SPEAKS LOUDER THAN WORDS

... Yet the success of direct action also raises the issue of its democratic legitimacy.

(STL 25 June)

In all of the above examples, the 'threat-to-democracy' frame is the newspaper's own, not that of a quoted primary source or of a guest writer. The first quotation is taken from a *Telegraph* editorial, the second from an article by its Industry Editor, and the third from a feature article by the *Sunday Telegraph*'s Environment Correspondent.

Framing Greenpeace

Greenpeace and its campaigners were generally referred to as 'Greenpeace', 'protesters', 'campaigners' and 'activists'. However, the *Telegraph*, in keeping with the anti-Greenpeace tone already indicated, and consistent with what linguists have described as the phenomenon of overlexicalisation, deployed a rather wider and clearly more negative set of descriptors.[1]

Greenpeace and its actions were described variously in terms such as 'nuisance', the formulaic phrase 'single-issue + politics/campaigners/group/pressure group', 'self-righteous', 'rebels', 'bearded', 'doleful', 'extreme eco-warriors', 'eco-sentimentalists', 'emotional', 'misguided', 'militant group', 'undemocratic', 'irresponsible', 'propagandists', 'arrogant', 'more fervent than competent' (DTL 7 September) and 'bullyboys'. A Greenpeace spokesman 'gibbers', rather than speaks, in a *Sunday Telegraph* article (25 June). Where the *Mail* and the *Mirror* tended to portray the battle between Greenpeace and Shell in terms of a struggle between 'daring', 'heroic', 'homely', 'idealistic' protesters and a 'huge', 'large', 'multinational', greedy 'giant', the *Telegraph*, particularly conscious of the potential representation of the battle over Brent Spar as a David (Greenpeace) versus Goliath (Shell) encounter, endeavoured to expose this as a fallacious and mythical representation by repeatedly focusing on the size, (business) value and power of Greenpeace itself as a multinational organisation:[2]

THE BRAINS BEHIND GREENPEACE VICTORY: Oil Rig success proves power of £9M group

(DTL 21 June)

NOTEBOOK: Giants fight and the nation loses

(DTL 24 June)

The framing of Greenpeace as a powerful and threatening organisation (to business, democracy and the public) was further emphasised by the metaphoric labelling of its politics as 'environmental jihad' (DTL 24 June), 'harassment' (DTL 21 June), a 'black art . . . seducing or bullying public opinion by media manipulation ranging from hype and distortion to public demonstrations and criminal disobedience' (DTL 5 October).

Previous research on media coverage of social movements and pressure groups has noted that one of the key problems is to keep media coverage focused on campaign issues, as opposed to personality clashes among movement leaders, movement organisation, internal schisms and break-away groups (Gitlin 1980; Kielbowicz and Scherer 1986). While analyses of other newspapers (Hansen 1993a) have indicated Greenpeace's past success in keeping media attention focused on its campaign causes and issues, the *Telegraph* in particular focused much of its reporting on Greenpeace as an organisation. Much of the Brent Spar coverage, as already indicated, centred on demonstrating that Greenpeace was not the idealistic grassroots 'David' of the moral high ground, but instead a powerful, undemocratic, multinational and multimillion pound organisation (e.g. DTL 21 June):

> SUNDAY COMMENT: Why we should back the French atomic tests – Greenpeace is not about the environment but the exercise of power, argues William Oddie.
> . . . It [the battle] is between democratic politics – with all its faults – and a well-funded, undemocratic, unaccountable and irresponsible internationalist politics, which is growing disconcertingly in its power. I refer to the ecological movement, here epitomised principally by the rich and powerful transnational lobbyist Greenpeace.
>
> (STL 13 August)

In contrast to the *Telegraph*'s negative framing of Greenpeace, the *Mail*, although by no means uncritical or uniformly positive, generally framed Greenpeace protesters in a way which showed them as devoted, daring (only the *Mail* and the *Mirror* ever referred to Greenpeace's occupation of the Brent Spar as 'daring'), committed and ingenious.

DAWN MISSION PAYS OFF FOR THE LADY FROM MONTANA: Fiasco over Brent Spar

The woman pilot who landed the last two Greenpeace activists on the Brent Spar was the toast of the crew on the Solo yesterday. Paula Huckleberry, a former US Army pilot, had caught Shell's minders off guard with her dawn raid.

Her daring mission took just 40 minutes and, by the time the oil company's water cannons were trained back on the platform, she was on her way back to the vessel.

(DML 21 June)

THE BAR-ROOM BATTLE PLAN SCRIBBLED OUT ON BEER MATS
. . . He and his fellow activists talked through their various options time and again and Captain Jurgens jotted down the main points on the back of a couple of beer mats.
He could not have known then that those scribbles would be the blueprint for a battle that would herald the environmentalists' finest hour.
. . . We basically prepared the general outline of the campaign and as we didn't have anything but a ballpoint and beer mats, that's what we used.
. . . The campaign was masterminded from the Greenpeace UK office in London

(DML 21 June)

The portrayal of Greenpeace as potentially 'threatened', 'peaceful demonstrators', rather than as a threatening, powerful organisation was further underlined by the *Mail*'s revelation in several articles that the government had authorised Royal Marine Commandos to be on stand-by to help Shell evict the Greenpeace protesters from the Brent Spar platform:

MYSTERY OF 'SBS MISSION TO BRENT SPAR'
A commando force of around eight men from the Special Boat Squadron may have been on stand by to storm the Brent Spar oil platform shortly before Shell abandoned plans to sink her in the Atlantic, according to an MP last night.

(DML 22 June)

ANNE'S HUSBAND WANTED PROTEST RIG STORMED: Secret memo reveals Marines poised to evict Greenpeace.

(MOS 25 June)

GOVERNMENT ADMITS MARINE TASK FORCE TARGETED GREENPEACE

(DML 15 July)

The incompatibility of this particular news angle with the *Telegraph*'s framing of Greenpeace as a powerful and manipulative organisation may help explain why it received no mention in the *Telegraph*.

In sharp contrast to the wide range of negative terms and labels used by the *Telegraph*, glorifying battle-terms such as 'hero/heroes/heroic', 'army of green warriors', 'Greenpeace commandos', 'fighters' and 'daredevils' were unique to the *Mirror*. From the outset, the *Mirror* painted the controversy as a fight between the brave and heroic Greenpeace ('HEROES DID GREAT JOB: Fishermen pay tribute to Greenpeace over Brent Spar', DMR 23 June; 'OIL RIG HERO GETS SHELL DISCOUNT CARD', DMR 24 June; 'DEMO MAN WANTS HUG FROM LOVE: Brent Spar hero Al Baker arrives back in the Shetlands', DMR 24 June) fighting on behalf of us (the readers) and nature against a greedy, powerful, inflexible and irresponsible multi-national company.

> GREED THAT'S POISONING OUR SEAS: Shell's sinking of the Brent Spar oil rig.
>
> (DMR 20 June)

> WE SHELL NOT BE MOVED: Dumping of Brent Spar could be the first of many – there are 350 rigs in the North Sea.
>
> (DMR 20 June)

> MR GREEN TARGETS BRITAIN: As Britain is tagged the dirty man of Europe, green heroes talk of North Sea ordeal: European greens target Britain's polluting companies.
>
> (DMR 22 June)

The *Mirror* went further than simply legitimising Greenpeace's actions. In a manner typical of the particular mode of readership address often adopted by British tabloid papers (see Hall *et al*. 1978) the *Mirror* cast itself in the role of representing, speaking for and campaigning on behalf of its readers. Thus, the *Mirror* not only claimed to be the first to have reported on the scandal and problems of dumping, but also portrayed itself as having been largely instrumental in bringing about the Shell U-turn on the dumping of the Brent Spar.

> GLAD OIL OVER – DAILY MIRROR VICTORY AS PETROL GIANT HALTS RIG SINKING: Greenpeace were jubilant when Shell dropped the plans to dump Brent Spa [*sic*].
>
> (DMR 21 June)

> HOW WE DID IT: Brent Spa [*sic*] scandal was first revealed by Daily Mirror which highlighted potential diaster.
> JUNE 20: A day of drama ends in Shell's climbdown.
> 10am: The Mirror contacted Shell to find if they meant to continue with the dump plans. Shell confirmed that explosive charges were set. . . .

4pm: The Mirror quizzed Shell over claims that a Dutch company offered to dispose of the rig 'on shore for £19 million' – not Shell's £46 million-plus. Sea disposal was costing around £11 million.

6pm: Shell announced its U-turn and revealed they will bow to pressure from Greenpeace, the Mirror and the public.

(DMR 21 June)

VICTORY FOR THE PEOPLE: Mirror comment on Shell decision not to sink Brent Spa [sic]

(DMR 21 June)

Unlike the other papers, the *Mirror* rhetorically constructed an active role for its readers, a sense of participation, by characterising Shell's change of mind as a result of 'people power' (DMR 22 June, 27 June). This was accomplished by inscribing its readers into the same general 'battle' language used for describing the conflict between Shell and Greenpeace.[3] Readers were referred to as 'the *Mirror*'s army of readers', relationships were constructed between Greenpeace and *Mirror* readers (Greenpeace was quoted as thanking the *Mirror*'s readers for their support – DMR 22 June), and readers were directly addressed using the personal pronoun 'you', for example '£700M: YOU SHELL OUT TO CLEAN UP 200 RIGS: YOU'LL PAY £700M FOR OIL FIASCO (DMR 22 June).

Risk, science, scientists and experts

Claims-making about the Brent Spar hinged centrally on the ability to demonstrate, with science, whether it posed a serious and significant pollution risk. Although claims-making about the Brent Spar did not draw solely on a scientific discourse (other important discourses included moral, legal, economic discourses, and 'a right to know/open to public scrutiny' discourse), science, research evidence, and scientists were pressed into service by the key players (Greenpeace, Shell, and the government) as well as by the newspapers themselves. Significantly, the role of science in the news coverage was very much one of 'asserting facts' or of bolstering of the arguments for or against dumping by invoking scientific expertise and authority. Newspapers offered very little information about how 'science' goes about establishing whether deep-sea dumping would harm marine life, or on what scale such harm might occur. There is nothing particularly extraordinary about this; indeed, research has frequently shown that the media deal mainly in the 'facts' of science and are far less well equipped to convey an understanding of how science works (Nelkin 1995; Long 1995; Hornig 1990) or of how risk is assessed (Dunwoody and Peters 1992).

The use of science and scientists varied across the three newspapers much in line with the general variation in stance already indicated. Thus, the *Mirror* generally and faithfully reproduced and elaborated Greenpeace claims that the Brent Spar contained large amounts of very toxic materials which, if the installation were dumped at sea, would cause serious pollution, contamination and harm to marine life. This was the key frame of the *Mirror's* first report of the Greenpeace action:

> MURDER AT SEA: Scandal of dumped rigs that may wipe out marine life: Greenpeace seize oil rig to highlight danger of leaving deserted rigs to rot at sea.
> . . . Experts fear the millions of tons of steel, copper, lead and waste oil from old rigs could wipe out many species. They threaten fish stocks, seals, whales and dolphins. Greenpeace say their studies have already shown the shattering impact of pollution on marine life.
>
> (DMR 1 May)

Once adopted at the beginning of the coverage, this dramatic frame remained in place in the *Mirror's* reporting throughout the sample period. While reference was made in passing to studies supporting dumping as the best solution, the *Mirror* unambiguously promoted the pollution of the sea frame both by seeking out and drawing attention to other incidents of pollution (which would otherwise have remained singularly un-newsworthy) and by headlining scientific experts' warnings against dumping:

> EXPERTS WARNED MINISTERS OF OIL RIG DISASTER TWO YEARS AGO
>
> (DMR 20 June)

Most significantly perhaps there were no reports in the *Mirror* of the later (September) admission by Greenpeace that some of their measurements and calculations regarding the amount of toxic material in the Brent Spar had been erroneous – an admission widely covered in both the *Telegraph* and the *Mail*.

While not ignoring concern about pollutants and the potentially harmful implications of dumping (e.g. 'SEABED MUST NOT BECOME RUBBISH TIP', DTL 20 June), the frame promoted by the *Telegraph* and the *Mail* stressed scientific arguments that dumping was the environmentally least damaging solution. It was also a frame which put great faith in science (see particularly the first and last quotes below) and called on science as the only reasonable alternative to what was described variously as 'emotional', 'irrational', 'hysterical', 'uninformed', 'manipulative', 'ideological' and 'dogmatic' propaganda and claims:

> A TRIUMPH FOR THE FORCES OF IGNORANCE: In the wake of the Brent Spar oil rig fiasco, one of Britain's most distinguished Nobel Prize-winning scientists savages Greenpeace.

The problem of Brent Spar was easy to state: how to dispose of an oil platform with the least possible damage to the environment. For three years,
scientists working for both Shell and the Government studied that practical and important problem. They would have examined all possible ways
to achieve the end: for that is the method of science. I am horrified that a
scientific study which took so much time and analysis to prepare should
be overturned in a few hours by a group of terrorists appealing not to reason but to ignorance and emotional blackmail.
. . . Science tackles a problem logically and comes up with the best answer
that the human mind can devise.
. . . The reversal was based not on science nor on logic nor on reason. It
was based on a popular appeal to unreason and anti-science.

(DML 22 June)

LEADING ARTICLE: DEEP WATERS
. . . Many people have considerable sympathy with Greenpeace's aims, if
not its methods. But these aims should be based on rigorous scientific
analysis, not emotion.

(DML 6 September)

LEADING ARTICLE: GREEN FOR DANGER
. . . Shell's decision has allowed emotion to triumph over reason.

(DTL 21 June)

GREENPEACE BRENT VICTORY 'A SAD DAY'
A leading academic yesterday hit out at Greenpeace's role in halting the
dumping of the Brent Spar. Aberdeen University principal Professor
Maxwell Irvine condemned the group's victory as 'one of the saddest days
in the history of the environmental debate'. Prof Irvine claimed Shell's last-
minute decision not to dump the disused oil platform in deep water was
the result of 'ignorance and one-issue campaign politics'.

(DML 8 July)

LEADING ARTICLE: GREENPEACE FIASCO
. . . Industry must resist misguided and emotional campaigns which
undermine its ability to operate profitable and essential businesses.

(DTL 7 September)

BELLAMY CALLS FOR SCIENCE OMBUDSMAN
The naturalist David Bellamy called for the establishment of a scientific
ombudsman to advise on complex issues such as the dumping of the Brent
Spar platform.
'The world is in desperate need of a science-based arbitration council that
can rapidly come to valid decisions of research and action on matters envi-
ronmental,' said Prof Bellamy, president of the British Association's
Biological Sciences Section.

(DTL 15 September)

In contrast to the *Mirror*, both the *Telegraph* and the *Mail* elected from an early stage of the coverage (and well before Greenpeace's discovery/admission that some of their calculations and measurements were wrong) to give considerable play, not least through headlining, to scientists' claims in support of dumping. As indicated by the first quotation above from the *Daily Mail* and in the quote below from the *Daily Telegraph*, much of the 'authority' of the scientific case for dumping was secured through reference to the number, cost and sheer 'scientific status' of studies conducted rather than through an examination of how science works or goes about establishing the implications of dumping:

30 STUDIES IN FAVOUR OF DUMPING
The Government and Shell say that more than £1 million and 30 scientific studies have gone into proving that dumping the installation at sea is the best environmental option and the safest.
. . . The Brent Spar contains 100 tons of sludge, which Greenpeace claims is toxic waste. The company says 90 per cent of this is sand, the remainder oil residues no different in composition as far as heavy metals are concerned from bitumen on the roads. The Brent Spar does contain naturally-occurring radioactive materials trapped in scales, like the inside of a kettle, but Shell says that these pose no risks if disposed of at sea while they might if dried out and inhaled on land. In any case they say that the radioactive materials are equivalent to a group of granite houses in Aberdeen. The structure is to be disposed of 150 miles out in the Atlantic, north-west of the Hebrides, at a depth of around 7,800 metres in a depression where, scientists say, the sludges it contains are unlikely to move far.
(DTL 20 June)

The emphasis on the Brent Spar as an alien (to the environment), dangerous, contaminated and hazardous structure, an emphasis promoted by Greenpeace and variously elaborated by the newspapers themselves, stood in stark contrast to a 'naturalising' counter-rhetoric, including that of several scientist sources, which stressed the 'naturalness' of the substances contained in the Brent Spar and the potential beneficial impact which the structure itself might have on fish life.

SCIENCE: DUMP THE RIG – AND BE DAMNED
. . . The large metal storage buoy will contain radioactive muds, but these were naturally occurring and have only been concentrated by drilling activity. There may also be traces of oil, but Dr Rice says the effects should be local and limited to within a few hundred metres. . . . 'Some animals – mainly worms and bivalves – will be killed. But people don't seem to ask how many millions of creatures – worms and so on – are killed when you build a mile of motorway or a hospital'.
(DTL 31 May)

DUMPING RIGS 'IS GOOD FOR SEA LIFE'
Dumping the Brent Spar oil platform at sea would have been good for
marine life, scientists claim. . . .   Professor Euan Nisbet and Dr Mary
Fowler of London University's Royal Holloway College say in Nature magazine that metals on board the rig are already present in huge quantities
on the sea bed.

(DML 30 June)

At the beginning of September 1995 Greenpeace admitted that some of its earlier claims concerning the amount of toxic materials inside the Brent Spar had
been exaggerated due to erroneous measurements and calculations. In addition
to devoting not only news coverage but also editorials to discussion of this
'admission', in both the *Mail* and *Telegraph* this also paved the way for the selection of further coverage of scientist claims that dumping would have been the
best solution:

N-SUBS 'GOOD FOR SEA LIFE'
. . .   An ecologist told the festival that Greenpeace was wrong to fight the
dumping at sea of Shell's Brent Spar oil platform. Dr Martin Angel, of the
Institute of Oceanography in Surrey, said Brent Spar could have been an
ideal habitat for marine life.

(DML 12 September)

BRENT SPAR PLAN 'WAS RIGHT'
Shell was right to want to dump the Brent Spar platform in the deep ocean
but it chose the wrong site, the conference was told. The company should
have selected a depth of more than 15,000ft rather than the relatively shallow depth of 6,500ft, said Dr Martin Angel, of the Institute of
Oceanographic Sciences.

(DTL 12 September)

BRENT SPAR WAS NO POLLUTION THREAT, SAY EXPERTS
(DTL 19 October 95)

From a risk perspective, the middle quotation above is particularly telling. All
previous coverage in the *Telegraph* and *Mail* uniformly conveyed an image of
the designated dumping site in the Atlantic as a 'trench' of very considerable
depth, which, precisely because of its great depth, would easily absorb any con-
taminants remaining in the Brent Spar. The seeming absoluteness of 6,500ft
as a suitable depth was now suddenly called into question by its description as
a 'relatively shallow depth' and by quoting a scientist arguing that more than
twice that depth would be required for safe disposal. This, however, did not
give rise to a wider questioning of the case for dumping in the two newspapers (including a questioning of its scientific robustness).
    By contrast, the admission of error by Greenpeace was portrayed in the *Mail*

and the *Telegraph*, not as a legitimate mistake, but as evidence of the 'slipshod', 'self-serving' and 'fatally flawed' (DML editorial, 6 September) science practised by Greenpeace, and a lesson that 'single issue groups are often not unimpeachable guardians of society's best interests, but highly motivated and well-financed zealots who play fast and loose with the facts' (DTL editorial, 7 September).

Conclusion

While 'commanding attention' (Solesbury 1976) and achieving media coverage are important to successful claims-making, it is clear from the analysis presented here that different newspapers frame and inflect the claims which they give coverage to in very different ways. While an environmental pressure group such as Greenpeace has the ability to secure media coverage for its claims, its capacity to influence or control the way its claims are framed and inflected by individual newspapers is more questionable.

All of the newspapers analysed here exercised a considerable amount of ideological work, not merely in terms of the differential accessing of sources and selective prominence (such as through headlining) given to particular sources, but perhaps more significantly, through their differential choice and promotion of particular lexical terms (Greenpeace as 'terrorists', 'a nuisance', 'undemocratic'), particular discourses (law and order, democracy, science), and, consequently, particular frames. It is especially significant that the core frames, characteristic of each individual newspaper's coverage, did not emerge gradually over the period of coverage or as a particular response to developments in the controversy (for example Greenpeace's admission of errors in its scientific claims), but were in place from the outset, indicating the limits to claims-maker influence. While successfully 'commanding attention', Greenpeace had much less uniform success with the second key task (Solesbury 1976) in the claims-making process, that of claiming or securing legitimacy.

Finally, a key question which this analysis invites, but one which cannot be answered on the basis of the period of coverage looked at here, is perhaps this: while Greenpeace did indeed draw media and public attention to the immediate problem of the Brent Spar and its disposal, did it succeed in constructing the general issue of decommissioning of redundant oil rigs and marine pollution as a problem for longer-term media, public and political concern?

Notes

1 Overlexicalisation or overwording: a concentration of interrelated terms signalling an intense preoccupation with some aspect of reality (Fairclough 1989) and resulting 'in certain meanings rather than others being repeatedly and routinely foregrounded' (H. J. Brookes 1995: 471).

2 'Formulae package concepts simply and memorably; they signify paradigms, model

ideas which can be applied to new "instances", however remote from the original referents' (Fowler 1991: 178).

3 Although all the papers drew on military/battle metaphors, these were particularly prominent in the *Mirror* and included such lexical choices as: siege, warriors, battered, fighters, commandos, green army, killing blow, victory.

Chapter 4

The burrowers

News about bodies, tunnels and green guerrillas

Maggie Wykes

Protest

In April 1997 protesters dug under the proposed site of a new stretch of the A30 at Fairmile, near Honiton in Devon, south-west England. Tree-dwelling protesters attracted considerable media attention but something about the action of those who 'burrowed' beneath the earth really caught the imagination of journalists. It also proved a very effective way of resisting eviction for these 'green guerrillas'. Planning approval for a second runway at Manchester airport was granted just as the protest collapsed at Fairmile:

> Swampy, and fellow eco-warrior, Animal, were hailed as heroes by many after they barricaded themselves in a tunnel for seven days and nights in order to try and stop the new A30 being built in Devon. On the day Swampy was presented to the media, TV crews turned out from Germany, France and Holland.
>
> *(Guardian* 6 May 1997)

My curiosity was aroused by the apparent empathy of many news journalists with the young eco-warriors and their single-issue politics. News reports seemed to go against the expected grain. Ample academic work since the early 1970s has associated representations of youth subculture with drugs, sex and rock 'n' roll (S. Cohen and Young 1973; Griffin 1993). However, political resistance has been theorised as mediated in terms of violence, criminality, *reds under the beds or the enemy within* and certainly not in terms of Britishness (Waddington *et al.* 1991; Young 1991; Reicher 1984). At Manchester politically resistant young people attempted to impose their views on the debate around green issues through direct action against 'legitimate' groups such as developers, the local authority, Members of Parliament (MPs) and a large proportion of the local population. Yet, the kind of castigatory and damning reporting familiar after urban and industrial disputes, such as the miners' strike in 1984–5 and inner city disturbances of the early 1980s, was missing from this scenario. Nor was there a moral panic about drugs, despite the concurrent media focus on ecstasy, youth and death epitomised by the case of teenager Leah Betts, who died after taking ecstasy.[1]

Something appeared to be different about this 'news' because the British media have not fundamentally changed. It was (is), as Tunstall (1996) claimed, steeped in the interests of dominance, whether middle class, Oxbridge, white, male and heterosexual as at the quality end, linking the interests of state and patriarchy or working class, macho and populist, as at the commercial tabloid end. The coverage offered of the environmental protests was often sympathetic – a component of news rare in itself and almost wholly absent from the accounts of anti-nuclear weapons protests at Greenham Common during the mid-1980s (Young 1991), which was in some ways a not dissimilar example of political resistance. It, too, was a non-violent occupation of the land in an attempt to conserve it for the future. Both involved protesters living 'rough', reliant on support from sympathisers and united in collective political struggle.

Admittedly years spent analysing the news media leads to a certain cynicism but I could not quite take at face value the apparent generosity of the British press. The *Daily Express* dressed Swampy in designer gear in a fashion spread; Charlotte Raven in the *Guardian* iconised him as the successor to 'new lad' and the *Independent on Sunday* agreed:

> Surprise, surprise – women don't fancy the eight-pints-and-a-curry man, reports Ros Wynne-Jones. The end of ladism is nigh long live Swampy! . . . 'Swampy's building a motorway through our ideas of masculinity' said Phil Hilton editor of *Men's Health*.
>
> (*Independent on Sunday* 13 April 1997)

Even British television's masters of crushing irony, *Private Eye* editor Ian Hislop and comedian Paul Merton, managed to be no more than gently patronising when Swampy failed to inspire on the television political quiz programme *Have I Got News for You* (BBC 2 May 1997). I could not believe that such accounts meant our journalists were aligned with the views of the tunnellers and tree dwellers and I saw no evidence of hacks abandoning their company cars and recycling their booze bottles. So what was going on in this reportage of environmental political struggle?

Data about dirt, danger and deviancy

Clearly 'burrowing' was on the news agenda for some journalists and editors. This was not a case of resistant activity being rendered invisible through *symbolic annihilation* (Tuchman 1978); this was controversial, even subversive, *and* reported. There was, however, a skewedness in the reportage because the two most popular tabloids the *Sun* and the *Daily Mirror*, the 'red-top' newspapers popular with working-class readers, did not publish any reports of the runway resistance that I could find. Instead during April and May 1997 both focused on the British general election, the Spice Girls, Diana, Princess of Wales, various soap opera stars and the sexual antics of a range of famous footballers. This seemed to confirm the *Daily Express*'s claim (28 May 1997) that the green guerrillas were 'middle-class warriors'. The conservative quality papers offered few accounts of the protesters whereas the liberal broadsheets were obsessed, presumably because they were deemed to be issues likely to appeal to the 'muesli' audience. Of the other papers, only the *Daily Express* ran with the story at least once each week during the siege.

The *Guardian's* copious coverage kept within a particular vein – a discussion of the popularity of the 'burrowers' with the media rather than any account of the environmental politics. Alex Bellos filled a page of the 'Media' section of the newspaper with the following:

> Swampy Fever . . . he's scruffy, jobless, rebellious – hardly the type beloved of conservative tabloids. But like the rest of the nation, they've fallen in love with him. So why has this anarchist become a romantic hero?
>
> *(Guardian* 12 May 1997)

Bellos' response was that Swampy has enabled the press to make environmental issues news because 'he is a media friendly personality – more accessible than Jonathan Porrit and less threatening than a hunt saboteur' (*Guardian* 12 May 1997). Swampy offered the human-interest element – 'he is such a nice bloke and his parents said he was wonderful'. Clearly the often acerbic Bellos agreed: 'the legacy of Swampy is that when we have forgotten him his influence will still be there'. This kind of adulatory coverage of the person, albeit 'justified' here as a critique of the 'other' papers, typifies the liberal broadsheet approach. Swampy was made a love object – a desirable earth man among new laddism – a star.

The *Independent on Sunday* went the whole way on the romance angle (see Figure 4.1). In this article, Ros Wynne-Jones quoted *Cosmopolitan's* editor:

> he's brave and courageous and wants to change the world. You'd have a far better sex life with someone like him than someone with the snotty arrogance of Chris Evans.
>
> *(Independent on Sunday* 13 April 1997)

This set sexual titillation in motion in the qualities and virtually none of the accounts that follow was without prurience about the sex lives of green protesters. Curiously, readers were reminded frequently that these new sex symbols were 'middle-class young people' and therefore in some way different from 'working-class' youth, so often castigated in the press for hooliganism and crime (Griffin 1993) or working-class adults deemed responsible by journalists for strikes and other political conflict (Hollingsworth 1986).[2] Charlotte Raven in 'New lads out, Swampy in' (*Guardian* 22 April 1997) commented 'his mother

NEWS

Swampy takes centre stage, sidelining such notable lads as (from left to right) David Baddiel, Frank Skinner, Eric Cantona, Paul Gascoigne, Danny Baker, Chris Evans and Ace from 'Gladiators'

Photomontage by JONATHAN ASTER

Lads limp off as girls swoon for sexy Swampy

Surprise, surprise – women don't fancy the eight-pints-and-a-curry man, reports Ros Wynne-Jones

THE END of laddism is nigh: long live Swampy! After many dark months of *Loaded* innuendos, fever pitch on the football terraces and men behaving sadly, woman have decided that what they really really want is a good old-fashioned hero with a soft centre. Daniel Hooper, 23, of Second Runway, Manchester, is the man for the new millennium.

"Women are realising that lads are good enough for flirting and drinking with, but an environmental warrior like Swampy is so much more sexy," says Mandi Norwood, editor of Cosmopolitan. "You might have to clean under his fingernails, but he's brave and courageous and wants to change the world. You'd have a far better sex life with someone like him than someone with the snotty arrogance of Chris Evans."

The rise of Swampyism signals a cultural change. Its Messiah possesses neither a Brit-pop haircut, nor a Pamela Anderson fridge-magnet, nor a season ticket to Highbury, and is more likely to be found sweating over a shovel than a vindaloo. "I was brought up with manners," he said in a recent interview. "If I burp I say 'Excuse me'. I don't put my elbows on the table. I want to be remembered as the person who succeeded in stopping the madness."

The evidence of a waning lad for lads is all around. Recently Newcastle Brown Ale, fluid symbol of male virility and all things Gazza, was caught sneakily repositioning itself away from testosterone-loaded slogans such as "Size Is Important". Pressed to explain how come the Broon was going soft, the brand director admitted that laddism had "peaked". This month saw the launch of a new ad for McEwans lager featuring six blokes on their way to the pub for a night out. One is late – not because he got laid on the way home from work, or because the match went into extra time, but because he was helping an old lady off the bus. One small step for men, a giant leap for mankind.

"The type of man we're depicting here knows who he is, is loyal to his friends and will stand up for what he believes in." says a spokeswoman for Scottish and Newcastle Breweries. Sometime a bit like Swampy? "Ooh, yes," she says. The new McEwans slogan is "It's what we stand for." Standing for something more noble than the right to fart in public is suddenly all right again.

"Swampy's building a motorway through our ideas of masculinity," Phil Hilton, editor of Men's Health magazine, says. He salutes the end of laddism. "Male and female roles are breaking down a little and that can only be a good thing. Men might be able to have some feelings or a healthy relationship. Women might feel more able to be sexually aggressive. Men might even start going to Jane Campion films...anything's possible."

A "symposium" on 22 April featuring editors of the men's magazines which are to laddism what such texts as The Female Eunuch are to feminism may be evidence that the market is running scared. Glossy breasts-and-soccer mags such as Loaded and Maxim, after all, have a vested interest in laddism, their senior staff the graduate lager louts who dreamed the whole thing up in the first place.

After several attempts at communication with the various lad titles have been deflected by voice mail, answerphones and soft-voiced girl receptionists, we eventually pick up the phone at Loaded. 'Laddism may well be dead elsewhere but it's certainly alive and well in our office,' she says. 'It's Friday afternoon. All the blokes are down the pub.'

A million miles away at Runway Two, Manchester Airport, Swampy's not available for comment either. Perhaps the new man for the millennium is down his local enjoying a pint of McEwans, the lager that helps old ladies? No, the eco-warrior's out there battling against the forces of darkness before another night in the tree-tops with his Finnish girlfriend, Merry.

Figure 4.1 Lads limp off as girls swoon for sexy Swampy
Source: Independent on Sunday 13 April 1997

taught him to be nice: "If I burp I say 'excuse me'" he said recently'. Raven dismisses Swampy's 'politics' completely with 'He thinks the world is bad because he doesn't understand it'. He is 'untainted, a-political "Forrest Gump" with manners'. Yet Raven also failed to help us understand the ecological issues of Manchester.

Instead, journalism during May featured the same things repeatedly: the mud; the living accommodation (the 'tunnels are really warm and cosy – not claustrophobic at all'); the stockpiles of food; the risk (natural and human made: emphasising the 'natural' dangers from tunnel collapse, lack of oxygen or hypothermia but often attributing the possible cause of these to the quasi-legal evictions); the names of the protesters and the camps; the courage of the protest and the effort to remain within the law. 'Camp dwellers show bravery and bravado' (*Guardian* 23 May 1997) was typical of the broadsheet headlines.

Eschewing any mention of the political and economic bases for the environmental protest, the liberal middle-class *Observer* Sunday newspaper had serious columnist Nicci Gerrard use the unforgettable headline 'Tunnel of love: For Denise and Grandpappy, the earth moved under Manchester airport' (15 June 1997) to introduce a couple's subterranean romance (Figure 4.2).[3]

This article began with detailed personal description. He had a

> ring in his nose and a tattoo of a howling [wolf] profile on his muscled right arm. She's the one with a red T-shirt whose insignia reads 'Surfers Against Sewage', alarming boots, a clatter of silver bangles, and a cropped brown head topped with a fluorescent orange-red plume.

Gerrard discovered the daily routine of the camp-dwellers included

> digging the shit pit . . . [and] constructing the fire pit, around which the protesters gather at the end of each day to eat from the communal pot, drink, smoke ('baccy, spliffs, whatever'), and sing. Of course there's romance, when a group of young and euphoric men and women get together over drugs and alcohol to save the world.
>
> (*Observer* 15 June 1997)

When told that Denise is pregnant (if the child is a boy they say they will call him Clay or Doug) what Gerrard wanted to know is how did they do *it* underground and did they not ever want 'a warm bath and a bed?' Only Denise seemed sensitive to the irony of these questions, commenting 'I can't believe you're asking this. This is the *Observer*, right?'

Among the papers I expected that this kind of fairly straightforward media conservatism would be most evident in the aspirant middle-class, right-of-centre *Daily Mail* and *Daily Express*. Yet the *Mail* ignored the protest and the *Express* offered a convoluted, repackaged version of the law and order mandate in order to support the protesters.

Tunnel of love

For Denise and Grandpappy, the Earth moved under Manchester airport...

I have no trouble in recognising them in the little pub in Aldersley Edge: he's the one in green combat trousers, with a crest of hair crowning the face which looks a bit like Oliver Reed's, a ring in his nose and a tattoo of a howling profile on his muscled right arm. She's the one with a red T-shirt 'whose insignis reads "Surfaces Against Sewage', alarming boots, a clatter of silver bangles, and a cropped brown head topped with a fluorescent orange-red plume. Her expression, under this burst of synthetic colouring and 'behind' her round tortoise-shell spectacles, is calm and sensible. He is Andy ('call me Grandpappy'), 27 years old, who once, in a different life, worked as a removal man and then on a market stall, selling fruit and vegetables: she is Denise ('no last name, thanks a lot'), who is 29 - 'he's my toy boy' she says cheerfully, pinching Andy's substantial thigh - and who once worked as a registered nurse.

Now, though, they tunnel together. They have joined the merry band folk heroes (or weirdos and misfits and unwashed layabouts - it depends on how you look at it) who roam the despoiled countryside, trying to save it from roads,runaways. Center Parcs, modernity: who have dreadlocks, big dogs, strange views, torn trousers, enigmatic tattoos; who live up in their trees like Tolkien's elves: who burrow mazes into the ground like the rabbits in *Watership Down*.

For five months, Denise and Andy have been tunnelling into hard clay, constructing the Cakehole, the labyrinthine series of interconnecting tunnels that descend 70 feet beneath the site of the proposed second runaway of Manchester Airport. For 11 days, Denise lived under the ground without coming up for air, while the bailiffs tried to evict her, chasing her through the burrow. One of her fellow protesters, Matt, is still down there the day that Denise and Andy and I meet, behind a series of steel-plated hider doors, ready to lock-on to a massive block of concrete when 'they' (the

scum, the scabs, the authorities) get to him. 'When you go down there,' says Denise, 'you have to tell yourself very, very firmly that you are not going to come out voluntarily. It's a promise that you make to yourself. But I did. I came out of my own will.' For down in her underground chamber, denise started vomiting. 'I couldn't even keep down a sip of water.' She grimaces, 'Morning sickness, which goes all day'. She puts her hand on her still flat stomach, an age-old gestures. Denise is pregnant. She and Andy have discovered that they are going to have a tunnel child. If she is a girl, they will call her Gaynor, after a resident near the Flywood Camp, who has donated food, offered baths, given generous hospitality to all the protesters. But if he is a boy they say that they will call him Clay. 'Or Doug,' says Andy, giggling into his pint of beer. 'Or Digby' So if you ever wondered what protesters do to pass the time down under ground, now you know. It can be a tunnel of love.

The couple met at the A30 protest in Devon, at a camp named Trollheim (all the camps are given strange names: the Sir Cliff Richard OBE Vegan Revoultion Camp, the Battleship Calactica, the Zion Tree, the Jimi Hendrix Camp, the wild Garlic Camp...), although Denise was not there all the time. 'I was reclaiming the streets of London then: so some of the time I reclaimed.' I start to laugh and then stop: she's not being ironic. They moved to Manchester at the end of January, arriving ('with about 30 other trolls') in a jacked-up jeep laden with 'tat': tarpaulins, ropes, axes and shovels. 'Tat' in the language of the protesters, means personal possons. Denise and Andy do not have much tat.

When they describe the five months there, at the Flywood Camp, the couple become animated, anecdotal, proud. They butt into each other's stories, with laughter in anticipation of what the other is about to say. I had though the protesters were like conwarriors, fighting a war to save the planet from the fat cats, the blind authorities, and the apathetic rest of

us, Andy and Denise say that it's more like a game: serious, but cheerful and definately fluffy.

Fluffy?

'Yeah fluffy. Fluffy means.........."

'Fluffy means nicey-nicey yoghurt weaver' says Andy incomprehensibly.

'Yoghurt weavers'

'No, Andy, not yoghurt weavers,' says denise firmly. 'Look fluffy - means well, at the A30 action, when a girl was dragged down from her tree. I saw her tackle the climber who was evicting her. That's Fluffy.'

The opposite of fluffy, 'says Andy.' Is spiky. Spiky is like when the police dragged us out of the tunnels of Trollheim, they handcufffr us and bumped us along the tunnels, and when we got out they kicked our heads in. That's spiky.'

The first few days were spent getting the camp in order, putting up benders (tents made from bent hazelnut poles which are covered with tarpaulin), including the sleeping benders and the kitchen benders, digging the shit pit ('very hygenic', says Denise firmly 'very environmentally friendly. We cover it all up with ash as we go along). Constructing the fire pit, around which the protesters gather at the end of each day to eat from the communal pot, drink, smoke (baccy and spliffs, whatever') and sing. of course there's romance, when a group of young and euphoric men and women get together over drugs and altchohol to save the world. The best known protesters, swampy, is apparently writing The

Eco Terrorist's Handbook - according to its publishers Fourth Estiae. The Sloane Ranger's Handbook for the Nineties - which discusses alongside tips for building and cleaning out the burrows the question of romance in the tunnels.

IN JANUARY it was muddy, rainy, windy, freezing cold. my head clouds with depression just listening to the litany of chill and discomfort. Didn't they ever want a warm bath and a soft bed?

'You can't think of things like warm baths when you've got the countryside being destroyed like this, can you?' says Andy severely.

'On yes, you can,' says Denise.

'We buddle up together, anyway. That helps.'

But soon Denise and Andy and their fellow Panses (Politically Active and Not Seeking Employment) started to digbacking into the clay with builders' axes, passing back the dislodged earth to the person behind them, who bags it and drags it back to the surface. Every two metres, the tunnel is shored up with wooden planks. When Denise and Andy describe the process, they are professional and precise; they really know what they are doing down underground with their cement and wood and their tools of the trade. Once a main tunnel has been established, the diggers can make their own individual tunnels that worm downwards, puckered with little chambers, stoppered up with boiler-plate doors.

'After a while,' says Andy. 'Its all you think about, your tunnel: where you're going to take it, how big. You get obsessed.'

'Tunnel fever,' says Denise.

'Tunnel fever.'

'It's your home and you make it with your blood and sweat and tears, and you decorate it whatever way you want, and even after you are evicyed it is yours and no one can take what it means anyway.'

'Everyone who came to visit the Cake-hole said it had a really nice feel about it,' says Andy, very house proud, brown eyes nostalgic and sweet. he doesn't really look so like Oliver Reed.

I ask if they ever feel claustrophobie.

'If you get claustrophobia, then you feel claustrohobic down there,' admits Denise. 'But I feel peaceful, safe in the earth Looked after somehow. It's very quiet down there, unless a plane is going by. It's an inner sanctum.'

'An escape.'

'Like a womb.

'We tried to make a double chamber but the earth fell in on us and covered our legs.'

While the tunnelling was going on, and before the evictions started, Denise would often escape the 'upper world' and go into her chamber. 'It's about this big.' - she shows me three foot with her hands – 'this tall,' (four foot) 'and oh, about eight foot long. 'Down there, she would read (Robbie Burns, Seamus Heaney – though she doesn't really go for him – and *Watership Down*, which she's already read about 50 times), sing, think, sleep, see Andy. 'I could get away from the world in the tunnel,' she says, 'though there wasn't much room down there.'

What about the, um, conception?

'I can't believe you're asking this. This is the Observer, right?', she says. Andy hoots.

'When we did it up in the tree, there was a woodpecker, pecking away,' he tells me.

'And remember that time in the filed she says. they snigger reminiscently.

Until this month, the diggers

movod betwen the earth and their underworld, sleeping in tunnels or in the benders, sitting round the campfire as the weather turned the warmer. Each day, they worked hard and in their spare time they played 'Flywood rounders' ('the balls are made of clay. one person bats and everyone else bowls at the same time, and it's called getting stoned.' says Denise). or they did the 'office run', or went skipping.

Excuse me?

'Skipping. Thats mainly how we eat ,' explains Denise. 'All the big superstores , they throw out good food at the end of each day. You can get all sorts. I once found a salami this big.' She measures the air proudly, like a fisherman telling a tall tale ' and a bottle of wine tc go with it

'I onct found 260 cans of lager outside Costcutter ,' says Andy.

'Yeah, and there were those 400 Madeira cakes, remember.'

'And bottles and bottles of water. thrown away because their lables have come off.'

'Dented tins sell by-date 1998'

'Roses chocolates, mmmm.'

'Easter eggs.'

Sometimes, though, the managers of the supermarkets douse the food in detergent to stop the skippers taking it.

'Seems strange doesn't it' says Denise.'They prefer to throw it away than give it away.'

The authorities clamped down on alchohol, so the protesters built a watkway in the trees and ferried it across, and the 'sea subs' (ocean saboteurs) floated cider, beer and wine down the river in rubber dinghies. 'Got to unwind' says Denise.

At the start of June, the evictions began. There were dozens of protesters at the flywood camp, but only five of them – Matt (who first put his shovel in the ground) , Muppet Dave. Tunneller Tim (the little Cambridge graduate and schoolteacher), and Neville- went underground, bolting sted doors behind them.

'Poor Neville'. says Denise fondly. 'He hadn't really done the digging, he'd never Continued on page 4

> If the child is a boy, they say they will call him Clay. 'Or Doug,' says Andy, giggling into his pint of beer

Photography by Andrew Testa

The *Express* went into great detail about the protesters' identities, stating 'many of those at the heart of the Manchester Airport campaign are articulate and well-educated' under the headline 'Middle-class warriors' (Figure 4.3).

Then the paper's Paul Gilbride offered a list of descriptions for them – 'astro-physics graduate; social worker; photographer; media studies student' adding for each detail on their parents 'middle-class background; retired school master; education officer; senior manager; engineer'. Only one sentence from twenty-nine in the main article addressed environmental politics while a second unsourced comment could not resist the claim:

NOW THE EXTREME LEFT TRIES TO HIJACK GREENS

The hard Left is wooing Green protesters to take on other social issues.

 The marriage could be attractive to both partners. Few new roads are being built, giving militant Greens little to campaign against. And the hard Left has been marginalised within New Labour.

               (*Daily Express* 28 May 1997)

This clearly linked environmental protest to Trotskyist groups, just as happened to the Peace protesters at Greenham Common (Young 1991) and made dupes of the 'burrowers'. This paper, unsurprisingly given its Conservative political allegiance, was one of the few to label the eco-warriors as left wing; none the less it was not particularly damning, taking instead a paternalistic line 'Are these middle-class echo-warriors brave and self-sacrificing or innocent dupes?'

That paternalism extended to repeated warnings that the protest might end in 'deadly conflict' (*Daily Express* 28 May 1997). This paper, more than any other, focused on the role of the bailiffs and raised issues about liberty and the law. Philip Norman wrote:

> There is indeed something alien and un-British about these squads of mercenaries – they are paid up to £25 an hour – moving through the undergrowth towards their objectives. Watching them evokes memories of cudgel bearing strike-breakers in America. Why can't the job have been given to the police?
>
>   (*Daily Express* 22 May 1997)

But the protesters did not get off lightly in the *Express*, dubbed by Norman 'that lank-haired, anorak wearing vegan class', but their 'democratic right to protest' was firmly stated and the dubious use of 'vague' laws was condemned. The *Express* managed to sympathise with the protest, condemn left-wing politics, denigrate veganism, ridicule the 'tree and tunnel rebellion' and support British law and order, at a stroke. The only explanation for its convoluted

Figure 4.2 Tunnel of love
Source: Observer 15 June 1997

THE EXPRESS: WEDNESDAY MAY 28 1997   NEWS 17

Middle-class warriors

But have they all been duped by the eco-thugs?

TO some they are folk heroes. But the latest campaign by Green activists could end in deadly conflict. Bailiffs clearing the site of a new airport runway have warned of booby-trap bombs, and protesters have admitted placing nails in tunnel walls. Caught in the middle are those genuinely concerned for the environment. Are these middle-class eco-warriors brave and self-sacrificing or innocent dupes? PAUL GILBRIDE speaks to three of them.

THE image of the typical protester is of a dole-scrounging drop-out living like a hippy at taxpayers' expense.

But despite their ragged appearance, many of those at the heart of the Manchester Airport campaign are articulate and well-educated.

And they come from all walks of life. Among the first to be evicted last week was **MARTIN PORTER**, an astrophysics graduate.

Martin, 27, a former public schoolboy with a BSc from Leicester University, comes from a middle-class background in Southport, Lancs.

He said: "I joined Greenpeace while I was still at school and when I went to Leicester I became a hunt saboteur. I then got actively involved in the Newbury bypass protest, and have been here in Manchester for two months.

"Throughout my career as a protester I have also managed to qualify professionally as a social worker, although I'm not working at the moment."

At first his parents — his father is a retired schoolmaster and his mother an education officer with the National Trust — opposed his activities. "But they now realise how vital what I'm doing is, and even came to visit me this week and brought along some food."

This is where the eco-warriors believe they are scoring their greatest success — wooing support among the middle classes.

Treetop protester **MARK CHADWICK**, nicknamed "Skin", has been here off and on for three months, hitch-hiking back and forth from his home in Bournemouth.

Mark, 34, who has a nine-year-old son and is studying for a diploma in photography, said: "There are all kinds of people here. My father was an engineer and my mother a housewife.

"But I am going to spend my life making a stand over the destruction of the environment.

"I have a duty to my son to save our countryside. I've got a mission to do this kind of thing for the rest of my life."

"Tinkie", real name **KIM WEBSTER**, 20, is a student at John Moore's University in Liverpool. She hopes to graduate next year with a degree in Media and Cultural Studies.

Her father is a senior manager for one of the privatised water companies. "The coun-

THE ENGINEER'S SON: Mark Chadwick

THE ASTROPHYSICIST: Martin Porter

tryside here is a natural treasure," she said. "If they wanted to bring more jobs to the North-West, they could have invested in Liverpool Airport instead. The area around there is already fairly derelict.

"At the moment we are locked in a vicious circle. How many more roads, runways or out-of-town shopping centres do we need?"

NOW THE EXTREME LEFT TRIES TO HIJACK GREENS

THE hard Left is wooing Green protesters to take on other social issues.

The marriage could be attractive to both partners. Few new roads are being built, giving militant Greens little to campaign against. And the hard Left has been marginalised within New Labour.

A top Green protest organiser said yesterday: "The hard Left wants to be seen associating with radical groups who hit the head-lines with their energy. It's the perfect recruitment ground.

"As it dawns on Green protesters that this government will avoid controversial road schemes, such as Salisbury's bypass, they will be amenable to taking on more social issues."

He said support from Reclaim The Streets, campaigners against urban congestion, for striking Liverpool dockers at a recent London rally were the first evidence of the new bond.

THE MEDIA STUDENT: Kim Webster's father is a senior manager

Figure 4.3 Middle-class warriors
Source: Daily Express 28 May 1997

approach might be the need to satisfy a readership of rather conservative, nationalistic green-belt dwelling *not in my backyarders* (NIMBYs) some of whom might well have been providing warm baths and hot meals to the 'empty headed hippies' at Manchester. Its sister paper, the *Daily Mail*, steered clear of the kind of turbulent ideological political effort adopted by the *Express* by ignoring the whole thing. Perhaps to their credit, neither of these newspapers got into bed (or into the bathroom) with the liberal broadsheets.

During the spring of 1997, television news regularly featured brief accounts. An edition of the Sunday evening religious and moral affairs television programme *Heart of the Matter* (BBC1 March 1997), which was broadcast before the Manchester occupation began, was the only media space where environmental protesters articulated their aims without being subjected to reinterpretation or ridicule, albeit these aims were rapidly sidelined in the main debate on whether ends justify means. One documentary was made specifically about the Manchester 'burrowers'.[4]

World in Action is a television documentary series with a reputation for hard-hitting, fact-filled investigative journalism yet its 30-minute programme illustrated the mobilisation of diversionary connotative discourses even more clearly than some of the press. The programme (ITV May 1997) was a clear example of the tabloidisation of the news (as was Gerrard's account) and the move to infotainment (B. Franklin 1997). It indicated a shifting of events into more newsworthy discourses in order to comply with news values, now dubbed 'dumbing down', and demonstrates explicitly a focus on conflict/violence and the body/sexuality in accordance with the populist sex and personality agenda of much contemporary journalism.

The first of these shifts was manifested by a lack of coverage of issues of environmental protest and a subtle shifting into explanatory discourses which did not construct the tunnellers as deviant (politically or criminally) but as daring, dirty defenders of the earth. Commensurate with this, journalists identified risk and threat in two contexts: to the protesters from the 'army of security men' and 'bailiffs' on one level and, more subtly, from nature itself as the tunnellers aligned themselves literally with the earth against the march of technology – the developer's bulldozers and the aviation corporations. The 'science bit' of the programme justified the 'dig-in' in terms of polluting aviation fuels and global warming. This made technology (not capital) the enemy and nature (not a political collective) the embattled resistor to attack. The names of the protesters even mimicked the natural as they allied with it – Animal, Swampy, Muddy, Slidey – and covered with dirt they are camouflaged as the earth and share the risk posed to the earth.

To this particular model of violence *World in Action* added the personalisation of the protesters as newsworthy. This was achieved particularly through a focus on those strange and evocative names, their relationships with one another and the individual risks they took 'burrowing', becoming nature. Interviews in the programme focused closely on the danger in the tunnels, the illness and risk of injury, the dependence of the youngsters on local women for support (surrogate mothers?) and the love affair between Denise and Grandpappy, as featured in the *Observer*. Some ten minutes of the programme were dedicated to showing the couple bathing together in the home of a local supporter. A final shot lingered on the muddy, pink suds whirlpooling around the plug-hole. This was a 'dumbing down' of the political aims and goals of the protest by romanticising, personalising and metaphorically 'cleaning up' the political message whilst the activists were literally cleaned.

In contrast, a scientist offered lucid evidence to contradict the minimally put 'green' claims and the response from the aviation company was advanced authoritatively by a man in a grey suit – people want jobs, cheap travel and convenience, which the runway development will provide for them. Britain, we were told, is a free country. If people preferred to pay the price for environmental conservation they could use their vote to elect green politicians. The protesters were portrayed as scientifically naïve, anti-democratic and anti-populist. Like the *Observer*, the *World in Action* programme was prurient about sex and cleanliness. Collective activity was personalised; dirty bodies were cleansed; significantly science was debunked and the populist argument for travel, freedom and employment was strongly put.

Theorising mediations

Trying to come up with an explanation for the puzzle of the nature of news about 'green guerrillas' led me to some rethinking about the plausibility of current media theory in relation to these stories. Media representation has been, and still frequently is, theorised (popularly and academically) as propagandist by such unlikely bedfellows as the ultra-conservative right and censorious radical feminism. Its thesis is a simple one: those who control the media create messages that sucessfully tell passive audiences what to think. Critical spawnings have included disparate positions, including models of resistant, autonomous, pleasure-seeking consumers (Hartley 1996) free to accept or disregard the media, and the absolutist media propagandism of Noam Chomsky (1989), which argues that mass media cannot be 'free' even in democracies.[5] However, neither the simplistic state propagandist model nor Chomsky's more subtle version of power-propaganda appeared to apply to the news about 'burrowers' which seemed neither to serve the interests of either the law (on behalf of the state) nor the developers (on behalf of capital) in any obvious, uniform or direct way.

Journalists themselves have resisted the concept that the media can offer only a *necessary illusion* of objectivity whilst having the real effect of serving the interests of the powerful. Journalists' self-worth requires an integration of some belief in the effectiveness of their role (otherwise why bother) and resistance to the idea that they are mere propagandists on behalf of power. This has influenced a second theoretical model of the media as agenda-setting. Agenda-setting's premise is that '*the press may not be successful much of the time in telling people what to think, but it is stunningly successful in telling its readers what to think about*' (B. Cohen 1963, emphasis added). Its origins are American and relate to attempts to link the content of news media to the interests of state policy (Lippman 1922) so as to demonstrate convergence of interests and hence claim a potential for propaganda. McCoombs and Shaw (1972; McCoombs 1981) offered an indirect 'softer' model of state control of the media. The focus was a mutuality of interests between policy-makers and press, leading to a hierarchy of topic foci or agenda, shared by both state and media, in relation to the public sphere and closely linked to sources and authorities. Journalists then rigorously report from all angles those agenda items, so telling people what to think about and orchestrating a scale of public interest priorities.[6] This perspective assumes unbiased reportage about selected topics with any skewing of media representation being structural rather than ideological – dependent on reporters' need for sources, news values, access, competition and commercial popularity. In a sense journalists are let off the hook, free to write what they wish but not about the topic they wish. Indeed, because politics is on the agenda, journalists monitor the political environment and may highlight issues which lead to policy change arguably giving them a crucial role in democracy (Dearing and Rogers 1996: 100) as in the Watergate affair. Yet the placing of politics on the agenda is not, it is argued, something about which the media have any freedom of choice.

In the case of environmental politics and accompanying protests, the issue is that not all the British media saw them as agenda issues, which queries the notion that journalism is *per se* constrained to comply with a proscribed kind of news hierarchy. Moreover, those who did put it on the agenda rarely put it on the political agenda; instead news about burrowers turned up in lifestyle sections, in the review section, alongside crime news, in the media supplement, in comment and on the women's pages. This suggests that journalists may be rather less structured and more interpretative than the concept of agenda-setting might formally suggest.

Certainly the stories about the young greens were sympathetic and in some ways apparently anti-state and capital but the 'true' issues were barely featured and certainly not featured in the same way in the plurality of accounts, texts and contexts. Diversity in the volume, placing and meaning of stories made agenda-setting seem a rather inadequate tool with which to investigate the protest stories.

The confusion of exclusions, representations and readings could not be accounted for by the genericism of propagandist and agenda-setting theory. However, focusing on what Barthes (1957) called a second linguistics – myth, metaphor, genre and narrative of discourses – has been illuminating in this research (Lévi-Strauss 1958; Propp 1958). Narrative structures and mythic content arguably work as *naturally predictive* devices for the interpretation of meaning. The media uphold and recycle these discourses because they are our cultural capital, our heritage, identity and community. Journalists recycle existing modes of expression but these are normally already steeped in the interests and values of dominance because the exercise of power is necessary to make meanings conventional (Foucault's (1979) normalisation process); the powerful have greater access to the knowledge of recording (for Derrida (1968) writing is violence) and they have the authority to confer legitimacy, reverence and conservation (Williams' (1961) selective tradition).

More recent models of such dominant power see it not merely as class-based, economic authority but reflecting the diversity of sociocultural power norms such as heterosexuality, whiteness, patriarchy and maturity (Segal 1994; Gilroy 1987; Weedon 1987; Grossberg 1986) as well as class. Moreover, texts, though apparently discrete discourses in form, are not opaque, solid and fixed in terms of meaning but semi-transparent, web-like and tenuous, allowing other inferences and discourses to 'slip, slide' (T. S. Eliot 1968) around and behind the more overt realisations. Barthes (1972) calls this potential a third or mythic level of interpretation – shaping, highlighting and closing down possible readings in our subconscious 'structured like language' (Lacan 1976). The effect is powerful not least because a text may appear to be liberal, empathic, resistant and critical at the denoted level but be working against those very positions connotatively – either by diversion or by omission. Events that involve different interests and values in conflict – as the burrowers versus the bailiffs – increase the potential range of representations, interpretations and contradiction.

News discourses: sex 'n' violence

Such conflict makes news – the more violent the better and if there is a sexual aspect, better still for newsworthiness. Conflict metaphors underpin many everyday discourses, particularly sport, sexuality and politics in British culture.[7] Conflict delivers many of the components which Galtung and Ruge (1965) originally found to constitute news values.[8] It is rare yet continuous, relevant, negative, unambiguous and intense. Few of us experience violence whether in riot, war or personal attack but it has a high knowledge threshold – we all know about it. As well as offering newsworthiness, conflict has a further advantage for journalism – there are always two sides (or more) to conflict. This services the ideological demand that our press should be unbiased, objective and investigative; it also satisfies narrative demands for villains and heroes, lost and found, and good and evil.

Sexuality adds a further frisson to conflict stories. Unlike violence this is an area we all have experience of and curiosity about (though some may be in denial) and it is the discourse which probably more than any other underwrites our identity. The centrality of sexual to social reproduction and respectability has made sex a site of conflict over control of the body. Symbiotically, state and church have underwritten a moral discourse, traceable to the Victorian period (Foucault 1979), which places legitimate sex in the home, between husband and wife and for the purposes of reproduction. Sex was cleaned up, morally. It was also cleaned up, literally, in the quest for physical health at a time of increasing medical and popular understanding of disease. The middle classes removed themselves from the contagion of the streets and provided public baths, hospitals and asylums to deal with the dirty masses. But as Foucault (1979) argued this 'repression' nurtured a continuing fascination with the forbidden that in turn supports a whole industry in 'other' sexuality. This often hovers on the borders of the law, adding further 'spice' to the heady mix of forbidden pleasure available for a price – money or/and the risk of disease.

Today, our sexual norms are still largely Victorian and violence remains both a mystery and fascination confirming our everyday 'normal' security (life is arguably much safer now than a century ago, despite the myth of the violent society). The call to the 'normal' was evident in news about tunnels. It was worked through in accounts of conflict and the body (violence and sex), woven around and behind the issues of environmental politics, which actually impelled both the 'real' events and the media 'representations'. The broad news accounting paradigms of sex 'n' violence formed a meta-discourse beneath which sex 'values' were satisfied around metaphors of 'earthiness' and 'dirtiness'; violence was most often transformed to personal danger – political collective resistance to authority was less the focus than was the individual body at risk from burrowing and bailiffs. In many ways the earth which the protesters sought to defend was transformed into risk; the dirt they dug into to protect the environment became the metaphoric vehicle of curiosity and condemnation within the sexualised account and the source of threat in the violence account. The first shift dislocated the debate from the public to the private; the second allowed the transfer of risk causation to the 'mercenary' bailiffs and nature rather than state and capital – disconnecting the protest from politics and economics.

Conclusion

Such discursive shifts around meaning may be partly explained by the kind of class account rather disparaged in post-Marxist academia yet apparently alive and well in journalism, where green activism was divided along class lines in these stories – both in terms of the producers of news reports, protest participants (if the news is to be believed) and also in relation to audience. The environment is apparently neither a working-class nor a populist cause. These were 'nice' young people – not unlike the sons and daughters of the journalists on the quality newspapers. The very middle-classness of the protesters alongside the middle-classness of most journalists (Tunstall 1996) offers much in the way of explanation for the coverage they got. Taboo and forbidden myths were mobilised because these people were not doing it in the accepted middle-class manner – at home, in private, in bed and with plenty of hot soapy water at hand to wash away the 'dirt' preferably before and after.

Making Swampy a romantic hero was the motif which allowed the whole protest to be shifted into such a different discursive space. The issues became not those of political protest but of youthful passion. Add to this exotic names – Animal, Muddy, Muppet Dave, Posh Pixie and Randy Hippy and the overt links to the culture of drugs, protest and rock 'n' roll – and some of these news stories could have been written in the 1960s (when some of the journalists may well have been engaged in not dissimilar behaviours).[9] This naming and the potential to identify and focus on individuals facilitated a shifting of the account from the serious to the frivolous and from the collective to the personal. In news value terms the 'story' was no longer a threatening conflict between deviance and authority but individual young people doing what young people do – falling in love, having sex, not keeping terribly clean, being a bit rebellious (but probably led astray by the wrong crowd), being idealistic and taking chances.

The complexity of this news places it outside of the scope of agenda-setting, nor is the class account discernible directly commensurate with Chomsky's model of the media unitarily propagandising economic and state power. Certainly, though, there are representations here which served the interests of power. The values of the various audiences seem to have shaped the news accounts differently but in ways which were likely to retain sales for journalistic products (micro-capital) and any possible collective political critique of state transport policy was made invisible, safeguarding the position of the state (and ultimately macro-capital via the aviation corporation). Because in the case of the burrowers macro middle-class values (state and capital) were often in conflict with micro (the NIMBYs, the right to protest, personal safety, law and order) the discursive field was repositioned to a site where such conflict could be articulated – middle-class culture rather than politics and economics.

Named bodies experiencing dirt and danger allowed the debate on the Manchester runway to be transformed from one about 'high risk economic decisions in terms of the expectation of a probable high gain' (Douglas 1992: 41) to one about risk as a 'trait of individual personality and not a culturally shared attitude' (1992: 44). Once risky action was personalised it could be psychologised and even pathologised: any political account became redundant. Audiences and citizens needed in Douglas' terms to be given a 'way of putting the isolated risk issue into the context of the larger system' (1992: 50); at Manchester that should have meant economic and environmental issues. Instead journalists framed risk in culturally resonant personal terms, not far distant from their own sociocultural profile, focusing on the body.

Sex underground risks danger; dirty conditions signify disease. Cleanliness, health and sexual purity are inextricably linked in middle-class British culture. Cleanliness is a boundary marker: to be dirty is to be 'other' such as homeless, criminal, promiscuous, diseased or a Greenham Common lesbian (Young 1991). At Manchester the taboo of dirt was seen to be made even more dangerous by the proto-official evictions. The context supported the very particular cultural response among newsmakers that Douglas (1992) identified:

> Danger in the context of taboo is used in a rhetoric of accusation and retribution that ties the individual tightly into community bonds and scores on his mind the invisible fences and paths by which the community co-ordinates its life in common. By grace of their concern for these lines and boundaries they can share their territory and muster resources to protect it.
>
> Douglas (1992: 29)

Douglas also pointed out that dangers to the body, to children and to nature 'are available as so many weapons to use in the struggle for ideological domination' and 'it would be strangely innocent nowadays to imagine a society in which the discourse on risk is not politicised' (1992: 13) particularly in the kind of 'individualist culture which sustains an expanding industrialised system' (1992: 28). But given that such a system pivots more and more around sophisticated, mass-mediated information to a highly media literate audience, it would be equally innocent to imagine that such a process of politicisation would manifest or succeed as overt propaganda on a discreet and closed agenda.[10] Instead, the middle classes closed ranks around cultural norms and values: lost children were brought safely home; dirty bodies were scrubbed clean; legitimate law and order were restored; individual heroes were paraded in public and given tokens of recognition (Armani suits in Swampy's case); 'democracy' was served and everyone will soon be able to fly off on holiday from the new runway. In this fairy story middle-class interests of all types justifiably live on happily ever after.

The methodological potential to elicit and critique such *mythic narrative* is the reason I would argue that something particular is gained in news analysis by paying close, systematic attention to language, especially at this time of globally and technological burgeoning production and consumption. Language is at least empirical data with a specificity of form whereas attempting ethnographic work on the practices of journalists (increasingly plural and/or inaccessible) or theorising the role of media institutions (increasingly diverse and/or impenetrable) are becoming ever more ephemeral analyses. Although by no means a transparent route to knowledge, language necessarily, by its very role in communication, however awkwardly and imperfectly, shares meanings within language communities. For Fairclough (1995), language is a *social barometer*: 'The value of such a view of texts is that it makes it easier to connect the analysis of language with fundamental concerns of social analysis' (Fairclough 1995: 17). Add to this a post-structuralist view that

> Different languages and different discourses within the same language divide up the world and give it meaning in different ways which cannot be reduced to one another through translation or by appeal to universally shared concepts reflecting a fixed reality.
>
> (Weedon 1994: 172)

and a powerful investigative tool is made available. The importance of analysing news such as that about the 'burrowers' is that it can reveal that even in accounts which are not overtly denigratory or exclusive, which may even appear laudatory and pervasive, the interests of the subjects of the accounts may not necessarily be being served. Mass media forms even at their most empathic with politically resistant, 'green' youth were not here supporting anything that was not commensurate with mature middle-class culture, values and authority.

Analysing the language of these texts indicates the power and the mutability of discourse. Analysing the texts *discursively* in relation to ideas and social identity shows their authority but, because of that exposure, to some extent weakens their potential. Foucault (1979: 100) pointed this out: 'Discourse transmits and reproduces power; it reinforces it, but it also undermines and exposes it, renders it fragile and makes it possible to thwart it.' In terms of how to thwart it – the 'burrowers' are clear on one thing when it comes to environmental resistance – the media are unlikely to help. Kate Evans' (1998) *Copse: The Cartoon Book of Tree Protesting* contains 'an illustrated page on how to build a tunnel' with the footnote:

> *Don't show the tunnel to newcomers or journalists.*
> (*Observer* 21 July 1998, emphasis added)

Notes

1 Media reporting of deviant youth and the abuse of drugs and/or alcohol has long been a source of interest to media academics, most seminally perhaps in the work of Cohen and Young (1973) in relation to the media amplifying issues to the point where they cause a moral panic in the popular arena.

2 It is worth noting here that media reports of English fans rioting in Marseilles during and after the World Cup match against Tunisia in June 1998 initially referred to the hooligans as youths. It was only after arrests were made and they were revealed to be employed men in their mid-20s to late 30s, often married with children, that youth was replaced with terms like violent criminal. No accompanying critique of mature, heterosexual, solvent English masculinity appeared in place of the misplaced demonisation of youth.

3 Only the *Big Issue* offered a 'politicised' account but provided the jokey headline 'Swampy's tunnel of love' duly adopted by the *Observer* a month later. The *Big Issue* is a paper sold on the streets by homeless people; it often features sympathetic and very well researched accounts of social and political issues relevant to those excluded from the mainstream of British life.

4 This was the first and only time I came across the argument that a primary goal of 'burrowing' was not necessarily to prevent any single project, whether at Newbury, Honiton or Manchester, but to add so substantially to the process of construction in terms of time, publicity and finance that future projects either would not be undertaken or would be sensitive to environmental issues. The main body of the programme, however, took a very different turn with little reference to the environmentalist's degradation. The debate was about the right to protest and rapidly descended into a slanging match among the male panellists. Here there was some sympathy with the goals of the resisters but not the acts themselves (criminal) nor those involved in them (anti-democratic deviants). This was in many ways, in its second part, the closest to the kind of media account I was expecting to find more generally – space was given to oppositional views and yet the different perspective lost out to a barrage of political conservatism and moral denigration. In other words, this was more like news as commonly theorised, blending the superfice of journalistic balance with fairly obvious dominant hegemony. The fact that this occurred on the BBC's flagship religious affairs programme rather than elsewhere in news journalism is a curiosity beyond the scope of this chapter.

5 Chomsky's position derives from his critique of the relations between the media the state and capital in the USA. In Britain, Rupert Murdoch's papers are currently 'bullying' the state to defer from entry into the European monetary system. Murdoch's *Sun* accused Blair of being 'the most dangerous man in Britain' in the week beginning 22 June 1997. The *Guardian* a week later suggests 'Mr Blair may

be too anxious about the influence of Mr. Murdoch's media empire to risk alienating him over regulation of his business interests' (29 June 1998).

6 This ranking of agenda in the media is seen by environmentalists as evident both in politics and the media. Green issues are seen to be consistently under-addressed or ill addressed, hence their espousal of direct action on single issues rather than the democratic process (*Heart of the Matter* BBC1 23 March 1997).

7 *In Metaphors We Live By*, Lakoff and Johnson (1980) go so far as to suggest that conflict is our dominant cultural metaphor, effectively underwriting all our institutions and relations. This seems an overstated claim until they suggest how different our experiences and understandings might be if the dominant sense-making metaphor was dance.

8 Interestingly this work was first published in the *International Journal of Peace Research* 1. Galtung and Ruge (1965) isolated twelve components common to accounts of foreign conflict in Cuba, the Congo and Cyprus.

9 With a certain presumed (self) irony the protesters even called a site the Jimi Hendrix camp.

10 Obviously there are major issues around audience not dealt with in this chapter. Fairclough (1995: 198–9) agrees that mediated discourse 'can usefully be regarded as a domain of cultural hegemony' but that 'consumption/reception of media discourse raises a number of issues'. He suggests that 'it is essential for effective citizenship that people should be critically aware of culture, discourse and language, including the discourse and language of the media' (Fairclough 1995: 201). I agree and would argue that this would be a more useful way forward for academics as analysts and teachers, rather than continuing to pursue the mythical holy grail of effects.

Part II

Denaturalising risk politics

Chapter 5

Environmental pressure politics and the 'risk society'

Alison Anderson

This chapter examines the media politics of environmental reporting within the wider context of the study of new social movements. Over recent decades the environmental lobby in western Europe has witnessed some profound developments. A few powerful environmental organisations have become significant players in the global policy-making arena and have become highly attuned to the demands of the news media. At the same time a proliferation of locally-based grassroots networks have emerged, often pursuing their own distinct agendas and holding a somewhat ambivalent relationship with the mainstream news media. The symbolic content of environmental actions involving, for example, protesters burrowing underground tunnels or chaining themselves to trees has acquired a new significance in a society increasingly dominated by the circulation of images and signs. A number of social theorists, such as Melucci (1994, 1996), suggest that these developments may be conceptualised as forms of a new culture.

The chapter offers a critical analysis of new social movement theory in relation to processes of mass communication and the globalising of modernity. It draws upon some semi-structured interviews I conducted with environmental campaigners and policy-makers in Devon, south-west England in 1995 (this formed part of a wider study on local press reporting of environmental issues in Devon and Cornwall). The discussion considers recent examples of grassroots action and particular consideration is given to symbolic politics, media packaging, and issues of time and space. What is novel about contemporary forms of collective action? To what extent has a new-style politics emerged? And can this be seen as part of a large-scale cultural shift in the politics of risk in western society?

New social movements

I want to begin by considering some of the issues concerning defining new social movements (NSMs) since this is crucial in order to evaluate the different approaches that are taken in the literature. Social movements are defined here as organised forms of collective action representing a broad mobilisation of interests around a specific goal. Although they are outsiders from mainstream political institutions they may have some access to formal channels of influence, for example through lobbying activity. Within the literature on social movements and theories of 'risk society' environmentalism is viewed as a particularly strong illustration of a new social movement. NSMs may be characterised by the following: grassroots activism outside of formal political structures; informal, relatively unstructured, network forms of organisation; and, finally, an emphasis upon direct action and identity and lifestyle politics (see A. Anderson 1997).

In the UK and the USA environmentalism evolved from a limited number of conservation and wildlife preservation organisations which had a relatively narrow focus. It was not until the 1960s and 1970s that campaigning organisations were established, such as Friends of the Earth and Greenpeace, which were concerned with a wider set of issues. Increasingly, such groups became involved in campaigning about global environmental risks such as those associated with nuclear technology, global warming and acid rain. Also, in contrast to many of the earlier traditional organisations, they adopted a proactive approach towards generating public sympathy and political support. Television had become an increasingly important source of information about politics and was seen as a powerful means of influencing public opinion. Spectacular stunts during the 1970s aimed to capture the strong visual requirements of this medium. However, the reliance upon pseudo-events is certainly not new and there are examples of this sort of symbolic activity taking place in the first part of the twentieth century (A. Anderson 1997).

During the 1980s and 1990s globalisation and the growing impact of new media technologies led to a new emphasis on global marketing. With the gradual institutionalisation of environmentalist demands, large-scale environmental organisations, such as Greenpeace International, increasingly came to operate virtually as transnational corporations. As such groups adopted more proactive approaches and their resource base became stronger, they took on highly skilled professional staff with public relations backgrounds. These individuals were often very adept at tapping into particular sociocultural climates and generating more wide-ranging support for environmental issues through moral/symbolic appeals. Direct-mailing became a major source of revenue for such groups which meant that it was vital that they maintained a high public profile.

At the same time there has been a significant increase in localised, grassroots environmental action across Europe. These much looser networks of the 1980s may be differentiated from the formally organised movements of the 1970s in a number of respects: they do not have a fixed fee-paying membership; they mobilise relatively sporadically and do not have a hierarchical structure or fixed leadership; finally, they bring together a wide range of individuals from different social and cultural backgrounds who are united only, it seems, by a deep political cynicism and a strong sense of moral outrage (Hegedus 1990).

There are also major cultural influences upon expressions of collective action in Europe and the types of environmental risks which individuals mobilise around. Nas and Dekker (1995) found that there were major variations between and within countries when they examined data on the composition of environmental movements in Belgium, the UK, Germany and the Netherlands. They found that attitudes towards environmental groups were significantly more polarised in Germany compared with the other countries. Also, the degree of responsiveness of established political parties was an important factor in influencing expressions of collective action. In the Netherlands, for example, there was less opposition to green issues which was partly due to attempts made by the Pacifist-Socialist Party (PSP) and the radical party (PPR) to respond to the issues and develop close links with NSMs. The environmental 'movement' therefore embraces elements of both old-style and new-style politics. Action is mobilised at a variety of different levels including local, national and international. While grassroots networks tend to stress identity and lifestyle politics and expressivism, many formal mainstream organisations have developed more and more links with statutory authorities and often operate in conjunction with them. It is misleading to speak of environmentalism as a NSM without acknowledging these differences of structure, value-orientation, strategy and approach. A number of diverse influences upon the growth of the environmental movement can be discerned including romanticism, socialism, religious fundamentalism, the peace movement and anarchism. Accordingly, an adequate definition of social movements must be capable of embracing these various elements (see Goldblatt 1996).

NSMs and sociocultural change

A number of different explanations have been offered to account for the rise of the mass environmental movement in western society. Perhaps one of the most widely known is provided by Beck (1992a). He views social movements as representing the emergence of a new form of politics in a society which is based upon conflicts around risk. Such movements constitute a reaction to objective and subjectively perceived dangers or threats, and to related contradictory processes of individualisation in late modern society:

> on the one hand the new social movements (ecology, peace, feminism) are expressions of new risk situations in the risk society. On the other, they result from the search for social and personal identities and commitments in detraditionalized culture.
>
> (Beck 1992a: 90)

The work of Beck has had a considerable influence upon current thinking about environmentalism and social change. Increasingly, it is held, political activity is taking place outside the confines of the formal centralised spheres. For Beck, this is reflected in the arenas of 'sub-politics', for example the media, the judiciary and citizen action groups. Beck's prognosis of contemporary society has a number of parallels with that of other European theorists. Beck and Giddens both identify a new radical departure towards 'reflexive modernisation', although this is interpreted in rather different ways. In essence, they suggest that the old order is being shaken up by social institutions starting to adopt self-confrontational, critical engagement with the downside of industrial society. However, Beck's writings suggest that the mass media play a much more central role in risk society and reflexive modernisation than is the case in the work of Giddens (Cottle 1998a).

For both theorists the politicisation of the environment is taken as a key illustration of this emergent culture. Beck (1998), for example, claims it was grassroots citizen initiatives that forced environmental issues onto the political agenda of many western countries during the late 1980s. The mobilisation of public opinion was therefore, according to Beck, the key factor which forced Europe's major political parties to respond. Both Beck and Giddens observe an increasing uncertainty over the future opening up of the critique of science.

Similarly, Castells (1997) views the rise of environmentalism as inextricably bound up with fundamental shifts in the structure of society:

> I propose the hypothesis that there is a direct correspondence between the themes put forward by the environmental movement and the fundamental dimensions of the new social structure, the network society, emerging from the 1970s onwards: science and technology as the basic means and goals of economy and society; the transformation of space; the transformation of time; and the domination of cultural identity by abstract, global flows of wealth, power and information constructing real virtuality through media networks.
>
> (Castells 1997: 122)

Environmental concern in itself is clearly nothing new; generations of people have voiced anxiety over local conditions in one way or another. However, in my view Beck is right to observe that what is new about current environmental concern is that many of the problems exist on a global scale and the new immediate and personal 'sub-political' level encourages individuals to 'feel' environmental threats. In other words, discourses of risk and risk assessment are more pervasive. Also, Beck is right to recognise that perceptions of risk are selective and different environmental issues have varying degrees of cultural potency and mediagenic dying trees and seals, for example, allow us to glimpse the bigger picture (see Beck 1995: 47–8).

Although a number of contemporary theorists consider NSMs and the media to play a pivotal role in late modern society (see, for example, Beck 1995; Castells 1998; Melucci 1996) much of what has been written is at a highly generalised level. This is particularly evident in Beck's recent accounts of shifts in the political arena. While Beck views the mass media as the key site whereby ideas about risk are socially constructed, to date he has provided little in-depth analysis of their role. As Cottle (1998a) observes, his theory of the media is underdeveloped and contradictory at times. In particular, it fails to consider the complexities of the cultural mediation of risk and audience responses. Moreover, it treats the media as homogeneous while empirical research demonstrates that the news media are highly differentiated (see A. Anderson 1997: 188).

Castells's (1997) 'network society' has significant parallels with Beck's (1992a) 'risk society'. In his three-volume work on *The Information Age*, Castells (1996, 1997, 1998), like Beck, views the media (and in particular new media) as occupying a central place within late-modern society. In brief, Castells's argument is that fundamental changes have occurred since the 1960s which have resulted in a new capitalist mode of development which he labels the 'information society'. Castells analyses the emergence of what he labels 'network society', characterised by the rise of network forms of organisations, together with the transformation of time–space relations and virtual reality brought about by globalisation and the impact of new media technologies.

For Castells (1997), traditional divisions based upon social class have declined in importance and the locus of power is no longer concentrated within capitalist corporations, the institutions of the state, or in ideological state apparatuses such as the media and religion. Instead, Castells maintains that it has become more diffused and NSMs play a prime role in the generation of new cultural codes: 'The new power lies in the codes of information and in the images of representation around which societies organise their institutions, and people build their lives, and decide their behaviour. The sites of this power are people's minds' (Castells 1997: 359).

Castells's treatment of the media (although requiring further elaboration and empirical support) is considerably more developed than that of Beck. He recognises that the relationship between the new media and the political sphere is complex and that effects are contingent upon a number of diverse factors: 'Overall, the media are rooted in society, and their interaction with the political process is highly undetermined, depending upon context, strategies of political actors, and specific interaction between an array of social, cultural and political features' (Castells 1997: 311).

A concern with cultural codes and the information society is also a major theme running through the work of Melucci (1994, 1996). He suggests that contemporary social movements have an essentially communicative role in that they allow us to capture key aspects of social changes which are currently under way. However, Melucci challenges the view that social movements should be understood in the context of reacting to the powerful forces of global capitalism. He argues that power relations are more fluid and ambivalent than tends to be recognised by many neo-Marxist approaches (see Melucci 1996: 176). For Melucci the rise of the 'information society' has shifted old balances of power and conflict is increasingly played out in cultural arenas:

> Social movements of modern and premodern historical periods were deeply
> rooted in the material conditions of their environment, and their capacity
> for a symbolic elaboration and representation of this specific context was
> comparatively lower than it can be today. The capacity for symbolisation
> and for cultural representation of social action evolves directly in propor-
> tion to the social capacity to produce symbolic resources. A society which
> is highly dependent upon its material environment consequently possesses
> a lower capacity to produce an autonomous cultural sphere.
>
> (Melucci 1996: 177)

It is not clear how such claims could be tested empirically; Melucci (1994)
himself recognises that the novelty of this aspect of collective action could be
called into question but claims that this is making the mistake of regarding it
as a 'unitary empirical object'. However, it is possible to draw some tentative
conclusions from an analysis of the contemporary use of symbolic resources
among social movement organisations involved in campaigning about environmental issues. Much of what has been written concerning 'risk' has been
based upon the implicit assumption that environmentalists have not played a
significant role in the framing of environmental knowledge (see Jamison 1996).
However, in my view environmentalists have played an important role in a
cognitive as well as a political sense. The next section examines environmentalists' perceptions of the rise of what has become labelled as 'DiY politics' and the relationship between NSMs and the media.

DiY politics

The growth of the new grassroots networks of the 1980s can be seen as one
aspect of a broader phenomenon which has acquired the label, DiY culture.
'Do it Yourself' culture, as the name suggests, concerns individuals becoming
frustrated with the alienating forces of globalism, coupled with the ineffectiv-
ity of mainstream political channels and taking things into their own hands to
bring about real social change. In Britain, much of the action developed in the
context of protesting against the Criminal Justice Act of 1995, which gave
police new powers to prevent obstruction and trespass on public land.

One of the few books to focus upon this is McKay's (1998) *DiY Culture*,
which brings together the reflections of a range of activists on the contemporary protest culture in the UK. This collection of pieces provides a fascinat-
ing (largely biographically based) insider account of the development of this
counterculture which has a number of diverse roots in, among other things,
anarchism, paganism, New Ageism and humanism. Like all life history
material, sensitivity towards the subjectivity of the accounts is necessary.

McKay places DiY culture within a long tradition of radical mobilisations
among youth, particularly drawing upon the Anarchist movement. He views
DiY culture as a 1990s counterculture, following the earlier countercultures of

the 1960s (McKay 1998: 2). Of course, a feature of recent grassroots protests is that they represent something more than a narrowly based youth culture since they have mobilised a broad cross-section of the public. Also, they cannot be seen as simply a reflection of the concerns of the professional middle classes (see A. Anderson 1997: 95–6). However, it is possible to discern a number of perceptual shifts underpinning the new consciousness-raising networks of the 1980s which reflect wider sociocultural changes. One important feature of the grassroots networks concerns their conception of time which, as McKay maintains, tends to be marked by a concern with immediacy and some degree of disdain for rationalising action or thinking about it in philosophical terms. One activist described it thus:

> Unlike other political issues and historical moments, being a radical environmentalist at the end of the twentieth century gives one a very fixed time frame, one which looks out on an incredibly fragile future. Even the Armageddon fears of the peace movement were always based on *if* – *if* there was a Third World War, if a nuclear warhead is dropped – out of the ordinary events. But ecological collapse is not based on if but when: business as usual, growth economics, globalisation, etc. [. . .] is all normal everyday activity, all leading to collapse. Time means something completely different to DiY culture – time is short – and that is why there is an obsession with the collective present. There can be no long term strategy when there is no long term.
>
> (cited in McKay 1998: 13)

In some respects this has parallels with the time frames of millennial cults. The new consciousness-raising networks of the 1980s fundamentally challenged traditional conceptions of time. The global environmental crisis was seen as requiring a completely different perspective since it is an actuality.

Another important element of the new networks concerns perceptions of space and place. Protests have tended to be highly localised and yet global dimensions have been strongly emphasised. Recent grassroots protests in the UK around live animal exports (in 1995), protests in support of striking trade unionists in which the radical group, Reclaim the Streets, participated together with Liverpool dockers (1996) and demonstrations over the Manchester airport runway expansion (1997) all brought the local/global dimension to the fore in their intensely local, but also international, appeal (McKay 1998). More recently (1999) protests against genetically modified foods have also encompassed these dimensions. In some senses, then, recent forms of collective action can be seen as representing resistance to the globalising forces of late modernity.

A further significant characteristic lies in the tendency to favour direct action and cultural politics as opposed to participating in political institutions. The proliferation of grassroots consciousness-raising networks during the 1980s and 1990s can, in part, be seen as representing a response to the institutionalisation of environmentalism, and a growing disillusionment over the perceived lack of channels open to ordinary citizens to get actively involved at the local level (see Wall 1999). Even organisations such as Greenpeace, which is well known for its direct action approach, has shifted its focus increasingly towards lobbying (see Yearley 1994). At the local level, environmentalists are often involved in working in tandem with councils to promote Local Agenda 21. For example, West Devon Environmental Network was set up in 1994, and was initially partially funded by the council, to co-ordinate environmental activity in the area. An officer for West Devon Borough Council explained: 'we decided that there was a need for a sort of co-ordinating function at arm's length from the council, that's where the idea of a West Devon network came up' (interview, July 1995). Also, many local authorities now have official environmental committees, and some have environment forums which include local councillors, local government officers, representatives of local environmental groups and interested members of the public.

This emphasis upon behind-the-scenes lobbying activity, representation on councils and a recognition of the complexity of the issues appears to have resulted in groups of individuals feeling isolated, frustrated and powerless. An environmental co-ordinator in Devon County Council, who had previously campaigned with Friends of the Earth, commented:

> When I joined the group six years ago we thought it was just fine to talk about don't chop the trees down in the rainforest and that was campaigned about and we would do little hand written letters and now the rainforest campaign is massively complex . . . and someone comes along to a group and wants to do something about the environment, you say right we're going to have to get to grips with the structure plan, transport policies programmed for the county and they go ugh! So basically the issues have become far more complex and the whole thing has become professionalised. . . . There is an increasing recognition that it's about fundamental political and economic things in our society and a lot of people are just not comfortable getting spirited off to strategic levels.
>
> (Interview, June 1995)

She went on to explain how a once-vibrant local Friends of the Earth group in the early 1990s had dwindled to only a handful of activists. At the same time many community-based initiatives have grown in strength; for example, Local Exchange Trading Schemes (LETS), which aim to introduce a non-sterling economy through bartering goods and services. Also, as environmental pressure groups have become increasingly sophisticated in targeting their messages, and actively included in the policy-making process, they have shown a greater willingness to make concessions over issues. This contrasts with grassroots networks which typically show little willingness to compromise over their principles. But it must be acknowledged that even here there are lots of splits and differences of approach. In sum, there are a number of diverse factors which have played a part in these shifts and it would be reductionist to view the growth of grassroots networks simply in terms of structural factors (see A. Anderson 1997).

A final feature of contemporary grassroots networks lies in their role in the production of knowledge and attitudes towards publicity channels. While in some respects they are highly critical of technology, many protest networks have been at the forefront of developing new forms of political action through the new communications media. At present, relatively little is known about the use of new media technologies by grassroots campaigners. In the UK, Small World was set up in the early 1990s by a handful of activists with a film-making background to provide assistance to campaigners in the effective use of video as a political tool. Thomas Harding, a director and co-founder, describes how the birth of what he calls 'video activism' emerged:

> The major shift came in the late 1980s with the introduction of the small format 8 mm and VHS camcorders. These were very easy to use, high quality, relatively low in cost and widely available.[. . .] Three factors converged at the same time: an emergence of a vibrant form of activism; the availability of the new camcorders; and the failure of mainstream TV to adequately cover the boom in grassroots politics.
>
> (Harding 1998: 83)

The views of contemporary protest activists are characterised by a profound ambivalence towards the mainstream media. Although the potential power of the global capitalist media is recognised and considerable use is made of new media technologies, there is often a reluctance to work with the media in the pursuit of their broader goals. This in itself is not new; the 1960s countercul-ture was equally embracing of new media technologies of the day, such as off-set litho printing (McKay 1998). What is different, however, is the new possibilities for networking opened up by globalisation and new computer tech-nologies. As Castells (1997) maintains:

> Through these networks, grassroots groups around the world become sud-denly able to act globally, at the level where main problems are created. It seems that a computer-literate elite is emerging as the global, co-ordinating core of grassroots environmental action groups around the world, a phenomenon not entirely dissimilar to the role played by artisan printers and journalists at the beginning of the labour movement, orienting, through information to which they had access, the illiterate masses that formed the working class of early industrialisation.
>
> (Castells 1997: 129–30)

However, these possibilities are constrained and the result of interacting on the web may be the individualisation of politics bypassing intermediary groups.

There are fundamental inequalities of access and distance which inevitably polarise people's experiences (Bauman 1998).

Gamson and Wolfsfeld (1993) provide an interesting analysis of power transactions in media–movements relations. They argue that the relationship between social movements and the media tends to be based upon unequal power relations since social movements are more dependent upon the media than the media is on social movements. Also, they suggest that movements often have different cultures which conflict with mainstream media and political cultures. This relationship is characterised by what they call a 'fundamental ambivalence'. 'Movement activists tend to view mainstream media not as autonomous and neutral actors but as agents and handmaidens of dominant groups whom they are challenging' (Gamson and Wolfsfeld 1993: 119).

While this may apply very well to many organised pressure groups, it is less appropriate when considering looser grassroots networks. It is questionable whether they are always more dependent upon the media than the media are on them. In some cases, campaigners are actively hostile to the mainstream media and rely heavily upon their own underground channels of communication. For example, grassroots protesters in the UK have developed their own alternative outlets such as *Squall* magazine and *Aufheben* magazine (both founded in 1992) and the radical group, Earth First!, known for its 'monkey-wrenching' tactics, has its own publication entitled 'Do or Die'. According to Jim Carey, co-editor of *Squall* magazine, it is designed to reflect: a serious attempt to provide a more socially relevant representation, unfettered by the usual sycophancy to advertisers and spin doctors; an attempt to rejuvenate the independence, accuracy and liveliness of British journalism' (Carey 1998: 59). In addition, these magazines have their own websites which often replicate material in their publications. At the same time, though, where mainstream media seek to cover the opinions or activities of some of the grassroots communities, such communities tend not to be well represented: they tend to lack power because they are not likely to have any pre-identified spokespersons. However, by no means all contemporary elements of DiY culture seek to separate themselves completely from the mainstream media. For example, some of the production team of *Squall* magazine are part-time freelance journalists and spokespersons for the magazine have made several media appearances (Carey 1998).

Castells (1997) is right to observe that the electronic media have come to play an increasingly central role in structuring the whole process of politics. Organised pressure groups and grassroots networks have acted in proactive ways to these developments. McNeish's (1999) study of anti-roads protests and survey of members of Alarm UK (a London-wide alliance against road building formed in the late 1980s) demonstrates the importance of the use of the Internet by both grassroots networks and established groups. Movement identity is to a significant degree shaped by how collective values, norms and action are refracted in the media. Different events and elements of a 'movement' or grassroots 'culture' are brought together and dramatised in the media. For example, it is hard to imagine the roads protests in Britain without 'Swampy', the underground tunneller who came to personify the conflict. In my opinion, politics and the media are inextricably bound together and episodes like Greenpeace's action against the Brent Spar oil tanker in 1995 illustrate the potential power of mobilising public opinion through graphic visual images.

Conclusion

Clearly, new sources of identity have emerged through the growth of non-party based networks and community groups which often tend to be concerned with localised environmental issues, offer the opportunity for shared emotional release, and tend to be non-hierarchical with a relatively rapid turnover of people (Macnaghten and Urry 1995; Castells 1997). It appears likely that such explanations apply to particular subsections of the population but it is still necessary to explain why it is that environmentalism is so appealing compared to other community-based movements through which individuals may gain a powerful sense of identity. Popularised moral issues and values, for example, may be a major motivation of individuals within animal welfare and anti-cruelty movements (Goldblatt 1996). Also, explanations that focus solely upon identity and general value shifts among the population run the risk of divorcing expressions of environmental concern from real world events.

There are a number of limitations with NSM theory and it has not been the intention of this chapter to provide an exhaustive discussion since this has been well covered elsewhere (see Diani 1995; Yearley 1994). Instead, the chapter has focused upon the symbolic content of environmental action and the framing of collective action through the media. In this respect, it is questionable as to how far contemporary environmentalism can be seem as radically differing from older forms of protest; in my view an overly dichotomous picture has tended to be painted in contrasting old and 'new' social movements. For example, Eder (1996) and Jamison (1996) invest the contemporary environmental movement with a heightened significance in terms of what they see as their increasing dependence upon mobilising symbolic resources. As Szerszynski *et al.* (1996) point out:

> [. . .] both imply that the movement's contemporary reliance on symbolic and identity politics represents a qualitative departure as if an earlier purity of ideological commitment has been displaced by an institutionally driven need for careful, but ultimately instrumental, media self-presentation. Yet surely environmental groups always were 'cultural pressure groups', as much concerned with the iconic as the mythic as with the propositional or narrowly normative statements, and with the construction of themselves as authoritative social actors – but through complex processes of self-invention that cannot be reduced to the narrowly strategic.
>
> (Szerszynski *et al.* 1996: 22)

The growth of grassroots environmental networks which exist alongside established pressure groups illustrates some of the contradictions inherent within
the forces that shape modernity and countermodernity. For example, diverging
responses to the rationality of scientific reasoning; strategic thinking and the
relativisation of the temporal sphere through challenging notions of clock-time
and replacing it with new 'glacial' and 'virtual' conceptions of time. In particular, they represent fundamental tensions concerning identity, symbolic politics
and strategically oriented action. Many of the international environmental
pressure groups operate like transnational corporations and have become
increasingly sophisticated in knowing how to put a spin on issues. Whilst grassroots networks often exhibit deep suspicion of the mainstream media, they are
increasingly forced to package their actions in media friendly ways if they are
to avoid political marginality. This raises a whole set of dilemmas about the
ways in which issues are framed to fit into established news values, opening up
possibilities for subverting these through the use of the internet and alternative channels of communication.

There is some evidence, then, which suggests that a large-scale shift has
occurred in relation to the cultural politics of risk; new grassroots groups
emerged in western Europe during the 1980s and 1990s and have become a
highly significant force in politics. However, there are dangers with treating
social movements alone as the carriers of a new form of society. In particular,
the emphasis upon identity and symbolic politics is not entirely novel and
masks important ambivalences and contradictions.

Chapter 6

'Industry causes lung cancer': would you be happy with that headline?

Environmental health and local politics

Peter Phillimore and Suzanne Moffatt

> Air 'link' to cancer: report warns women.
> *(Teesside Evening Gazette* 6 December 1995)

> No evidence of asthma link to air pollution.
> *(Northern Echo* 7 December 1995)

> Illness: it's not the Teesside air. Poor health cannot be blamed on pollution, says new study.
> *(Northern Echo* 7 December 1995)

This is an account of the politics of pollution in Teesside, a conurbation of over 400,000 in north-east England.[1] The quotations above were the contrasting headlines in local news coverage after publication in December 1995 of a research report which examined the impact of industrial air pollution on the health of some of Teesside's poorest neighbourhoods. *Health, Illness and the Environment in Teesside and Sunderland* ran to 400 pages, and was based on nearly four years of research (TEES 1995). We were both members of the team which conducted the study.[2]

National newspapers did not cover publication of the TEES Report. However, the environmental health trade press did, echoing the differences shown in local news reports. 'Teesside health study links lung cancer with air pollution' was the headline in the *ENDS Report* (December 1995). 'Teesside health study takes the blame off industry' was the contrasting emphasis in the *Environment Information Bulletin* (February 1996). The following month (March 1996) the *Bulletin* returned to the topic following a letter sent by three of us involved, under the headline 'Teesside study "misinterpreted" say researchers'.

In this chapter we explore the context in which this ambiguity arose. If the outcome was unanticipated confusion as to what the story seemed to be, this can be only partly attributed to the complexity of findings couched in the cautious language of epidemiology, or the absence of 'hard facts' surrounding the health risks of industrial air pollution (see Taubes 1995).[3] An additional factor was the determination on the part of the main local institutions to ensure that the public portrayal of the findings was carefully controlled, and perception of the risks to health minimised (see MacGill 1987). How that was done is our main theme. Our interest is not so much in media coverage itself as in attempts by major institutions in Teesside to steer and guide this coverage. These efforts have a long history.

Prior to publication of the TEES Report, several clues suggest considerable unease about the findings and possible public responses. A draft version of the report was leaked anonymously to a group representing industry interests by 'a concerned doctor' two months in advance. When members of this group received advance briefing of the findings of the study, the presentation met with this reaction: ' "Industry causes lung cancer!" Would you be happy with that headline?' Yet after publication, as time elapsed, a different tone became apparent. The following remarks, all made by representatives of industries in Teesside, reflect a more confident expectation that potential difficulties had faded (cited in E. Hudson et al. 1998: 1).

> We were expecting the equivalent of World War Three.

> I thought the publicity was well balanced, positive for Teesside, the best publicity for many a year. It put the air pollution debate to sleep.

> Prior to publication of the findings, whenever our organisation responded to requests for financial support, generosity was interpreted as 'guilt money'. . . . Since the TEES study findings were published, it's easier to breathe out there.

As researchers, we ourselves were not disinterested spectators content to let our findings 'speak for themselves' – epidemiological findings do not speak for themselves. Attempts to clarify and correct press statements were made (as mentioned above). More particularly, we each also had a hand in editorial compromises over the various summaries of such a large body of data (including, crucially, the press release) which helped to pave the way for the re-presentations which occurred. As social scientists, the two of us have been intrigued as much as dismayed by the manner in which our findings have been remoulded, and used as a basis for apparently authoritative claims about pollution and its impact (Burgess and Harrison 1993). More clearly than in other work we have done, the politics of epidemiology has been revealed (see MacGill 1987; Nash and Kirsch 1988).

This puts us both in the position of participants and commentators, with an epidemiological perspective to present while we also reflect sociologically about the processes that have created the necessity for this epidemiological rescue work. The dual role means that alongside epidemiological analyses (Bhopal et al. 1998; Pless-Mulloli et al. 1998) we are also writing sociological accounts which take the controversy surrounding interpretation as the focus of attention

(Phillimore 1998; E. Hudson *et al.* 1998). Central though the idea of risk is to both disciplines, a chasm nevertheless divides the epidemiological search for 'risk factors' from the sociological exploration of how 'risk' has emerged as a central cultural construct in the twentieth century.

Air pollution in Teesside

For a century, air pollution has been a sensitive topic in Teesside with both sides of the River Tees recording some of the highest levels of smoke, ferric oxide and sulphur dioxide in the country since national monitoring began in the 1950s and 1960s. Built first around iron and steel, and after the First World War around chemicals as well, the Teesside towns of Middlesbrough, Stockton, Thornaby, Billingham and Redcar were initially notable for their extra-ordinarily rapid growth (Briggs 1963; Beynon *et al.* 1994; R. Hudson 1989). The conurbation remains identified with steel and petro-chemicals in the 1990s, with ICI the dominant corporation on the chemicals side and British Steel the present-day inheritor of a number of separate steel-producing companies. These industries are visible from almost every angle in Teesside, as dominating physically as they are economically and figuratively in Teessiders' lives.[4]

It is *industrial* air pollution, moreover, which has excited greatest concern in Teesside. Since the 1980s traffic pollution and non-local sources have entered the equation, setting the scene for contention over the relative importance of different kinds of air pollution. On the principle that responsibility shared is responsibility reduced, it has been politically expedient to de-emphasise local industrial emissions by highlighting other pollution problems, typically those which Teesside shares with almost every other British conurbation (we return to this theme later in the chapter). Yet if Teesside (more specifically Middlesbrough) is at the forefront of national developments in air quality monitoring, it is not because it is *like* other places but because it is in crucial respects *unlike* them – the difference being its concentration of industrial processes which necessitate the atmospheric emission of toxic gases.

In Teesside, investigation into links between industrial pollution and the health of the surrounding population invariably has been controversial. By the same token, empirical research which finds no clear-cut evidence to link pollution with ill-health provides a shot in the arm for industry and local government, eliciting comments such as 'gratifying', 'reassuring' and 'allays anxieties'. Yet one person's reassurance may be another person's whitewash, and in neighbourhoods where preoccupation with air pollution is strong, negative or inconclusive evidence is liable to be discounted (see Belsham 1991). 'No link established' is not read as 'there is no link' (as public authorities and the industries concerned find it convenient to read it) but as 'they failed to find the link that is there'.[5] Usually underlying this response is a sense of cynical resignation that local knowledge and experience has, once again, been ignored (Phillimore and Moffatt 1994; see Hobart 1993). We agree with Wynne

(1996a) that the 'lack of overt public dissent or opposition towards expert systems is taken too easily for public trust . . . the reality of social dependency on expert systems should not be equated with positive trust' (Wynne 1996a: 50).

Alternative readings of the epidemiological evidence

The latest phase of concern with environmental health in Teesside coincided with evidence that mortality in poorer areas was unexpectedly high (Phillimore and Morris 1991). The new study concentrated on the poorest neighbourhoods, which were grouped into zones based on differential proximity to the main industries (Bhopal *et al.* 1998; Pless-Mulloli *et al.* 1998; TEES 1995). The slim possibility that pollution effects might be apparent across Teesside led us to include several comparably poor neighbourhoods in Sunderland, twenty-five miles to the north. We examined mortality and morbidity. The strongest evidence for a link between industrial air pollution and health proved to be in relation to deaths from lung cancer and other respiratory diseases. While analysis of deaths appears to offer less scope for ambiguity than analysis of illness and morbidity, several paradoxes were nonetheless evident. For example:

- Why was the gradient across zones from female lung cancer and respiratory disease mortality not paralleled to the same extent among men?
- Why did the pattern of variation observed among women for these causes of death disappear or even reverse over the age of seventy-five years?

This is not the place to go into the case for one interpretation rather than another, though we doubt very much whether it is justified to account for lung cancer and respiratory system mortality variations across Teesside without reference to a significant causal role for industrial air pollution (Pless-Mulloli *et al.* 1998). In the original report our conclusions about the lung cancer evidence were expressed in these words:

> On their own these data *do not demonstrate that industrial pollution caused* the excess lung cancer mortality (over and above already high rates across the study zones) apparent in areas close to industry. Nevertheless, they add significantly to a substantial scientific literature, including local research, that **historical levels of air pollution from industry are likely to have contributed to lung cancer** deaths. Given the long latency period characteristic of lung cancer, and the limited data available on historical patterns of air pollution, it is *impossible to be more precise about the mechanisms* underlying the association. We consider that, until better explanations are offered, **the evidence points to a causal role for industrial emissions**

in the strong lung cancer gradients observed among women. (TEES 1995: 284, contrasting emphases added)

The scope for divergent readings of this statement is made clear by the contrasting emphases we have highlighted. This is almost inevitable in assessing health risks from exposure to environmental hazards, where long time-scales are involved. The long duration of exposures to pollutants, the long time-lag between cumulative exposures and medical symptoms, and the chronic nature of ill-health once symptoms manifest themselves, militate against confident claims about causation in epidemiological studies (Adam 1995; 1996, Das 1995). An inevitable consequence is a high degree of caution and qualification in environmental epidemiology. These uncertainties make it easy for those whose interests are at stake to disregard evidence or place upon it an interpretation which suits their needs. With this in mind, we take issue with the uniform insistence in local government and industry in Teesside that the new data provide 'reassurance' that industrial air pollution is not linked to ill-health.

On publication of the epidemiological report, ICI released a 'General Position Statement', one point referring to lung cancer:

> There is a theory in the report that air pollution in the past may have contributed to high incidences of lung cancer in women. On this question, however, no cause has been established in the report, and ICI has no evidence that our activities have or are causing ill-health. ICI believes this situation requires further careful research to allay concerns.
>
> (ICI press statement 6 December 1995)

Her Majesty's Inspectorate of Pollution (HMIP) adopted a similar line:

> HMIP also notes that the report can not explain the high rates of lung cancer in women living in residential areas close to current industrial complexes and there is a need for more research in this area.
>
> (HMIP press statement 6 December 1995)

Organisations which had funded the study used their joint press release to start reinterpreting the findings, to cast doubt on any link between industrial air pollution and mortality and to re-emphasise the adverse effects of smoking:

> 'The results do reveal, however, an increase in deaths from lung cancer among women living in the areas closest to industrial sites . . . It should be noted that these areas do not correspond well to the major sites of industry 20–30 years ago when the disease would be developing and tobacco is by far the most potent cause of lung cancer. Rates of smoking are still

rising in young women and this needs to change if we want to see reducing rates of lung cancer in women.

(Tees Health, Middlesbrough and Langbaurgh Borough Councils press statement, 6 December 1995)

The implication that we had overlooked the gradual migration of industry down-river through the twentieth century was in our view unfounded, and all the more curious as staff from these organisations were part of the research team.

Middlesbrough Borough Council additionally put out a press release of their own. This highlighted the issue of poverty, locally less contentious than industrial pollution:

The report says that current air quality on Teesside is good, but also strongly reaffirms the link between poverty, smoking and ill-health. Said Middlesbrough Council's chair of Public Protection and Trading Standards:

Action must also be taken at Government level to reduce the yawning gap between health in some of Teesside's most disadvantaged communities and the rest of the UK. That assistance should not be confined to advice on lifestyle, helpful as that might be. It must come in the form of measures to alleviate the hardship and poverty which is literally killing people.

(Middlesbrough Borough Council press statement, 6 December 1995)

Faced with this guidance, it is not surprising to find the same emphasis in local news reports. The *Evening Gazette* noted:

A new report claims past industrial air pollution may be a contributory factor [to lung cancer]. But health chiefs stressed smoking is still the major cause of death for this disease.

(*Evening Gazette*, 6 December 1995)

The *Northern Echo* quoted the chair of the Middlesbrough Public Protection Committee as saying that the report 'helps us nail the myth about local air quality' (7 December 1995). Local media coverage took its cue from the strong steer provided in the press releases of the main Teesside institutions. The following remarks from a local government officer illustrate how much this was the outcome sought:

Fortunately our past experiences with the local media helped us to prepare for the public launch in ensuring that a balanced view was represented to the public and the 'bad news' was not unduly emphasised. Our views as officers are that the research findings need to be minimised. So we were pleased with the low key media response. The fact that people don't know much is good news, we're pumping millions into the area, we don't need more bad news about Grangetown. For the council it's a double edged sword. We need to breathe confidence into the area and attract industry, we need jobs.

(quoted in E. Hudson et al. 1998: 26)

Depicting and moralising Teesside's air pollution

Pollution may be a recurring motif in Teesside's image of itself as a place, but its stacks have always conjured up contradictory associations: of economic vitality, but also of the associated pollution (Briggs 1963; Beynon *et al.* 1994). In an area where the major national recessions of the twentieth century have hit hard, the long-term risks associated with exposure to pollution have invariably been set alongside the risks of job loss and economic insecurity. The following remarks made by Teesside citizens are current illustrations of an old dilemma:[6]

> I think that the lack of employment is causing far more havoc than anything and in my mind even supersedes having a cleaner environment.

> I think it is ridiculous how industry in this area gets away with the amount of pollution they pump into the air and rivers. In my opinion it is industry that is to blame for the amount of chest problems people suffer from in this area.

Yet as wider national and international concerns about environmental pollution have grown since the 1970s, Teesside's image as a place beset by abnormally severe air pollution has dogged it. Several disparate examples will illustrate the point. The first relates to the tobacco industry's own interest in Teesside's air pollution. For instance, in the 1950s the tobacco industry was not slow in spotting that Teesside offered a useful laboratory which might assist its efforts to deflect attention from the rising tide of evidence linking tobacco consumption with lung cancer and respiratory illness. Accordingly, research started in the 1950s, funded by the Tobacco Research Council, to examine 'environmental factors associated with lung cancer and bronchitis mortality' (Wicken and Buck 1964). A follow-up study continued this work through the 1960s (Dean and Lee 1977). The conclusions of these studies need not concern us here. The relevant point is that Teesside was seen to provide a suitable testing ground for determining the impact that atmospheric pollution might have in relation to diseases increasingly being associated with smoking. This in turn had the potential to offer the tobacco industry valuable ammunition in its attempts to counter its increasingly exposed position, neatly illustrating Beck's (1992: 227) observation that risks which provide a problem for one industry can be another industry's opportunity.

An incident in 1981 highlighted Teesside's image as a polluted place in a quite different way. An advertisement for Crown Paints in the trade press suggested that exposure to the Teesside air offered the most demanding test conditions that the company could find for one of its products. The implication that the air along the River Tees was heavily polluted brought an angry response, with an official complaint to the Advertising Standards Authority and, after an unfavourable response, the eventual intervention of local MPs.[7] Fears were voiced that inward investment may be deterred, especially as this incident came at a time of dismay about economic collapse and unemployment. As the minutes of a Pollution Control Committee insisted:

> It is not merely a matter of local pride that caused us to pursue this matter – it is difficult enough already to attract new industry to the area, and nationally circulated advertisements which perpetuate the myth of the grimy North East certainly do not assist the local authorities in their efforts.
>
> (Borough of Cleveland Pollution Control Group 1982–3)

Our final example is more recent, and reflects both the continued sensitivity of air pollution in Teesside and also the official endeavours to combat this image. In 1996, a leaflet was circulated to thousands of households in Teesside by local authorities and industries (funded partly by the Department of the Environment). Entitled 'Air Quality Today', the following extracts illustrate its message:

> Smokey old Teesside?
> Fact: Teesside used to be one of the most polluted places in Britain. In the 1960's it suffered from some of the worst air pollution in the country, due partly to domestic coalburning.
> Fact: it used to be – but not any more! . . .
> The latest analytical techniques available have shown that our air is as good as other towns and cities in the country – and in many cases a lot better. Take airborne particle pollution for example, which is the most significant local pollutant nowadays. National statistics show that in 1994 Middlesbrough had the lowest reported levels. . . .
> Our biggest air quality problem on Teesside is one of perception.
>
> So, do we ever get poor air quality?
> Yes. On about a dozen occasions through the year. Sometimes these occur in the summer when we get PHOTOCHEMICAL SMOG drifting into Teesside from as far away as Europe.
> Despite great care being taken with industrial processes, there are occasions when locally-produced short-term emissions of pollutants do occur.

. . . Thankfully these episodes are quite rare. You might also be interested to know two things:

1 Peak pollution levels occur on 5th November.
2 Nowadays, much of our local air pollution comes from road traffic.

Do you get annoyed when people talk down Teesside? If we have wrong perceptions of our area, WE CANNOT BE SURPRISED IF OTHERS DO AS WELL. A wrong perception could mean people do not invest in our area. . . .

The way forward involves everyone getting together to challenge wrong perceptions.

This leaflet was ironically part of a strategy of increased openness and improved provision of information to the public. In it we can identify several strategies which have been employed in official efforts to deflect attention from industrial pollution in order to promote an image of Teesside as a 'clean' environment, attractive to investment by high-tech industries (see Burgess and Harrison 1993). One line has been to acknowledge that Teesside has had a history of heavy pollution, using the contrast between past and present to highlight the improvements that have been made. A second has been to emphasise the role of traffic pollution. A third has been to place stress on the contribution to poor air quality of air pollution from outside the region – whether imported from the power stations of South Yorkshire or from across the North Sea. Finally – and implicit in the consortium of bodies publishing the leaflet – local authorities and industries have increasingly been taking a joint approach not only to pollution control but also to public education about pollution also. The objective has been to secure improved air quality, and public knowledge about this improvement; but one consequence has been to tie local authorities more closely to the industries' interests and their own gloss on developments.

Conclusion

The leaflet 'Air Quality Today' aptly displays how different issues surrounding pollution can be 'moralised' (Lowe et al. 1997) for propagandising or public education purposes. In it, poor air quality in the past was associated with domestic coal-burning, while poor air quality in the present is associated with traffic exhaust fumes, imported pollution from Europe, and even Guy Fawkes night. By verbal sleight of hand local industrial emissions are (almost) removed from the picture, though indirectly they survive in the assertion that Teesside's biggest air quality problem is one of perception, and in the exhortation to challenge 'wrong perceptions'. By the same token, Crown Paints provoked official anger locally with its advertisement in 1981 not because it drew attention to Teesside's unique traffic problems, nor its special exposure to European pollution, but because of Crown's tacit reference to Teesside's chemical and steel industries.

One thread running through this larger story of the representations of air pollution in the Tees conurbation, in which our epidemiological research has been caught up, has been the protection given to the industries on which Teesside has been built (Beynon *et al.* 1994; R. Hudson 1989). Close public, political or media scrutiny of atmospheric emissions and their possible effects on people's health has invariably therefore proved a sensitive issue. Critics may view our argument as recycling old and outworn stereotypes of Teesside, another in a long tradition of writing that 'perpetuates the myth of the grimy North East'. Not surprisingly, we do not see it in that light. Our view is that there is no reason to take at face value the official images being presented of Teesside. Precisely because environmental pollution has been a matter of extreme sensitivity there, official discourse about its impact has been highly politicised, and we ourselves have witnessed the efforts which went into promoting an official line on what our research signified.

A year after publication of the TEES Report, it would have been easy to surmise that the epidemiological research had made little impression upon the place it investigated, either in local government or among local residents. The comments of industry representatives quoted earlier reflect the satisfaction at that outcome. Yet ironically, events elsewhere led to the first attention in the national press, and drew renewed attention to the work in Teesside itself. After ICI had been criticised by the Environment Agency, the new national regulatory authority, for contravening discharge standards at a site in north-west England, the *Sunday Times* ran a report under the headline, 'Revealed: the chemical giants polluting Britain'. Reference was made to death rates from lung cancer among women in Teesside being four times the national level in areas close to industry, and Suzanne Moffatt was quoted as saying: 'We concluded that the most plausible explanation was exposure to industrial pollution' (*Sunday Times* 1 June 1997).

This example is symptomatic of the way in which wider concerns about pollution, safety and risk in Teesside continually resurface in the media. The TEES Report was published at the end of 1995. That year alone had seen summer concerns about smog and high levels of benzene and small particles (PM_{10}s) (*Northern Echo* 2 August 1995), fresh doubt about dioxins released in the steel industry's blast furnace operations (*Northern Echo* 13 February 1995) and five incidents involving the county emergency planning team. The largest of these was by all accounts the biggest fire in Teesside since 1945, started in a BASF warehouse of plastics at Wilton. In the aftermath of this fire, described in media images such as 'on the brink' and 'very nearly the accident we've always dreaded', one dispute centred on the toxicity of the fumes. The different perspectives were reflected in statements in *Northern Echo* news stories:

> last night BASF insisted it was always under control and as it was non-toxic posed no danger to the public.
>
> (*Northern Echo* 10 October 1995)

A spokeswoman for Cleveland police said: 'If anything burns and gives off smoke then it can be said to be toxic. It wasn't a toxic cloud full of petrochemical by-products. If we had told people to evacuate because the smoke was toxic there would have been panic.'

But a spokesman for Friends of the Earth, in London, said: 'Polypropylene is toxic by ingestion and a respiratory irritant. It gets into the blood stream via the lungs. In such circumstances it is pointless telling people to remain indoors unless their homes are fitted with an air purification device.'

(*Northern Echo* 11 October 1995)

The context here may be one of accidental rather than routine pollution, but the toxicity of fumes is precisely the issue that underlies much of the ongoing debate about air pollution generally in Teesside.

Taken together these examples highlight the context within which our epidemiological study was done. Epidemiology cannot be neatly separated from the political and cultural 'noise' which surrounds environmental health risks and insecurities (MacGill 1987). It was always likely that argument would surround interpretation of the evidence presented in the TEES Report. Industry and local authorities in combination have long been able to present the authoritative account of safety and risk in Teesside, and it would be naïve to think that a mere research team might have free rein to present an unchallenged account of environmental health risks in the area. In this process, industry and local government were undoubtedly assisted by our collective failure as researchers to summarise key findings effectively for the media and therefore ultimately for public consumption. It is hardly surprising, then, that the first reports of local media and trade press alike should convey contradictory verdicts; or that the local media should subsequently rely upon official statements and briefings which steered towards a 'reassuring' reading of the evidence. If this was the desired outcome in industry and local authorities, it was certainly not an outcome which could have been taken for granted in advance of publication. The anxious enquiry which forms the title of this chapter alludes all too clearly to official concerns in the run-up to publication – concerns which were then allayed not so much by the findings themselves as by re-presentations of the findings. As examples above have shown, local government in particular seized on the evidence of poor health, in order to emphasise the significance of poverty, deprivation and personal lifestyle at the expense of any emphasis on the effects of pollution. Any suggestion, however, that these events have helped to 'nail the myth about local air quality' are, we suggest, unlikely to be fulfilled. For the link between pollution and health continues to provoke public disquiet and unease in Teesside, particularly in areas close to industry (Moffatt *et al.* 1998), while more generally, media interest in pollution and its risks is growing, not waning.

Notes

1 Themes discussed here overlap with work by two colleagues, Eve Hudson and Dawn Downey (see Hudson *et al.* 1998). We warmly acknowledge their contribution.
2 The research team had over a dozen members, drawn from the universities of Newcastle, Durham and Teesside, and from Teesside local and health authorities. The size of the team and its diverse composition created problems of its own in reaching consensus.
3 Epidemiology is the study of disease patterns within populations. The language of epidemiology takes much of its character from procedures used to distinguish association from causation. In assessing the case for and against causation, the concept of 'confounding' is central: for critical discussion of some of the implications of this central term, see Moffatt *et al.* (1995) and Phillimore (1998).
4 Even in a footballing context these associations can be evoked (*The Independent* 21 October 1995): 'The cooling towers and chemical works of Middlesbrough shouldn't come as too much of a shock for the newly arrived Brazilian footballer, Juninho. He has effectively transferred from ICI's South American headquarters in Sao Paulo to their British base on Teesside'.
5 It is interesting how commonly popular views about health causation are couched in such positivistic terms (see Lash and Wynne 1992: 5).
6 Respondents were invited to make additional comments to a postal questionnaire on self-reported health conducted in 1992–3 as part of the Teeside Environmental Epidemiology Study (1995). THe issue if environmental versus economic insecurity is explored in Phillmore and Moffat (1999).
7 One irony was that, in choosing Teesside as the setting, Crown was encroaching on the territory of ICI, makers of Dulux, its paint rival.

Chapter 7

The media timescapes of BSE news

Barbara Adam

Bovine Spongiform Encephalopathy (BSE) in British cattle, commonly known as 'mad cow disease', is considered by many to have been the greatest disaster in the European food industry in the second half of the twentieth century. As such it presents an enormous challenge at every level of sociocultural organisation: farming and the food industry, science, politics and policy, public health, the media, and last – but by no means least – those at the receiving end, that is, consumers. Yet, despite the enormity of the disaster, BSE would not be on the public agenda had it not been for the media, which transformed this highly complex, intractable issue of scientific and political concern into public news.

BSE is a risk issue *par excellence* and yet it does not fall neatly within the conventional bounds of risk. As a socio-environmental hazard whose probabilities are unknown it confronts us with taken-for-granted assumptions about risk, choice and safety. It brings to the surface implicit expectations about the role, for example, of the media, science and politics. Moreover, it foregrounds for our attention temporal issues that tend to be disattended in this contradictory matter of social concern. It is these assumptions and expectations I want to unravel in this chapter. This means I am not concerned to disentangle the complex interactive web of the science-politics-media triad where each component, in turn, is subject to interests of a professional, economic, political and personal kind, all of which have a bearing on the story presented to the public. I leave this task to media researchers who are successfully grappling with these relations – many of whom are presenting their insights elsewhere in this volume (see also A. Anderson 1997; C. Carter *et al.* 1998; Chapman *et al.* 1997; A. Hansen 1993b). Instead, as a social theorist and time researcher, I am interested in giving a temporal inflection on the media politics associated with BSE and its posited link to the new variant Creutzfeldt Jacob's Disease (nvCJD), which turned a scientific veterinary problem into a public health issue and economic matter of transnational concern.

Of risks and hazards, un/certainty and in/decision

The language of risk is traditionally associated with dangerous activities, with the economic world of trade and insurance, and with the medical world of health professionals and their clients. Here, specific risks are conceived with reference to the physical, mental, social and/or economic welfare of individuals, families, companies and/or the nation. In these traditional risk situations, the risk potential of certain actions is assessed. Decisions and choices are made in the light of their risk appraisal. This perception of risk entails a particular relationship to an essentially unknown future whose likelihood of coming about nevertheless can be calculated on the basis of extrapolating from past occurrences. Risk assessment of this kind is a question of mathematics and calculations of the probability and intensity of harm, of the weighing-off of pros and cons, dangers and gains, and the likelihood of coming to grief (J. Adams 1995). As such, the domain of risk assessment is the realm of rational action and scientific certainty, of clear distinctions between safety and danger, truth and falsity, past and future. Importantly, it is a world in which individuals can make choices and act in the light of those risk assessments.

BSE, this most pervasive of risks, does not fit this conception of risk. Its probabilities are unknown. Ignorance and uncertainty surround questions about its causes, its consequences and its remedies. What is known about it is highly disturbing and threatening but the language of risk seems to be largely inappropriate. Let me explain by drawing on the work of BSE specialists (Dealler 1998; G. W. Jones 1997; R. W. Lacey 1994; Owen 1997). BSE is fatal. In the UK some 167,000 cases had been identified by the spring of 1996. To date, a brain biopsy after death is the only means to confirm the presence of BSE. Its incubation period is variable and may or may not be dependent on the dose of infective material. There is certainty neither about the infective agent nor how it enters the body. The hypothesised prion protein (PrP) as infective agent has not been empirically verified. Yet, it appears that the infectivity is resistant to heat, chemicals and radiation. The same uncertainty applies to nvCJD, whose lesions in the human brain tissue are similar to those found in BSE infected cattle. By autumn 1998, twenty-nine cases of nvCJD had been officially confirmed in the UK. On the eventual size of the infection in humans, however, the jury will be out for at least another twenty years. On the basis of a wide range of scientific models, Stephen Dealler, one of the key scientists studying the BSE epidemic and its possible effects on humans, postulates a possible number of nvCJD victims for the early part of the twenty-first century that ranges from 2,000 to 2 million. 'Neither of these methods are satisfactory,' he acknowledges, 'but it is unlikely that we will get more exact predictive figures for several years' (Dealler 1998: 49).

This overwhelming uncertainty puts BSE outside the conventional range of risk issues in which experts calculate the probabilities for economic, public and private use. Where I can choose to smoke, drive a car or take up a dangerous sport, I have no choice in the issues surrounding BSE and nvCJD: hundreds and thousands of infected cattle were consumed which means that infective material found its way into products before the general public were informed that there is a possible danger to human health. The decision not to go skiing eliminates the risk of a skiing accident. The decision not to eat beef, in contrast, does not safeguard against nvCJD: some of the victims were vegetarians, others were infected by blood products. While conventional risks are subject to calculations of probability, public hazards such as the BSE–nvCJD conjuncture cannot be encompassed by the traditional conceptions of risk since the unknowns far outweigh what is known.

Clearly, scientists now know much more about BSE and nvCJD than when these diseases were first identified. But, even so, the extensive and indeterminate time-scales involved mean that the significant relations are not bounded in time and space and thus can neither be grasped through the rules of causality nor safeguarded, remedied or compensated. As Leach (1998: 128) notes, 'the BSE event offers no narrative closure, no ending by which the truth is recovered, boundaries stabilised, or uncertainties made certain'. Instead of predictability and demystified futures, the world of 'manufactured risks' (a term used by Anthony Giddens and Ulrich Beck to differentiate risks created by the industrial way of life from natural risks such as hurricanes or ice storms), of the kind associated with BSE and nvCJD, is both more messy and substantially less amenable to individual choice. Choice, in this context, is no longer an individual option for high-risk activities. Instead, it is socially imposed on the basis of scientific, economic and political decisions.

At the societal level, however, the BSE risk requires responses, demands decisions and necessitates the dissemination of information. In the face of its catastrophic potential, political action is absolutely vital as it might include life-or-death decisions. Yet, as the need for more complex and more precise calculations rises with the increased indeterminacy of risk, so does the impossibility of establishing such calculations. This means that the capacity for providing unambiguous information and making clear decisions is increasingly disabled. As Beck (1999) points out, 'at the very time when threats and hazards are seen to become more dangerous and more obvious, they become increasingly inaccessible to attempts to establish proof, attributions and compensation by scientific legal and political means'. Or, to put it differently, proportional to the increasing societal need for information and certainty, the potential for calculation and certainty decreases (Adam 1998; Ford 1996; R. W. Lacey 1994; 1998, Ratzan 1998).

This is the social context that Beck (1992a, 1995, 1996a, 1997b) encompasses with the term 'risk society' – a society that can no longer contain and handle the risks it engenders and where, consequently, a new system of articulations has emerged between capitalism, media, science and politics. The BSE case, claims van Loon (1999), illustrates one of Beck's strongest claims:

> that in the risk society the calculating of probabilities collapses under the weight of our collective inability to conceptualize the consequences. Scientists who were called upon by the British government could not estimate the exact probability that eating possibly BSE-infected beef results

in CJD. However, whilst admitting the incalculability of this possibility, the science-politics conjuncture simultaneously resulted in the slogan that British beef was completely safe for consumption because the risk was very small.

(van Loon 1999)

In Beck's risk society, we are inescapably subject to manufactured risks which those charged with our safety are unable to know in their full extent and incapable to bring within the bounds of the appropriate conventional institutions. This has an erosive effect on the authority not only of politics but also of the scientific establishment and leaves all knowledge-creating practices in a state of permanent instability: certainties become contingent, particular and thus temporary.

The scientific community seems to have accepted this new knowledge context to the extent that being uncertain has become 'the mark of the respected scientist' while being certain is likely to brand one as a 'quack or snake-oil salesman' (Leach 1998: 124). In the world of politics and news reporting, in contrast, the demand for and valorisation of certainties remain undiminished. For the media, this creates what Gareth Wyn Jones (1997: 75–6) describes as a potent and unpredictable 'witches' brew' of scientific uncertainty, desire for certainty where none exists, increasing concern about food safety, widespread distrust and disenchantment with the conventional providers of truth and safety: scientists and politicians. Moreover, the double paradox of un/calculability and un/decidability generates a pervasive context for public anxiety and distrust, on the one hand, and political displacement strategies which project a sense of security onto the dense complexity of risks, on the other.

In the mass media, the articulation of the uncertain nature of manufactured hazards tends to be handled by either silence or denial, or by asserting that risk assessment and risk management are possible and attainable, if not already accomplished, by 'scientific experts' (Adam 1998; Adam *et al.* 1999; van Loon 1999; Wynne 1996a). What therefore tends to be perpetuated is the denial in public discourses of the fundamental ambivalence and indeterminacy of the risk(s) associated with BSE, with the effect that anxiety and complacency, distrust and assurances chase each other in a complex web of reflexive media politics. This clearly places the news media in the domain not only of inescapable interpretation but also, more pertinently, of political struggle. 'This struggle', as van Loon (1999) points out, 'not only concerns the definition of the risk in terms of its probabilities and implications, but affects the very core of the problematic of what the "actual risk" is and what "being at risk" is supposed to mean'.

'Environmental news': challenge and media response

The characteristic features, outlined above, which pertain not only to the BSE–nvCJD link but also to many other manufactured risks such as radiation and ozone depletion, pose difficulties for definition and representation. Consequently, they present major challenges not only to politicians and policy-makers but also to the news media which are charged with the task of keeping the public informed. A first cluster of difficulties relates to the media's diminished capacity for factual reporting since such hazards destabilise traditional assumptions about what constitutes a 'fact' and 'causality' which, in turn, affects the definition of a problem and its solutions. A second cluster relates to the difficulty of encompassing such environmental matters within the traditional confines of 'news'.

With respect to the first difficulty of factual reporting there is the problem of deciding what constitutes an 'objective fact' given that the contamination tends to be invisible until it materialises as a symptom after indeterminate periods of latency. The disease will have been developing subclinically over a very long period but it is not until some of the by now characteristic features of 'abnormal bovine behaviour' occur that BSE or nvCJD are suspected. The question is whether something that cannot be known, something that is inaccessible to the senses and scientific measurement, can be a 'fact'. Closely related is the difficulty of establishing verifiable connections between symptoms and their causes, that is, for example, between lesions in the brain tissue of BSE infected cattle carcasses and the contamination of feed stuff, milk or meadows, between the disease and its origins. During the invisible periods of latency, the provable links have been broken and causal connections severed. This discontinuity has implications not only for the irrefutable establishment of causes but also for the definition of a problem and the formulation of potential solutions. Taken together, these features of invisibility, latency and high-level ambiguity place BSE and the BSE–nvCJD link outside the sphere of 'factual' reporting. Phenomena of this kind therefore require theory and analysis rather than recounting, explanation rather than description, understanding and interpretation rather than mere technical translation.

The second difficulty – environmental risks as news – relates primarily to the fact that socio-environmental hazards tend to be long term and chronic. BSE is no exception. With respect to the conventional meaning of 'news', therefore, such events fall outside the definition of 'news' because news means events of public interest and concern that are pertinent here and now, such as accidents, disasters or crimes (Dunwoody and Griffin 1993). Moreover, 'newsworthiness' tends to be associated with specific temporal characteristics such as novelty, timeliness, recency, immediacy and urgency (Bell 1995; Tuchman 1978). These news values rarely apply to globally dispersed and time-space distantiated environmental phenomena that reside nowhere in particular and go on for years without resolution. Long-term, chronic contaminations, such as those associated with BSE, do not allow journalists to limit their story to the here and now. Instead, they require historical contextualisation since, without such wider historical background, the information at any one point in time may be meaningless. Furthermore, such matters of social concern demand frequent coverage which, in turn, needs to be carefully planned with respect to what angle to take and which aspects to cover at what point in the series so as to avoid telling the same story many times over.

Environmental 'news', therefore, is almost a contradiction in terms. In the case of BSE and the BSE–nvCJD link, the long-term continuous pertinence of possible danger constitutes a major challenge to newswork: news as the delimited here and now of events has to be rethought in the context of the long-term and continuous manufacture of these hazards as inescapable by-products of the industrial way of life in general and industrial food production in particular.

At the practical level, BSE similarly poses significant difficulty for the tradition of news production. The complexity of the issues and the substantial level of uncertainty involved frustrate the journalists' need to be fast and succinct under deadline pressure. The speed of turnaround, the competition between papers and channels, and the need to sell maximum copy, or to have maximum listening/viewing figures, do not bode well for such hazards and risks getting the treatment and attention they ought to have, given their social pertinence.

Moreover, as I have just indicated, complex environmental 'news' such as the BSE crisis necessitates a shift in emphasis from description to analysis, from accident-oriented information gathering and event-based reporting of isolated facts to interpretation, explanation and analysis of conflicting data, ambiguities and unknowns. This dramatically complicates and complexifies newswork. At one level, the news media remain mere channels of information, at another level they define the parameters of the issues and, at a further level still, they are the constructors of knowledge and risk. Through their mediation, interpretation and translation of otherwise inaccessible knowledge into a publicly accessible form, newsworkers are not only prime sources of public information but also the principal social theorists of contemporary industrial societies. As such, they carry a heavy burden, a responsibility that they are poorly equipped to provide and that does not sit comfortably with their own self-perception, that is, their understanding of themselves as harbingers of news, disseminators of matters of human interest and providers of a critical perspective on the more shady aspects of sociopolitical and socio-economic life. A complex array of temporal issues is centrally implicated in this contradictory context of environmental news and an explicit focus on those issues provides us with a novel perspective on the matter.

The timescape of 'hard' and 'soft' news

In an article on 'News time', Bell (1995) develops the well-rehearsed argument that news reporters tend to differentiate between two kinds of news – 'hard' and 'soft' news – and gives it a distinct temporal inflection. Like Tuchman (1978) before him, Bell (1995) suggests that 'hard' and 'soft' news each have their own distinct temporal characteristics. According to Bell's typology, 'hard' news encompasses the factual and temporally bounded realm of accidents, crimes, disasters, conflicts, one-off events, statements and outcomes of actions that are newsworthy today. Such now-here phenomena tend to be perishable. They have a limited life as 'news' since, as Bell points out, 'the next edition renders them obsolete' (Bell 1995: 306). 'Hard' news accounts operate within the replacement cycle of hourly bulletins, fixed daily reports and papers published on a daily and weekly basis. 'Soft' news, in contrast, is a phenomenon with a longer shelf-life. 'Soft' news accounts cover issues of public concern for which it often does not matter whether they are reported on today or the week after.

Environmental hazards tend to fall predominantly into the category of 'soft' news. Given that most of them are of a long-term nature, the specific time and day chosen for their discussion is not that important. Irrespective of their degree of significance, environmental concerns tend not to 'pop up' today and be gone tomorrow. Instead, the social pertinence of socio-environmental hazards is long term, chronic and often cumulative. This gives them an air of relatively stable and predictable continuity, punctuated only by political actions, new research findings and the emergence of unexpected symptoms arising somewhere, some time, at which point they would change status from 'soft' to 'hard' news. While 'hard' news requires almost real-time reporting – the faster the better and instantaneity is best – 'soft' news environmental topics, from ozone depletion to pesticide contamination of soil and water, do not command the same sense of urgency. Instead, during the 'stable' phases, environmental risks are often seen by the news media as useful filler items for the days when there is nothing more urgent, timely or pertinent to report.

Over much of its ten-year history, the contamination of UK cattle with BSE belonged to the category of 'soft' news. However, the shock announcement on 20 March 1996 by Stephen Dorrell, the UK government's Health Minister at that time, that there is a likely link between the consumption of BSE infected meat and the nvCJD catapulted the issue into the category of 'hard' news. Overnight it became an urgent now-here phenomenon that touched profound public fears and had the potential to destroy livelihoods. The spectre of a link between BSE in cattle and nvCJD hit Britons and the citizens of continental Europe like a bombshell. Everybody recognised themselves as implicated: meat eaters and their children, vegetarians who were told that foods such as cheese, fromage frais and fruit jelly contain beef products and people who had undergone growth hormone treatment during childhood. Moreover, while everyone clearly had choices to make about the future consumption of beef, the biggest risk relating to nvCJD was tied to past actions, thus outside today's parameter of individual choice and control.

At this level, therefore, one can easily see how the announcement of the possible BSE–nvCJD link corresponds with news values of now-here recency, immediacy and timeliness, of the unexpected, the shocking, and the socially pertinent. Its emotiveness is unquestioned. Its dramatic content and the potential for personal disaster are enormous. Pictures of staggering cows, empty cattle auctions and young people reduced to a vegetative state are emotive symbols that do not only fuel people's fears but also point to the conflicts of interest that permeate the manifold outcomes of this socio-environmental hazard. With Stephen Dorrell's announcement the long-term, periodically newsworthy story had been transformed into a lead story that was to stay at the top of the news agenda for weeks and refused to fade into the background for the months and years that followed. As such, it received the 'treatment' meted out to any major news story: it got coverage from all possible angles ranging from human interest to economics and science, from personal accounts to macro-economic data.[1]

At another level, however, this socio-environmental hazard does not conform to the 'ideal type' of news: it is not a once-off or even a short-term 'continuing news' story. It is not an event that is bounded in time and space. After a long history of sporadic CJD and thirteen years of publicly recognised BSE, this particular threat to public health is not all that novel and unexpected either (see R. W. Lacey 1994, 1998; Dealler and Lacey 1990; Ford 1996; Lang 1998; Ratzan 1998). Second, as I have already indicated, unlike the quantifiable facticity associated with more conventional 'hard' news, there is little about the BSE–nvCJD link and the two diseases' respective causes that would count as incontrovertible 'fact'. Instead, this hazard is shrouded in mystery, permeated by uncertainty, marked by scientific disagreements and notorious for the persistent denial of its existence by the relevant government departments. A significant proportion of its 'facts' are as yet missing and it is consequently open to almost limitless hypotheses, conjectures and speculations. Third, the story seems destined to 'roll on' even though the media are periodically showing signs of fatigue and burnout, eager to move on to the more familiar ground of less intractable news, keen to let this public health issue fade from the limelight back to the more manageable sphere of soft news. Moeller (1999) identifies the process as one of 'compassion fatigue'. 'There's no great interest in what-could-be's,' she suggests. 'The hypothetical nature of the threat to humans ultimately chilled the coverage' (Moeller 1999: 79; see also Kitzinger and Reilly 1997). Finally, both BSE and CJD have a history that forms an essential part of their present as news. Without this history, the significance of the present coupling of BSE to nvCJD cannot be adequately understood.

'Historical news'

Despite the public's need for knowing the histories of those two diseases as well as the agricultural, political and medical actions associated with their respective developments, providing information on the historical background is generally not considered to be an integral part of newswork. News, as I suggested above, is associated with a succinct and factual presentation of clearly delimited now-here phenomena rather than their history (see also Allan 1997). 'News' and 'history' seem to be incompatible and 'historical news' a contradiction in terms. In the case of BSE it means that the media in general and the press in particular were and still are exclusively concerned with the material outcomes of the invisible time-distantiated processes and actions of BSE and CJD. That which gave rise to the symptoms, in contrast, is largely neglected and thus negated. In a context of news reporting it could hardly be otherwise.

Moreover, the solutions which have been developed to deal with the difficulty of repetition – reducing the history to one standard, contextualising sentence that acts like a signature tune to the story – further simplify an already extensively simplified complex issue and give BSE reports an air of certainty. As Demko (1998) elaborates:

> The effect of 'boiling down' the history of the crisis into a single sentence clearly omits important factors in the case, such as the degree of uncertainty involved in the announcement, the lack of conclusive data leading to it, and the controversy surrounding the decision to make the announcement. By choosing only to repeat the announcement itself, each article which describes another aspect of the crisis (i.e. the trade war, culling plans) serves to contribute to a sense of certainty surrounding the link to CJD by taking the 'link' for granted.
>
> (Demko 1998: 159)

An exception to the rule are media reports on the Parliamentary Inquiry into the BSE crisis which was set up by the incoming Labour government to uncover the history of events that led to the fateful announcement about a possible link between BSE and nvCJD and the subsequent handling of this disaster. We are reminded by *The Independent* that:

> The inquiry, chaired by Sir Nicholas Phillips, is not designed to accuse people of professional failings but to 'reach conclusions on the adequacy of the response, taking into account knowledge at the time' and report this to ministers sometime next year.
>
> ('Getting to the root of BSE', *The Independent* 13 October 1998: 4)

In this case, the newspapers are happy to report on the history of the BSE 'saga' as it unfolds in the course of the inquiry. No longer front-page news, the fudges, the bending of research to suit the political and economic agenda, and the conflicts of interest within and between governmental departments are reported on as 'historical facts' – without comment, critique or condemnation. With the inquiry by Lord Justice Phillips, BSE and the link to nvCJD have been transformed from a discomfiting rogue and hybrid news topic demanding explanation into a conventional factual history that lends itself to objective reporting and recounting.

The distinction between the factual context of history as it is emerging from the official inquiry and the ambiguous ongoing hazard requiring historically aware analysis and explanation is particularly evident when the two dimensions are reported on in one and the same paper, during the same week, on the same day and even in the same article. Thus, for example, the article entitled 'Getting to the root of BSE' (*The Independent* 13 October 1998: 4), quoted above, simply notes: 'What has emerged is a complex tale which is always better told with the benefit of hindsight. The single most important message is that when a politician said it was "safe" to eat beef this did not mean there was "no risk".' The article ends on a partisan and patriotic note extolling the safety of British beef. In answer to its own question 'Is beef safe to eat?' it states:

> Britain has the most stringent safeguards in the world to protect cattle and the public from BSE. Any risks there might be pale into insignificance compared to other risks of dying that people are exposed to every day. It is fair to say that eating beef on the continent – where BSE rules are not so stringent as in the UK – can in theory carry more risks than eating British beef.
>
> (*The Independent* 13 October 1998: 4)

There is no mention here that the numbers of infected cattle involved differ substantially between the UK and countries of continental Europe. According to the figures released in 1996, the difference then was in the order of 167,000 cases in the UK and some 400 cases elsewhere in Europe. Neither is it noted that most countries of continental Europe have a policy of destroying all infected herds. On the next page Jeremy Laurance comments on 'the latest spat over BSE', pointing out that 'these are decisions with huge financial implications that cannot be shirked. They require careful judgement guided by science and tested against public will' (*The Independent* 13 October 1998: 5). These are noble demands which sadly stand in stark, almost schizophrenic, contrast to the historical events as they emerge, in the same broadsheet, from reports on the inquiry. They testify to an inappropriate faith in science to provide facts, in public servants to put public safety above economic expediency, in guardians of public safety to be able to make 'careful judgements' in a context awash with ambiguity and uncertainty.

Relations of definition and the centrality of framing

When we look back over the representation and framing of BSE in British broadsheet newspapers, we find that the risks were defined, recounted and discussed in a number of ways. From being reported as a science and veterinary matter, BSE turned into a health hazard, was reformulated into an issue of European politics and, finally, stabilised as a 'beef crisis'. (For a North American perspective on the shifting definitions and perspectives on BSE, see Moeller 1999.) Within that media career of BSE, stories abound about scientific discovery, competition and protectionism, government incompetence and cover-ups, competing approaches to health regulation in continental Europe and the UK, beef wars and bankruptcies, innocent victims and human suffering (Anand 1998).

The diversity of interpretations can be understood in a variety of ways. For Demko (1998) in the USA, they connect to conflicts of interests and stakeholder positions, which means that governments, consumers, scientists, food producers and journalists all have interests to protect with reference to BSE. For van Loon (1999), British responses were an indication 'that there were different risk positions involved': consumers facing previously unacknowledged health risks, whilst the beef industry is confronted with the collapse not just of beef sales but the entire industry. I would like to offer a third way of understanding the stabilisation of media reporting on the BSE–nvCJD link as a 'beef crisis' within days of Stephen Dorrell's announcement about the potential connection between the consumption of contaminated beef and nvCJD.

The risk of contracting nvCJD from beef contaminated with BSE constitutes a health hazard of *potentially* epic proportions, a modern-day equivalent of a cholera or pestilence epidemic with an unknown period of incubation. And yet, of the many hundreds of newspaper articles written on the subject, very few indeed were focused on the risk to public health. Instead, the newspapers were and still are full of calculations about lost export revenues, the impact on gross national product (GNP) and the costs to farmers and retailers, as well as the rendering and slaughter industries. This particular representation has significant consequences. Once the BSE–CJD connection is framed in those terms and viewed from an economic perspective, a raft of implications follow: citizens' concerns about a potential health hazard are sidelined. The government can legitimately concentrate exclusively on the material task of rescuing a dire economic situation. The entire issue can be dealt with from the firm basis of facts since (it is wrongly assumed) economics is not afflicted like science by the malaise of uncertainty. Awkward questions about the industrial methods of food production can be avoided. Blame can be externalised.

The British press have – to varying degrees – gone along with this political reframing of the issues not because they were necessarily on the government's side or were in some way tricked into this perspective. Rather, the 'beef crisis' frame of reference brought this rogue news issue back within the fold of the familiar news world of reportable statements and events, describable disasters and quantifiable economic facts and figures. It provided journalists with an effective way to report on a matter suffused with uncertainty in terms of tangible, material outcomes and the now-here world of political wrangling in the politico-economic present. With the 'beef-crisis' frame of reference, the news media were back on familiar territory: answers to questions about when, where, what, who, why and how could once more be factual, clear and unambiguous.

Furthermore, the 'beef-crisis' perspective enabled the news media to sidestep the challenge of informed analysis and avoid the need for continuous and unrelenting, careful and considered explanation of the nature and extent of the risk over a period of years, probably even decades. It meant that journalists did not need to worry about historical contextualisation, wider social issues, arbitration between rival theories, questions about their educative role. The shift in perspective saved them from the challenge of engaging with something that is an ongoing process – indeterminate, immanent, in/visible, non/concrete, time-distantiated, latent, contingent, non/linear and not easily quantified – something that is timely without being recent and novel.

Conclusion

With the emergent health hazards associated with the BSE–CJD link, citizens have been confronted by tangible, multiple institutional failures. In the face of this inter/national crisis, neither the former UK Conservative government and its scientific advisers nor the British news media rose to the challenge of their public responsibilities. Instead, they largely carried on their respective businesses as usual, which meant translating this intangible future-based health hazard into an economic issue and a matter of national pride, thus effectively silencing all and everything that threatens the status quo. While in spring 1996, during the height of the crisis, political hyperactivity and intense news coverage indicated the importance of the matter, inactivity and media silence did and do not mean all is well. They simply mean(t) that other news topics have taken over, or that editors judged the story to have exceeded the public's interest span and thus to be threatening paper sales. The 'beef crisis', after all, still belongs to the long-term environmental issues that run on and on. As newsworthy 'history', the BSE 'crisis' is retrievable whenever the need arises and it can always be updated from one now-here present to the next: objectively, factually and with certainty.

Acknowledgements

This chapter arises from research conducted during an ESRC Fellowship under the Global Environmental Change Programme 1994 (L32027312593) entitled 'Mapping the Environment: Temporal and Spatial Problems for the

Social Sciences'. For an extended discussion on several related issues, see my *Timescapes of Modernity* (Adam 1998, especially Chapter 5).

Note

1 The UK newspapers I consulted in the course of this research included the *Daily Express*, *Daily Mail*, *Daily Mirror*, *Daily Telegraph*, *Farmers Guardian*, *Financial Times*, *Guardian*, *The Independent*, *Observer*, *South Wales Echo*, *Sun*, *Sunday Times*, *The Times*, *Wales on Sunday* and *Western Mail*. There were marked differences in the press coverage of BSE and its link to nvCJD between the 'quality' broadsheet newspapers and the 'tabloid' popular press which are not touched upon in the analysis here. For an interesting account of the gendered dynamics of the tabloid press's treatment of the issues, see R. Brookes and Holbrook (1998).

Chapter 8

Reporting risks, problematising public participation and the Human Genome Project

Peter Glasner

If, as C. Wright Mills (1970) suggested, the essential project of sociology is to use the imagination to 'grasp history and biography and the relations between the two in society', we must accept his stricture to uncover the relationships between 'the personal troubles of milieu' and 'the public issues of social structure'. This means that we must 'range from the most personal and remote transformations to the most intimate features of the human self'. Mapping and sequencing the human genome, while constituting an example of de Solla Price's (1963) 'big science' project, is unlike many of the new technologies in that it directly affects all of us at a very personal level. It poses a threat to the boundary between ourselves and the world in a way quite different from, for example, the virtual realities of the new electronic technologies (Bloomfield and Verdubakis 1995; S. G. Jones 1995; Glasner 1996), which only temporarily liberate individuals from their particular social and biological characteristics (gender, class, ethnicity, age and so on).

In geno-technologies, the connections are obscured, and the boundaries defined by (predominantly) scientific and medical experts (Gieryn 1994; S. Carter 1995). The issues of risk and danger are uncontrolled, and not subject to expert assessment. The impacts may be irreversible and unforeseen. The public is often characterised as ignorant about the complexities of these risks, and how they might directly affect people now and into the future. Attempts to rectify this state of affairs range from providing new institutional forms within which to transfer knowledge, to, more radically, challenging its epistemic basis.

Much of the public's understanding of the development of the biomedical sciences has been historically derived from literature and the media (Durant *et al.* 1996; Turney 1998). The Frankenstein myth has come to permeate twentieth-century stories about biological and medical discoveries in the popular mind. Scientists are regularly portrayed as entering Faustian pacts with the devil in their search for the secret of life. The cinema's long-standing affair with the works of Mary Shelley (the Hammer films notwithstanding) has brought the myths to a wider public. Widespread and mainly negative reactions to the application of cloning techniques to humans have been more recently fuelled by speculative press accounts of the risks associated with the new genetic technologies couched in similarly mythic terms.

This chapter begins with a brief discussion of the social and ethical issues which surround the Human Genome Project (HGP) and then locates these in the context of life in a 'risk society' (Beck 1992a), where risks and hazards are ubiquitous and uncontrollable. It goes on to relate the discussion to the changing role of scientific expertise, and its relationship to lay knowledge, particularly as it is framed by the media. This is followed by an analysis of some different forums within which these complex issues can be informed by discussion and negotiation. The chapter concludes, perhaps pessimistically, that relatively little real progress can be made until it is recognised that the boundaries of the acceptable are not neutrally drawn.

The Human Genome Project (HGP)

HGP, an international programme costing billions of dollars, has been likened to the biological science's equivalent of landing on the moon (see, for example, Cook-Degan 1994). It is an attempt to map and sequence all 3,000 million base pairs which constitute the human genome. It aims, in its metaphorical search for the 'holy grail', to write the 'book of life'. In 1988, an organisation called HUGO – the Human Genome Organisation, described as a United Nations for the Human Genome – was established *inter alia* to encourage public debate on the ethical, social, legal and commercial implications of the project (Bishop and Waldholz 1990). These include fairness in the use of genetic information in, for example, employment; the impact of knowledge on the individual through stigmatisation and labelling; issues of privacy and confidentiality; impact on genetic counselling and reproductive decisions; issues of education, standards and quality in medical practice; the past uses and misuses of genetics; and commercialisation and other intellectual property rights. HUGO, at this time, has failed to address these in any concerted fashion (Glasner 1993).

Others have been less reticent, writing about, for example, the reductionist nature of the project (Lewontin 1993), with its attendant danger of a resurgence of eugenicism; its impact on reproductive technologies (Stacey 1992); its use in employment and insurance areas (Nelkin and Tancredi 1994); its application to policing and the law (Lander 1992); its gendered ramifications (Haraway 1997; Rose 1994); and the possibilities which arise from commercial exploitation – patenting 'life' itself (Cook-Degan 1994). Less seriously, we can perhaps now join the couple standing by their car at a desert cross-roads, with the driver triumphantly holding up a picture of the double helix and exclaiming: 'We're not lost. Here's a map of the Human Genome.'

British scientists initially involved in the project generally argued that the HGP posed no new ethical problems for society to address. At the Royal Society meeting on Genes, Ethics, and Embryos in 1991, the view expressed was that this research did, however, place emphasis on *existing* dilemmas (Brenner 1991) even if no new ones were apparent. In a 1996 survey, a substantial proportion of scientists involved in the UK HGP were of the opinion that their work did indeed pose *new* ethical problems (Glasner and Rothman 1998). The views of these respondents, working away from the political epicentre with its policy-oriented concerns for the shaping and funding of research in molecular biology, are probably more representative of laboratory scientists. One suggested that opinion about the novelty of ethical issues in this area depended on whether the focus was on the present use of discoveries already made, or the use to which they may be put in the future. It is the former which should exercise the public more.

Living at risk

It is probably also true to say that modern industrial society is in some ways a less dangerous place than it was during industrialisation in the nineteenth century, or even in the predominantly agricultural economies which preceded it. Those of us fortunate enough to live in the global North are a great deal safer (not to say wealthier) than those in the South. We also have greater expectations concerning the levels of safety we experience, greater controls over them, and ultimately greater responsibility for their management. However, Giddens (1991: 84) has noted the ubiquity of crises in modern life, defined as those occasions when activities concerned with 'important goals in the life of an individual or a collectivity suddenly become inadequate'. He concludes that for most of us, 'Apocalypse has become banal' (Giddens 1991: 183).

One major reason for the perception that modern life is in crisis comes from the fact that we appear to be living in a global laboratory. Whereas in previous epochs, the hazards affronting our eyes and our noses were susceptible to the senses, today's risks escape direct perception as they appear in toxins in foodstuffs, or in fallout from nuclear accidents. This is not to deny that the great plagues of Europe appeared equally hazardous for those living in the Middle Ages (Turner 1995: ch. 12). More importantly, according to Beck (1992a), today's risks and hazards are no longer clearly tied to their place of origin. They have become global threats for which the associated medical precautions we expect to deal with them, and normal accident insurances, are no longer adequate.

> The focus is more and more on hazards which are neither visible nor perceptible to the victims: hazards that in some cases may not even take effect within the lifespans of those affected, but instead during those of their children; hazards in any case that require the 'sensory organs' of science – *theories, experiments, measuring instruments – in order to become visible or interpretable as hazards at all.*
>
> (Beck 1992a: 27, emphasis in original)

These 'sensory organs' of science can empower many who are not scientists at all. The result is that the claims of science to a monopoly of expertise become more difficult to sustain in the face of competing claims, interests and viewpoints, including those from the lay public who wish to participate in decision-making and influence policy decisions.

Genomic research and public understanding

In the spirit of Mills' sociological imagination, we might, therefore, usefully address the issue of public participation in decision-making in this key area. Initially, we may surmise that the efficacy of participation may be correlated positively with knowledge and public understanding of science. It has been suggested (Durant *et al.* 1996: 235) that medical science is 'paradigmatic for the popular presentation of science in Britain' and therefore a greater public understanding of the new genetics might contribute to greater public participation in decision-making. We already know that within Europe, public knowledge and concern about the impact of the new genetic technologies is differentially located (BEPCAG 1997). Thus, for example, the Northern European countries tend to be more active and informed than those in the South. We also know that within the former, the issues are given greatest prominence in Denmark and Germany. The best informed groups in Europe are men, the young and the financially better off (Marlier 1992; Terragni 1992). In comparison with the USA, however, the Europeans are much less critical about scientific and technological advances in general, and medical advances in particular (G. Evans and Durant 1989; Zechendorf 1994). HGP straddles all three areas: science, technology and medicine.

We recognise, however, that the public understanding of the new genetic technologies is often framed by the media, and particularly by the press. A study by Riechert (1995) of the Associated Press coverage of the Human Genome Project in the USA, over the ten years between 1984 and 1994, showed an increase in the number of relevant articles from zero in 1984/5 to 43 in 1992/3 and 40 in 1993/4. Content analysis revealed that in her sample of 246 cases, 'scientist ' was mentioned 42 times and 'scientists' mentioned 363 times. This contrasted sharply with 'citizens/consumers', which were mentioned only 7 times. She discovered that the large majority of articles exhibited a strongly positive slant with an emphasis on hope and promise, with only relatively few discussing risk. Most were concerned to show how the new genetic technologies would lead to the prevention, diagnosis, treatment or cure of many inherited diseases, thereby prolonging and improving the quality of life. Only a few articles addressed issues of individual ethical or legal rights, although several patent debates were covered.

In their case study of the British public's understanding of HGP, Durant *et al.* (1996) discovered that there was no prior awareness of, or knowledge about, HGP among non-specialist interviewees. However, there was knowledge about a number of closely related core topics such as genetic engineering or DNA finger-printing. Within these core topics, the researchers were able to identify prominent 'anchors' (for example Down's Syndrome or rape and murder cases).

These were then grouped, together with the results of their content analysis of a sample of the output of the British press over a four-year period, into either discourses of great promise or of concern. Significantly, HGP appeared to exist in the minds of the public only as a 'virtual reality' through a 'network of associations' with these adjacent and better-known core topics. As in the USA, the press coverage was generally couched in the discourse of great promise, while the results of interviews suggested that the public located their knowledge more in the discourse of concern.

Related studies have confirmed that applications of genetic research associated with humans or animals are more likely to raise concerns than were those involving plants or micro-organisms (Wheale and McNally 1996). Bloomfield and Verdubakis (1995) describe this distinction as symbolising the boundary between what is acceptable to self-identity (the language of expectation) and the what is not (the language of anxiety). However, in the context of understanding HGP and playing an informed part in its future development, the public is sometimes treated as if disenfranchised through ignorance. The front cover of an issue of *The Ecologist* (September/October 1996) conveniently summarised much of the ill-informed nightmare vision with its illustration of the six-foot high chimera combining parts of a rat, beagle, pig, sheep, cow and chicken, symbolising the splicing together of genes from different species, developed for the campaign against genetic engineering in 1995 (see Figure 8.1).

While all this recognises the contextual nature of public understanding, in the 1990s studies in the sociology of science and technology have begun to dispel the simplistic view of an 'ignorant' public faced with a superior array of technical experts whose mission is to fill their deficiencies of knowledge (Hilgartner 1990; Irwin 1995; Irwin and Wynne 1996). We have learned that what counts as a risk is actually problematic, and should be seen as situated, contextualised and negotiated. Any discussion of risk is as much about culture, institutions, perceptions, control and activity as it is about how risks are framed by experts (Douglas 1985). Studies have shown that disputes between experts are not only normal but often conducted in rhetorical rather than empirical terms (see, for example, Nelkin 1985).

Significantly, for both Giddens (1990) and Beck (1992a), expertise is also a temporary phenomenon, since the development of new knowledge coupled with the new reflexivity, results in a continuing process of expert replacement. Knowledge, for Giddens, becomes valid only until further notice. Much the same can be said, as Wynne (1992) notes, for contextual knowledge which is also subject to alteration and regular rethinking. In this way, in a culture faced by society-wide hazards, the concept of 'expert' becomes problematic. Experts in the fields of medicine, as well as science, may be held to be no more expert than knowledgeable and informed lay people in certain circumstances. As Giddens (1990) notes, while the key to late-modern, risk society is knowledge, such knowledge may not be distributed equally. In addition, it is likely to be rooted in differential experience, and may be, as a result, opaque in practice.

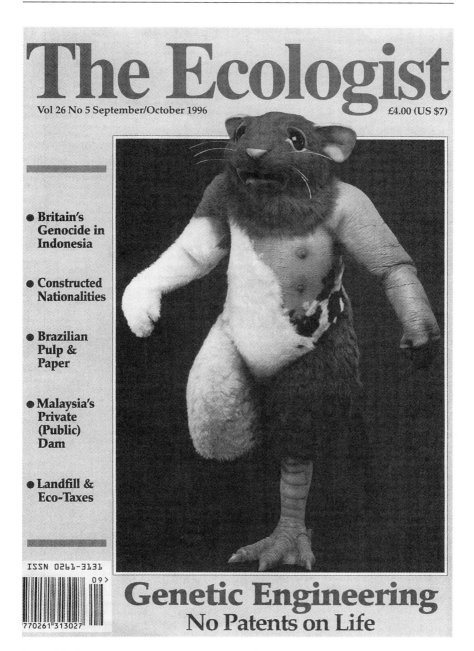

Figure 8.1 Genetic engineering: no patents on life
Source: The Ecologist September/October 1996

A good example of this can be found in the handling of the BSE crisis and its relationship to a possible future outbreak of nvCJD among humans. Wynne (1996a) notes that the danger lies as much in the social dependency engendered by our science-policy culture as it does in any real risk *per se*. The matter is complicated by the wide range of issues involved:

> The tortured United Kingdom relationship with the European Union; the over-industrialization of agriculture and food supply; ideological obsessions about de-regulation and government ministries' scandalous proximity to sponsorship of private industrial interests; fast-eroding public identification with official science policy bodies and their pronouncements; and the distinct whiff of political control of science arising from recent changes in the UK research and education structure.
>
> (Wynne 1996a: 13)

Public controversies like this one are not simply based on differences between 'experts' on the one side and the lay public on the other. Often experts also disagree (Limoges 1993).

We thus appear to face the uncertainty of whether or not thousands of us who innocently enjoyed a diet of hamburgers in recent years are already infected with a life-threatening disease for which there is as yet no cure. It is not, according to Wynne, sufficient to suggest, as British government ministers now do, that the risks were never as low as initially indicated by those directly concerned, even though the policy implications of the cattle-feeding programme were based upon this assumption in order to gain public acceptance (though not without concerns being expressed by some scientists such as Professor Richard Lacey; see S. Pain 1990). The public is on the whole more mature about risk and uncertainty than scientists or politicians are willing to admit.

Similarly, the perceived risks associated with mapping the Human Genome are not part of a futuristic, Jurassic-Park inspired, doomsday scenario (Nelkin and Lindee 1995). To think that the public perceives them as such is to fall, as some scientists seem to, into stereotyping the public in a most unscientific way. Kerr *et al.* (1997) make it clear that the twenty-six senior geneticists they interviewed saw the public as a homogeneous group. They go on to state: 'Without exception, all of the interviewees saw the public as ill informed' (Kerr *et al.* 1997: 291). Wynne (1996b) summarises this position succinctly:

> According to this widespread view, expert systems have unmediated access to nature hence peddle only natural knowledge, whilst lay publics are epistemically vacuous, and have only emotional wellsprings of culture and ephemeral local knowledges.
>
> (Wynne 1996b: 76)

Of course there are no new ethical problems associated with HGP if you think that those who pose them are, so to speak, 'off the wall'. The events at Newbury in Berkshire illustrate this perfectly, with an almost silent, official response to those local protesters who presented in suits and cardigans, and the generation of a moral panic around the less sartorially conservative, and more actively concerned with opposing the development of a new bypass. When the exclusiveness of traditional science is broken down through 'reflexive modernisation' (Beck *et al.* 1994), then, according to Eden (1996):

> The politicization and democratization of science allows people, primarily activists within environmental NGOs, to become 'counter-experts' who are scientifically competent through self-education, but also employ traditionally 'non-scientific' forms of argument, such as morals and emotions, particularly where the issues under discussion could have enormous public impact.
>
> (Eden 1996: 194)

Public participation in decision-making

The issue, then, may be how best to constitute forums in which better informed as well as less stereotypical exchanges can take place. The list is extensive, ranging as it does from science shops, citizens' courts and scenario workshops to public representation on advisory groups and consensus conferences (Irwin 1995). On the only recent occasion when scientists voluntarily called a halt to their research, following the publication of the 'Berg letter' calling for a moratorium on experiments using genetic engineering techniques in 1974, public involvement in the USA took the form of local, lay, citizens' courts (Krimsky 1982), while Britain involved representatives of 'the public interest' (laypersons selected from the great and the good) in its national, Genetic Manipulation Advisory Group (Bennett *et al.* 1986: 153 ff.). Here, their impact was largely symbolic with lay members acting mainly as a 'safety net', ensuring that sufficient 'checks and balances' were seen to operate. Their input into technical decision-making was, according to respondents, limited by their lack of specialist knowledge, although they always felt free to ask the awkward questions.

Consensus conferences originated in the USA in the late 1970s with the first dealing with breast cancer screening. The UK held its first national Consensus Conference on Biotechnology in 1994 in London, but this focused on plants rather than humans or animals (Joss and Durant 1995). It consisted of a lay panel of sixteen chosen from replies to advertisements in the local press, who then chose a group of experts and a group of counter-experts from pre-selected lists. This framework, opposing lay and expert knowledge, revealed the importance of the neutral chair in framing the context and the nature of the ensuing debate. In particular it ensured that (as its name suggests) the Conference reached a consensus in its final report. This was not without cost, as Purdue (1995) concludes:

> The goal of manufacturing a 'National Consensus' out of a diversity of opinion on such a highly contentious topic as biotechnology was impossible to achieve without silencing dissenting voices.
>
> (Purdue 1995: 172)

Citizens' juries have also been promoted as an alternative to the more conventional approaches to improving public participation in decision-making, although the first attempt to extend this model to encompass representatives of a large and culturally diffuse geographical area (the Principality of Wales), on the topic on genetic testing for common disorders, has stretched this method to its limits. This has been particularly evident in the use of medical scientists as supposedly neutral expert witnesses, the problems of obtaining representativeness with a jury of fifteen or sixteen, and the need to guarantee that action is taken on jury recommendations by sponsors (Dunkerley and Glasner 1998).

In February 1997, the departure lounge of Terminal 2 at Manchester airport saw the opening of The Gene Shop. Organised by the Centre for Professional Ethics, the University of Central Lancashire and the Royal Manchester Children's Hospital, and funded by the European Commission, it is conveniently located between the Body Shop and the Prayer Room. It aims, according to its advertising, 'to provide an opportunity for the general public to find out more about genetics and how it can affect everyday life'. Open between 8.30 a.m. and 2.30 p.m. on most days of the week, it provides an information service, with interactive computers, permanent and short-term displays, a Saturday lecture programme, and staff available to answer questions about all aspects of genetics. It suffers, however, from its relatively inaccessible location.

All of these different methods of attempting to include the public in decision-making about human genomes exhibit both strengths and weaknesses. The most participatory (by lay people) clearly suffer from lack of representativeness, and reach only a small number and proportion of the public (Fiorino 1990). They also suffer from the conceptual imbalance noted by Wynne (1996b) in the work of *inter alia* Giddens (1990) and Beck (1992a, 1995), which draws an absolute distinction between lay and expert knowledge, and privileges the latter consistently over the former. This may be further overlaid by those with the power to establish agendas as against those who are relatively powerless. However, they do provide, albeit rare, opportunities for public debate on issues normally reserved for the privileged few in science, government and industry. They also encourage a culture in which openness, debate and the sharing of knowledge become more the norm rather than the exception. Irwin, in describing what he labels 'citizen science', notes that the challenge is to 'integrate scientific expertise with other assessments, problem definitions and expertises; to acknowledge diversity as a positive element within sustainable development and to appreciate the inter-connectedness of "social", "environmental" and "technical" issues and concerns' (Irwin 1995: 173).

Conclusion

These examples, as we have seen, do not prevent experts defining the boundaries of risk. However, they can help the public identify the existence of such boundaries in an environment which attempts to reverse the coercive (Douglas 1985: 59) privileging of 'boundary' over the 'connections' between adjacent spaces such as 'us' and 'them' (S. Carter 1995). These connections, as I suggested earlier, are more obscure as well as more personal in the geno-technologies. As illustrated in a *Time* magazine story on the hereditary characteristics of breast cancer in women, the problems are as much about whether to find out if you are genetically predisposed, and with what associated risk, as they are about whether to have a double radical mastectomy (L. Thompson 1994). The danger lies in assuming that the experts in such a situation have, in some ethical way, *privileged* knowledge and understanding of the complex issues involved. They may be in a better position to provide an answer, based upon the scientific and technological knowledge at their disposal. But then, again, they may not.

C. Wright Mills' injunction to link personal troubles with the public issues is thrown into stark relief when scientific and technological advance poses questions of such complexity, ignores the fact that those who receive them may or may not be poorly equipped to come to their own conclusions, and sidelines further discussion as the responsibility of the professional ethicist. Beck (1995) notes that there appears to be an obligation by society to cross the boundary between safety and risk before being in a position to make even a qualified decision about its appropriateness. The injured of Chernobyl are not all even born yet. The space in which even to hold a debate is, it seems, only infrequently available and imperfectly constituted. I am irresistibly reminded of the words of the rocket scientist who joined the US 'Space Race' after the Second World War, and who is purported to have justified his work with the observation: 'I aimed at the stars, but I hit London.'

If we do, indeed, live in a 'risk society', and are confronted with ecological changes which will affect future generations in unknown ways, then another boundary, that between nature and the self also needs revisiting. Rheinberger (1995) notes that biology has lost its innocence and is as much about inventing facts as it is about discovering them. 'On the microscopic level, technologies are being developed that may alter the genetic program of an individual's biological constitution.' He concludes that 'Given these prospects, it is no longer possible to distinguish between nature and culture' (Rheinberger 1995: 261). Such a *Gestalt* switch of paradigms would indeed be worthy of Kuhn's description of a scientific revolution.

We must, however, end on a pessimistic note when contemplating the furore generated by the cloning of the adult sheep, Dolly (see *Nature* 27 February 1997), and its reporting in the national press. The broadsheet *Sunday Times* (2 March 1997: 14–15) even printed a centre spread by Bryan Appleyard entitled 'The runaway gene genie', in which he asked whether 'Dolly the sheep raises the possibilities of cloning children, growing new limbs and tuning the human species to higher levels of intelligence'. Fortuitously, the new UK Human Genetics Advisory Commission met shortly after the announcement and its chairman, Sir Colin Campbell, made it clear that Dolly was very much on their agenda, reminding the British public that cloning human embryos for research was illegal. The US President, Bill Clinton, rushed to call for a moratorium on this and related work, noting that no similar law existed in the USA. He gave the National Bioethics Advisory Panel ninety days to review the implications. It was left to the editor of *Nature* (27 February 1997) to point out that 'At a time when the science policy world is replete with technology foresight exercises, for the US President and other politicians only now to be requesting guidance about what appears in today's *Nature* is shaming.'

Interestingly, Martin Woolacott (1997) suggests that we are more in danger of being over-informed:

> Pick up the newspapers or turn on the television almost any day and you will experience that increasingly common thing, the arrival of the wearily familiar future. We live in an over-anticipated world in which virtually every scientific or technical change, every developing social trend, has been studied, sermonised, fictionalised and even parodied in cartoon and advertisement before it actually happens.
>
> (Woolacott 1997)

He feels that, while 87 per cent of Americans polled by ABC News were against human cloning, both the majority, and the minority 6 per cent who are personally ready to be cloned, are 'still mainly reacting in terms of fantasies – replicant soldiers like dragon's teeth advancing in their minds, or the thought of a spare me kept in the cold store – rather than reality.' However, evidence for his view is outbalanced by much of the hard research discussed earlier. In the context of public participation in shaping the direction and application of the Human Genome Project, at least in Britain, reactions to the arrival of Dolly the sheep are indicative of what Durant *et al.* (1996) describe as the public's discourse of concern. The dearth of successful models for breaking down the traditional barriers between scientific and lay conceptions of knowledge, does not make the problems of participation in decision-making insuperable. As Irwin (1995) notes, much depends on developing a truly 'citizen science' and rejecting the privileging of the former over the latter through extension of the peer community. He quotes Funtowicz and Ravetz's (1993) paper on 'Science for the post-normal age':

When problems lack neat solutions, when environmental and ethical aspects of issues are prominent, when the phenomena themselves are ambiguous, and when all the research techniques are open to methodological criticism, then the debates on quality are not enhanced by the exclusion of all but the specialist researchers and official experts. The extension of the peer community is then not merely an ethical or political act; it can possibly enrich the processes of scientific investigation.

(quoted in Irwin 1995: 172)

Meanwhile, public participation in the future development of the new genetic technologies cannot be hampered by the breakdown of trust in scientific expertise, the framing practices of the media, or the many problems posed by current participatory experiments. We may be helped in following C. Wright Mills' stricture to dissolve the boundaries between the 'public issues of social structure' and the 'personal troubles of milieu' by the recognition that they are not neutrally drawn.

Part III

Bodies, risks and public environments

Chapter 9

Selling control
Ideological dilemmas of sun, tanning, risk and leisure

Justine Coupland and Nikolas Coupland

Bodily exposure to the sun entails a biomedical health risk, aggravated by ozone depletion in the upper atmosphere. Growing awareness of the risk of skin cancers caused by sun exposure has both stimulated and been stimulated by several relatively new media practices, at least in summertime in the UK. These include the publication of burn-time information in national TV weather forecasts, a steady stream of print media features on sunbathing and skin care, and a welter of advertisements for 'sun-care products', particularly sunscreens and blocks. It is this last set, product ads in print magazines targeted at women, that we focus on in this chapter.

Our intention is to identify the ideological work done in the texts of these sun-care product ads, and how they engage with broader societal themes of health, risk and leisure. The texts promote their products by naturalising specific value systems and resisting others. They work, for example, to undermine what we could call the discourse of avoidance – the simple logic that if exposure to the sun is dangerous, one should avoid it, and the associated value system that sun exposure is outdated and naïve. They posit ideological dilemmas, particularly desire for hedonistic leisure while avoiding risk, to promote expensive, technologised and packaged solutions to them. These meanings are communicated for the most part implicitly, in the subtle semantics of the texts' language and visual imagery.

Our analyses centre on how agency and control are negotiated in these texts – how consumers and products are in various ways constructed as being *in control* of the social processes linked to body tanning and risk avoidance. A semantic analysis can show, for example, how various forms of risk (to people as potential victims and therefore affected objects) are edited and reformulated as forms of social control (by people as agents using technological products) in pursuit of identity and personal-social goals. Control is in some senses an opposing force of risk, and advertisements which can convincingly package control as inherent in their products can succeed in domains of risk. But their effect is, more generally, to redefine risks and to give them new cultural, and indeed commercial, relevance.

The specific themes and instances we take up in this analysis may be of wider interest. They may illustrate how popular appreciation of specific clusters of risk phenomena is promoted through media texts, but also how this appreciation is refashioned ideologically. Because ozone depletion is of course the global risk behind the discourses we are considering, there is also the issue of how matters of environmental concern can be reinterpreted as lifestyle choices and patterns of consumption.

Before turning to the analysis itself, we briefly introduce the data set. We then overview the ideological dimensions which make up the background to the advertisement texts. It is in support of these values or in opposition to them that the texts build their meanings.

The data set

Data are drawn from a corpus of fifteen high-circulation UK magazines: *Best*, *Company*, *Cosmopolitan*, *Family Circle*, *GMTV*, *Good Housekeeping*, *Marie Claire*, *New Woman*, *Options*, *Prima*, *Vogue*, *Woman*, *Woman and Home*, *Woman's Journal*, *Woman's Own*. The sample was taken in June and July 1997. We focus on selected advertisements from these sources, all of which are aimed at predominantly female readerships. The products being promoted include those marketed by Estee Lauder, Hawaiian Tropics, Lancaster, Nivea and Malibu. While we do not try to argue any particular distributional case, the advertisements we examine had, at the time of sampling, high prominence in the market and the ads themselves are known (from magazine circulation statistics) to have reached large readerships.

In the following section we comment on some semantic features of the general set of ads. For the main analysis of agency we consider five individual advertisements, and reproduce their language texts in full. Magazine advertisements of course depend as heavily on visual as on linguistic forms, and we comment on some of the visual strategies used. But our main concern is with the linguistic representation of risk and control.

We also refer briefly to data from interviews on the theme of sun use conducted with people at seaside resorts in New Zealand and in Wales (discussed in more detail in J. Coupland *et al.* 1998).

Ideological dimensions

As texts, sun-care ads exist in a highly contested ideological arena. Is body tanning safe or dangerous, naïve or cool? Is it yesterday's version of public leisure or one of the most obvious manifestations of contemporary body culture? Is promoting sun use sexist and ageist or a force against repressive political correctness? Does it encourage the use of new health technologies or of expensive cosmetic products? Our intention is certainly not to resolve these disputes, although we inevitably bring our own judgements and commitments into the debate. We intend to show how the ads generate meanings and values relative to a complex cluster of competing discourses, and in fact express varying moral stances when featuring different products and targeting different readerships.

The following themes can be seen as the ideological strands which particular advertising texts invoke and recombine (see also Coupland and Coupland 1997).

Body culture

Working against a traditional (liberal humanist, sometimes religious) discourse that seeks to purge the body of any real significance, ideological forces in late modernity have been argued to give the body remarkable symbolic status. Some critics have argued that the body is the single most potent signifier of selfhood in modern society (see, for example, Featherstone 1991; Giddens 1991; Shilling 1993). The ads we are concerned with are clearly part of media promotion of body culture, with the importance of bodily beauty as a 'taken-for-granted'.

Ads predominantly feature visual images of tanned, naked or near-naked bodies. The words 'body', but more particularly 'skin' and 'face', are of course frequent textual items: 'Nivea sun face, all your skin needs'; 'face and body suncare'; 'Heliotan stimulates skin's natural ability . . .'; 'rejuvenates your skin'; 'protects the skin from sun ageing'; 'your skin's worst enemy'.

Gender and sexuality

The visual images are almost uniformly of women, and these ads appear predominantly in the magazines we have sampled (those pitched at women). Although women are occasionally addressed in the ads in their roles as mothers, encouraged to be vigilant about their children's exposure to the sun, the dominant projection is that tanned female bodies are sexually alluring. Visual images in the ads are often eroticised, with sweat-beaded brows and facial expressions suggesting abandon or fulfilment. Linguistically too, there are implicatures or suggestions of transcendence ('become one with the sun') and sensuous indulgence ('TAN MAXIMISER is soothing, moisturising'; 'golden delicious'). Overall, there is significant meaningful overlap between the imagery of sun usage, as promoted through the ads, and popular media interpretations of female sexuality.

Youthfulness and health

In addition to imagery centring on portrayals of youthful female bodies, the ads frequently refer, explicitly or implicitly, to the risk of 'premature ageing'. In this context, youth and health are deemed equivalent. The word 'damage' could in principle refer to either health risk (melanoma) or spoilt appearance and ageing effects. But wrinkles and ageing are referred to explicitly in these texts, while cancer/melanoma never is. 'Damage' in its aesthetic/self-presentational aspect is therefore what is salient in the ads: rejuvenates your skin . . . improving the overall condition of your skin; minimise the damage; a major cause of skin damage and premature wrinkles; free radicals, the primary cause of skin ageing; more crow's feet . . . more liver spots, more thinning skin and more premature ageing.

The ads clearly equate the signs of ageing with diminished aesthetic appeal and are therefore thoroughly gerontophobic (see Woodward 1991 on the 'unwatchability' of old age; also N. Coupland *et al.* 1991).

Brown is beautiful

The tacit assumption in all sun-care promotional texts is that brown or golden skin has aesthetic advantages over white skin. There appears to be a reticence to use the colour vocabulary itself; 'golden delicious' and, in the same text, 'all the gold without the guilt' is the only reference in the sampled texts, other than 'tan' as a colour, for example 'the only colour you'll turn is tan'. Rather, the priority is established visually, in the skin tone of female models portrayed and in the colour of product packaging. In terms of what the colours signify, gold is powerfully associated with warmth and richness, just as brown skins are associated (in the northern hemisphere) with southern skin types and cultures. Urry (1990) comments on how sunbathing was uncommon before the 1920s, when it became a newly fashionable leisure practice, associated with resorts like Cannes and Biarritz and with the cultural values of the 'presumed spontaneity and natural sensuality of black people' (Urry 1991: 37). Values attached to 'tanned' and 'golden' skin obviously contrast with 'pale' or 'white' skin, which might be deemed aesthetically preferable in other contexts, and with 'burnt' and 'damaged' skin, as represented in the discourse of avoidance.

Leisure/asceticism

Sunbathing is often taken to be the quintessential way of practising leisure, and the ads certainly invoke images of relaxation and passivity (reclining bodies with satisfied facial expressions; 'you can enjoy the sun and achieve a wonderful tan, feeling safe and secure'; 'continue to enjoy the sun'; 'enjoy the sun today with no regrets tomorrow'). In an earlier discussion (Coupland and Coupland 1997; see also Urry 1990) we have shown how traditional British summertime leisure centred on 'having fun in the sun' is often invoked in newspaper representations of the weather and holiday-making. Key signifiers are ice-cream, beaches, deck-chairs, bathing, heat, inactivity and time-out. As part of this ideological set, sun-tanning, at least traditionally, was a bodily marker of having achieved summer leisure, as a short break in the working routine.

Contemporary sun-care product ads, on the other hand, overlay a new asceticism on top of this version of passive sun enjoyment. The sun is still to be enjoyed, but the imperatives of body culture require far more awareness and control than simply 'laying out'. Perhaps this is the most striking ideological inconsistency in these texts, to which we return in detail below. 'Spending time in the sun' is reconstituted as an active and controlled form of sun use. The phenomenon central to the ads, sun care, is constructed as a moral obligation upon responsible hedonists. Sensuous and passive leisure, it is implied, now have to be earned through active engagement with new and dedicated forms of science-based knowledge ('enhanced UVA protection and a wider range of SPF levels'). This informed and technologised leisure must be bought and implemented, by acquiring and deploying the products developed to service the leisure 'need'. We are told that attentiveness and monitoring, therefore asceticism of a sort, will improve the leisure experience ('enhancing and pro-longing your tan'; 'a new revolutionary after sun booster which increases your tan by up to 50% in just four days').

Representing agency and control

Agency can be represented either through explicit denotative or referential lin-guistic forms (expressions like 'causes', 'produces', 'achieves' or 'is responsible for') or through clause-level syntactic patterns involving specific verbs. The semantics of agency at clause level were originally explained via case grammar, formalised in the theoretical work of Fillmore (1968). In this approach, broadly defined cases or participant roles (Hurford and Heasley 1983) are identified to specify how animate or inanimate items (represented by noun phrases) are related to actions or processes (represented by verb phrases). In the most sim-ple instance, a clause like 'Judith cut the peach with a knife' is semantically analysable as the verbal action of cutting being specified by Judith as an agent, the peach as an object affected by the action, and a knife as the instrument or means by which the action is performed. This general approach has been taken up and developed within systemic functional linguistics as a key aspect of, in Halliday's (1985, 1990) terms, the transitivity system of a language.

A contextually based focus on language use (a pragmatic perspective) is needed to capture the complexities of representing agency, since there is no fixed relationship between syntactic form and role function. For example, gram-matical subjects are not necessarily agents in relation to verbal actions. In the clause 'Judith bled', Judith is arguably the affected object, or at least the expe-riencer of the action, and need have no causative or agentive semantic role. Verbal actions may have no specifiable agents, as with verbs like 'be', 'seem', 'appear', 'turn', 'become' (verbal copulas). A grammatical subject will often specify an instrument rather than an agent, as in 'The car knocked them down'. Expressions often place reified physical forces, like wind, fire, rain or sun (J. Lyons 1977), in the syntactic slot we associate with agency. In the clause 'Rain stopped play', no direct physical link is actually proposed between the event of it raining and the event of the cessation of play, although the grammar constructs rain as the 'causer' or causative agent (Quirk *et al.* 1972: 743 ff.). Lyons (1977) similarly suggests that we have a natural tendency to identify causativity with agency, even in the case of inanimate objects incapable of intentions.

This set of semantic issues around agency, control, causativity, responsibility and instrumentality can be used to show how product ads linguistically represent 'sun use', although of course that very expression already defines the social process as instrumental and motivated. Texts position the sun, the person, the body and chemical creams and lotions in various semantic relations to one another, and these connect directly to the ideological issues we overviewed earlier.

If we consider the elementary semantics of 'tan' and 'tanning' as lexical items, we might predict a specific set of participant roles to be featured. Tanning represents a process where the sun is causative and possibly agentive, and where people or their bodies are the affected objects or patients: sun-tans-people. But these semantic relations are not at all conventional in any common context of use. 'Tanning' as an intransitive verb (a verb which can be used without an object: 'I tan easily') is more common, but is again rare in the product ads. In the intransitive form, tanning itself is 'naturalised' as an apparently agentless, recurrent process which people experience, rather than being affected by an activity performed on them by an agentive, causative force.

Common syntactic strings in the product ads involve 'a tan' as a nominal, that is as a 'product' rather than a 'process', for example 'your tan'; 'a perfect, uniform tan'; 'an even, controlled tan'; 'a natural-looking semi-permanent tan'; 'a healthy-looking tan'. 'Getting' or 'achieving' a tan is a frequent structure: 'You can enjoy the sun and achieve a wonderful tan, feeling safe and secure'. In our interview data too, respondents most commonly represent tanning in this way: 'I like to get a bit of a tan'; 'my friends are saying "I'm going to have a better tan than you this year"'. 'Tan' therefore appears in a resultative semantic role, brought into being through the actions of 'getting' or 'achieving', with agency most obviously attributable to the consumer. 'A tan', as a nominal, is then interpretable as a commodity ('having a tan', 'a healthy-looking tan'), but also as a commodified state – 'achieving a tan' is equivalent to achieving wealth or status. 'Tan' as part of a product name, such as SuperTan, suggests both process and result.

'Tanning' as a verbal nominal ('tanning technology') is also common in the ads. In the process depicted through this usage, the sun is displaced as a potential agent or instrument. The identified instrument is more likely to be chemical/technological than a natural phenomenon (the sun). So where is 'the sun' in consumerised tanning discourse? We find it in expressions such as 'suncare' (often lexicalised as one word), as a general nominal or as part of a product name ('Face and Body Suncare'; 'Lancaster's new suncare line') and in expressions like 'sun protection' ('Sun protection you can trust'). 'Suncare' is a dense collage of implicit participant roles. The bought product is the instrument by means of which consumers are 'cared for' as patients or affected objects in the context of a risk-process. But the product, or its parent company, may also be implied to be the controlling agent. The sun as a hostile agent threatening damage to consumers (again as affected objects) is the source of risk which occasions the need for care.

A general characteristic of the ads, therefore, is the construction of semantic structures which identify consumers as being at risk, but also claim to control their risk levels by a form of protection. We can highlight the particularities of these processes, and strategic differences between different types of ads, by looking at specific examples. Text 1 is shown in Figure 9.1.

The phrase 'between you and the sun', the last phrase before the contact details at the foot of the text, refers most literally to the product as a cream barrier, an intervening item, which may also intervene chemically, as a 'block' or a 'sunscreen'. This phrase juxtaposed to a visual image of whole body exposure conveys the marketable paradox of bodies being exposed and yet protected. The naked female pictured is therefore vulnerable but cared for (see the phrases 'UVA protection' and 'Suncare' and the adjectives 'safe' and 'secure'). The implied risk, in line with the general pattern we commented on above, is specified as premature skin ageing. The primary agency relation in the text has the female predominantly as a passive 'experiencer', placed in a resultant state of security through the instrumentality of the product.

But the product is constructed more as an agent than as an instrument. In particular, agency of the action of *protection* is by the product itself. At one level the product retains its instrumentality in the service of the consumer, but not as a 'blocking' instrument under her control. After all, a newspaper or a T-shirt would be cheap physical barriers to the sun's rays which the consumer could put to use. The product is constructed to be multiply agentive in its own right. Its chemistry 'works to neutralise free radicals', which would themselves be hostile agents/causes in the risk process of premature skin ageing. The product's chemistry is a catalyst to a 'natural' process whereby the skin 'produces pigment' (agency triggering agency). It also works in 'enhancing and prolonging your tan'.

The product, in the text's semantics, takes over, leaving the consumer to lie down and *enjoy*, as experiencer not as agent, 'safe tanning', a process which is suggested to be both natural and highly technologised. Passivity is symbolised by the visual image of the body floating, nude, in contact with the sky, and 'one with the sun', cosseted by an invisible protective agent. The sun is usefully elided as an agent in this text; the body is projected as being 'with the sun', not affected by it.

Very similar semantic alignments are constructed in other product ads of this sort (which we reproduce here with little commentary), such as Texts 2 and 3 (see page 153), promoting other companies' products. Agencies relative to caring and protection are again central, and ascribed to the products or their company names. The consumer, always addressed as 'you' in this genre, is associated only with the verbal actions of 'trusting', 'assessing' ('you'll know whether the sun protection you've chosen for your face has done its job'), 'having fun in the sun' and 'wearing' – not agentive roles in any case, but rather experiencer roles.

Figure 9.1 Becoming one with the sun
Source: Lancaster advertisement

The dominant configuration is in fact well summarised in Text 3's final text-line: 'We'll add the protection. You have the fun'.

Text 2
AT THE END OF THE
DAY, SUN PROTECTION
YOU CAN TRUST.
By sunset, you'll know whether the sun
protection you've chosen for your face has done
its job. Because, when it comes to caring, and
protection from harmful rays, NIVEA, the skin
care expert, is the one to trust.
Active Cell Protection from NIVEA SUN FACE
protects against harmful rays and free radical
damage, which can cause premature skin
ageing. And provides intensive moisturising
action.
You can trust NIVEA Sun to protect your face, all
day long.
NIVEA SUN FACE.
ALL YOUR
SKIN NEEDS.
[Text arranged above and below close-up of face of reclining, young,
tanned female, smiling.]

Text 3
added
    protection
      extra fun . . .
Three way protection for twice the fun.
Hawaiian Tropic's unique Triple Defence System means you
can
have fun in the sun while wearing the best protection.
1. UVA, UVB & Infrared protection.
2. Exclusive time-released Vitamin
    Plus complex A, C & E.
3. Waterproof for up
    to 8 hours.
In factors up to 35, our sun protection
formulations are made from the purest
ingredients for better protection
against sunburn and skin
damage.

Hawaiian Tropic. We'll add the protection. You have the
fun.
[Text arranged above and below visual of young, tanned female,
laughing.]

Sun-tanning

'Tanning technology' in one set of cases eclipses the sun totally from the tanning
process – in so-called 'self-tanning'. Text 4 illustrates how what it calls 'Self-
Action tanning technology' products are promoted.

Text 4
The only colour you'll turn is tan.
Estee Lauder invents
Self-Action
Sunless SuperTan
Incredible but true. This new Sunless SuperTan out-tans
the original. How? New, exclusive Self-Action tanning
technology turns your skin a deeper, more natural tan
colour.
New easy-on formulas – Lotions and Sprays – dry fast,
tan fast, last longer and they're streakless. So go ahead.
Your tan starts in one hour.
And looks real . . .
without the sun
damage, or the peel.
[Visual of product]
ESTEE LAUDER
[whole page visual in parallel, face and arms of a tanned Liz Hurley]

Again the product and the company are represented as active agents in some
respects – 'inventing', 'turning your skin' and in 'out-tanning the original'
(which we take to be the sun). But the semantics of the expression 'self-tanning'
and 'Self-Action' bring the consumer into greater potential agentivity. The
expressions are ambiguous: it is not clear whether they should be expanded
into 'products which allow you to tan yourself' or 'products which act on your
skin by themselves'. The first of these implicates the user in an explicitly agentive role, consistent with the text's exhortation to action: 'So go ahead.'

To the extent that 'tanning' is a process based on the sun as agent or instrument, 'sunless' products confront a fundamental problem of reference. The 'tan'
they generate is not 'a tan', or at least not a 'natural' or sun-achieved tan. The
text of the ad is systematically ambivalent on this. The process involved is certainly referred to as tanning ('tan fast'; 'Super Tan') and its outcome is referred
to as 'a tan' ('Your tan'). But the text then obfuscates its definition of tanning

in its expressions 'looks real' and 'tan colour'. These semantic devices, which we might call inauthenticity flags, are reminiscent of how fruitless concentrated cordials cannot be labelled 'fruit' cordials or squashes but have to be labelled 'fruit drinks' which 'taste fruity'. The effect is to construct a self-action tan as a commodity or quality which, while thoroughly hedged as to authenticity and naturalness, is efficient ('fast', 'easy-on') both chemically and aesthetically. By implication, Sunless SuperTan is a truly instrumental product. It does not need to offer the agentivity of protection and it offers itself to agentive consumers who want to deploy its effects in the domain of bodily self-presentation.

The foregrounding of risk

As a final instance, we can consider a sun-care ad which addresses the responsibility and agency of parents to protect their children's skin from sunburn. In these cases, the risk element in sun exposure is referred to directly, without the mitigating reference to tanning for the body project. Children are not presented as wilful, agentive tanners but as innocents, naturally enjoying playing and swimming out of doors. This is the only type of advertisement where semantic relations of the sort 'sun-burns-people' are represented as text.

Text 5, shown in Figure 9.2, is an advertisement for Malibu For Kids High Protection Lotion. Although the term 'ritual' may imply unmotivated recurrent action, the text aggressively imposes agency on mothers whose action damages children: 'Your mum did it to you. Her mum almost certainly did it to her.' The impact of the ads is precisely to accuse mothers of irresponsible agency, in contrast to children who have limited physical capacity to resist the damage of sun exposure. Children are represented as patients in both grammatical and medical senses ('children tend not to get sunburn once, they tend to get burnt often').

Strikingly different from the previous instances we have considered, the text adopts the register of health promotional campaigning. We have 'burning' in place of 'tanning', 'cancer' in place of 'damage'; 'product' and 'lotion' in place of 'system' or 'formula'; explanation of technical terms (melanin, the brown pigment that protects the lower layers of the skin) rather than 'blinding with science'; obligation ('children should wear a hat. . . . Children should always wear a waterproof sun lotion') in place of indulgence.

The promotional function is an attempt to impose a new, more aware form of agency upon mothers: 'Here's how to stop the ritual taking place'. The agency/responsibility clearly attaches to mothers ('should be kept out of the sun', 'should be reapplied often') and the action of buying which is implicit in the phrase 'more expense'. The product's and manufacturer's agency is downplayed. It is a product which only 'helps protect your children', implying once again that the dominant agency is the mother's. Other similar ads, which we have no space to consider in detail, repeat this apportioning of responsibility; for example an ad for Garnier Ambre Solaire Kids begins: 'We always protect the ones we love . . . but some do it better than others.'

Figure 9.2 Mums in child burning ritual
Source: Malibu for Kids advertisement

Conclusion

We have seen how sun-care product advertisements are able to construct several different semantic roles for consumers, relative to the health risks and pleasures of tanning. The principal strategies in advertising sun-blocking and screening products involve detaching consumers from significant agency. The products themselves take on more than instrumental functions, seeming through their technologies to dictate and control 'safe tanning'. Consumers, according to this discourse, are freed up to function purely as passive experiencers of the sun and of a regulated tanning process.

In self-tanning, on the other hand, chemical products are projected to be more instrumental, meeting the aesthetic goals of agentive consumers. Both groups of products deliver 'a tan' as a commodified and marketable attribute.

The ads cast the sun in the contradictory agentive/causative roles of a facilitator of tanning (except in the self-tanning case) and a source of biomedical threat. In the case of the child-burning mothers text, the threat is overtly and baldly referenced as cancer and burning. In the ads targeting women as potential tanners, the sun's threat remains implicit, so as not to detract from the promise of sensual body exposure.

Women are therefore targeted in radically different ways in these ads, with parenthood marking the boundary between two moral codes or ideologies. Women as non-mothers are offered roles as eroticised nudes, luxuriating in the chemical protection that their product purchases have legitimised. Women as mothers are challenged to confront their moral laxity as unthinking agents of torture, and to take more responsibility and change their ways.

'Sun-care products' therefore claim to provide bought solutions to different sets of ideological dilemmas. Perhaps the central dilemma lies in the contradictory appeals of exposing the body for self-display in the interpersonal marketplace while protecting the body from the known risks of 'damage'. Texts like Text 1 (Figure 9.1) are very direct attempts to claim that their products resolve this dilemma: 'you can trust'; 'you can enjoy the sun'; 'you can have fun'. They are texts of legitimation.

Ozone layer depletion, as it has been interpreted in the mass media (Bell 1989, 1991; Coupland and Coupland 1997), is therefore an environmental concern which has suited the sun-care industry admirably. It may have turned some people away from a habit of unquestioning sunbathing (more clearly in the southern than in the northern hemisphere). But it has also created a vast sales opportunity for those who can claim to offer ostensible solutions to apparently new problems. Many of the ads in our sample have to be seen as feeding, as well as feeding off, the ideology of hedonistic 'fun in the sun' which has maintained high melanoma rates for many decades. The fact that certain ads espouse an entirely opposing ideology (along the lines of 'skin cancer is an avoidable consequence of unnecessary exposure') is just another example of advertising's facility of comfortably accommodating blatant intertextual contradiction.

As we noted earlier, body exposure and skin tanning as part of leisure are a recent innovation – sometimes credited to the early days of Hollywood film-making and even to Douglas Fairbanks Jnr as an innovator of sunbathing. Urry's (1990) analysis of the history of tourism and about the role of nature in tourist activities (see also Macnaghten and Urry 1998) also provide an important context. The tourist consumption of the sun, through the growth of package holidays to sunny places and designing leisure into sites where bodies can be legitimately bared, is itself historically and socially very specific. In the UK, there has been, for example, a definite social class dimension to the practice of sun tanning. It is not surprising that people with restricted leisure and limited funds and mobility should have been in the forefront of sun-tanning culture. With changing patterns of work and leisure, and with changes in social class configurations, we might indeed expect sun tanning to be viewed as outdated and naïve. While we have no direct evidence of change, the seaside interviews we have conducted in New Zealand and Wales certainly show very wide-ranging public responses on the theme of sun use as a core criterion for leisure (J. Coupland et al. 1998). A good proportion of the sample of 80+ interviewees do recycle health promotional information about sun avoidance and the use of sun-blocking creams and claim to follow it.

It seems to us that the broader role of current product advertising in this area is therefore to resist the demise of fun-in-the-sun ideology and the discourse of avoidance. These ads, taken together, attempt to reinvent traditional practices of sun use as contemporary ones, largely by adding new dimensions of control and choice. After all, the traditional British working-class week's holiday by the sea was, from one point of view, a resolutely eyes-closed experience. There were no conventional restrictions on sunbathing to those with confident own-body images. If we ignore a measure of inevitable voyeurism, bodily exposure to sun and sea was not essentially a display activity; people sunbathed with their eyes shut. In today's body-cultured times, sun use is not merely conventional hedonistic leisure behaviour. According to the advertisements, at least for women in their non-mothering role, it is a lifestyle choice made through patterns of consumption. Consumers have their eyes open – to health risks, which sun-care products purportedly control for them, and to the presumed aesthetic benefits of brown bodies. What might once have been, for some people, the 'natural delights' of exposure to the sun have been reinterpreted as motivated and technologically supported body management. Self-tanning is, by this account, the most contemporary of available strategies, sequestering (Giddens 1991) even more radically the natural basis of tanning.

It remains to be seen whether the sun-care industry's creative fusion of hedonism and asceticism continues to engage consumers, or whether melanoma statistics and health promotional campaigns can interrupt its rhetoric. All we have done in this chapter is unpack some of the design principles of this rhetoric, particularly those relating to risk and control. Risk – in this case the represented risk of unmediated sun exposure and of ignorance of technological solutions – turns out to be a powerful premise for marketing solutions. The texts of most of the ads we have considered refer rather obliquely to risk and give over most of their language to expressing the agency of either products or consumers. It will require several further forms of consumer agency for people to resume responsibility for what they do to their bodies and for how they define their leisure, let alone for containing the ozone hole problem.

Acknowledgements

A collaborative project 'Public Discourses and the Natural Environment' was initially funded by a grant from the British Council, New Zealand. We gratefully acknowledge its support. The interview corpus was designed in conjunction with our New Zealand colleagues involved in the project, Allan Bell, Janet Holmes and Chris Lane. The UK interviews were conducted by Pam Perkins. We are grateful to these colleagues for their input, although the interpretations we offer in this chapter are ours alone.

We also acknowledge permission to print copies of original magazine advertisements granted by The Lancaster Group and Euro RSCG WNEK Gosper, on behalf of Malibu.

Chapter 10

Exclusionary environments

The media career of youth homelessness

Susan Hutson and Mark Liddiard

Youth homelessness hit the headlines in 1989. Over the next few years it was a popular subject in the broadsheet and tabloid press. Images of young people sleeping rough on the streets of London were common, particularly in the Sunday press. Youth homelessness featured in women's magazines and the subject matter lent itself to a number of television drama documentaries. This chapter traces the media career of youth homelessness – the way it entered the headlines and, later, how the reporting changed. However, before looking in more detail at this, the question needs to be answered: why, in a book about environmental risk, is an analysis of youth homelessness relevant? The main answer is that an analysis of social issues and the media has much to tell us about environmental issues and the media. The boundaries between 'social' and the 'natural' environments are porous. For example, it is obvious that political decisions over the distribution of economic and social resources are intricately connected with political decisions over natural resources. Broadly, what a society does with its people is likely to reflect what it does with its natural environment. Policies, be they environmental, economic or welfare, can produce a fall out. In youth homelessness this resulting 'pollution' is essentially social or human.

Central to this chapter is the idea that environmental and social issues are both identified and socially constructed in a public arena, the precise processes of which we will look at in relation to youth homelessness. Beck (1992a, 1997b), in his analysis of 'risk society' and 'reflexive modernisation', makes many references to the way in which 'risks' are introduced and defined within the public arenas of the media by contesting groups. While Beck was talking primarily about environmental 'risks', his analysis is relevant to broader social 'risks'. For example, many of the environmental 'risks' identified in later modernity are invisible and their consequences lie in the future. This gives them the status of 'virtual reality'. Youth homelessness is also largely invisible, as are the social and economic factors which cause it. For this reason it is, like many other social issues (Hilgartner and Bosk 1988; Cottle 1993a), very much open to social construction. However, to say that youth homelessness is socially constructed (Hutson and Liddiard 1994) is not to imply that it is an illusion any more than studies around the social construction of death (Sudnow 1967) deny its reality.

The process of social construction is dynamic and this chapter focuses on the 'media career' of youth homelessness. In tracing this process, we shall show, on the one hand, why youth homelessness was so attractive to the media and, on the other, how these media images shaped the public conception of the problem. We suggest that the particular configuration of youth homelessness and the press was influenced by the dominance of the voluntary agencies. Such an analysis, of the intersection between a social issue and the media, is equally relevant to many environmental issues.

Youth homelessness first became widely reported in the British news media in 1989. In 1998, the Labour government appointed a 'homelessness tsar', demonstrating that it regards homelessness as a serious social problem. Youth homelessness can be seen as the fallout from global change – recession and then economic restructuring which left little employment for young school leavers – coupled with broad monetarist politics which exacerbated unemployment and led to cuts in welfare benefits. Benefit cuts were targeted on under-25s and triggered an increase in the numbers of homeless young people after 1988 (Hutson and Liddiard 1994). These cuts were fuelled by fears that a generation was leaving home to live on benefit (Brynin 1987). One aim of the cuts was to push young people back into their parental homes. Through the 1990s, youth homelessness grew despite the fact that the voluntary sector set up housing and support projects and the duties of social services towards care-leavers after the Children Act (implemented 1991) were increased. Despite the current Labour government's rhetoric of 'social exclusion' and the 'New Deal', single young people are generally still not housed and therefore youth homelessness continues to be a pressing social issue (A. Evans 1996).

The 'media career' of youth homelessness shows a different pattern of progression. In 1988, a report was published about homeless young people staying at the Centrepoint hostel in London (Randall 1988). The public interest and the media response to this report surprised the involved agencies, who then realised that youth homelessness had considerable potential for publicity (personal communication from R. Strathdee). Youth homelessness stayed in the headlines and the issue was regularly raised in parliament. The homeless young person sleeping under the arches of Charing Cross railway station became 'the symbolic image of the modern British adolescent' (*Observer* 26 March 1989). Media coverage peaked in the summer of 1990 and this publicity worried the government. The Bullring in London, where many were sleeping rough, was cleared and a £15 million package for the voluntary agencies called the 'Rough Sleeper's Initiative' was announced. Both moves were undoubtedly designed to take youth homelessness out of the headlines and, in this, they were successful. Media coverage declined and changed, but familiar images of youth homelessness still appear at Christmas and in media-led charity events such as Children in Need.

'Mediagenic' issues

What elements were there in youth homelessness to attract the media? As a subject, it clearly had the elements of negativity and unexpectedness identified by Galtung and Ruge (1965) in their influential research on western news values. Our analysis (Hutson and Liddiard 1994) highlights the pictorial nature of the subject. In the first place, stark contrasts could be easily presented in the images. For example, the oft-quoted report and picture of George Young, the then Conservative Housing Minister, stepping over 'huddled bodies' as he came out of the opera (*Sunday Correspondent* 14 January 1990) neatly pitches destitution against power and luxury. The juxtaposition of children and street life was shocking. This deliberate use of childhood was characteristic of the early reporting. For example, a two-page article in the *Sunday Express* (24 June 1990) headlined 'THE LOST GENERATION' promised a crusade to find 'a lost generation of children'. Inside, the account of a 15-year-old girl is headlined 'LAMBS TO THE SLAUGHTER', indicating both childhood and innocence.

Young people have always been popular 'folk devils' with the media primarily because of the 'sex, drugs and rock and roll' with which they are associated (S. Cohen and Young 1981). Moreover, the public nature of their activity made them more accessible to journalists. Cardboard shelters, dogs on strings and mohican hair cuts feature in the pictures. Two later reports show the continuing pictorial symbolism of homelessness. Figure 10.1 shows a young man in a model pose and his dog with the headline 'Hip to be home-less' (*Guardian Weekend* 15 February 1997). This article reported on a photographic exhibition of homeless people after which one young homeless man was offered a modelling job with Calvin Klein. The *Guardian* (26 January 1995) reports on another photographic exhibition, with photos taken by homeless people themselves, with the headline 'SHAMEFUL IMAGE THAT NEVER FADES'. This mixture of art and the unusual is also typical of the serious Sunday papers.

Youth homelessness also has plenty of potential in terms of human interest stories, which are so attractive to the media (Curran *et al.* 1980). The lives of the young people are full of pathos and shock, and most press reports contain personalised accounts. Youth homelessness is often presented on TV via a drama documentary, the most common narrative being an individual arriving in London. Through the weeks or months, the audience follows his or her experiences (*Johnny Go Home* 1995; *Street Kids* 1998). As far back as 1979, Beresford commented on the way in which the complex economic issues around homelessness are merely reduced to 'a matter of runaway kids and the dangers awaiting them in the big city' (Beresford 1979: 157).

The pictorial and symbolic potential of youth homelessness can be easily paralleled in the environmental movement (A. Anderson 1997) where the faces of the seals in 1988, the sinking of the Greenpeace vessel, *Rainbow Warrior*,

Figure 10.1 Hip to be homeless
Source: Guardian Weekend 15 February 1997

in 1985 or the exploits of Swampy and the road protesters in 1997 have raised and symbolised environmental issues. Both the social and the natural environment can be packaged for the consumer. As Alexander Wilson (1992) comments:

> Alongside the environment of the biosphere, though, there is now also an environment of promotion and advertising and speech about nature — its management, its protection, its fragility, its sacredness, its marketability. . . . It is also an environment in which we must intervene.
>
> (A. Wilson 1992: 86)

Gamson and Modigliani (1989: 9) suggest that 'packages succeed in media discourse through a combination of cultural resonance, sponsor activity and a successful fit with media norms and practices'. It is possible to be only speculative about 'cultural resonance' because of the difficulty of measuring the latter. However, youth homelessness images resonated with a general dissatisfaction with Conservative policies in the late 1980s, particularly in terms of unemployment and public spending cuts. Youth homelessness was often used to symbolise the failure of these policies. Looking at the environment, Anderson (1997) agrees that issues are taken up because of their 'fit' with existing values but further stresses the action of entrepreneurs in influencing the media career of an item. Let us look at these 'entrepreneurs'.

Agencies and the media

A new kind of pressure group emerged in the 1960s which consciously exploited the media in order to influence politicians and civil servants with whom they were in dialogue (A. Anderson 1997). The housing pressure group, Shelter (D. Wilson 1984) and Child Poverty Action Group were two examples. In the environmental movement, Greenpeace and Friends of the Earth were the major players. Prominent in youth homelessness, from the 1990s, were the large children's charities such as Barnardo's and National Children's Homes. In terms of youth agencies, Centrepoint, the early specialist youth homelessness agency, was joined by the Young Men's Christian Association (YMCA). All these agencies were attracted by the media potential of the issue. For the children's charities, the rise in youth homelessness coincided with the rundown of their previous work in child residential care.

The dominance of the voluntary sector in youth homelessness is related to the limited responsibilities of the statutory sector. When the Homeless (Homeless Persons) Act 1977 was passed, statutory responsibility extended only to homeless families. Young single homeless people were not seen to be a problem and so were not included. Although, later, the Children Act (implemented 1991) gave social services some responsibilities for care-leavers and other 'children in need', services were limited and, if set up, were usually in partnership with the voluntary sector. This dominance of the voluntary sector is directly linked with its media prominence. Charities have a long tradition of advertising as their funds depend on public response which is not the case with statutory agencies. As Beresford (1979: 152) perceptively points out: 'The media are crucial to the agencies for the part their publicity can play in legitimising them and their version of the problem, gaining them resources and ensuring their survival.' In contrast, the reticence of statutory agencies and their reluctance to enter a public arena is well known. If youth homelessness had been a statutory responsibility, its press career would have been different.

What was the link between the agencies and the press? Essentially, the agencies fed the press with the stories of youth homelessness. Agencies wrote press releases which were often reported word-for-word. The media used the agencies for their expert views and for access to homeless people for stories and photographs (personal communication from P. Toynbee). Youth homelessness agencies were certainly: 'adept at providing the media with pre-packaged material that suits the journalist' just as were the environmental pressure groups commented on by Porritt and Winner (1988).

This agency activity resulted in youth homelessness being reported in a particular way. In the 1980s, Brandon and colleagues commented on how the homeless agencies were competing among themselves and with other social causes to promote the cause of tackling homelessness. Brandon *et al* (1980: 26) felt that, at the time, these reports presented 'an alarmist picture of the extent and dangers of homelessness'. Moreover, as they pointed out: 'The problem is packaged in black-and-white terms to ensure easy public assimilation and to provoke ambivalent feelings of anxiety, pathos and guilt' (Brandon *et al*. 1980: 192).

Similar reports can be given of environmental pressure groups in the presentation of their issues. Chris Rose, a former director of Media Nature suggests, in 1990:

> What Greenpeace are very good at is that they've invented, if you like, a sort of morality play. . . . You've got to have pictures . . . which is one reason why they've stuck with boats on the high seas. . . . Issues are simplified, they're global problem issues and they're David and Goliath, a sort of pantomime I suppose.
>
> (quoted in A. Anderson 1997: 126)

A media career

Any analysis of media images must be dynamic and there are several theories describing the way in which issues are reported. Downs (1972) suggests a cyclical pattern. Hilgartner and Bosk (1998) say that symbols compete which each other in a number of arenas. Anderson (1997) points out that such theories do not take into consideration the actions of the agents and she perceptively adds that the media lose interest once an issue is sucked into the bureaucratic process. There is little doubt that youth homelessness fell from media prominence after 1990. Several reasons for this can be suggested. Once the resources from the Rough Sleepers' Initiative had been announced, the immediate prize had been gained and agency attention necessarily moved to spending the money. Secondly, with the closing of the Bullring, access to homeless people by reporters and photographers was more difficult. One can also speculate that media attention moved to the outdoor activities of the road protesters to fill the 'outrageous youth' slot. A similar decline in interest in environmental issues is reported by Anderson (1997), quoting a BBC Television News correspondent, speaking in 1993:

> You got to the stage, I think, where you got environmental fatigue. . . . People say 'not again, we've heard it before' . . . to sustain a news operation you have got to have new stories, and campaigns are all very well but they tend to lose their impetus after a while.
>
> (A. Anderson 1997: 176)

Interestingly, as the numbers of reports in the press dropped after the summer of 1990, there was a change in tenor (Wardhaugh 1996) which echoed a more vocal and negative government stance. Two high-profile statements about aggressive begging produced a flutter of media activity. In 1994, the then Prime Minister John Major said that beggars were offensive 'eyesores' who needed to be removed from the streets. In 1995 Jack Straw, the then Shadow Home Secretary, expressed concern about 'aggressive begging by squeegee merchants, winos and addicts' (*Guardian* 9 September 1995). Later Tony Blair, in an interview with the homelessness magazine, *Big Issue*, four months before his election as prime minister (13–26 January 1997), said of beggars: 'Yes, of course they are doing something problematic for other people. . . . King's Cross is actually quite a frightening place for people'. Over the same period, homelessness and begging was being increasingly criminalised, first with the use of the Vagrancy Act 1824 to make arrests and, later, through the Criminal Justice and Public Order Bill 1994. The link between begging and wider crime was consciously drawn in 'zero tolerance' policing, by both Conservative and Labour governments in the UK, following practices in the USA (Kelling 1995). As the government became more authoritarian, the media coverage shifted from 'street children' to older vagrants.

However, if we look at current media coverage of youth homelessness, we can see that the more positive agency reporting of 'street children' continued but was relocated from the press headlines after 1990 to the reporting of annual media and charity events. Youth homelessness enters the millennium as a popular UK charity cause, reaching the television screen at Christmas, on Red Nose Day or in the week of Children in Need. What was initially a media issue and what failed to become a sustained political issue has now become predominantly a charity issue. This reflects, no doubt, the fact that it was predominately children's charities which were driving the earlier media campaigns. Throughout our research, we have noted the propensity for agencies to migrate to new fields and to flag up new issues in order to gain new funding and further publicity. In a society where the media are so important in catching the attention of the public and the politicians, it is likely that voluntary sector charities will tend to follow mediagenic issues. For example, within youth homelessness, Foyers and Self-build are both such new directions bringing new potential for publicity (Hutson and Jones 1998).

The impact of media hype

It would appear that the media hype of 1991 did bring the government's acknowledgement of the problem of youth homelessness as well as resources to the voluntary agencies in terms of the Rough Sleeper's Initiative. A *Times* correspondent reported that, through press headlines, young people had become 'A talking point for visitors and a deep political embarrassment for the Government' (*The Times* 18 June 1990). Ever reflexive, the journalist reported the next day: 'The alarm and pity this causes to the populace has at last communicated itself to the government, which has responded with a mixture of proposals' (*The Times* 19 June 1990). A similar link, between media hype and policies, can be identified between the coverage of the road protests and the announcement of a reduction in the government's road-building programme in the summer of 1997.

However, a broader perspective leads one to ask why the early media hype over homelessness brought so few changes in the political policies which had, in fact, caused youth homelessness – namely labour market, benefit and housing policies (Liddiard 1999). In the Housing Act 1996, the rights of all homeless people were reduced and no effort was made to improve the situation of the increasing numbers of young, single, homeless people. Benefits were not restored to under-25s despite this being a clear cause for the rise in youth homelessness and destitution. The Criminal Justice and Public Order Act 1994 criminalised begging. Although unemployment rates improved by 1999, many of the new jobs are skilled and young homeless people are not in a position to compete for them. While New Deal training initiatives are targeting young people, training is linked to outcomes which many young homeless people are unable to deliver. There is evidence that the situation of young homeless people has worsened, that the age of homeless people has lowered and even that rough sleeping itself has increased (A. Evans 1996). It is ironic that, as the issue falls from the headlines, the situation on the ground worsens. This suggests that the media career of a social issue may not coincide with its empirical course.

Before understanding the effect which media coverage has had on homelessness as a social issue, it is important to consider further the kind of images which have been produced. It is undoubtedly true that rough sleeping is the predominant media symbol of youth homelessness. For example, an early article (*Guardian* 3 March 1987) was concerned with young people trapped in their parents, homes because of increasing property prices. To illustrate this article, which had featured young career couples, was a picture of a muffled shape sleeping on the pavement with the caption: 'Out In the Cold. For Some Who Escape, the Streets are Paved Only With the Meanest Bedclothes'. Although it is very unlikely that any of these couples would end up sleeping rough, the powerful image of rough sleeping can used to illustrate any problem in the housing market. The reasons for this are undoubtedly because rough sleeping represents both the drama and the contrasts so liked by the press and also because it is accessible to photographers.

Reports show, however, that most people in youth homelessness surveys are not sleeping rough (Hutson and Liddiard 1994). Many are sleeping on friends' or relatives' floors. Some may be in, or recently evicted from, unsatisfactory private rented accommodation. Many, when interviewed, are staying in homelessness hostels or projects. Young people who leave home at the age of 16, often because of conflict in the family, may fall into this mixture of temporary and unstable accommodation (G. Jones 1995; J. Smith et al. 1998). They may be blocked there for months or years because they have neither sufficient money to secure permanent accommodation nor a relationship with a parent or a partner to gain them a home. As single people, they are unlikely to qualify for local authority housing. Rough sleeping may occur sporadically as part of this unstable, homeless phase. It may be a night here or there or it may extend for several months or longer. Longer-term rough sleeping is most likely to occur when a young person's links with accommodation become broken, through dislocation from mainstream life due to the length of time spent homeless (Hutson and Liddiard 1994) or through having a disturbed background, often from being in care (Fitzpatrick and Clapham 1999).

One effect of this emphasis on rough sleeping is to remove youth homelessness from the experience of everyday people (Beresford 1979). In so doing, the risk of homelessness for the majority is distanced. In fact, it is not uncommon to be without secure accommodation. As a student or, following a partnership break-up, many people move in with friends, or even spend a night in the car. A number of people have been repossessed after defaulting on a mortgage. But if homelessness is visualised simply as rough sleeping, then far fewer people have experienced it. It becomes seen as an outside normal experience and, ultimately, the people who sleep rough are not seen to have normal identities. This latter point is related to the fact that media images, because of their emphasis on extremes, tend to simplify the complexities faced by homeless people. Moreover, through the human interest emphasis, stories become personalised. Under these conditions, it is easy to place personal blame for a situation which rests on economic and policy decisions. Such personalised images of homelessness will therefore suit governments.

A further result of this emphasis on rough sleeping is to locate homelessness exclusively in city centres. This association is continued by the presence of *Big Issue* sellers in this location; this street newspaper was set up in the early 1990s to give homeless people a way of making a living and also to keep the issue visible to a public. Other social problems, such as prostitution, violence, drug and alcohol use, are also popularly located and visible in city centres. Thus rough sleeping, and so homelessness, is given a distinctive location within the urban environment. This is at odds with reality as the typical young homeless person is more likely to sleeping on friends' floors in his or her local suburb (Fitzpatrick and Clapham 1999).

Youth homelessness and 'risk'

In Beck's (1992a) terms, youth homelessness can be seen as a 'risky' element in late capitalism, resulting from a decrease in family support and the removal of state provision in terms of full employment, benefits and housing. This 'risk-iness' has a double edge. On the one hand, homelessness places young people personally 'at risk'. Because they are unable to gain access to a 'home' with the physical and social protection this affords – they are at risk particularly in terms of health (Fisher and Collins 1993) and sexual exploitation. The poor personal environment which homeless people face each morning is summed up by one 16-year-old girl living in a poor private rented flat (Hutson *et al.* 1995): 'Every morning I look around and think "O God". A better environment would make a big difference.' On the other hand, as we have seen above, homeless people are often presented by the media as, themselves, creating 'risks' for the public. It is particularly in the city centre that homeless people add risk to an already dangerous environment. The 'street child' has been replaced, in certain con-texts, by the 'aggressive beggar'. As Wardhaugh (1996) points out: 'It is the visible presence of marginal people within prime space that represents a threat to a sense of public order and orderliness' (Wardhaugh 1996: 706).

In the late 1990s, the contrast, alluded to in this quote, excites fear rather than the pity which was aroused a decade before. In saying this, we would add that both slants on reporting can coexist even though one may tend to domi-nate (Liddiard and Hutson 1991). In the practical world of housing allocations, a negative slant has direct implications. Young, single, homeless people are often presented as extremely 'risky' tenants by the statutory authorities under pressure to house them and often by the neighbours around them. Stories of trashed houses, abandoned tenancies, public dirt and violence are commonly used to justify the exclusion of young single people from mainstream tenancies (Hutson and Jones 1997). Ironically, when the 'pollution' is human, then the victim can be blamed.

Conclusion

Parallels can be drawn between the media politics of a social issue such as youth homelessness and the media politics of many environmental issues. In both, dangers and risks are caused by global changes and national policies which can create physical or 'social pollution' – be it oil on the coast or young people sleeping on the streets. Where these end products are mediagenic and, even more importantly, where there are agencies to pick them up and present them to the media in attractive packages, then an issue is identified publicly and prominently. Such publicity pushes the government into action, mostly to clear the symptoms rather than to alter the underlying processes. The media careers of such issues are short, as the press moves on to other images. The risk may continue but the media spotlight has moved. This may well suit the government which needs only to wait until the media hype drops. The way in which these issues are constructed – to fit media agendas – means that they are conceived in black and white terms. Such representations produce a mismatch between the image and actuality. In youth homelessness, the emphasis on rough sleeping removes the problem from the experience of the ordinary person. It also places homelessness in the city centre rather than in the more ordinary venue of the suburb. Whilst earlier media images of homeless children showed the 'risks' they faced on the street, later reports – of aggressive beggars and troublesome tenants – can make it appear that it is us, as ordinary citizens, who are 'at risk' from the homeless.

Acknowledgements

The observations about youth homelessness come principally from a number of studies carried out by the authors at the University of Wales Swansea and funded by the Children's Society, Joseph Rowntree Foundation and Welsh Office between 1987 and 1998. The research rested primarily on interviews with young homeless people and agencies but a collection of video documentaries, agency literature and press articles (mostly from broadsheet daily and Sunday papers) informs this chapter. The authors would also like to acknowledge the contributions of Stuart Jones, Margaret Sutton and Jaqui Thomas, who worked on research projects cited in this chapter.

Chapter 11

The female body at risk

Media, sexual violence and the gendering of public environments

C. Kay Weaver, Cynthia Carter and Elizabeth Stanko

> It makes me nervous, living on my own and knowing if you go outside you're not safe. And even in your own home you're not safe. If I have to walk home and it's dark — I'm looking everywhere. Even to go round and shut the entry door, I look in and see if anybody has climbed in - the bloke could be hitched on the top [of the wall]. People will say 'She watches too much telly'. But I know what these people are like. Men are out there and they do do these things.
>
> (English Afro-Caribbean woman, with experience of violence)

> I feel [when] I set out in the dark, I'm taking a risk every time. I've never been attacked as such, but how do I know that I won't be? There's always the feeling there.
>
> [English white woman, with experience of violence]

Reports of sexual violence in the British media typically encourage audiences to believe that females are most at risk of becoming the victim of a violent attack in public environments at the hands of male strangers.[1] This is despite overwhelming statistical evidence which confirms that women face much higher risks in private spaces from males whom they already know (Home Office 1998; see also Stanko 1998; Stanko *et al.* 1998). By accentuating the risks that women face when they enter public environments, the media help to construct such spaces as profoundly gendered ones in which women are urged to be unceasingly fearful for their personal safety and therefore never at ease (see Massey 1994; R. Pain 1991). Through the creation of a sense of public environments as places overtly hostile to women, and particularly so at night, the media assist in cultivating a gendered alignment between public spaces as inherently masculine spheres of operation and power (political) and private ones as feminine (domestic). Reports of public forms of sexual violence, in particular, operate discursively to put women 'back in their place' (the private sphere), especially those women whom journalists deem to have exhibited 'risk-taking behaviour' — wearing clothing which is 'too revealing', walking on the streets alone at night, being loud, aggressive or inebriated in public, to name only but a few gendered 'indiscretions'.

Feminist cultural geographers have argued for the need to understand how 'space' and 'place' help to shape gender relations (Massey 1994; R. Pain 1991, 1993; Valentine 1989). As Massey (1994: 179) has suggested, severe restrictions on women's mobility in public spaces have been crucial to the perpetuation of their subordination in western societies. In her view, patriarchal attempts to confine women to the private sphere represent both forms of gendered spatial control as well as efforts to delimit the range of feminine identities available so as to maintain women's close alignment with domesticity. Above all, it is women's perceptions that they are most at risk of becoming the victim of sexual violence in public environments which place strict limitations on their use of such spaces (see Valentine 1989). Furthermore, as Pain (1991) points out, it is largely because of these perceptions that women tend to take 'social and lifestyle precautions which are most costly in terms of personal freedom' (R. Pain 1991: 420). Thus women's fears are central to the reproduction of their unequal participation in society.[2] Agencies of socialisation, such as the media, are important in this respect because they are seen to contribute to the construction of a (public) world in which the unceasing risk of sexual violence is understood to be an inevitable part of women's everyday life or, as Pain (1991: 423) puts it, 'part of the natural environment' (see also C. Carter 1998a; Stanko 1990, 1997, 1998).

Women's fears of being physically attacked in public spaces have real material effects in their lives since such fears are used to encourage them to confine most of their activities to private spaces, and preferably in those where a man is present to protect them from (outside) harm. Although growing numbers of women have been entering public spaces to seek paid employment over the course of the century, feminists have argued that their increased physical presence in public has done little to alter their continuing gendered identification with, and responsibilities within, domestic spaces. The gendered division of space into work (public) and home (private) has therefore become less significant to the maintenance of unequal gender relations than the continuing ideological separation between them. Instead, Pain (1991) maintains: 'Perhaps the most important determinate of men's continuing dominance in public space is now sexual violence, and ideologies which surround sexual violence which have the power to restrict women's movements and activities' (R. Pain 1991: 424).

To investigate these and related claims, this chapter begins by exploring the ways in which various groups of women responded to a televisual crime reconstruction portrayal of sexual violence (*Crimewatch UK*). Their reactions, we suggest, offer important insights into how and why women are encouraged by the media to define certain activities as 'risk-taking behaviour'. The data demonstrate that in relation to crimes of sexual violence which occur in public environments, notions of risk are discursively very closely associated with, if not inseparable from, notions of 'provocation'. Yet even when such discursive readings are not foregrounded, many women interviewed in the televisual reception study still provided 'victim blaming' interpretations. This demonstrates the extent to which women have 'bought into' patriarchal explanations of violence against women which deem the female body as, by its very (reproductive, privatised) nature, a form which is at risk of violation and therefore in need of 'protection'. Such discourses impact considerably on both women's understanding of their right to operate in public, how women express themselves in that sphere and, finally, the strategies they employ to negotiate such spaces as safely as possible.

From there we offer a broad examination of some of the conclusions drawn from recent research on news reports of sexual violence (see, for example, Benedict 1992; C. Carter 1998a, 1998b; Carter and Thompson 1997; K. Clark 1992, Cuklanz 1996; Meyers 1997; Soothill and Walby 1991; Wykes 1998). Specifically, we take a look at how certain forms of sexual violence (murder and various categories of rape) tend to dominate press reports of this type of crime, and how the male stranger is constructed as the single most common and therefore most feared type of sexual offender. We then consider how these news reports help to construct certain commonsensical prescriptions of gendered normalcy which are rooted in assumptions about women's proper roles and responsibilities within private environments. It is here that we examine how certain ideological assumptions consistently underpin such reporting, which often result in placing blame on women and girls who fail to live up to the demands of domesticised, privatised forms of femininity.

The final section of this chapter directly examines how the risks of sexual violence reported in the media are internalised and operationalised by women when they enter public environments. Here we argue that women draw upon the same recognisable social and cultural expectations about women, as do the media. While all the available evidence suggests that women are most at risk to known men (especially men with whom they are or have been intimate), women speak about public space as possessing the most danger of criminal violence. We illustrate this through Stanko's (1990, 1997) research on women's strategies of crime avoidance. As we show, the discourses of crime prevention often embrace the same type of imagery that is regularly used by the media.

(Re)constructing female risk

Crime reconstruction programmes which have proved highly popular with audiences in the 1980s and 1990s, as exemplified by *America's Most Wanted* in the USA and *Crimewatch UK* in Britain, underscore women's perceptions of the public sphere as dangerous. Research demonstrates that such programmes have particular consequences for women in terms of increasing their fear of crime and/or concern about their personal safety (BBC Broadcasting Research 1988: 18; P. Schlesinger *et al.* 1992: ch. 3; Wober and Gunter 1990: ii).

Here we draw on an audience reception study of one of these programmes,

Crimewatch UK, to illustrate how crime reporting plays a part in the patriarchal construction of public space as 'no safe place for a woman'. This reception study comprised ninety-one women formed into fourteen focus discussion groups, with half of those groups comprising women with experience of physical, sexual and/or domestic violence, and half with no such experience. Groups also varied in terms of social class (working class and middle class), ethnicity (white, Asian and Afro-Caribbean) and nationality (Scottish and English). These focus groups viewed an edition of *Crimewatch UK* containing a report on the sexual assault and murder of a young female hitchhiker. The report was accompanied by a reconstruction which depicted the last hours of this woman's life, and which appealed to witnesses to come forward with information which might assist the police in solving this crime.

In terms of how the women in the reception study generally evaluated *Crimewatch*, there was an overwhelming belief that it performed a valuable informative function in that it made women aware of the risks of associated with public environments. For example:

> I think it's good because it highlights crime and makes you more aware of [what] can happen to you. Just to be more cautious and everything.
>
>   (English Asian woman, with no experience of violence)

> I watch it and I hope that it's highlighted that particular risk area. This woman has been murdered and hopefully somebody has learnt something from it.
>
>   (English Afro-Caribbean woman, with experience of violence)

> It's showing . . . what crime is and really how it's happening. I think they're really making us understand how bad it could be.
>
>   (Scottish white woman, with experience of violence)

Regarding the report on the sexual assault of the young female hitchhiker, the respondents also felt that *Crimewatch* performed an important service in illustrating the specific risks of hitchhiking for women:

> People have got to be made aware. Some 17-year-old lassie could have watched it and said 'Well if I'm in the same situation I'd better not do that'.
>
>   (Scottish white working-class woman, with no experience of violence)

> It's just highlighting the danger of her being a woman and hitchhiking.
>
>   (English Asian woman, with no experience of violence)

> That is something I wouldn't do. That is something I wouldn't encourage any of my children to do and that's something I definitely would say to friends who are thinking of it, 'I wouldn't do that if I were you'.
>
>   (English Afro-Caribbean woman, with experience of violence)

Such responses demonstrate how this programme encourages women to anticipate danger, and seek ways to inhibit their activities outside of the home as a way to avoid it. As we suggested earlier in the chapter, women tend to place more restrictions on their use of public environments, and do not consider themselves as having the same freedoms as men in such spaces (Gordon and Riger 1988; R. Pain 1991). However, several respondents in this study were highly critical of *Crimewatch* for communicating this 'risk' message to women, and argued that it unfairly placed the burden of responsibility for violent attacks against women on the victims, rather than on the perpetrators of such crimes:

> What they actually said about hitchhiking was wrong. . . . The first thing they said is 'This is what happens when you hitchhike' basically. Why should we be the ones to stop hitchhiking? They should be catching the people that are murdering these people. . . . I've done some hitchhiking in my life and you meet some nice people. It's not us that are at fault because we hitchhike. It's them, it's their minds. They made you think that you shouldn't hitchhike, because this is what will happen to you.
>
> (English white woman, with experience of violence)

It is noteworthy that this response came from a woman with experience of violence. These interviewees were more sensitive to the manner in which women are represented in the media as blameworthy for not taking precautions that might have prevented a violent attack. Women with experience of violence were also more likely to identify reports of violence against women as highlighting women's alleged vulnerabilities:

Respondent 1:   Have you noticed it's usually women that are [reported as] getting attacked? . . .

Respondent 2:   It sounds worse if it's a woman than if it's a man. If a man's been stabbed in the street [they say] 'a man's been stabbed'. But if it's a woman [they say] 'Oh God, a woman's been stabbed!'

Respondent 3:   It's more sensational isn't it because women are supposed to be the weaker sex.

Respondent 2:   'The helpless female'. . . . They're making us out to be wee meek and mild mice and that we can not stand up for ourselves. A lot of us can.

(Scottish white women, with experience of violence)

Yet, there were a few women interviewees with no experience of violence who protested against *Crimewatch*'s construction of hitchhiking as a 'risk-taking' activity and who were highly critical of how the threat of male violence works to regulate women. For example, one such interviewee asked:

Does it mean all women are not allowed to go because somebody might come along and murder them?

(Scottish white working-class woman, with no experience of violence)

Even when it was felt that women should be able to participate in an activity such as hitchhiking, doing so could be regarded by others as taking 'unnecessary risks':

My own personal opinion of society is that women should be able to go and do what they like without being attacked. However the reality of it is if you're hitchhiking along a dark road people will say 'silly devil, what on earth are you doing out there?'

(Scottish white middle-class woman, with no experience of violence)

We're told there's only a few of these nutters around, so on the one hand we're being told carry on, live your life normally, but then if you're a so-called 'idiot' you just take the risk.

(English white woman, with experience of violence)

For the most part, however, this study found that women negotiated their everyday lives privileging a gendered distinction between public and private spaces. In these terms, the research findings are highly comparable to Valentine's (1989) examination of women's fear of male violence and their perception and use of public space. Valentine states that 'whilst women identify specific isolated places as frightening during the day, they express a fear of all public space alone at night' (Valentine 1989: 388). Indeed, this fear is overtly expressed in the following comment:

My advice would be to people that do walk the streets at night is to look where they're going and keep an eye out – I don't see anything wrong with walking at night and looking around you all the time because that's way you've got to be these days.

(Scottish Asian woman, with experience of violence)

One of the consequences of this association of risk with public space at night is that women 'participate less in public activities and spend more time in the home and seek more public protection from men' (R. Pain 1991: 423). This is confirmed in this discussion among one of the groups of Asian respondents:

Respondent 1:   I think Asian women are more careful than white [women] especially in late night. We don't go out alone.
Respondent 2:   We are not allowed that's why.
Respondent 3:   Yes we are brought up like that and that's why we can't go alone. [If] we should go [there are] two women and sometimes

a man and woman go, sometimes son and mothers go. We can't
go alone after eight o'clock, we are brought [up] like that. You
know you are not. Like [white women] brought up like that.
You always go alone.

(Scottish Asian women, with no experience of violence)

For these women then, Asian culture is seen to provide certain (familialised)
benefits for women. Male family members are responsible for ensuring that
women avoid the risk of violent attack from male strangers in public spaces.

The above findings taken from the study of women's responses to media portrayals of violence indicate how women associate public spaces with personal
risks. Such risks are associated with being female (Stanko 1997; Tulloch,
Chapter 12 in this volume). Yet, this is not to say that women necessarily feel
safe from the risk of violent attack in their homes. A number of women
espondents did reveal a sense of considerable unease about their safety in their
homes when they were home alone at night unprotected by a male partner or
relative. Such fears were expressed by some women as especially aroused when
watching *Crimewatch UK*:

It frightens me. My husband was on nights when I watched it this week.
I had my house alarms on. That's the only thing that reassures me – I've
got real brilliant alarms in the house. That's the only way I feel safe in my
house.

(English white working-class woman; with no experience of violence)

They have shown a lot of scenes where things have happened within [peo-
ple's] homes – where people have come in when you could be in bed. It
makes me nervous, living on my own and knowing if you go outside you're
not safe.

(English Afro-Caribbean woman, with experience of violence)

It is perhaps somewhat surprising that this study of *Crimewatch UK* generated
discussions of women's fear of crime only in relation to attacks by male
strangers, especially given that many of the respondents had experience of
domestic violence committed against them by male intimates. Yet this further
demonstrates the ways in which patriarchal assumptions, through the particular types of discursive strategies used in crime reporting, encourage women to
'adopt false assumptions about their security when in places falsely deemed safe
for women, such as the home' (Valentine 1989: 385).

In the next section of the chapter, we examine Pain's (1991) claim that ideologies which shape our understanding of sexual violence are now the most
important determinants of men's continuing dominance in public environments. We discuss the ideological role that the media play in shaping women's
sense of the risks they are taking when entering public spaces which encourage

them to restrict their movements and activities. For as Massey (1994) points out, the ideological and physical restriction of women's activities within the private sphere helps to both secure their continuing performance of domestic roles and exclude them from 'entry into another, public, world – a life not defined by family and husband' (Massey 1994: 179–80).

Stranger danger

Media research has established that there are patterned, predictable ways in which journalists and their sources comment on incidents of sexual violence (see Benedict 1992; Caputi 1987; Cuklanz 1996; Finn 1989–90; McCormick 1995; Meyers 1997; Soothill and Walby 1991; Voumvakis and Ericson 1984). A repeated finding is that there is a distinct over-representation of the threat posed by male strangers in relation to their officially recorded occurrence. For instance, official homicide statistics in Britain for the year 1995 (Home Office 1996) indicate that only 13 per cent of female victims were killed by a male stranger, while Carter's (1998a) research on the British tabloid press sampled over two months illustrates that during that period, 40 per cent of all news of sexual violence fell into this category.[3] Carter also found that murder is the most common type of violence against women reported in the tabloid press, accounting for nearly half of all sexual violence news items in her sample. Against this, Home Office (1996) records suggest that women's greatest risk of violence consists of 'less serious wounding', representing over 60 per cent of all violent crime against females.[4] However, Carter's (1998a) study documents that only 30 per cent of sex-crime news in the tabloid press during the two-month sample period she examined could be categorised in this way.

Media researchers have also established that victims of sexual violence are routinely described in terms of their physical attractiveness, dress, hair colour, marital status, social background and demeanour (see Benedict 1992; K. Clark 1992; Voumvakis and Ericson 1984). Moreover, the language that journalists and news sources recurrently use is organised, in part, to legitimise the patriarchal control of women within both public and private spaces. As Clark (1992) explains, news reports of sexual violence are rendered unthreatening to 'normal' men by placing beyond discourse men whose violence is deemed to be excessive and female victims whose suffering is seen to be *undeserved* (that is women who did not transgress the spatial and ideological boundaries of patriarchal definitions of femininity). Thus, labels like 'monster', 'fiend' and 'animal' are employed to refer to some offenders in order to individualise and personalise the violence. The use of such terms invites the reader to divert blame away from individual men as well as a patriarchal system which perpetuates structural gender inequalities based on the economic, social and cultural subordination of women. Newspaper readers are recurrently encouraged not to see certain sexual offenders as 'real men'. Where victims are discursively constructed as 'faultless victims', the terms used to describe them include 'wife', 'mother' and 'grandmother', among others. Such labels serve to establish for the reader a female victim's discursive connection to gendered roles and behaviours which may be regarded as being closely aligned with the (culturally sanctioned) feminised and domesticised private sphere.

As Voumvakis and Ericson (1984) argue in their study of news reports of attacks on women, such stories are invariably embedded within a patriarchal, 'consensual worldview'. This worldview is a product of a dialectical relationship between certain ascendant cultural ideologies as well as the occupational ideologies within which journalists operate (see also Allan 1998; Croteau and Hoynes 1992; Holland 1987; Kitzinger 1998; Rakow and Kranich 1991; Skidmore 1998; Steiner 1998; van Zoonen 1994, 1998). The news media therefore contribute to the construction of a social consensus (albeit one which is provisional and always changing) around particular patriarchal values, morals and ideals. This consensus includes a condemnation of violence against 'good' women and girls and acquiescence around sexual violence against 'bad' girls and women, or at least those whom the journalist considers to have taken 'unreasonable risks'. As Voumvakis and Ericson (1984) explain:

> Attacks on women, within the consensual world view, is [sic] not a phenomenon that is an inevitable outcome of the ways in which this particular society is structured; rather, it is easily explicable in terms of individual or organisation problems: the victim's carelessness, the offender's pathology, the police department's inefficiency, inadequate legislation, etc. The dominant culture which shapes particular attitudes toward women, which permeates the way women are portrayed, and which may ultimately contribute to attacks on women, remains largely unquestioned and unexamined.
>
> (Voumvakis and Ericson 1984: 43)

Furthermore, journalists contribute to the (re)production of this consensual paradigm by both personalising sexual violence (Meyers 1995, 1997) and simplifying it (Benedict 1992). Sexual violence is personalised and simplified through its attribution to 'individual pathology'. Wider social conditions and structures of socio-economic gender, racial, sexual and spatial inequality are rarely cited as possible antecedents to violence (Finn 1989–90; Meyers 1997). An emphasis on individual responsibility for one's actions, successes and failures forms the basis of western law, governmental legislation and social policy. Journalists operate within these assumptions resisting suggestions that structural inequalities, which are largely beyond any individual's control, might help to shape an offender's actions. One important consequence of this is that journalists tend to over-simplify incidents of sexual violence in their news reports. As a result, rather than agitating for wider socio-economic reform which is needed to tackle the root causes of sexual violence, journalists typically support calls for greater repressive social control, such as increased numbers of police, tougher sentencing and so forth (Sasson 1995).

We now return to a discussion of the ways in which women's fears of sexual violence, many of which are encouraged by current forms of reporting in the British media, are internalised by women, particularly when they enter public spaces. Here we make certain connections between gendered media accounts of crime prevention and the strategies for personal safety women employ every day in order to avoid potential risks of sexual violence.

Public spaces, female fears

> I've never been fearful. But whenever I've gone into any area . . . I would do things [like go out at night or have a social life]. But I think I always went with a sense of being ready, just in case, you know. Avoid dark alleys, walk in the middle of the road, [I felt] safe where it's lighted, be careful where you park your car. I think there was always that kind of watching.
> (62-year-old professional, white widow, USA)[5]

There are many existing meanings linked to explanations about the nature of crime, fear, danger, blame or responsible citizenry (Douglas 1992), and these are typically left out of contemporary debates in media research (Sparks 1992a; Walklate 1997). Fear of crime – and especially women's fear – has great value in popular cultural portrayals of good and evil (Sparks 1992a). So regardless of whether fear stems from *actual* crime or its risk, ignoring whether the danger is real or imagined, women are increasingly encouraged by the state to be literate about crime prevention as a way to combat both. To avoid the dangerous, lurking male menace (the other), we are advised how to travel locally ('with petrol in our car') and afar, how to dress, how to walk, how to talk to a potential intimidator, how to appear assertive and in control of our modern lives (Gardner 1988; Stanko 1990). At the same time, our precautionary strategies for minimising men's violence are practices that display an awareness of the relationship women have to men – the dangerous 'other'. But awareness of our relational insecurity *vis-à-vis* men is not restricted to crime prevention advice; it is embedded within women's routine consciousness about being respectable women in contemporary life. What is at *risk* for women, in an encounter with any potentially violent man, is a sullied self. The women who watched the *Crimewatch UK* reconstruction (discussed on pp. 173–8) provide ample evidence of the strength of this expectation to remain 'respectable' by avoiding the danger of men.

As we have already noted, both officially recorded crime and the studies of the vast, hidden violence against women suggest that women's assailants are commonly known to them. Women are most likely to be injured, raped and require medical attention in assaults from known assailants (Mirrlees-Black *et al.* 1996; Stanko 1998; Stanko *et al.* 1998). Feminist research has emphasised the instrumental impact of serial, intentional and directed violence by men on women in intimate settings (Dobash and Dobash 1979; Hoff 1990). Further evidence shows that men do not sustain the same level of serious injuries at the hands of intimates, unless women they batter kill them, often in self-defence (see Wykes 1995). Women (or those acting on behalf of women) ask police for help in 90–95 per cent of requests for assistance in domestic violence.

Crime prevention discourses about danger largely deny the main risks to women and instead draw upon conventional (patriarchal) social and cultural knowledge about women's respectability, such as those provided in the news media. Such discourses make it very difficult to problematise the safety of heterosexual unions – and label them as potentially dangerous (see C. Carter 1998b; Wykes 1995, 1998). That women are most likely to be assaulted or killed by known men is still explained as a natural course disaster for some intimate relationships. It is ironic, then, that crime prevention advice primarily targets the potential danger to women from men in public environments.

Despite over twenty years of sustained campaigning, feminist work in the fields of media and criminological research has not shifted journalistic attention away from thinking about the danger of strangers. Women are still being told about being careful walking on the streets at night. Even highly publicised cases of random murder against women have given rise to media commentary that 'no woman alone is safe in public'. Observations from such feminist commentators as Caputi (1987) or Cameron and Frazer (1987, 1994), who argue that sexual murder is not just an unfortunate event, but part of systematic violence against women, are not to be found in these public comments. The evidence about women, violence and victimisation is overwhelming, its implications about danger are denied. Only 'beasts' hurt women. Yet we now know that most violence against women is perpetrated by 'nice guys', not 'beasts'. As the evidence mounts that women lead more socially and spatially restricted lives and use greater caution when out in public, the impact of violence against women must be acknowledged as a *collective harm against all women.*

Shifting our understanding of the danger of heterosexual intimacies is still far from the development of new social policies on crime. We continue to separate the danger of known men from that of the so-called dangerous stranger in media and criminological debates, and this is reflected in popular media and television accounts of sexual violence. In part, this separation is supported by the documentation about women's greater worry about safety in public places found so consistently in studies about fear of crime. Beyond any doubt, the gender differential is the most consistent finding in the literature on fear of crime. Women report fear at levels that are three times that of men, yet their recorded risk of personal violence, especially assault, are lower than men's, according to official sources. Indeed, there is a mismatch between women's and men's *reported* risk of violent criminal victimisation and their fear of falling victim to such violence. Those who admit feeling safest, young men, reveal the greatest proportion of personally violent victimisation. But we cannot fully explain women's fear of crime by examining crime data alone. Women's concerns about public danger receive support via the media's representation of violence against women.

The study of the fear of crime neglects the domestic nature of a vast majority of men's violence to women. Women are treated as if they need fear only the unknown male stranger. As Pain (1993) found, despite disclosing a variety of domestic and intimate assaults, her interviewees spoke of potential violence as 'stranger danger'. Such concern about danger begins early in life, suggests Goodey (1994). The schoolchildren she interviewed took safety precautions, especially with strangers; girls took more precautions than boys did. Stanko's (1990) research on safety and violence avoidance strategies of adult women and men illustrates how early lessons in danger become part of a lifetime of negotiating danger, inside and outside the home. Yet when one asks women about danger, their fears translate into concerns about the danger lurking in the physical environment: car parks, public stairwells and public transport, for instance, are typically named by women as dangerous places in community safety audits collected by campaign groups or local crime prevention initiatives.

Conclusion

In this chapter, we have examined how media reports of sexual violence are shaped by an ideology of the 'respectable' (domesticised, privatised) woman who adheres to traditional expectations for women under any patriarchal regime. Home, family and sexual propriety are expected to shield women from harm. But exactly the opposite is true. Moreover, women acknowledge the potential of sexual violence – whether from known or unknown men – as a core component of their *being female*. The danger and risk is managed through a wide range of everyday, mundane routines and is a mechanism for avoiding the potential violation of sexual integrity. What women define as a violation of sexual integrity, moreover, is not confined to what is statutorily defined as rape. Sexual humiliation and degradation are clearly included in women's list of what to avoid. Further, women are expected to behave as if not only are they aware of these potential dangers, but also they are expected to acknowledge the naturalness of these dangers arising from men's behaviour toward and attitudes to women.

As a consequence of this state of alert, women police themselves by restricting their activities in public environments because of their anxieties about potential violence. Research shows women use more safety precautions than do men (Gordon and Riger 1988; Gardner 1995; Stanko 1996). The voices of women presented earlier in this chapter attest to the strength of how the use of precaution is justified as reasonable for 'respectable' women. The routines of precaution, though, become an invisible and worrying commentary about the unspeakable: it is largely men who are supposed to be the protectors, the intimates, the sources of support, who are the source of danger. Many women prepare themselves to avoid men's violence as an 'impending disaster'. Such preparation has become a routine and expected part of being a woman (Stanko 1997; see also Madriz 1997; Tulloch, Chapter 12 in this volume). This has occurred despite radical feminist challenges: the acceptance of this normalisation is an acceptance of subordination. Second-class citizens should not expect to walk the streets unhindered.

As this chapter has demonstrated, the media clearly play a key role in socialising women to accept their subordinate status by way of constructing the female body as a site of risk. While feminist cultural geographers such as Massey (1994), Pain (1991, 1993) and Valentine (1989) have insisted that the media assist in socially constructing gendered spaces within and between public and private environments, news media research has generally failed to make use of this insight. Such an omission places a detrimental limit on understanding the ideological and material effects of media representations of crime and violence on women, who are so often depicted as victims.

Notes

1   The media examined for the purposes of this chapter include a two-month sample of six tabloid format (including 'popular' and 'mid-market') British newspapers over a period of two months from late 1993 to early 1994 as well as the British crime reconstruction programme on BBC television, entitled *Crimewatch UK*, which has been on the air since the mid 1980s to the present. The reception study of *Crimewatch UK* was carried out for the publication *Women Viewing Violence* (Schlesinger *et al.* 1992). We are grateful to Philip Schlesinger, Rebecca Dobash and Russell Dobash for allowing us to draw on this research here.
2   We concur with Tulloch (in this volume) that women's fears of sexual violence occurring in public spaces should not be viewed as being 'irrational' simply because statistical evidence has demonstrated that they are less likely to be attacked in public than men. Indeed, as Tulloch suggests, it is the potential indicators of sexual violence ('the man across the carriage staring fixedly at you, the man in the seat next to you whose knee nestles into yours each time the train lurches, the nervousness of sitting in an empty carriage at night, or worse, with that one unknown man sitting at the back of the carriage') which form part of the everyday reality of being female which often inhibit women's movement into and within public spaces.
3   Although the sample used in Carter's (1998a) research covered only the period of two months from mid-November 1993 to mid-January 1994, past studies in both Britain and the USA which have included longer term (including yearly) samples generally concur with Carter's findings (see Meyers 1997; Soothill and Walby 1991; Voumvakis and Ericson 1984).
4   'Less serious wounding' (defined in *Criminal Statistics, England and Wales* reports) primarily refers to physical assault without an explicitly sexual element (e.g. 'battering').
5   Interview contained in Stanko (1990).

'Landscapes of fear'
Public places, fear of crime and the media

John Tulloch

A 'bad' rail story . . . will always get a run, particularly in [the tabloids], and probably on television if they can get pictures. A 'good' rail story is really struggling even to get into the local papers. For instance, we've upgraded the lights at Cabramatta [notorious for its 'Asian gangs', drug dealing and station crime] . . . and that still hasn't been publicised in the local press.

(Sydney CityRail manager)

I think the media could play a major role by having a positive attitude towards using the trains. . . . Because what the media has done so far is to . . . encourage [people] to avoid the trains and I think it's the wrong attitude. We give up and we hide ourselves and give the space to the intruders. I think the media should reverse this attitude and tell the people to protect themselves but go ahead and not be hiding. We are the many, we are the people who should fight them and we should go out in masses and show *body*, not hide.

(Senior citizen, Sydney)

Both of these statements make two assumptions: that certain public environments are 'landscapes of fear' and that the media have a powerful influence in setting public perceptions of these risks. As such they might be taken as 'lay' parallels to recent 'expert' discourse from within academic sociology. For example, the Sydney, Australia, CityRail manager's comment about 'bad' replacing 'good' rail stories reminds one of Beck's (1992a, 1996a) view that the controlling logic of modern industrial societies' discourse has shifted talk about the distribution of 'goods' (of 'public services' like state-run train travel and better lighting at stations, for example) to one based on the distribution of 'bads' (the 'risk society'). At the same time other academics take much further our Sydney senior citizen's concern with the negative role of the media, to argue that the discourses about criminality she describes may be 'the perfect metaphor for post-modernism'. Thus, Osborne (1995: 27–8) argues that 'media narratives encode crime and disorder as the representations of fragmentation rendered coherent'. In his analysis, the 'obsessive . . . and hysterical replaying of the possibility of being a victim and staving it off' (Osborne 1995: 29) that marks the boundaries of our senior citizen's comment, has become systemic in the media's attempt to institutionalise the postmodern condition.

There are, in fact, some grounds of agreement between theorists of post-modernism and of 'risk society'; most notably in their critique of the 'grand narratives' of the Enlightenment tradition (such as science and Marxism). Like Baudrillard and other postmodernists, Beck argues for a global society in which we are increasingly free from controlling and normative expectations, whether those of class or of modern institutions. For both Baudrillard (1984) and Beck (1992a, 1996a), the condition of the individual in this situation of fragmenta-tion is 'schizophrenic'. Baudrillard speaks of everything becoming 'undecid-able' and Beck emphasises the 'incalculability' of risk among all sectors of society.

But their comments on the relation of the undecidable and the incalculable to the media and environmental risk also indicate their significant difference. In Baudrillard's postmodern world, environmental risk and media signification fuse. The nuclear meltdown at Three Mile Island has no 'core' reality beyond television's images of it, the television event having 'supremacy . . . over the nuclear event which itself remains . . . in some sense imaginary' (Baudrillard 1984: 18). In Beck's 'risk society', the environmental hazards produced by sci-ence and technology – Chernobyl, Bhopal, the greenhouse effect, pollution, global warming – are clearly not simulacra; and far from TV *becoming* the world in an endless fragmentation and succession of images (as in Baudrillard's vision), the media form one of many institutions of 'experts' (together with science and the law) which define and circulate the politically salient discourses of risk.

For Beck (1996a), risk society sees a systemic transformation of industrial society in which the intellectual and discursive relationship of society to the hazards which it is producing and which are exceeding its own conceptions of security has led to all sectors of society – business, the law, academia, the media and politics – now talking 'risk' discourse. But they talk in conflict, as competing 'experts'.

> Insurance experts contradict safety engineers. . . . Experts are relativised or dethroned by counterexperts. . . . Ultimately industries responsible for damage (for example, the chemical industry for marine pollution) must even expect resistance from other industries affected as a result (in this case fishing and the business dependent on coastal tourism).
>
> (Beck 1996a: 31–3)

It is this emphasis on risk society as a compilation and circulation of 'expert' rhetorics that has been criticised by another 'risk' theorist, Brian Wynne. He rebukes both Beck and Giddens for 'not problematising the boundary between expert and lay domains of knowledge and epistemology' (Wynne 1996a: 76) and in his study of Cumbrian farmers faced by British government scientists' research into the effects of the Chernobyl disaster, Wynne emphasises the contextual, situated and 'adaptive "control"' . . . which is exercised with personal agency and overt responsibility' (Wynne 1996a: 70) that is symptomatic of specialist lay knowledges. Although Wynne's analysis applies to a rather restricted social group (Cumbrian hill sheep farmers), it will be readily apparent that his emphasis on agency, on local and contextual knowledge, and on 'the adaptive coping with multiple dimensions in the same complex area' (1996a: 70) is equally important in other areas, such as risk in public environments.

The Centre for Cultural Risk Research at Charles Sturt University in Australia conducted a major 'fear of crime' research project, adopting a qualitative approach to the 'micro-narratives' of 'lay knowledge' (Tulloch *et al.* 1998). Here we were confronted by the very different multiple (time/space) dimensions of the 'adaptive coping' among the women we interviewed: for example, an older woman who boards the daytime train with her knife (in case of muggers), her apple (to legally 'justify' the knife) and her crochet needle (to keep her busy), compared with the variety of nighttime strategies by younger women on the train – such as the teenage girl who told us how she would meet three other women friends after work to catch the train home, and how they had nervously experimented with each of them sitting in a different carriage for a short while to help them control their fear.

These are not 'irrational' women with 'mistaken impressions' of their 'objective risk' on the train, as conventional statistical surveys of fear of crime tend to suggest. The kind of decontextualised and 'universal' expert-driven approaches that Wynne is criticising are very common in fear of crime research. Typically, individual survey questions like 'Do you feel safe walking alone in your neighbourhood at night?' are used to measure fear of crime in this research.

There are at least three problems with this kind of survey question. First, it is too hypothetical and ambiguous. Many older women, for example, will tell you that they do not feel like going out at night since their partner died, and even if they do, they may be as afraid of falling over an uneven pavement as of being mugged. So what does 'afraid' in this question mean? And what is especially apparent when you talk with older people is, of course, a feature with all age groups. There are a range of factors other than incidence of crime that contribute to an individual's perceptions of their own risk. Some of these are local, physical and direct (like an ageing body, or a younger, sexually harassed body). Others are more indirect or systemically long term, depending on experience of a declining environment or social exploitation. The single 'safe in your neighbourhood at night' question does little to explore these complexities.

Secondly, the responses to this question are used as evidence of the so-called 'risk/fear paradox'. But this notion – that women and older people who have less 'objective' reason to fear (based on the statistical profile of crime victims) actually fear most and are thus 'irrational' – founders on the everyday reality of being female or of growing older. It is not simply a matter of many crimes going unreported, but (as many young women said to us) of the whole spectrum of *cues* to fear – the man across the carriage staring fixedly at you, the man in the seat next to you whose knee nestles into yours each time the train lurches, the nervousness of sitting in an empty carriage at night, or worse, with that one unknown man sitting at the back of the carriage – which are underpinned by daily experience on and off the train. Only a few of our respondents spoke of actual sexual assault, but they consistently reported potential *indicators* of it. To argue (as senior New South Wales (NSW) transport managers did to us) that the gap between statistics of crime in NSW generally and crime on NSW trains not only indicates an irrational public ('it often comes down to just a pinch on the bum'), but also is 'caused' by a sensationalising media, misses this subjective reality and clings to a long outmoded model of communication, where people are seen as inert and passive 'receivers' of media messages.

The third problem is a complete undervaluing of human agency. Young women and older people have a wide range of strategies which they apply when they choose (or choose not) to go out in 'the neighbourhood at night'. So, too, do the group supposedly at the heart of the 'risk/fear' paradox – young males. Members of each group do fear public places at night and actively employ strategies of 'resistance' to these fears. But the active response of late-teenage boys is different from that of late-teenage girls. The latter articulate a variety of gender identities in their strategies for dealing with their fear of the unpredictable male stranger: going out in groups, surveying the carriage via reflections in the train window at night, sitting at the back of the carriage near the exit, and so on. But whereas young women adopt various active surveillance strategies targeted at one object – male (of any age) threat – late-teenage boys perceive a veritable anthropology of subcultural threats (whether from 'rednecks', 'westies', 'footies' or 'homies'), but then describe precisely where and when that threat resides, and what discursive strategies to adopt in response. The 'homies' are most feared because they target the trains as central to their own economy, and because young, non-car-driving males often need to travel by train to their gigs, movies, parties and so on.

So, to return to the narratives of our older lady with her crochet needle and the three younger women trying out sitting in separate carriages at night, these are women who, faced almost daily with a wide range of gendered inequities and minor harassments, are seeking a 'kind of adaptive "control"'. The young woman who told us this story also described the continuous harassment of a female colleague at work who was followed home via bus and train by a male, until she actually changed her job. These are real exploitations, to which the young women are finding whatever partial and 'fragmented' answers that they can.

'Lay knowledge', public environments and the media

How then can we employ this Wynne-style emphasis on the agency of 'lay knowledge' in the area of media and public 'landscapes of risk'. Virtually nothing has, to my knowledge, been done in this field. The classic studies of the media and fear of crime by Gerbner and colleagues were, in their own way, top-down, emphasising the public's fear of crime as an effect of mass television watching of a diet of 'mean world' content; and much of the debate around this work has been within an empiricist, top-down paradigm also (see Tulloch *et al.* 1998: vol. 1).

In contrast, Sparks (1992a) has criticised Gerbner's 'cultivation thesis' precisely because of its top-down and 'objectivist' assumptions. For Sparks a common limitation of both 'administrative' criminological and cultivation theory's worries over the mass media and fear of crime is the calibration of levels of fear against indices of exposure to risk. This is a legitimate but not exhaustive concern, because fear is not simply a quantity to be measured. It is, rather, a mode of perception which is constitutive of personal identity. To this extent it is not accurate to speak of fear as simply being 'caused' by a specific precipitating event. One should always see fear of crime as not 'irrational' but as *intelligibly* summarising a range of more diffuse anxieties about one's position and identity in the world (Sparks 1992a).

But despite Sparks' emphasis on multiple identities and the *lived experience* of fear-of-crime problems, and despite his critique of both 'cultivation' theorists like Gerbner and 'selective exposure' theorists like Barrie Gunter for a similarly reductive interpretation of texts, Sparks himself has not conducted empirical research to examine how 'lived experience' of fear of crime is woven through different people's media reception; or, to put it differently, how the perceived risk of crime is implicated in daily and routine practices. In the final section of this chapter, I give some examples of this kind of analysis from our fear of crime research. I shall look a little more systematically at responses to the media in focus groups in the city of Sydney, the tourist belt of the Blue Mountains and the rural town of Bathurst, New South Wales. These responses will take us a bit further with Sparks' agenda in examining

> different senses of the term 'fear' [that] may be operative for different circumstances and groups of people, so that women's fear might differ from men's, or the fears of the elderly from those of the young, not just in 'quantity' but in kind.
>
> (Sparks 1992a: 11)

My focus here is on interviews with older people only, mainly for reasons of space, but also because, as Pain (1997) has argued, there has been a systematic ageism built into many institutions (academic no less than media) in starting from the assumption of older people as 'elderly victims'. We might see the issue of older people and fear of crime differently if we start from the opposite assumption, as articulated in one of my opening quotations – of older people as agents.

All our focus group and long interview respondents were asked a series of questions about their media uses and pleasures, particularly in relation to the 'cynical, mean world' thesis of Gerbner *et al.* and also in relation to Sparks' interests in the narratives, iconography, genres and scheduling of crime on television. There is space to discuss only a few of these questions here: relating to crime 'experts', 'lay' experience or risk and 'landscapes of fear'.

Fear of crime, older people and the media

In choosing some of our focus groups we deliberately started from the assumption of situated agency. For example, the 'Combined Pensioners' focus group that we conducted in Sydney was primarily composed of working-class, long-term union activists. In addition, there was a woman, born in Ireland, who had experienced unemployment during the Depression of the 1930s, had been widowed young after coming to Australia and had then been 'forced to fight [her] own way in a new country'. Among our many other focus groups (chosen for their apparent differences in terms of age, gender, sexual preference and so on), here was one which might be expected to speak to Beck's emphasis on 'the exhaustion, dissolution and disenchantment of collective and group-specific sources of meaning' (1996a: 29), especially class consciousness). Or, to put it in Wynne's terms, to what extent would this group retain the specialist lay knowledge adhering to a lifetime of imposition?

This group of seniors emphasised strongly to us that they did not regard themselves at the 'passive' individualised end of the spectrum where Beck tends to position his risk citizens.

> We *do* discuss these things, and we *do* write letters that don't get printed . . . because we tell the truth about things. There was a big article of half a page attacking older people in the *Sun Herald*. . . . They were saying that the young were paying for the old. We wrote a letter giving them the statisticians' figures. . . . What we said is that it's not the young or the old that's causing these sort of things, it's the people escaping tax, and we named Packer and Murdoch as two that doubled their assets. But it wasn't printed. . . . In order to understand anything you've got to look at both sides of it. You've got to look for contradictions in things. . . . We've got to talk to other people, and we've got to unite with other people to band for our common interests. When we do that we'll start to get somewhere. But we're not going to get that with the press only looking at one side.
>
> (Male senior)

If the young and the old instead of being separated like that, they got together more.

(Female senior)

Clearly this is a rather 'militant' group – in Beck's world they have what Williams (1977) called a 'residual' structure of feeling. However, we could also see them as the collective equivalent to the 'emergent' grey-power conscious- ness of the woman I quoted earlier, who wanted to win back public spaces by 'going out in masses and showing *body*'.

Not all (or even most) older people speak this way, of course. The following conversation from two Bathurst seniors was more 'typical':

Husband: I guess I like to insulate myself. . . . I feel I want the good things in life, and I don't want all the bad things that are happening around the world constantly being thrown at me on television. It spoils the evening. It spoils everything for me – whether it's a con- stant lot of murder or whether it's Bosnia or whatever. So I'm some- thing of a chicken about it, I guess. I like to smell the roses.

Wife: I'll watch [the TV news] and I'll face it and I know that that kind of thing is going on. I'm not going to put my head in the sand like an ostrich and pretend it doesn't happen, nor do I think that it just couldn't happen here.

Husband: If I could qualify what I just said, I think the thing that triggers my attitude is that I feel *so* helpless in every one of these spheres – whether it's murders, whether it's drugs, whether it's poverty overseas, what- ever it is I just feel *so powerless* against all the forces that are around the world, and I guess that I just back away from it, sorry . . .

Wife: As I was growing up I never had this fear of crime. But now all I can say is that you're not safe – even in your own home or out at night, and I will not go out at night. . . .

Husband: I just think that our generation and our society has completely lost the battle as far as crime is concerned.

Though there is some variety of opinion in this Bathurst group of older peo- ple, none of them feels empowered: it is just that some watch the media more than others in order to know what to be fearful about in their own commu- nity. It is important to emphasise, though, that even among these more 'privatised' older people, most are not terrified into passivity by fear of crime.

No, we're not terrified by it. We feel sad about it that it's come to this sort of thing, that life's not as easy as it used to be.

In most cases, even the more 'privatised' seniors still move around public envi- ronments in the daytime, using a range of strategies: a whistle in the pocket, an apple and a crochet needle on the train, a purse hidden in an inside pocket when travelling down to Sydney, waiting in the bank if there is 'a mob of young people outside', never taking house keys to Sydney and so on. A married couple in their early 80s from Sydney actively sought out Asian restaurants in (the much feared) Cabramatta when their friend from the country visited; only rarely did we find an older woman like the one in Bathurst who had made her house into a fortress since her husband had died, and who no longer watched crime (in any genre), because it made her terribly fearful of 'home invasion'.

Yet, even as she privatised her life and turned off her TV, so this older woman scanned all the more avidly the local newspaper's court cases. There she found ample 'evidence' to support her view that unemployment and 'drugs' among young people led to the attacks on older people she was so fearful about. In other words, even while turning off one media form, she was actively turning to another circuit of communication to order conceptually at least, if not control, her fear. She was perhaps an extreme example of Beck's 'individualised' members of 'risk society', repeatedly discovering and justifying her outer world 'in personally changing constellations' (Beck 1996a: 30). But she was not 'fragmented' in a hyperreal world of simulations. As she turned away from Baudrillard's (1984) 'TV is the world' scenario, she reached actively for new logics-of-use in other media forms.

The point is that in all of these cases, from the long-term unionists (and their critique of multinationals and economic rationalism) to the frightened older woman in Bathurst (with her social equation: youth unemployment → drugs → home invasions), our respondents were – as Wynne (1996a) would predict – using 'systematic theory' as a central part of their 'adaptive coping with multiple dimensions in the same complex area'. The difference from Wynne's analysis, of course, is the role of the media itself in helping construct their 'lay knowledge'. Despite his critique of lay 'romanticism', there is a sense in which Wynne's hill farmers are both romanticised and constructed as single (if adaptive) entities, as though they, too, are not part of the complex and mediated processes of late-modernity.

There is insufficient space in this chapter to take this analysis of 'local' and 'mediated' knowledge very far. But by discussing two focus groups in particular – and their responses to specific questions about 'expert' sources of knowledge and about 'landscapes of fear' – perhaps I can begin to describe how this 'agentive' yet 'mediated' relationship can work.

Question: overall enjoyment of police series: do these make them feel better or more ill at ease about the world, or make no difference?

The focus group of Sydney seniors is a strong example of Sparks' point that fear of crime, far from being simply the result of direct experience of crime cannot 'be separated out from other experiences and hazards and troubles'

(Sparks 1992a: 12). This group of four men and three women (all 60+) was dominated by three men and one woman who regarded economic rationalism as the cause of crime through creating unemployment. Consequently, they argued that there is far too much focus on the effects of crime, rather than its causes, namely unemployment, the drug problem, power brokers and the big corporations. For some of this group it was the Australian media magnates who 'are the real criminals', doubling their assets in one year while 'economic rationalism is putting workers out by thousands'. They argued for an independent Australian Broadcasting Corporation (ABC), since this is the only channel where economic rationalist propaganda *may* not be peddled.

The group's choice and enjoyment of police shows tended to flow from these broader socio-economic worries. Most enjoyed *The Bill because* it is on the ABC ('I am opposed to privatisation, so I support the ABC') and because it is 'realistic . . . made in the streets, the police force as they are'. In contrast US police series were rejected because the group disliked the power of advertising on young people.

The Bathurst group of seniors (two men and four women of 60+) also liked *The Bill*, and contrasted the ABC shows with the (mainly US) police series that show too much graphic violence. But whereas the Sydney group contrasted the 'cause' (economic rationalism) and 'effect' of crimes and violence, this group contrasted 'after the crime' series (like *The Bill*) with 'before the crime' (mainly US) series which 'show people how to do it'. They worried that children are impressed by 'before the crime' police series and there was quite a high degree of worry in this group about rising crime rates among young people.

In other words, different 'systematic theories' underpinned these two groups' local and contextual knowledge, even though they both liked *The Bill* and disliked American cop series; one group was no less active than the other in adapting their lay theory from either media or experiential knowledge.

Question: pleasures in narrative: do they prefer shows where the police always win?

The Sydney group preferred good to win; but they defined 'good' as the opposite of 'the acquisitive society, where it's really big to make money . . . exploit your fellow man'. They would like to see television show the better side of people, helping each other. The Bathurst group also preferred it when good prevails, because 'it makes you feel better'. Overall, they worried that so many TV programmes are directed towards crime and violence, and thought that it is young people (in their 30s and younger) who want it. They believed these young people may thus become desensitised to violence. One woman, picking up this theme, described her grandchildren who come from a country property and 'only want guns' because their parents shoot kangaroos.

Again, each group actively chose its 'stories' in constructing their own theory of the 'risk society'.

Question: perception of a 'mean world': are images of the police (and crime) becoming more cynical?

The Sydney group once more focused on unemployment and the way in which the Australian right-wing One Nation politician, Pauline Hanson, is able to exploit divisions between Asians and others as a result. Further, 'the news media are concentrating on division', because that keeps the wealthy in power. There was agreement (via the woman who originated from Ireland) that there have always been divisions in Australia (between Catholics and Protestants, for example), always 'ghettos', and that immigrants have always brought crime problems with them. But there was also a feeling, via the discussion of Hanson, that things have become more cynical, partly as a result of media coverage of the Wood Royal Commission on police corruption. No one in the group was surprised at the corruption this revealed. For these older people, institutionalised crime is a systemic effect of power and monopoly control. One man spoke darkly of a friend's daughter who died on drugs: he told the police who the dealers were, but they did nothing.

The Bathurst group was quite sure that the world is much more mean because of television violence. One man described how his daughter (in her 30s) is so desensitised to violence that she recommended to him a film with 'appalling' violence in it. 'But my life has been insulated against it. And that's how I want to keep it. I don't want violence in my lounge room every night.' This is a group that tended to adopt a Gerbner-like mass mediated version of a 'mean world', unlike the more situated response of the Sydney group. But they also perceived generational differences. There was general agreement that the younger generation have been brought up on a diet of television crime and violence by 'TV as baby sitter' (and now via computer games), and so have less compassion and understanding about the reality of violence. Hence younger people will 'go and knock somebody on the head or kill somebody for a pair of joggers'. The feeling was that older people have a compassion that younger people have lost.

Question: feelings about crime representations of people and place: would they prefer crime shows that deal with their own or 'other' environments?

The Sydney group argued that 'the media doesn't accommodate our style of life' because of its need to sensationalise. Again, there was an emphasis from the men on the propaganda role of the media: 'the role of the media in our society is to mislead the ordinary Jack and Jill', hence the Hunter Valley miners' strike was not covered in its everyday reality but gave the 'Rio Tinto view'. As regards the urban environments that the media emphasise, two broad points were made by this group: first, that there has been far too much media focus (because of developers' interests) on further concentration of people into the coastal cities (one man compared this with Middle Eastern Arab countries which develop desert areas using artesian water); second, that media and advertising create consumerist expectations among the young, so that small inner-urban cottages which once everybody could afford are being torn down and 'grass castles' put up. There was also some emphasis on the 'society' orientation of media urban stories rather than about 'your ordinary Jo Blow'.

The Bathurst group emphasised the fear of AIDS and drugs (and the 'city' environment) that the media have brought into their country lives. One woman said she fears being raped at night in bed and getting AIDS; her experience of escalating violence on suburban trains ('No one is game to move to help anybody because you don't know when you're going to be jabbed with a needle') has added to this. 'I mean . . . if this reaches out into Bathurst, the same fear I and my family have in Sydney, then heaven help us.' A man said he feared break-ins much more now because drugs make burglars more unpredictable and dangerous. 'I've had no experience with drugs directly. But the television has taught me that people under the influence of drugs that break into your house are just maniacs. That's my biggest fear.' Others agreed with this, saying that it is the graphic images of television (rather than just reading about it in the local newspaper) that makes you aware of it. The general emphasis of the Bathurst seniors was of city and country life coming (unpleasantly) closer together via things like drug crimes, youth violence and AIDS.

Question: feelings about public space and 'big event' crimes

Because a top-down, all-powerful media theory (such as Gerbner's) might suggest that the saturation 'bombarding' of the public with 'big event' crimes (like the Port Arthur and Dunblane massacres, or the Atlanta Olympics bombing) would make the televiewing public even more convinced about a 'mean world', we asked people their responses to these televisual events. The Sydney group men felt that the main effect of the Port Arthur massacre was to increase the prime minister's popularity at the cost of the public as he peddled a rhetoric of 'gun reform', whereas guns in general are the result of the 'armament kings' making money. This led on to a discussion of imperialist countries using guns to control Africa, Europe and so on. 'Multinational capital is at the back of it', controlling for example development in Peru orAustralia, generating terrorism and so on. As regards the safety of public spaces, they argued for a routine return to 'more cops back on the beat', rather than any 'panic' law-and-order responses to the 'big event' crimes.

The Bathurst group spoke of being made much more fearful by events like the Port Arthur and the Strathfield shopping plaza massacres. One woman said that 'I found I couldn't go in a shopping centre. . . . I was petrified. I'm looking up and down escalators thinking who's going to blast us.' The women in the group would not contemplate going to Sydney during the Olympics for fear of terrorism. 'No one's going to tell me there won't be another Port Arthur.' One woman recalled visiting a friend in Sydney some years ago: 'All the windows were all guarded up, all with mesh and everything, and I thought, fancy having to live in a house like that, but now it's quite normal for people in Bathurst.'

Question: knowledge of the police: preferences vis-à-vis type and style of police series

There was quite a lot of direct experience of the police in the Sydney seniors group, particularly in relation to trade union matters. There was some agreement that many a young, local police officer 'will do his best to do the right thing' (though one man worried about the types who choose to go into the police force). The problem, they argued, was at the top because 'when the chips are down the job of the police is to protect capital, to protect big business'. They discussed different police attitudes to union marches and demonstrations. There was some agreement that media images of the police are positive (though some gave the example of news items on the Wood Royal Commission into police corruption against this).

The Bathurst group all had a positive image of the police, though they recognised the full spectrum 'from corruption to good police work'. Their preference was for British-style 'after the event' police series, rather than the more violent US series. They also worried about the violence on the news (including the ABC). 'Why do we have to see it over and over and over again, the same incident, night after night?'

In this section I have deliberately contrasted very different 'positive' and 'negative' responses to the possibility of agency among older people in controlling public environments, and in response to the media. More generally, as our quantitative data indicated, the negative view prevailed.

> We've lost the battle, it's gone. . . . I just think that our generation and our society has completely lost the battle as far as crime is concerned, and I think that the next twenty, thirty, forty, fifty years is going to be so bad that we're just going to lose it. We've got Asian organised crime coming into our country now and I think that the police are just powerless to cope with . . . the drug situation. . . . How I feel for my grandchildren is what I end up on: I think that our new generation coming on have just lost the battle, they're going to have terrible things happen. We lived in the best generation.
>
> (Male senior)

Older people, when they look past their own weakening bodies, also look both backwards and forwards, on behalf of their grandchildren. What they see is not a pretty picture: unemployment, crime, drugs, AIDS, corruption in high places, a widespread loss of ethics. According to their location and knowledge system, though, seniors inflect their reading of those problems (and with it their particular fears and anxieties) very differently. The result may make them either more or less determined to be active in the years they have before them.

Conclusion

I have not chosen to contrast the 'leftie' older group with the country seniors to indicate either a 'right' or a 'wrong' agency (though obviously our individual opinions on this will vary depending upon our own 'systematic theory'). Nor is the comparison meant to represent that one group draws on its own rich 'lay knowledge' in engaging the media while the other is 'bombarded' by the media into passivity. In fact, both groups draw on their own experiences to underpin their 'theory' – since the Bathurst woman who talks of her grandchildren shooting guns is drawing on personal experience just as much as the Sydney man who complains about the *Daily Telegraph's* article on older people.

If there was more space, I could have indicated the richness of 'lay knowledge' in many different, but contextually situated, locations; comparing for example the responses to these questions of older and younger people, of women and men, comparing gay teenagers living together in a refuge with heterosexual teenagers dependent on their parents to bring them back safely from the train station late at night, and would discuss their similar-but-different responses to the dual threat – from 'homies' and 'sharkfuckers' (surfies), or from police and train security guards – in public places around Sydney. In all of these lay micro-narratives and adaptive strategies, 'landscapes of fear' were symbolically situated in everyday pleasures and practices, and media genres and representations were reflexively negotiated.

If analysts of postmodern media are right that criminality and risk have become the metaphor for the condition of postmodern fragmentation itself, it is important to remember the many (but experientially *situated*) micro-narratives via which people actively negotiate this condition. On the one hand, they add to the 'fragmentation'; but on the other they remind us as 'experts' to 'return to questions of the effects of the mass media at the social level in lived culture' (Osborne 1995: 43). That will require not only a critique of top-down 'scientific' expert discourse (as in Wynne 1996a), but, as Osborne says, also a critique of postmodernist theory.

A problem with both Baudrillard's and Beck's approaches to media and risk is that neither has a situated theory of the media. For Baudrillard, the world *is* TV. For Beck (1992a: 137) the 'networked media world' is just one of the autonomously operating 'subsystem rationalities' of reflexive modernisation, via which individuals 'self-confront' the contest between expert and counter-expert groups. The individual seems more passive than ever, as the experts dump their contradictions and conflicts at the feet of the individual and leave him or her with the well-intentioned invitation to judge this critically on the basis of his or her notions. With detraditionalization and the creation of global media networks, the biography is increasingly removed from its direct spheres of contact and opened up across the boundaries of countries and experts *for a long distance morality*. . . . [The] continual excessive demand [of world society] can only be tolerated through the opposite reaction of not listening, simplifying, and apathy.

(Beck 1992a: 137)

This is all too passive and pessimistic at the everyday, individual level. I argue that an approach to media and risk via the situated analysis of 'lay' micro-narratives not only re-emphasises the agency of individual adaptive control and 'lay systematic theory' (as Wynne argues), but also indicates that the biography (far from being 'removed from its direct spheres of contact') is still in local, daily affiliation with social identities of class, gender, sexual preference, age and ethnicity (as well as contesting any one of these 'prisons' of identity; see Ang 1996: ch. 7). These, as much as the single issue 'pragmatic alliances in the individual struggle for existence' that Beck (1992a: 101) emphasises, continue to be central to people's self-understandings and sense of control in the face of public 'landscapes of fear'.

Part IV

Globalising environments at risk

Chapter 13

Communicating climate change through the media

Predictions, politics and perceptions of risk

Kris M. Wilson

Global climate change may be the greatest environmental risk of our time. Of all time. It has the potential to affect all of Earth's inhabitants, like previous climatic change has, but perhaps in a shorter time-frame and on a larger scale. It could alter life as we know it in many arcane, unpredictable ways. Notice the careful phrasing – 'may be', 'potential', 'perhaps', 'unpredictable' and 'could'. These words are used *not* to diminish the threat that this environmental risk portends, but only to highlight the dynamic state of climate change science and the careful way scientists' phrase their findings. Unlike previous climatic changes, this one is being observed, predicted, studied, analysed and perhaps adapted to because of scientific discoveries.

Most world citizens will not learn about climate change research directly from the cautious lexicon in scientific journals, however, but rather from the mass media. Increasingly it is the media's responsibility to translate complex, scientific concepts to the 'lay audience'. For the public, the reality of science is what they learn from the media (Nelkin 1987). Research confirms this is especially true with the science of climate change (K. Wilson 1995; Bell 1994b). It is a large responsibility, one that the modern media, bereft of environmental reporters and specialists, is challenged to meet. Often what are portrayed in the media are not carefully worded scientific findings, but rather dramatic, eye-catching, entertaining stories that attract audiences but do little to enlighten them about the risks associated with climate change.

'SCIENTISTS SAY THERE'S NO GREENHOUSE EFFECT' screams the egregious headline of a daily US Midwest newspaper. Regretfully, this reporter, or more likely the headline writer, has misunderstood basic atmospheric science and exacerbated public confusion about climate change. While there is debate about the models used to predict future climates, all scientists agree that life on Earth is possible only with the greenhouse effect. The greenhouse effect is the most established theory in all of atmospheric science (Kellogg 1991). While it is a poor metaphor for how our atmosphere actually functions, no credible scientist would ever say there is no such thing as a greenhouse effect. The body of this news report successfully discerned the research which showed no significant warming of the continental USA at night during the twentieth century, but the headline writer got it wrong and yet another erroneous communication occurred. This chapter analyses underlying causes for why these errors and inaccuracies in environmental reporting may occur and how they have affected public comprehension of climate change.

Added to the scientific and journalistic quagmire is the increasingly fractious political milieu of climate change. Precisely because climate change is directly related to how we live, the issue strikes raw nerves. US President Bill Clinton announced in the summer of 1997 that the 'global warming science is clear and compelling', and proceeded to direct US policy leading up to the December 1997 Kyoto Summit. This marked a dramatic shift in policy from previous administrations and brought about a strong response. Reporters in the USA are now inundated with 'news releases' from a variety of invested sources seeking to get their climate change position heard in the press. Perhaps the most pervasive, *The Climate Report* (published by the University of Virginia and edited by Patrick Michaels), is sent free to hundreds of US journalists. Michaels is an outspoken critic of current climate change science, while often neglecting to mention that his publication is funded by Western Fuels Corporation, a major energy provider in the USA. Headlines in his benignly named bi-weekly glossy scream, 'ABC-TV, [vice-president AL] GORE IN GLOBAL WARMING LOVE STORY', 'TOP TEN GLOBAL WARMING MYTHS' and 'IPCC HEAD DOWN UNDER'. Like many headlines, they certainly grab attention, but work on the same principles Michaels publicly deplores about mass media coverage of climate change.

The Climate Report spends much of its time criticising the Intergovernmental Panel on Climate Change (IPCC) research. The IPCC consists of more than two thousand of the world's leading atmospheric scientists charged with creating climate change consensus. Scientific consensus is rarely achieved, and Michaels and a handful of other scientists remain unconvinced that climate change can be proven to be a real threat and have created their own sophisticated public relations machine to contradict the messages from the IPCC. Many reporters, untrained in science and scientific research methods, are caught in the middle of this seemingly contentious scientific debate. Too often, reporting has promoted an ersatz 'balance' of the scientific debate.

Global climate change has evolved into a scientific and political lightning rod, challenging us to develop new connections among science, public policy and journalism. This chapter begins with a synopsis of the science of climate change, including a discussion of why the scientific debate about modelling occurs. An analysis of some of the constraints to good climate change journalism follows; then a brief discussion of two pieces of recent relevant research are considered with recommendations on how to improve the process of climate change communication through the media.[1]

The science of climate change

The greenhouse effect is not a new scientific theory. As early as the nineteenth century, some scientists began to speculate on the effects of increased carbon released into the atmosphere by the burning of fossil fuels (Arrhenius 1896). Nevertheless, the intriguing idea that humanity could raise Earth's temperature seems at first to have attracted surprisingly little attention in the scientific community and even less in the public media (Kellogg 1988). This pattern continued even into the 1960s, identified as an era with high interest in environmental issues (Nelkin 1987). In 1965, the President's Science Advisory Committee (PSAC) published the first government report to recognise that climate change could be caused by human activities and that this would have important consequences for the world (PSAC 1965). Two years later, the first of more than a hundred atmospheric models predicted that a doubled carbon dioxide content should raise the average surface temperature of Earth 1.5 °C–3 °C (Manabe and Weatherald 1967). Those estimates remained largely unchanged in the mid-1990s (IPCC 1995).

The climate of Earth has always fluctuated. Eighteen thousand years ago vast expanses of North America were covered in ice sheets at the peak of the last glacial maximum. Six thousand years ago the planet was warmer than it is today, what some scientists refer to as the climatic optimum (Kutzbach and Guetter 1986). Current concern is not with the natural variations of Earth's climate, but a possible anthropogenic change that could be unprecedented in its rapid onset, making adaptation for many plant and animal species (humans included) difficult or impossible.

The Earth's climate operates on a balanced energy budget. So-called greenhouse gases, which include carbon dioxide, methane, nitrous oxides, various chlorofluorocarbons (CFCs) and water vapour, help to keep Earth habitable by trapping long-wave radiation and preventing it from escaping to space. The delicate balance keeps Earth's temperature at roughly 15 °C (Lindzen 1989). The amount of greenhouse gases in the composition of the atmosphere is relatively small. Currently carbon dioxide comprises only 0.03 per cent of the atmosphere, and the remaining greenhouse gases are in even smaller concentrations (IPCC 1992). All scientists agree that the amounts of these trace greenhouse gases are increasing in the atmosphere (Schneider 1990a). The consensus also concurs that a global temperature increase of 0.45 °C ± 0.15 °C has already occurred since temperature records began (IPCC 1995). This temperature increase could indicate the beginning of a period of global warming or merely reflect the natural variation of the climate. Unlike journalism with its daily deadlines, scientific analyses of these kinds of data will only be accurately interpreted over time. The temperature record remains part of the scientific consensus, but has been criticised by some because of its short duration, changes in methods of recording, and gaps that occur over the vast expanse of the oceans (Michaels 1997).

The task of predicting future climate change is extremely complex. Perhaps the most common approach to understanding future climate involves the use of General Circulation Models (GCMs). These are three-dimensional representations of the atmosphere that can require treatment of some 200,000 equations, with each equation then requiring extensive calculations (MacDonald 1989). More than 100 independent estimates of average surface temperature increase have been made since the 1960s using increasingly sophisticated models, and almost all of the estimates lie in the range of a 1.5 °C to 4.5 °C temperature increase with a doubling of carbon dioxide (M. Schlesinger and Mitchell 1985). Revisions from model sources have lowered the predicted temperature increase to 1 °C to 3.5 °C (IPCC 1995).

The models also all agree that a warmer world will be a cloudier world through increased evapo-transpiration (Henderson-Sellers 1989). The models disagree, however, on whether the increased cloud cover will be primarily low level stratus, which will reflect more of the sun's rays and lead to a negative feedback, or whether they will be predominately higher level cirrus clouds leading to a positive feedback and exacerbating the warming. How clouds are treated within the models leads to much of the variation in predicted temperature increases. Climate change sceptics also say they have concerns about how the GCMs atmosphere interacts with the oceans, soil, ice and vegetation (Michaels 1997; Lindzen 1989).

Finally, and perhaps most importantly with regards to news reporting, although the models do show consistency with respect to increased global temperature and precipitation, regional predictions of temperature and precipitation remain problematic due to the large grid size (Hansen and Takahashi 1984). Unfortunately for journalists, local angles to global stories are often the 'hook' they desire for their reports. Focusing on the predicted local effects of global climate change, however, is a recipe for 'the duelling scientist scenario'. That is the tendency for reporters to play one scientist against another in a colossal debate about the future, each one peering into his or her own crystal ball, through the use of GCMs, to try and predict small-scale changes decades in advance. Even with the latest high technology Doppler radar, forty-eight hour local weather forecasts remain problematic, let alone prognostications a half-century into the future.

This focus on possible future effects began immediately when global warming first came to public attention. Even though scientists have been studying the thermal capacities of increased greenhouse gases for almost a century, the topic did not make most news agendas in the USA until June 1988. Not until a top US National Aeronautics and Space Administration (NASA) scientist, James Hansen, testified before the US Congress that he was 99 per cent confident that global warming was here, did the story make the front page of most national newspapers. Perhaps serendipity played an important part in that timing since the USA was embroiled in a long, hot summer that culminated in a prolonged drought. If the weather had not been so extreme, some say the media and the public would not have listened any more closely to Hansen than they had to previous reports (Hertsgaard 1990). Other events, such as the Kyoto Summit, El Niño's dramatic return and the eruption of Mount Pinatubo have also contributed to the fluctuation of climate change reporting. Although not part of his study, climate change reporting could also suffer from the cyclic reporting of environmental issues that Downs (1972) discovered.

Global warming reporting began with catastrophism, with dramatic overstatements at the beginning of a new finding as a news hook, and now uncertainties are being overstated as part of a new hook to a story that is generally accepted (Moorti 1991). Too often the coverage focused on unrelated weather events and whether they were linked to anticipated global warming, and many times scientists instigated this kind of reporting.

Duelling scientists

Some scientists say the media have already accepted global warming as fact and have not given enough attention to the unanswered questions (Lindzen 1989). Other scientists suggest that the press has spent too much time focusing on statements by a handful of global warming sceptics (Lashoff 1990).

> Scientists are quick to condemn the media, to criticise the quality of science reporting, and to attribute negative or naive public attitudes toward science to the images conveyed in the press. . . . Yet they are often unable to document their complaints, to specify what is wrong.
>
> (Nelkin 1987: x)

Several studies have sought to do just that. Tankard and Ryan (1974) documented greater numbers of errors and inaccuracies in science reporting than in general news reporting. Tichener (1970) measured scientists' satisfaction with press stories of their own research compared with general science story accuracy, and Bell (1994b) distinguished between six different types of inaccuracies in climate change reporting.

To many journalists, the biggest constraint to good reporting is in the jargon of science and with scientists themselves (Detjen 1991). Most journalists place the blame for poor science journalism on their sources of information, that is with scientists and their institutions (Nelkin 1987). Another science writer described the uneasy relationship this way:

> Scientists think that whatever they tell a reporter is bound to come out wrong. Most ordinary reporters would practically cross the street to avoid running into an expert since they consider scientists to be unemotional, uncommunicative, unintelligible creatures who are apt to use differential logarithms against them the way Yankee pitchers use inside fast balls and breaking curves.
>
> (Burrows 1980: 15)

In some cases the lines between scientist and journalist blur. 'The current global warming debate: is it science or just media hype' (Schneider 1990a: 31)? Even Schneider, one of the pre-eminent climate change scientists, cannot find an easy answer to the question, since he is part of both the hype *and* the science.

> Scientists need to get some broad-based support, to capture the public imagination. That of course entails getting loads of media coverage. So we have to offer up scary scenarios, make simplified, dramatic statements, and make little mention of any doubts we might have. Each of us has to decide what the right balance is between being effective and being honest.
>
> (Schneider 1990a: 33)

Certainly this cantankerous atmosphere among scientists is accountable for some of the miscommunication to and within the media about climate change, but there are some other intrinsic characteristics of journalism that also contribute.

Journalistic hazards

Climate change is a difficult story to recreate for a daily news budget, while a short-term drought episode (or any other weather event) is much easier to visualise and portray. The global warming story is one of the most complicated stories of our time. It involves abstract and probabilistic science, labyrinthine laws, grandstanding politicians, speculative economics, and the complex interplay of individuals and societies (Stocking and Leonard 1990). The global warming story is also affected by a number of journalistic constraints, such as deadlines, space, one-source stories, complexity and reporter education.

Ninety seconds of testimony is dull video for television, but images of scorched land, sweaty brows on farmers and shots of the blazing sun all add the requisite spice to the climate change story. Mother Nature co-operated in the summer of 1988, providing the visuals of drought as scientists warned about possible future droughts in an enhanced greenhouse world. Whether the two are actually linked is impossible for current science to evaluate, but the images are now part of the televised portrayal of a greenhouse world. These pictures, visual metaphors, set the television agenda of a greenhouse world. More than simply a source of information about science, the press plays a significant judgemental role (Nelkin 1987). By their choice of words and metaphors journalists convey certain beliefs about the nature of science, investing them with social meaning and shaping public conceptions.

Common metaphors used in television coverage of climate change included comparisons with nuclear war and the 1930s dustbowl (Wilkins and Patterson 1991). This focus on possible consequences set the stage for continuing media debates about the uncertainty of future predictions, while relegating what is known and agreed upon to scientific journals. Hansen never said that he was 99 per cent confident that increased greenhouse gases had caused the record warmth and drought of 1988, but according to some scientists, such an inference was drawn and widely reported in the media (Schneider 1990b). Finding 'good pictures' constrains television coverage of many important science stories, and in the case of climate change, television's visual portrayal was a key element in promoting the 'duelling scientist' debate over global warming.

Content analyses of print coverage of climate change also showed inconsistencies in reporting. National papers tended to address the national and international ramifications of climate variability, with regional papers focusing on local effects (Moorti 1991). Science writers used the term 'greenhouse effect' as a label, while non-science writers preferred the term 'global warming' (Wilkins 1993). Differences in media portrayals were found to correlate with knowledge disparities noted among a population of college students in the surveys to be discussed later.

As the term implies, news is the desire to find a new angle to stories. This hunger contributes to the well-known issue-of-the-month syndrome. It allows persistent and growing environmental problems to slide out of sight if there is nothing 'new' to report (Stocking and Leonard 1990). The climate change story fits this category well. Often the only time that climate change becomes news is when a fresh study on predicted effects is released, which either corroborates previous work or contradicts it. In the constant effort to present a 'balanced' view, a reporter will seek an opposing opinion and controversy is created once again. The underlying causes and long-term consequences are often overlooked in the day-to-day grind to find a new angle by deadline. After Hansen's testimony on Capitol Hill, many journalists around the USA started calling scientists, wanting to know if global warming was responsible for the drought. Good scientists explained that one particular drought could not be linked to global warming (Schneider 1989) and good journalists reported the story that way (Wilkins and Patterson 1991).

Another influence on good climate change reporting is the overwhelming pressure of deadlines, which tends to make the stories overly simplified and one-sided. Under the pressure of a deadline, it is easy to rely on one source (Dunwoody 1986a), which can alter the balance of a story and lead to a duelling scientist scenario. In the early 1990s, research suggested that sources are not constant. One study found climate change sources initially were scientists and then official government sources (Wilkins and Patterson 1991). Another uncovered a substantial shift to policy-makers increasingly being used as information sources (Moorti 1991).

The complexity of the climate change story also acts as a constraint to good reporting and increased public knowledge. Reporters tend to explain their tendency to oversimplify as necessary to keep their readers' or viewers' attention (Nelkin 1987), which may also perpetuate the perception that the media gloss over complicated stories like climate change. Climate change is a complex issue, nearly impossible to relate in 20-second soundbites that pervade the industry. This complexity acts as a constraint because journalists may not know how to recognise what is important and may, therefore, miss a newsworthy story.

Complexity is a serious problem for reporters with little or no science back-ground and for news organisations that rely on general assignment reporters to cover climate change. At most US news operations, science stories are usually covered by general assignment reporters who are expected to handle a wide range of stories, but who also lack any kind of scientific training. Lacking both training and experience, they are less able to evaluate what they are reporting (Nelkin 1987). Science-trained journalists can be more critical about shoddy research methods and are less likely to take what they are told at face value than their untrained colleagues (Dunwoody 1986b).

Climate change is also an example of a story that requires not only good journalism skills and scientific literacy, but also an understanding of political dynamics. Media coverage of political issues is not a one-way street, but rather it influences both the public and decision-making elites in obvious and more subtle ways (Wilkins 1990). With regards to climate change reporting, Wilkins notes that the science writers knew the science, and in both 1987 and 1988 they reported the science accurately, but the science writers either did not understand the politics of global warming, believed that politics was not per-tinent to what they were reporting or were unwilling to tread on some other reporter's beat to get the political side of the story. This unwillingness to grapple with political questions came despite the fact that at least some scientists were insisting that global warming had important political ramifi-cations. The political and economic writers' stories reflected the same problem: because the science was not covered, the politics lost its edge (Wilkins 1990). This is especially problematic today, and into the future, as the issue becomes even more politically polarised.

Finally, the portrayal of risk provides a unique nexus between journalism and other disciplines, such as psychology and sociology. Particularly in psychology research, one common thread that applies to climate change is concerned with decision-making during uncertainty and perceptions of risk (Krimsky 1982). Research suggests that the relationship between reports of risk and audience responses can also be quite complex. Perceptions of risk are affected not only by the science, but also by feelings of worry or dread about the threat, and by the extent to which the threat is understood (Slovic 1992). Research has discovered a divergence between objective, measurable risks discerned by sci-entific experts and social perceptions of those risks and insinuates that media coverage of risk is largely responsible for the disparity (Viscusi 1992).

A variety of risk threats have been studied including nuclear incidents, asbestos, food tampering, water safety and environmental catastrophes (earth-quakes, floods, hurricanes). Climate change has not yet received such extensive attention, but is the focus of this chapter.

Results and recommendations

Despite extensive media attention since the summer of 1988, global climate change remains a challenge to lay comprehension (Kempton 1990). Ethnographic interviews with a small sample of Americans were conducted in Kempton's study to determine how ordinary citizens conceptualised global warming. Twelve of the fourteen individuals sampled had heard of global warming, but all held fundamental misconceptions about the process. Kempton (1990) made a leap of faith when he connected the lack of lay comprehension to media coverage because his study made no attempt to determine from where those individuals had received their information.

Two surveys, one of college students and another of environmental reporters, were used to measure climate change knowledge and sources of knowledge. The student survey confirmed the important role of the media in disseminating climate change information. About half of the students (50.7 per cent) said the media were their primary sources of climate change knowledge, in spite of consistent research (Roper 1998) which indicates that college students are notoriously low consumers of media. Students preferred television as a climate change source over print sources by a two to one margin. This figure was higher than has been reported in previous mass communication research on sources of information; earlier 53 per cent of college students identified television as their primary media source for information (Lucas and Schmitz 1988). Reliance on classroom sources of knowledge was also very high and allowed for the creation of three cohorts (television, print and classroom) for comparisons of knowledge acquisition based on source of knowledge.

Most of the 649 students (94 per cent) said they were familiar with the term global warming, but follow-up questions discovered that most students were confused about its meaning. Almost half of the students (48 per cent) incorrectly thought that global warming and the greenhouse effect were the same thing (Figure 13.1). Only 15 per cent of the students acknowledged the scientific agreement on the theory of global warming, but more thought that the topic was still strongly debated among scientists.

Additionally, less than half of the students acknowledged the scientific certainty of the greenhouse effect (Figure 13.2). The foundations for the duelling scientist scenario are already apparent, even in areas where there is no debate.

Reporters also exhibited confusion about the science of climate change. Several factors have now been identified that affect reporters' climate change knowledge and their ability to report on it effectively (K. Wilson 1998). In this chapter, reference to the reporters' survey will be made largely to elucidate the connections to student survey findings. Exactly the same percentage of reporters (45 per cent) as students correctly identified the greenhouse effect as a scientific certainty. About one-third of the reporters (34 per cent) answered correctly that the global warming theory is accepted by most scientists, and fewer reporters (30 per cent) than students incorrectly assumed that global

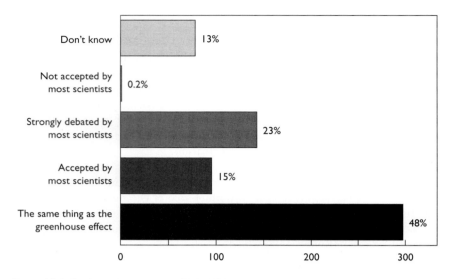

Figure 13.1 Student responses to 'Global Warming is ...'

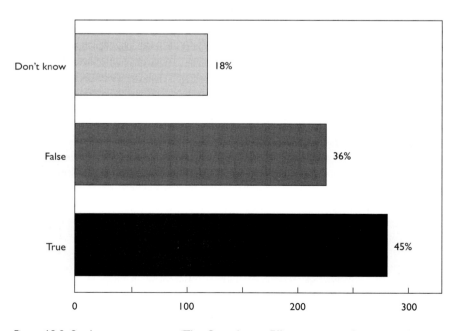

Figure 13.2 Student responses to 'The Greenhouse Effect is a scientific certainty'

warming and the greenhouse effect were interchangeable terms. More reporters (32 per cent) than students, however, believed that the theory was still strongly debated. These numbers help explain why so much climate change reporting has focused on the small area of scientific debate, creating 'he said, she disagreed' reporting. Controversy is great for ratings and circulation, but obviously constrains effective climate change reporting and public education.

These misconceptions may also be related to improper use of terminology and contribute to the inaccurate headline noted earlier. Global warming and the greenhouse effect are not synonymous terms. Enhanced greenhouse effect is more accurate nomenclature as it acknowledges the scientific foundation of the greenhouse effect. Global warming can also be problematic vernacular because it focuses on just one effect of increased greenhouse gas concentrations in our atmosphere, but its use is widespread and generally accepted. Global climate change is the most fitting term because it includes the wider range of resultant effects and more accurately depicts the science.

Another contributor to both student and reporter confusion may be the inflamed rhetoric used by sources. Given the polemic language some scientists and politicians use, it is not surprising that confusion about basic climate change concepts is so widespread: 97 percent of both students and reporters thought that the public was confused about global warming (and their own survey results confirmed this). Both groups, however, were reluctant to specifically blame either scientists or the media for such confusion (Figures 13.3 and 13.4), but politicians scored the highest as individual sources of confusion in both surveys. In Australia, the media and politicians were viewed as most responsible for public confusion about global warming (Henderson-Sellers 1989).

Other areas of ignorance and misunderstanding were noted in both surveys. High numbers of students recognised certain greenhouse gases, such as carbon dioxide (60 per cent) and CFCs (59 per cent) and their sources, automobile emissions (87 per cent) and aerosol propellants (83 per cent). There was broad ignorance, however, about other important greenhouse gases, such as methane (40 per cent) and nitrous oxide (28 per cent) and their sources, cattle production (45 per cent), fertilisers (33 per cent) and rice agriculture (14 per cent). As a group, the student population tended to inflate the scientific predictions of increased drought and hotter summers in the USA, while seriously underestimating the scientific consensus about increased global precipitation and cloud cover. Those students who said that they relied on television, especially local television news, had the poorest contextual basis for understanding climate change. Students who relied on these sources had less cognitive knowledge about greenhouse gases and their sources, and the most inaccurate view of future risks associated with climate change. Clearly the television portrayal of the inflammatory debate and focus on predicted effects has left an indelible impression on these viewers.

When considering perceptions of risk, measuring attitudes and values in the affective domain provides supplemental illumination to the acquisition of

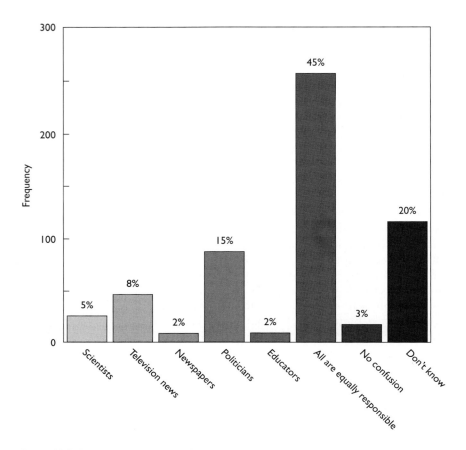

Figure 13.3 Student responses to 'Whom do you think is most responsible for public confusion about global warming?'

cognitive knowledge. In this study, students responded to eighteen Likert scale questions to discern their attitudes and values about global warming. Students in all three cohorts strongly agreed that global warming is a serious problem (Figure 13.5). Follow-up questions showed that students had very little awareness, however, of possible responses to this potential risk and by their own measure, students in all three groups felt unprepared to influence public policy on global warming (Figure 13.5).

Akin to the cognitive domain, students who said that they relied on television demonstrated some unique traits in the affective domain as well but not with the same patterns as in the cognitive domain. Students who relied primarily on local television news were least convinced of the seriousness of global warming (Table 13.1). The t-test of means showed that the mean for local TV

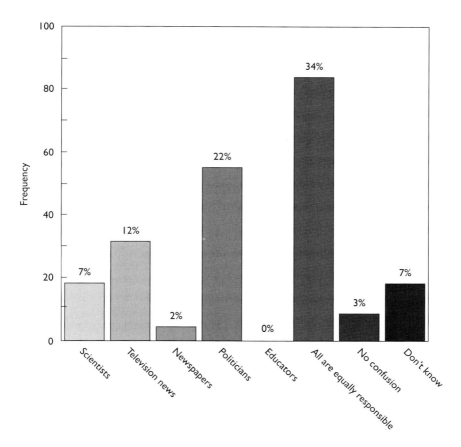

Figure 13.4 Reporter responses to 'Whom do you think is most responsible for public confusion about global warming?'

viewers was statistically significant with every other group of students. Duelling scientists strike again!

Very few students relied on public television to inform them about climate change, but those who did were statistically more aware of individual responses to potential climate change than all other groups (Table 13.1). These public TV viewers could be self-selecting in terms of their individual propensity to seek out longer form programming, but these findings could also suggest that it is exactly that kind of journalism that leads to greater affective understanding of climate change. Instead of a 60-second local news story that focuses exclusively on two disagreeing scientific 'experts', public television can present a 60-minute programme that not only includes that scientific debate, but also adds other necessary details to help the audience understand the political and

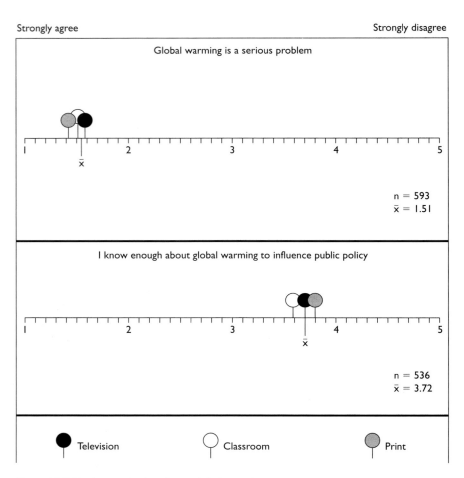

Figure 13.5 Student attitudes about global warming

scientific context of climate change. Even though few students relied on public television, all students held public television in highest regard as a climate change knowledge source, while rating both local TV news and newspapers as equal but significantly less valuable sources of knowledge.

This research discovered that it is not accurate or appropriate to indiscriminately blame 'the media' or even 'television' for public confusion about climate change. Results suggest that it is *how* television journalism operates that affects the transference of information to the audience, not just the medium itself. Summary results from the reporter survey illuminate several of these 'how's' that contribute to quality climate change reporting.

The reporters with the most accurate climate change knowledge were found

Table 13.1 Differences between means with student attitudes about global warming by
source of knowledge

| Source (n) | $\bar{x}$ | *Global warming is a serious problem* | | | |
		Source (n)	$\bar{x}$	t	p
Local TV (52)	1.81	Public TV (47)	1.36	3.06	0.003
Local TV	1.81	National TV (93)	1.46	2.75	0.007
Local TV	1.81	Newspapers (58)	1.50	2.08	0.04
Local TV	1.81	Classroom (248)	1.49	2.72	0.007
		As an individual I can do very little about global warming			
Public TV (43)	4.16	Classroom (237)	3.79	−2.37	0.019
Public TV	4.16	Newspapers (61)	3.62	−2.42	0.017
Public TV	4.16	Local TV (46)	3.47	−2.91	0.005
Public TV	4.16	National TV (90)	3.79	−2.21	0.029

to be full-time environmental specialists who primarily used scientists as sources. Unfortunately there were few reporters who fit this description. While the student population said they primarily relied on television for climate change knowledge, reporters said they preferred newspapers (37 per cent) and then scientists (20 per cent) as primary sources. These findings mark another shift in the use of climate change sources, from scientists (Wilkins 1990), to policy-makers (Moorti 1991), to now newspapers. This is a startling finding that has implications for the audience. Instead of going to direct sources of information, in this case scientists, these reporters say that they prefer previously published media reports. Reporters who said that they relied on newspapers were found to be significantly less knowledgeable about climate change than reporters who primarily relied on scientists. Any error or miscommunication in a previous media report could be passed along this 'news food chain', exacerbating any public misconceptions or misunderstandings. Science training and background was found to be less correlated with reporters' climate change knowledge than being a full-time specialist and using scientists as sources.

Given the overall poor showing of students who said they relied on television, statistical tests were also designed to measure differences in reporter knowledge based on job classification. About 9 per cent of the reporter sample said that they were employed in television, which is exactly TV's composition of The Society of Enviromental Journalists membership. While that qualifies as a valid sample, the overall low numbers of TV reporters made further statistical comparisons unreliable. Patterns of lower knowledge among local TV news reporters were apparent, but could not be confirmed statistically. This finding alone presents a pernicious predicament. Students, and by inference the public, are relying on television as their primary climate change knowledge source, yet the medium is poorly prepared to meet that responsibility. Not only are there few environmental reporters employed in television, but their numbers continue to decline (Detjen 1997) and very few are full-time, the attribute found to most positively influence reporters' climate change knowledge.

A final recommendation, synthesising previous research findings in conjunction with results from these two surveys, is embodied in a proposed five-part print or electronic media series on climate change (Table 13.2).

This model is not meant to be prescriptive, but merely act as a template that can be adapted for specific needs. It may be especially useful for general assignment reporters who are expected to cover climate change without significant science background or training. It is based on a decade of my own television news experience, a doctorate in geography with an emphasis in climatology and climate change, and a summary consideration of the research. From the journalistic perspective, this prototype works as a highly promotable series (especially during television's ratings periods) that can attract audiences from night to night. The reports can still provide the sensational, dramatic, contentious debate that content analyses say are common, but they also supply needed context. From the scientific perspective, the series provides important foundations to help the audience understand how scientific inquiry works and where and why scientific uncertainties exist. Instead of focusing exclusively on the debate over future modelling, an organised, extended series provides the necessary context that the survey results indicate are currently lacking.

Table 13.2 Proposed media series on global climate change

Monday	The science of global warming Scientific certainty – the greenhouse effect and global increases in greenhouse gases Scientific consensus – historical temperature records and predicted temperature increase with a doubling of greenhouse gases Scientific debate – magnitude, timing, and type of predicted effects
Tuesday	Explaining the scientific method How does the greenhouse effect work? Distinction between the terms greenhouse effect and global warming and enhanced greenhouse effect
Wednesday	Identification of greenhouse gases and their sources
Thursday	Analysis of the debate of predicted effects How do scientists predict future climates? Explanation of General Circulation Models and Paleoclimates. What do models agree on (global temperature and precipiation increases)? What are their weaknesses (regional predictions)?
Friday	Personal action responses Presentations of alternative energy developments, increased energy efficiency options, and the effect of increased energy taxes Creating personal empowerment to act in response to climate change

This five-part series ends with what communications research has consistently identified as the 'call to action'. Results from the student survey indicated a high recognition of the risk associated with potential climate change, but very low levels of understanding how to appropriately respond. This has created not only public confusion, but also a perception of impotency to properly respond to the risk of climate change. This proposed series is not recommending advocacy journalism, telling people what they should do, but rather presenting possible responses to the audience that allows them to make a decision about their own behaviours and how their policy-makers should represent them. Such a archetype has its roots in the growing civic journalism movement reflected in journalism today. Instead of a feeling of powerlessness about some highly debated esoteric scientific abstraction, this proposed series could empower an audience not only to understand the science more fully but also then to decide for themselves how serious an issue climate change is, and what personal responses, if any, are appropriate.

Other valuable, non-partisan resources exist for journalists. The National Safety Council and the Environmental Health Center (1994) have published *Reporting on Climate Change: Understanding the Science*, which is an excellent lay guide to the science and how to report it. Many organisations, including the Society of Environmental Journalists and the Radio and Television News Foundation, also sponsor workshops and training to assist reporters in covering climate change.

Conclusion

A well-informed public is essential to promote public policy on climate change (IPCC 1992). This chapter has confirmed the importance of the media, especially television, to provide this necessary information. Citizens need accurate and understandable information, but unfortunately, many of the recent articles on global change are either sensational, technical or too abstract for the general public, and do not help people make a connection between their everyday actions and the impending long-term global changes that will probably take place (Spranger 1989). This chapter has analysed several causes for this kind of reporting and offered recommendations on improving future media communication of climate change so that we can all be better prepared to make the kinds of policy decisions that climate change demands of us.

Note

1 The two climate change surveys referred to in this chapter include one administered to 649 undergraduate students at the University of Colorado at Boulder and a second of 249 reporters who were members of the Society of Environmental Journalists. The questionnaires were divided into two sections, one on personal information and media usage, and a second on knowledge of global warming. Those 76 questions were based on the IPCC scientific consensus. Both surveys were anonymous and confidential.

Chapter 14

Global citizenship, the environment and the media

Bronislaw Szerszynski and Mark Toogood

We live in an age when a combination of technological change and global economic restructuring means that environmental risks – especially those associated with ionising radiation, toxic pollutants and carbon dioxide emissions – are increasingly exceeding society's capacity to predict, control, geographically locate and causally attribute (Beck 1992a). At the same time, the growing reach of communications technology seems to be offering the possibility of a global civil society, a public space for debate, concern and action in relation to environmental and humanitarian issues of global scale or global distance (see, for example, Keane 1991: 135 ff.). The widespread, mediated awareness of global environmental risks, and the capacity for environmental groups to organise and communicate at the global level, has laid the grounds for a cultural 'remoralisation' in which individuals think and act in relation to global categories and values (Beck 1998b: 75; Albrow 1996: 83–4). A global civil society thus seems to be emerging as a conscious reaction and antidote to the growth of global corporate capitalism and environmental destruction.

However, we want to argue for a more complex relationship between the development of global consumer culture, on the one hand, and the emergence of critical globalist values and movements, on the other – a relationship characterised in terms not only of action and reaction, but also of irony and unintended consequences. The starting point for our argument is the centrality of the specifically *mass* media, such as television and radio, newspapers and magazines, in any emergent global civil society. The contemporary salience of these communications media bring certain emphases – of the visual and narrative over the textual, of the distant over the local, and of the non-dialogical over the dialogical – that are quite alien to dominant notions of modern citizenship, with their roots in the experience of face-to-face interaction in the Greek polis (see J. L. Cohen and Arato 1992), and call into question stark opposition between the 'puritan', disciplined modern citizen and the 'romantic', desiring consumer (Campbell 1987).

After developing this point in the first half of the chapter, we draw out two main implications of significance, both for researchers into media and politics, and for the institutions which act on this global stage. First, we argue, the one-to-many character of the mass media means that the 'staging' of global civil society is marked by a heightened salience of icons, motifs and exemplars – of condensing symbols of globality and interconnectedness, and of exemplary figures and stories which embody the notion of 'acting for the world'. This means that in order to fully understand the role the media might be playing in an emergent sense of global belonging and responsibility, one needs to expand one's attention away from a preoccupation with media genres which are predominantly informational and argumentative in character, so as to also embrace commercial and entertainment genres.

Second, the saturation of everyday life with the mediated experience of geographically distant places and culturally distant ways of life shifts the dominant cultural logic of global citizenship away from an emphasis on rational argument to one on 'sensibility' – from the linearity of claim, justification and refutation to the 'flow' of the televisual experience (Williams 1974). We thus argue that the very form of the mass media might be just as important as its informational content in generating the cultural ground for a global, cosmopolitan sensibility.

The global mediascape

Why might a putative notion of global citizenship be important in relation to the politics of the environment? A concept of responsibility and a sense of belonging that goes beyond our own locality and stretches to the world as a whole is implicit – and often explicit – in many political appeals from governmental and non-governmental institutions. Such appeals may request that people act locally in some way on behalf of the environment, and recognise the disparities between lives in richer and poorer countries. They might try to get us to reduce our fossil fuel use to avoid global warming, to use wood only from sustainably managed forests, or to buy coffee that has been produced by farms that have fair pay and conditions for their workers. Crucially, they take place in the context of an array of transnational processes and interlinkages that are encapsulated by the general notion of 'globalisation'. The idea of the nation-state as the institution through which individual citizens have duties and receive rights is thus being eroded by globalising processes that are producing global networks of organisations and actors, machines and technologies, risks and responsibilities, images and texts (Urry 1999: ch. 8).

A particularly significant global network is the mediascape of images and signs produced and marketed by the increasingly globalised culture industries. This flow of cultural products – film and television, branded products and advertisements – is frequently seen as at best irrelevant and at worse inimical to the creation of a environmentally and socially responsible global society. The seeds of a global civil society are seen as only surviving in the interstices of this mediascape, such as in the increasingly squeezed television documentary genre, and as constantly under pressure from market forces and the operation of corporate interests. Critical voices in civil society thus call for a defence of such genres against further contraction, and for them to carry an increased coverage of global environmental issues, in order to raise the level of public debate in this area (Committee for Interdisciplinary Environmental Studies (CIES) 1997; LaMay and Dennis 1991; Lay and Payne 1998).

Without wanting to deny that transnational corporations frequently play a key role in environmentally destructive and inequitable economic processes, nevertheless we want to suggest that the relation between the emergence of the global mediascape on the one hand, and that of global citizenship as a cultural ideal and as a cultural practice on the other, is more complex than this kind of account implies. In order to develop this claim further, in the next two sections we explore the role of this mediascape in developing people's sense of the global – of being members not just of one nation, generation or social grouping, but of a global community, and thus as bearers of rights and responsibilities in relation to the world as a whole. First, we present a critical summary of John Thompson's (1995) discussion of mediated interaction and its role in the constitution of a global public sphere and of a critical, deliberating global citizen. Second, we develop a hermeneutic account of citizenship, as crucially involving a cultural self-interpretation as being a member of a community of care and responsibility.

The mass media and the public sphere

Jürgen Habermas (1989) argued that in the eighteenth century a distinctive social arena, the bourgeois public sphere, emerged as a new social space, between the state on the one hand, and the private realm of familial life and economic relations on the other. This public sphere was one where private individuals could debate openly, rationally and critically about politics and social developments. Two developments were crucial to this process: the evolution of new social spaces such as the salon and the coffeehouse, and the emergence of the periodical press (Habermas 1989). But, as Habermas went on to argue, the emancipatory potential of this new public sphere was compromised by a process of 'refeudalisation', whereby the state started to intervene in the more 'private' realm of civil society, and as the media became dominated by large-scale commercial interests. Instead of being populated by autonomous individuals, debating together about society according to the principles of rational argumentation, the public sphere became dominated, rather like the medieval court, on the one hand with public figures and institutions bestowed with aura and prestige, and the other by a passive and uncritical population of consumers of 'mass' culture.

Thompson (1995) is critical of what he sees as the nostalgia in Habermas' assumption that a public sphere must involve co-presence and dialogue, and suggests that the presence of the global mass media should be seen as transforming, rather than simply diminishing, the possibilities of interaction and dialogue in modern societies (Thompson 1995: 261). Thompson grounds this argument in a detailed exposition of the distinctively 'mediated' character of so much of modern experience. He highlights how, through communications media, distant experiences and conditions are re-embedded in other, divergent, conditions of reception, and thus how individuals can thus acquire similar experiences without sharing life contexts or locale. People increasingly experience phenomena which they rarely encounter in their immediate lives. Through the extension of the senses that the media provide, the capacity to experience is thus disconnected from the activity of encountering. Thompson's emphasis here is on theorising the use of the media in hermeneutic, rather than narrowly cognitive terms – as a process through which identities, meanings and relationships can be negotiated across space and time, rather than simply as a channel for information and argument.

Thompson develops a version of 'deliberative democracy' in keeping with this recognition of the highly mediated nature of modern life. Deliberative democracy, as Thompson says, is a form of democratic politics where 'individuals are called on to consider alternatives, to weigh up the reasons and arguments offered in support of particular proposals and, on the basis of their consideration of different points of view, to form reasoned judgements' (Thompson 1995: 255; see also Dryzek 1990, 1992). However, in contrast to the more conventionally Athenian models of deliberative democracy which typically picture it as taking place dialogically (even if they might separate it from conditions of co-presence through electronic forms of interaction), Thompson proposes that any realistic form of deliberative democracy for the modern age must be one characterised more by the highly mediated and non-dialogical forms of 'quasi-interaction' brought about by the mass media.

Other writers have also envisaged a central role for the media in reinvigorating the public sphere. Morley and Robins (1995), for example, argue that the media may be the catalyst in reviving public spaces and recreating a civic culture, but that the 'decentralised communities' constituted over time and space through mediated experience must complement lived experience and not stand as alternatives to it. For them, like Thompson (1995: 41), the media can be directed to create a new forum for public discourse. Thompson specifically argues that, 'by providing individuals with forms of knowledge and information to which they would not otherwise have access, mediated quasi-interaction can stimulate deliberation just as much as, if not more than, face-to-face interaction in a shared locale' (Thompson 1995: 256). Just as technological and economic development has increased the range of the effects of our actions, the growth of the media has expanded our awareness of this. Our awareness of the interconnectedness of the world forces us to expand our horizon of concern to include those remote in time and space – even the non-human world itself, which can no longer be taken for granted as a mere backdrop for human affairs (Thompson 1995: 262).

In keeping with this assessment, Thompson's vision for democratic renewal in the media age is a combination of two elements. The first is the securing of a range of different points of view within the mass media through the application of principles of 'regulated pluralism' – the deconcentration of resources within the mass media and a clear separation between media institutions and state power (Thompson 1995: 241). The second is the initiation of participatory mechanisms for incorporating the 'reasoned judgements of ordinary individuals', honed and refined by exposure to the multiple points of view present in the mass media, into society's decision-making processes (Thompson 1995: 258).

The only disagreement we would have with these accounts of a mediated, globally responsive deliberative democracy is that in relation to this particular domain Thompson does not work through the full implication of his hermeneutic approach to the media. If the reception of the mass media is a cultural process whereby individuals incorporate 'symbolic forms . . . into their own understanding of themselves and others' (Thompson 1995: 42), then the role of the mass media in the constitution of a global citizenry would involve much more than them simply being a conduit for 'knowledge and information' about 'actions and their consequences' (Thompson 1995: 262). As we argue in the next section, this implies a more complex picture of how we should understand what it is to be a citizen – in terms of a self-interpretation based on particular cultural forms and vocabularies, rather than simply as a 'natural' identity as a rational appraiser of arguments and validity claims.

Global citizenship and self-interpretation

Thompson's account of the mediated public sphere invokes a familiar picture of the individual *qua* citizen as a rational individual, taking part in a democratic forum within which the deliberation of alternatives leads to the formation of considered judgements. However, such deliberation always has to take place within the horizon of a particular cultural self-interpretation, that of 'self-as-citizen'. As Taylor (1989) argues, human beings are self-interpreting animals, who possess personhood by virtue of understanding themselves through a particular model of the human subject. To be an agent at all is to experience the situations which one encounters in terms of particular evaluative meanings and interpretations, ones that involve certain responses being better or worse than others. Moral responses are related to the situations that give rise to them hermeneutically, in terms of the particular cultural meanings used to frame the situation, and not just through brute causality or logical necessity. Responses and actions are appropriate or inappropriate to the situation, in terms of the meanings that the situation has for the agent in question (Taylor 1989).

This implies that we need to move from a 'thin' idea of citizenship, where a disembodied, rational self judges proposals and arguments on the basis of abstract rationality, to a 'thicker' account which emphasises the cultural work that stands behind the achievement of such a 'citizen identity'.[1] To be a citizen, according to this latter view, would not just be to possess certain 'natural' human characteristics, such as rationality or autonomy, but rather to interpret oneself and one's actions according to a particular model or vocabulary, grounded in a given society. As Macedo (1990) points out, even the liberal ideals of autonomy, self-reflection, reasoned argument and tolerance are based on the 'strong evaluation' of specific 'liberal virtues', embodied in a character ideal nurtured by the institutions and practices of liberal society.

The importance of this insight for the present argument is that the role of the media in the emergence of a global public sphere may not be simply that of allowing the circulation of information and arguments, but also in providing for different, less localised forms of self-interpretation. For example, when a news item about landmine victims invokes a response of concern in the viewer, the 'structure of value' that makes such a response possible may already be in place, and have been shaped by relatively non-discursive forms of communication and experience. As Murdoch (1970) puts it, 'if we consider what the work of attention is like, how continuously it goes on, and how imperceptibly it builds up structures of value around us, we shall not be surprised that at crucial moments of choice most of the business of choosing is already over' (Murdoch 1970: 37). The cultural work that engenders a particular construal of the self and the world – for example, of other peoples and other cultures as 'like us' in morally relevant ways – may thus have taken place in communicative contexts where the conveying of information and points of view may have not been uppermost.

However, Thompson's (1995) account of the global public sphere tends to emphasise the very media genres, such as news and documentary, most concerned with the conveying of facts, proposals, arguments and points of view. Ironically, this seems to suggest his vision is one of a neo-Athenian polis, stretched across time and space, in which the individual as global citizen digests the information and knowledge provided by the media. But if the media's role in relation to global citizenship lies not only at the cognitive level of proposals and argument but also at the hermeneutic level of meanings and self-understandings, then this implies a need to broaden out from a focus on such genres. Media content and form convey not just 'information' alone, but also particular framings of self and world, and it is through this latter kind of process that a sense of global belonging, global connectedness and global responsibility may be forged. A sense of global belonging might be supported by cultural resources that constitute a wider sense of community – a community of global citizens rather than purely members of one nation, generation, gender, class or ethnicity. A sense of a common global destiny might be created by a range of symbols and narratives of global interconnectedness and global responsibility, and by the very extension of the senses that the media make possible. In the next two sections we thus explore ways in which a sense of the global can be created not solely by such 'informational' modes of communication, but also by other genres – and, importantly, by the very form of the media itself.

Media genre and the global

In what specific ways might people have access to a mediated experience of globality? As Garnham (1992: 373–4) has argued, the creation of a public sphere should not be regarded as carried by political and rational forms of media content alone. Media genres conventionally thought of as 'entertainment' or 'marketing', and as having little or no direct relationship to the public sphere, may be of primary importance in forging relationships between people's 'life-worlds' and wider concerns. Such communicative experiences are therefore relevant to individuals' senses of themselves as citizens. Using examples drawn from a survey of broadcast images of global connectedness, we will suggest that the conventional links between the environment and development as news or documentary types might be fruitfully expanded to explore a wider range of content, and different ways of thinking about how such content does its cultural work. Such content may be available in ads, logos, music video, soap operas and other forms that, seen in conventional terms, seem at odds with any idea of rational, deliberative citizenship. This content may not be inherently global as such, but may comprise imagery, actions, people and scenes that invoke senses of responsibility or of belonging to a wider humanity, and that are framed as global by particular conventions.[2]

First, images which represent the globe as a *whole* offer one kind of experience of globalness suggesting that we all live on one planet. A common version of this is the image of the earth seen from space (especially using one famous NASA photograph – see Cosgrove 1994). Other uses of such imagery are seen in the animated globes that appear in news and current affairs programmes, telecommunications, soft drinks and airlines ads.

Nevertheless, second, images of *local* environments can also be framed as 'global', as settings for global action, or for globally significant or globally representative processes or events. Certain kinds of generic places can stand in for the global environment, such as deserts, beaches and rainforests. Local environments such as Chernobyl and Antarctica can also be 'typified' by making them stand for the global environment as *threatened*, by radiation, global warming and other environmental risks. Finally, iconic *animals* can also be used to dramatise questions about the human relationship with nature.

Third, collections of people can also be framed as standing in for the whole of humanity, by being gathered together in one place, or simply by being juxtaposed with each other by editing. This 'typification' draws on the iconographic conventions of 'the family of man', in which differences between people are framed as indicating a more profound shared humanity. The juxtaposed images are typically of people in different cultures and settings that indicate their difference, but in which each are engaged in universal activities such as eating, expressing joy or giving birth. Ads for Coca-Cola and Norwich Union, as well as trailers for CNN and appeals from aid charities, regularly use images in this way to mark the connectedness and similarity of geographically and culturally distant people.

Finally, individuals can be represented as global subjects, either in their responsible behaviour, or as victims and suffering others. In the same way that single places can symbolise the global environment or risks to it, certain people, such as Nelson Mandela or Chinese dissidents, can be presented as acting on behalf of humanity. For example, Diana, Princess of Wales was frequently represented as an exemplary global citizen in her humanitarian campaigning. The One 2 One advertising campaign for a phone network, ostensibly representing itself as linking people together, uses such exemplars, and as it does so provides a cultural commentary on how people draw on images of exemplary people to imagine and steer their own aspirations.

Having raised the question of the wider content of the mass media in relation to the experience of globality we shall now attend to questions about how such an experience might be fostered by the very form and flow of the media itself.

Media form and the global

There are a number of ways in which the very form of the mass media can contribute to a global sensibility. First, by extending the experiential reach of individuals, the media offer a space in which individuals can frame themselves differently in relation to the wider world. This can be particularly seen in the emergence of electronic media in general and particularly of the development of television. The shift from oral, to print, to electronic forms of communication illustrates how experience itself has expanded. Orality went hand in hand with the proximity of village culture. The advent of writing, and particularly print, was crucial in the constitution of more dispersed senses of membership – of the diasporas of faith communities, and of nation-states. Electronic communication, in its turn, has created a 'global village', reblurring the private and public, and making everyone else's business potentially our business (McLuhan 1962, 1964).

The televisual media afford visible access to other people's experiences and existences, thus dissolving the distinction between 'our' experience and 'their' experience. Through the media, people are exposed to social situations on a daily basis which hitherto would have been unavailable to them for reasons of gender, class, physical distance and culture (Meyrowitz 1985). By extending and altering the types of social situations to which people have access, the media dissolve the boundaries of geographical embeddedness and potentially enable them to reflect on their social roles and identities. The media have helped to reconfigure group identities by increasingly revealing the 'backstage' behaviour of other social groups to which we do not strictly belong. An example of this sort of representation is a television documentary in the Modern Times series called *Mangetout* which followed the path of the mangetout pea from a specific farm in Zimbabwe, through a UK supermarket, through to a dining table in Britain (BBC2 26 February 1997). Each part of this chain is available to the viewers' gaze – farm workers, supervisors and owners talking about their lives in relation to the British and their dining preferences, a representative of the British supermarket Tesco discussing terms of trade and consumer preferences, and a dinner party discussion about 'exploitation' and farmers' lives in less developed countries.

The ability of individuals or institutions to control their 'presentation of self' (Goffman 1959) and their definition of social situations is problematised by this 'backstage' access afforded by the media. Through mediated forms of communication, audiences are able to inhabit a kind of middle region where backstage and frontstage social behaviour both come into view and where the audience are able to see actors move between the two. For example, television viewers not only have access to the frontstage behaviour of Greenpeace, performing its social role of 'bearing witness' against environmental destruction, but also have been given backstage views of the planning and preparation which lie behind such media events.

Second, the very awareness of the sheer variety of places, ways of life and points of view that are available to us through the mass media might have the effect of disembedding us from local cultures, traditions and identities, in a way that is perhaps best captured in the practice or even the mere possibility of channel-hopping. Such sensations create an awareness of interdependence,

> 'that the flows of information, knowledge, money, commodities, people and images have intensified to the extent that the sense of spatial distance which separated and insulated people from the need to take into account all the other people which make up what has become known as humanity has become eroded.
>
> (Featherstone 1993: 169)

This tends to erode any unexamined attachment to any particular form of life, and encourages what Meijer (1998: 244) calls a 'cosmopolitan style', with an attitude of detachment towards specific, local styles.[3]

Third, by participating in the practice of consuming the media one can experience oneself to be a member of a dispersed, global civicness, united by the sense that one is watching, reading or listening to something at the same time that millions of dispersed others are doing so (B. Anderson 1983; Dayan and Katz 1992). Such simultaneity is reinforced by global reportage of news such as sporting events, and by the endless day of satellite television. On the one hand, the global mediasphere may, be viewed as a disorientating, yet liberating, world of surfaces, virtuality, instantaneity and depthlessness. On the other hand, the new global cultural space created by increasing flows of images and signs may provide resources for the constitution of new identities and the reimagination of solidarity and care at the global level.

Conclusion

We do not claim to have answered all the questions about the role that the media might play in encouraging global responsibility among the public. What we hope that we have done is to expand the terms of the debate – to suggest, in particular, that global citizenship depends on global sensibility, and that such a sensibility in turn depends on a cultural imaginary that can be nurtured by a wide range of media genres and processes, extending far beyond the factual and analytical. Such a broadening of focus clearly raises challenges for conventional distinctions between consumer and citizen identities, and between the public and the private spheres.

The objection may, however, be raised that it is the intention of the corporate-dominated media to create pliant consumers rather than active global citizens. However, with the mass media, 'intention' rarely directly determines 'effect'. Meyrowitz's (1985) discussion of the development of the feminist movement in the USA shows how 'intention' and overt content can be subverted by media form, producing quite unanticipated consequences. Meyrowitz argues that in the 1950s, despite its stereotypical representation of gender roles, the media opened up a cultural space in which women were able to view themselves as a distinct social grouping, with shared features of everyday life and shared interests, and not simply as individual women with individual problems. The discreteness of the private sphere of the home on the one hand, and of the public sphere on the other, was undermined by the increasing availability of experiences for women. Through television women could 'observe' and 'experience' a wider world, including both all-male interactions, and the lives of others similar to themselves. Thus, the social roles and models that defined them as individual women became open for consideration and reconfiguration (Meyrowitz 1985).

We want to suggest that consumer capitalism's dependence on global media and global imagery makes it, too, vulnerable to such unintended consequences. Drawing on the work of Douglas and Isherwood (1979), Meijer (1998) has explored how branded products and advertising can provide resources whereby people can situate themselves as culturally global. Reasoning from this perspective, she provocatively suggests that even Coca-Cola be seen as 'not just a very popular soft drink, not even the symbol for an ever expanding universal lifestyle for young people, but the expression of a new way of living and understanding of global cultural values' (Meijer 1998: 239). She cautions against perspectives that regard advertising and consumption as necessarily retarding the abilities of people to think and act as independent citizens, advancing instead the notion that consumer culture can serve as a source of civic 'capital'. In a similar vein, we have been arguing that the cultural dynamics of global citizenship cannot be divorced from those of global consumerism, and that sharp divisions cannot be made between the 'public' world of information, education and debate, and the 'private' world of advertising and entertainment. The globalised mediascape, while created by global capital, perhaps paradoxically may be creating the cultural conditions for the emergence of a critical global citizenry.

Acknowledgement

The authors would like to acknowledge the support of the Economic and Social Research Council, whose funding of the research project Global Citizenship and the Environment made possible the writing of this chapter. They would also like to thank their colleagues on that project, Greg Myers and John Urry, and also Mimi Sheller and the editors of this volume, for helpful comments on earlier drafts.

Notes

1 See Fraser (1992) and Honig (1992) for performative conceptualisation of publics that emphasise the symbolic dimensions of communication.
2 For greater detail about this analysis, and the survey of broadcast output that was used to generate it, see Toogood and Myers (1998).
3 This is consistent with the analysis by Newcomb and Hirsch (1984) of television as a 'cultural forum', where the constant juxtaposition of viewpoints produces an experience characterised less by the giving of determinate answers than by the constant raising of questions.

Chapter 15

Mediating the risks of virtual environments

Joost van Loon

> What has the essence of technology to do with revealing? The answer: every-thing. For every bringing-forth is grounded in revealing. . . . The possibil-ity of all productive manufacturing lies in revealing. Technology is therefore no mere means. Technology is a way of revealing.
>
> (Heidegger 1977: 12)

The aim of this chapter is to problematise the concepts of environment and media in an attempt to extend Beck's (1992a) risk society thesis to the virtual world of information and communication technologies. I argue that apart from a critique of media representations of environmental issues (for example, A. Anderson 1997; Chapman *et al.* 1997; Hannigan 1995, A. Hansen 1993b) and risks (Cottle 1998a), sociocultural theory also needs to engage in a more fun-damental problematisation of risk itself. I shall invoke the concept of 'cyber-risk' to open the scope of analysis to the material-informational technological processing of risks that comes before their discursive realisation in signifying practices.

Exposing 'the' environment

In his widely acclaimed *Rise of the Network Society*, Castells (1996) describes the contours of an informational landscape, which is characterised by a series of relatively smooth, globally operational, flows (of data, people, money, goods, services, images). This landscape, or what he calls 'space of flows', is the field in which global capitalism, with its geopolitics of the new world order, is able to bolster new heights in the accumulation of wealth and power. The space of flows, however, is further marked by an increased separation from what he calls 'the space of places' – the lived geographies of everyday life. It is the growing gap between these two landscapes, the space of flows and the space of places, that is the definitive condition of inequality in the informational society (Castells 1996: 428).

Irrespective of whether one agrees with Castells' vision of the future or not, his notion of an informational landscape is worth pursuing. It highlights the problematic of conceptualising 'the environment' in an age in which techno-science has already irreversibly imposed its own specific logic on to everything else. The environment is a label that is assigned to *that which remains*; it is the by-product of the technological enframing of the world that has been called 'modernity'. In this sense, the term 'environment' shares the conceptual space reserved for 'waste', 'dirt', 'residue', 'excess' and – for this chapter most significantly – 'risk'. It is thus intrinsically contingent upon that which enframes the world – the technologies of science, governance (including politics and law), media and commerce. These technologies make particular risks visible by drawing them out of the darkness of ignorance into the light of knowledge; they attribute meanings to them by submitting them to discursive regulation and symbolic association; and they commodify and valorise them for circulation on global markets. Risks are not only dangers, but also opportunities. It is the technologies of visualisation, signification and marketisation which transform 'the' environment from a residual category into a meaningful problematic.

There is a tendency within the social sciences to talk about 'the' environment as if it constitutes a self-evident, monolithic entity. 'The' environment (of course) refers to the planetary physical environment; often simply referred to as 'nature' (Chapman *et al*. 1997: 27; Macnaghten and Urry 1998; Meyerson and Rydin 1996). In the general sense, 'the' environment is always 'out there', externalised from ourselves as the world in which we exist. As 'nature', however, it is also more specific than that; it is the limit condition of that which is not artificial, that is, that which is not technologically induced.

At the same time, 'the' environment is also referred to as 'a [relatively] new subject area' (Chapman *et al*. 1997: 37; see also Hannigan 1995: 62–3). It is being subjected to scientific and journalistic, political, legal and criminal investigations. 'The' environment is thus discursively objectified, and subsequently subjected to narrative and discursive treatment; an arena for discussion and political debate; a venue for scientific career-making and economic investment; and a domain for surveillance, discipline and punishment. This environment, one could argue, is *produced* in multiple and contested discursive practices, symbolic exchange and the administrative and economic regimes by which the outcomes of these are being valorised (Hannigan 1995; Macnaghten and Urry 1998; Milton 1996).

Perhaps it is too simplistic to equate the first position ('the' environment as out there) with realism and the second ('the' environment as discursively produced) with constructionism, but these two epistemological extremes are the ones generally, even if only implicitly, invoked in many discussions about environmental issues and mass media (see, for example, Adam *et al*. 1999; Chapman *et al*. 1997; Hannigan 1995; A. Hansen 1993b; Macnaghten and Urry 1998; Milton 1996). Ultimately, such debates can be traced back to the very essence of 'media-representations'. The central issue is whether we conceptualise 'representation' in terms of a dualism between the sign and the referent (as in realism), or in terms of a practice of 'realisation' (as in constructionism).

It is my contention that both epistemologies presuppose each other and keep each other in balance as anchoring points of a particular ideological ellipsis (or what Foucault (1970) called 'episteme') of modern thought. It is the opposition between 'words' and 'things' that is called upon here as being fundamental. The difference is whether 'the' environment is primarily seen as a 'thing' or as a 'word'. Both ends meet in the unspoken assumption that there are words *and* things. However, this episteme of modern thought is quickly losing its ground as the digital age of the informational society is obliterating the distinction between words and things. For example, in hypertext, links can be seen as both words and as 'things' that open a new universe of word-things (data). In other words, the framework of modern thought, which strongly relies on a dualism between reality and representation becomes side-tracked in a universe where reality is representation and vice versa (van Loon 1999).

Information and communication technologies reveal 'the' environment for what it 'really' represents: a word-thing that remains in excess of our ability to 'capture it' as either a word or a thing. The space of flows of the informational landscape discloses 'an' environment that is endlessly deferred in its enframed 'out-there-ness'. The contingent singularity of this endless deferral, or differance (Derrida 1982), is nothing more than the actualisation of a particular technology or medium. The difference between modern thought and what may be called 'hyperthought' is that whereas in the first episteme, environment remained contingent upon integral or molar media forms (science, governance, media, commerce), in hyperthought environment is enacted by a perpetual differential or modular assemblage (a 'bringing-together') of media forms (science-becoming-governance-becoming-media-becoming-commerce).[1] Indeed, it is the modulation of the different flows that spatialise the informational landscape into particular media assemblages (disrupting the categories of modern thought and its institutional forms) that characterises this new hyper-contingent sense of 'environment' (N. Clark 1997). As McLuhan (1964) notes:

> The hybrid of the meeting of two media is a moment of truth and revelation from which new form is born. For the parallel between two media holds us on the frontiers between forms that snap us out of the Narcissus-narcosis. The moment of the meeting of media is a moment of freedom and release from the ordinary trance and numbness imposed by them on our senses.
>
> (McLuhan 1964: 63)

The deadlock between reality and representation, referent and sign, objectivity and subjectivity that constitutes the episteme of modern thought is suddenly broken with the advent of new information and communication technologies. Indeed, the world has changed in many ways. Of course, we still have capitalism, we still have nation-states, parliamentary democracy, disciplinary power, racism and patriarchy, but we must seriously question whether any of these catch-phrases still 'signify' the same 'phenomena' (and inevitably, whether the very catch-phrases 'signification' and 'phenomena' are what they used to be). It is the speed of information flows that has eroded the very possibility of maintaining any firm distinction between words and things. In the same movement, the distinction between the natural and the artificial finds an uncomfortable dissolution in, for example, the creation of 'virtual environments'. Here a naturalistic concept of environment is no longer only a logical impossibility, it is has also become highly impractical.

I have argued thus far that the space of flows, or cyberspace, is not only a particular type of environment, but also one which problematises the 'naturalistic' notion of 'the' environment. Instead, environments are continuously constructed and deconstructed in endless processes of simulation. This is not to say that they are 'merely' figments of our imagination (what is often denounced as 'social constructionism'). Simulation is a transformation of energy into matter and hence a 'modulation' of reality. Particular environments are realised through simulation, but their construction and deconstruction are highly skilful accomplishments (Hillis 1996) take that a great deal of energy and power; hence their 'enabling' and 'disabling' is never simply a matter of individual wish-fulfilment.

The telematic revolution of the 1980s has exposed the inherent flaws in conceptualising 'the' environment as an ecological 'natural' system (see also N. Clark 1997). It is the transcoding of flows (that is, the modulation of one particular flow into another) between the systems of science, governance, commerce and media that marks the current climate of conceptualising environmental risk. Whereas these systems may continue to operate on the basis of their own distinctive self-referential technologies, it has become obvious that the real power is exercised from the assemblage that emerges in-between/beyond them – in the assemblage of technologies of visualisation, signification, commodification and marketing. In other words, what we need to focus on next is the accomplishment of such a transcoding or assemblage. This brings us to a discussion of 'the' media.

Problematising 'the' media

If we can except the proposition that environments are relative to the systems from which they are being differentiated, then any question about the environment and the media has to start with another question: 'What is the environment of media?' This is not an uncommon question for those working in media studies and has not been neglected in relation to environmental issues (see, for example, A. Anderson 1997; A. Hansen 1993b; Mormont and Dasnoy 1995; see also Hannigan 1995 for a useful overview). It is the typical question asked by the major stream of media studies in Britain, which is that of political economy. Indeed, one cannot understand 'the' media without taking into consideration the dynamics of their production – dynamics predominantly determined by the logic of capitalism with a strong intervention (in most European countries at least) by the state. However, if capital and the state (governmentality) can be seen as primary defining forces that shape 'the' mediascape (which is 'the' media plus 'their' environment), one needs to ask the question as to whether there is anything inside the media system that mediates this imposed force? That is, do those agencies which operationalise 'the' media system also perceive 'the' environment as being enforced upon it?

Chapman *et al.* (1997: 38), for example, observe that whereas journalists are far less concerned with pleasing their public than with pleasing their editors, there is a clear case for arguing that many journalists have to be, to some degree, concerned with environmental issues if they are to provide adequate coverage. The authors place a cautionary warning here as the majority of journalists they interviewed emphasised that they did not, by any means, wish to be seen as environmentalists, let alone environmental campaigners. However, what becomes evident from this research is that journalists operate on the basis of a logic that substantially deviates from the logic of capital. That is 'their' environment is not as well organised as the political economic theory of the media tends to suggest. Apart from criteria that are directly derived from the logic of capital (audience ratings, editorial strategy, medium profile: a good story with graphic pictures) as well as the logic of a disciplinary state apparatus (operating within the legal framework of rules and regulations, including morality and 'good taste'), they also adhere to criteria that are rather less derivative from the logic of capital and the state. Examples include 'objectivity', 'fairness, 'neutrality', 'creativity' and 'quality', which may indeed (even if occasionally) place them at opposite ends to corporate enterprise and governmentality, especially when they are applied to the coverage of environmental issues.

Again, what is important here is ambivalence. In my view, it is conceptually unhelpful simply to declare that 'the' media system is subordinated by capital and the state. Media systems have effectively generated their own environments which, through the incorporation of ambivalence, have acquired a relative autonomy from the economic and political systems. Without that insight, one runs the risk of continuing to discuss media coverage of environmental issues as if this is a direct effect of its systemic embedding in the dual logic of capital and discipline. This forces analyses of the mediation of environmental issues either to conceptualise coverage as 'covering up', for example by containing risks through mystification, or by being completely contained by the state's own legislative environmentalism, which disciplines both production and consumption within the capitalist system. Such analyses fail to perceive the actual critical activities that many journalists are involved in when reporting about environmental risks. It was journalists who in the early to mid-1990s kept the pressure on the then Conservative government in Britain on issues of beef consumption and risks of BSE 'spreading' to humans. It was also journalists who made the Greenpeace campaign against Shell's plans for sinking the Brent Spar so effective.

This claim is not made in defence of journalism, nor is it intended to suggest that the journalistic ethos of objectivity, creativity and fairness defines practices of reporting. I am merely arguing that because media systems are relatively autonomous, journalists can – to a degree – engage in critical activities that may undermine both the logic of capital and (to a lesser degree) the logic of governmentality. In any analysis of media systems, we need to understand the ambivalence of its differentiation. 'The' media environment consists of a multiplicity of forces that may not always pull in the same direction. We need to pay attention to the ways in which economic, political, social, cultural and ecological environments intersect. These environments are not simply imposed on to media systems; rather, they are the product of ongoing dialectics between the media system's own self-referential differentiation and the incorporative forces that characterise both capitalism (through commodification) and governmentality (through discipline).

We can make a second observation. As with 'the' environment, it is extremely difficult to talk about 'the' media. As McLuhan (1964) argued, anything ranging from a car to a television set can be called a medium. Even if we limit ourselves to media of communication, such as stone, paper, telephone, cable-wire or satellite, we still find that media exist in quite a range of forms. If we further limit ourselves to media of mass communication (print, radio, television and the Internet), we still face the problem of media diversity. Print, radio and television, for example, all have a very different logic of engagement; they generate quite different environments for themselves. Although McLuhan has been widely criticised for his allegedly over-optimistic technological determinism (Stevenson 1995), it seems hard to ignore his basic thesis that each medium generates its own social form. Of course, literacy was not simply caused by print, but neither did the emergence of literacy and print accidentally coincide. We cannot simply talk about 'the' media or even 'the' mediascape unless we are willing to theorise how these different media have come to reinforce each other. In the advent of a new world information order, we are witnessing a rapid hybridisation of media forms which have sent panic waves of ambivalence throughout modern western societies, thereby undermining the fixed boundaries and classification systems through which discipline and capital could organise and valorise a particular social, cultural, political and economic order.

What characterises this mediascape is a growing uncertainty over the boundaries between, on the one hand, the real and the possible, and, on the other hand, the virtual and the actual.[2] The hybridisation of media has affected all 'domains' of disciplinary society: science, governance and commerce impinge on institutions, individual bodies and even genes. The blurring of the boundaries between the real and the possible has generated a crisis over realisation. Increasingly, government agencies and corporate bodies are operating on the basis of complete uncertainty about whether something can be realised or not, but they are forced to think the unthinkable anyway. Moreover, the blurring between the boundaries of the actual and the virtual has engendered *a crisis of actualisation*, one in which the distinctions between fact and fiction, or the referent and the signifier, have become increasingly void of any differentiating power. The speed with which these boundaries are being transgressed has caused a number of serious breakdowns in social organisation. One needs only to look at politics or stock markets to understand the volatility of signification (Doel and Clarke 1998).

This relates to a third issue regarding the centrality of ambivalence in the analyses of mediascapes: the ambivalence of representation. In analyses of media coverage of 'environmental' issues, what generates most attention is the 'representational' aspect of coverage, that is, the signs that are brought into presence in the place of whatever they are made to refer to. Coverage in this sense refers to a process of displacement: real environmental risks are replaced with signs; the signs are stand-ins for 'the real' (Eco 1977; Pêcheux 1982). 'Critique' in this sense often refers to the adequacy of this 'standing in' – do the created signs actually correspond to that which they have replaced? Indeed, the crisis of actualisation is redesigning many mediascapes and obliterates any firm grounding to distinguish between the real and the representational, since both can only be expressions of a limit-condition of the virtual. For example, to say that a computer program is 'real' or 'representational' makes little sense, as what is primarily important is what sort of realities it actualises. Every computer program creates its own virtual environment according to the principles it puts into operation.

Fortunately, most critical analyses go beyond this issue of real versus representation and ask the much more productive question of what such media coverage *does*. Here we enter into a second axis of understanding representation, this time not as a process of replacement, but one of displacement. Representation is then not so much a confinement of the real in signification, but a specific realisation of possibilities. Mediascapes are thus articulations of reality effects. Hence, the critique shifts from a question of correspondence to one of performativity – what is the coverage actually achieving? As mentioned earlier, because of a general lack of understanding of mediascapes within the academic institutions of media studies, answers are most often located in terms of 'covering-up'. Here, the media are seen as ideological state apparatuses that mystify environmental hazards and naturalise them (Coleman 1995).

I am not trying to argue that environmental hazards are not often 'naturalised' in mediascapes (see, for example, Allan 1999b). The point to make, however, is that 'coverage' or representation does more; it is not only an act of concealment, but also one of unconcealment (sense-making). This requires a more productive, or performative, understanding of mediascapes as particular technologies. Mediascapes operate on the basis of technologies of signification, thereby allowing other systems (including what we may call 'the public') to articulate and relate to perceived risks in particular ways – and thereby engaging in what may be called the (sub)politics of the risk society (Beck 1996b,

1997a). However, as we cannot speak of 'the' environment independently of the systems that have produced 'it', we must also avoid discussing 'the' media in terms of a monolithically imposed externalised logic (of capital and governmentality). Instead, if we are to discuss 'the' media system as a singular form, we need to centrally focus on the relationship between media and their 'own' environments (mediascapes). However, simultaneously, these mediascapes are being transformed by the telematics of information and communication technologies as they weld together the various data flows and technologies of signification through which mediascapes are operationalised. One peculiar consequence of this is the birth of the 'risk society'.

Virtual risks and cyberrisks

The final question I would like to pose in this chapter is: in what way can Beck's (1992a) risk society thesis speak to an 'environment' that has already been completely incorporated by technologies of mediation? My argument is that it is in the very ambivalent role of technology/mediation – as both a making-sense (unconcealment) and a re-presentation (concealment) of risk – that the risk society reinstates the paradox of modern life as an order of disorganisation.

The power of Beck's work on risk, in my view, resides mostly in its visionary ability to see how we are witnessing a cultural transformation of risk perception. This cultural transformation is predominantly, but not exclusively (see Lash and Urry 1994; Welsh 1999), organised around a particular crisis – the legitimation crisis of technoscience. Risk society calls upon the very same technoscience to both reveal and conceal the danger. The paradoxical consequence being that of technoscientific delegitimation and political indecisiveness, and a further eradication of the foundations of modern society.

It is now 'common sense' to associate science and technology with risk. Associated with both causes of and solutions to risk, science and technology have played an intricate part in the construction of economic, social, political and cultural conditions under which risks operate in modern society. As argued elsewhere (van Loon and Sabelis 1997; Adam *et al.* 1999), science primarily operates through technologies of visualisation – thereby generating particular perspectives and insights hence constituting the condition for (mis)recognising unspecified possibilities as 'risks'. Governance and mediascapes tap into that visualisation with their respective technologies of signification: governance by articulating a distinction between 'significance' and 'insignificance' (hence difference and indifference), mediascapes by articulating sense and cultivating sensibility, bearing witness to the event of visualisation and (governmental) signification as it unfolds.[3] It is often suggested that media invoke technoscientific 'sources' to grant legitimacy to the coverage (Coleman 1995: 68). The acquisition of such a legitimacy, however, is not the accomplishment of either science or mediascape, but of the assemblage between technologies of visualisation and signification – the first by giving insight, the second by granting meaning.

Take for example the very notion of *ecology*, which is often used by environmentalists, or perhaps I should say ecologists, as a more adequate term than either 'environment' or 'nature'. The very postfix *logy*, however, already points towards the presence of *logos*. Logos can be made to stand in for a range of other terms: language, law, logic, even reason or discourse. However, it thus also refers to 'coverage' or 'concealment'. When something is put under the heading of logos, it is given a name, it becomes an attribute of the name, and it becomes covered by the name. As Foucault (1970) pointed out, modern thought went even a bit further than merely 'naming' and 'classifying' and started to replace the name (language) with 'logic' (both in terms of causality and of law). We can clearly trace that shift in today's usage of the term ecology, which often implicitly refers to a carefully balanced 'natural' system in which the laws of nature work in a perfect symbiosis to establish harmony and homeostasis.

It is impossible nowadays to operate under the heading of ecology, in my view, without submitting oneself to the technologies of visualisation that characterise much of modern technoscience. Granting 'insight' as the basis of knowledge is the central focus. Even if there is a considerable and critical residue of knowledge outside of the technoscientific establishment (see Welsh 1999), one cannot underestimate the powerful impact of the technoscientific overcoding – or overexposure, as N. Clark (1997) calls it – of such knowledge. This is because technoscience has been very effective in symbiotically appropriating the force of technologies of signification. Technoscience has successfully induced both governance and the mediascape (as well as commerce) to be able to intervene in the differentiation between significance and insignificance. This form of 'sub-politics' does not engage with the same forms of accountability that characterise the political domain of representational democracy. What is nowadays called 'the public understanding of science' can be seen as a programme of inducing the mediascape in order to more effectively operationalise the technologies of visualisation (Irwin and Wynne 1996; Rose 1999).

What happens to environmental hazards when they are overcoded by technoscience is that they are being transformed into objects of visual desire. The desire to make visible the implicit causal link between substance A, malign effect B, and possible effective treatment C is a major motivation of contemporary scientific discovery (Welsh 1999). What happens as a result of this visualisation, however, is the generation of more technoscientifically accurate 'knowledge' about hazards, which, via the enrolment of governance and mediascapes, are transformed into (sub)political issues for decision-making (via signification). As a consequence, hazards become risks (Luhmann 1995; Beck 1999).

With 'the' environment already transcoded by the mediascape, and signification being overcoded by technoscientific desire, it is quite difficult to see any relevance in asking the question whether such environmental risks are real or constructions (Beck 1999; van Loon 1999). They are always 'virtual'. What matters is the way in which these risks are being transformed: 'environmental risk' becoming 'health risk' becoming 'economic risk' becoming 'political risk' becoming 'representational risk'. In a world of complete self-referential systems (such as the 'perfect' disciplinary society), such risks would remain enclosed within one (sub)system only. Once immersed in the mediascape, they can move relatively smoothly across a range of intersystemic boundaries and at high speed. The result is a hyper-intensified multiplication of risks. A good illustration of this is the relatively recent BSE crisis in the UK and Europe.

Hence, the third point I want to make is that environmental risks are no longer contained by any single particular system, be it that of science, governance or commerce. The telematic transfomation of the mediascape has allowed risks to flow across systemic boundaries, inducing a range of environments and further contaminating and corrupting systemic integrity. Indeed, far from being an event of technocratic supremacy, the assemblage that is currently being formed between technoscience, governance, media and commerce bears all the signs of a highly vulnerable and fragile stature.

It therefore seems perfectly logical to extend Beck's analysis of risk society to the domain of electronic communications. Just as there have been applications to nuclear, genetic and reproductive technologies, so can the risk society thesis be applied to the world of information and communication technologies. Particular examples of such risks would be moral panics (outbreaks of 'irrational fear' after particular broadcasts, such as deaths from the drug ecstasy and 'mad cow disease' brought forth by news media), information overload and noise (such as middle management stress), cyberaddictions and cybercults even resulting in mass suicide (HeavensGate), cyberfraud (for example credit cards) and of course the hallmark of cyberrisks, the computer virus, which represents, as Nigel Clark (1997: 79) puts it, 'a new generation of digital demons to suddenly render our entire datasphere into terminal gibberish'.

In the most basic terms, cyberrisks refer to the potential corruption or manipulation of information flows in mediascapes. These breakdowns are typically instigated by program errors, such as the millennium bug, or malignant programs such as computer viruses. Cyberrisks are simulations capable of engendering new information flows, even new life-forms. In other words, they are 'representations of risk' that actualise particular virtual environments. Cyberrisks are material and they are performative. Although they are principally engendered by computer systems, they have the potential to affect all realms of economic, political, social, cultural and biological life. As Clark (1997) writes:

> Computer viruses are predisposed to escape the jurisdiction of their creators, dispersed by integrated circuitry, and capable of utilising previously accumulated signifying material for their own explosive replication, and in these senses might be seen as the archetype of the superconductive event.
>
> (N. Clark 1997: 88)

The example of the computer virus is telling. The emergence of computer viruses in the 1980s coincided with the arrival of AIDS on the global mediascape. The very notion of computer virus is an adaptation of that of viruses such as HIV. Similar to virologists who describe and analyse virulence in terms of genetics, computer experts analyse malignant programs in terms of virulent behaviour. To them, the claim that cyberrisks are intelligent life-forms makes absolute sense (Lundell 1989). More specifically, the very image of HIV, which effectively operates (it is assumed) by misleading the body's immunity system, is the image of the Trojan horse (F. Ryan 1996). The computer virus is simultaneously disguised as something else, secretly imported into the system where it can wait and cultivate itself until it is ready to strike. The image of HIV, the body invader, returns in the image of the computer virus. In its wake, the world of computing is also contaminated with the metaphors that marked the commonsensibility of HIV/AIDS in the global mediascape.

Hence, being infected with a computer virus became associated with unsafe computing, or worse with deviant forms of computing. 'Borrowing' software from public bulletin boards became the equivalent of visiting San Francisco's public bathing houses. Indeed, infections with computer viruses were being associated with the allocation of guilt and shame. Safe computing became a moral issue. In other words, cyberrisks became instruments in the policing not only of 'proper computing', but more importantly of the commercial interests of software producers.

The point to make, therefore, is not simply that cyberrisks became closely associated with the risks of HIV/AIDS and 'deviant' sexuality, but that it was the mediascape itself that brought these associations into existence, and furthermore cultivated their wider sensibility. The mediation of HIV/AIDS, like the mediation of computer viruses, articulated risk sensibilities far beyond the technoscientific domain, and entered – one might say infected – wider popular cultural formations. Governance and commerce were always inherently part of this movement, as cyberrisks in particular are always matters of discipline and commodification.

Conclusion

In the midst of speed and irreversibility, the human has lost its self-proclaimed centrality. 'The' environment can no longer be the externalised projection of the centred human subject. It has surpassed our ability to master and control it, or to subject it to our programming of the future; instead, our futures are being programmed as we speak. This sense of loss manifests itself in the uncanny but perpetual return of the same debate over the merits and evils of cybertechnologies. On the one hand, the technophiles and technocrats cannot stop talking about the benefits of the virtual: we are no longer hampered by the inertia of the flesh, we can construct our identities as we please, and we are free to engage in whatever we like and become participants in a more open and equal form of civic society (Poster 1995; Rheingold 1994). On the other hand, the technophobes and neo-luddites do not stop complaining about the dumbing and numbing effects of telematics; telematics as nothing but an extension of capitalist exploitation, propaganda and mystification which turns us into apathetic, lethargic, brainwashed consumers of infotainment (Dovey 1996b; Robins 1996). Both extremes show a remarkable inability to sensitise the inherent ambivalence of virtual environments and cyberrisks, choosing instead to operate as if in a permanent neurotic narcosis (Hillis 1996). Both extremes are so caught up in their own humanist preconception of subjectivity as an integral primacy for action that they fail to induce an ethos of subversion; they cannot see life beyond humanity (Haraway 1990, 1997; Ansell-Pearson 1997).

The challenge posed by new information processing and telecommunication systems requires us to rethink not only what kind of existence marks our being in the world, but also what we 'are' as beings whose 'integrity' can no longer be taken-for-granted. What is at stake, therefore, is the issue of re-articulating the profoundly existential moment of disclosure and revelation with the ethico-pragmatics of being-in-the-world. This issue is deeply political and, in my view, strikes at the media politics of environmental risks. That is to say, the question of how environmental risks are mediated is fundamentally a question of how we relate to our own being-in-the-world. However, this question can be addressed properly only once our preoccupation with survival has been suspended.

Notes

1 This notion of a transition from molar to modular forms of power is central to Deleuze's (1992) short and unfinished excursion into 'societies of control'. Molar forms are self-contained and holistic, they operate on the basis of resemblance, and they are repetitions of the same. In contrast, modular forms are distributed and folded, they operate on the principle of multiplicity and are repetitions of a singular principle. An example of a molar form is the arabesque; an example of a modular form is the fractal.

2 This analysis is derived from Hardt's work on Deleuze (cited in Lury 1998: 182–3).

3 It is not coincidental that apart from the ambivalence of signification both governance and mediascape also share another ambivalent concept: representation. It is in this ambivalence that the notion of 'the public' operates (Dahlgren 1996; Hartley 1992; see also Tulloch 1993 for a very insightful historical analysis of the relationship between governance and information-management in post-war Britain).

Bibliography

Adam, B. (1995) *Timewatch: The Social Analysis of Time*, Cambridge: Polity.

Adam, B. (1996) 'Re-vision: the centrality of time for an ecological social science perspective', in Lash, S., Szerszynski, B. and Wynne, B. (eds) *Risk, Environment and Modernity*, London: Sage.

Adam, B. (1998) *Timescapes of Modernity: The Environment and Invisible Hazards*, London: Routledge.

Adam, B., Beck, U. and van Loon, J. (eds) (2000) *The Risk Society and Beyond: Critical Issues for Social Theory*, London: Sage.

Adams, J. (1995) *Risk*, London: UCL Press.

Adams, W. C. (1986) 'Whose lives count? TV coverage of natural disasters', *Journal of Communication* 36, 2: 113–22.

Albrow, M. (1996) *The Global Age: State and Society Beyond Modernity*, Cambridge: Polity.

Allan, S. (1995) '"No truth, no Apocalypse": Investigating the language of nuclear war', *Studies in Communications* 5: 171–214.

Allan, S. (1997) 'News from NowHere: Televisual news discourse and the construction of hegemony', in Bell, A. and Garrett, P. (eds) *Approaches to Media Discourse*, Oxford: Blackwell.

Allan, S. (1998) '(En)gendering the truth politics of news discourse', in Carter, C., Branston, G. and Allan, S. (eds) *News, Gender and Power*, London: Routledge.

Allan, S. (1999) *News Culture*, Buckingham: Open University Press.

Allan, S. (2000) 'Risk and the common sense of nuclearism', in Adam, B., Beck, U. and van Loon, J. (eds) *The risk Society and Beyond: Critical Issues for Social Theory*, London: Sage.

Anand, P. (1998) 'Chronic uncertainty and BSE communications: Lessons from (and limits of) theory', in Ratzan, S. C. (ed.) *The Mad Cow Crisis: Health and the Public Good*, London: UCL Press.

Anderson, A. (1991) 'Source strategies and the communication of environmental affairs', *Media, Culture and Society* 13,4: 459–76.

Anderson, A. (1997) *Media, Culture and the Environment*, London: UCL Press.

Anderson, B. (1983) *Imagined Communities: Reflections on the Origin and Spread of Nationalism*, London: Verso.

Ang, I. (1996) *Living Room Wars: Rethinking Media Audiences for a Postmodern World*, London: Routledge.

Ansell-Pearson, K. (1997) *Viroid Life*, London: Routledge.

Arrhenius, S. (1896) 'On the influence of carbonic acid in the air upon the temperature of the ground', *Philosophical Magazine* 41: 237–71.

Aziz, A. A. A. (1995) 'Safeguarding the population and environment through communication: The case of advertisement of unleaded petroleum in Malaysia', *Journal of Development Communication* 1, 6: 46–55.

Badri, M. A. (1991) 'Mass communication and the challenges on global environmental protection', *Journal of Development Communication* 1, 2: 1–16.

Barthes, R. (1957) *Mythologies*, London: Paladin.

Barthes, R. (1972) 'The rhetoric of the image', *Image-Music-Text*, London: Fontana.

Barthes, R. (1977) *Image-Music-Text*, London: Fontana.

Bateson, G. (1955) 'A theory of play and phantasy', *American Psychiatric Association Psychiatric Research Reports* II: 39–51.

Bateson, G. (1972) *Steps to an Ecology of Mind: Collected Essays in Anthropology, Psychiatry, Evolution, and Epistemology*, San Francisco: Chandler.

Baudrillard, J. (1984) *The Evil Demon of Images*, Sydney: Power Institute Publications.

Bauman, Z. (1998) *Globalisation: The Human Consequences*, Cambridge: Polity.

BBC Broadcasting Research (1988) *Crimewatch UK*, London: BBC Special Projects Report.

Beck, U. (1992a) *Risk Society: Towards a New Modernity*, London: Sage.

Beck, U. (1992b) 'From industrial society to risk society: Questions of survival, social structure and ecological enlightenment', *Theory, Culture and Society* 9: 97–123.

Beck, U. (1995) *Ecological Politics in an Age of Risk*, Cambridge: Polity.

Beck, U. (1996a) 'Risk Society and the provident state', in Lash, S., Szerszynski, B. and Wynne, B. (eds) *Risk, Environment and Modernity: Towards a New Ecology*, London: Sage.

Beck, U. (1996b) 'World risk society as cosmopolitan society? Ecological questions in a framework of manufactured uncertainties', *Theory, Culture and Society* 13, 4: 1–32.

Beck, U. (1997a) *The Reinvention of Politics: Rethinking Modernity in the Global Social Order*, Cambridge: Polity.

Beck, U. (1997b) 'The relations of definitions: cultural and legal contexts of media constructions of risk', paper presented to the Media, Risk and the Environment Conference, Cardiff University, July.

Beck, U. (1998a) 'Politics of risk society', in Franklin, J. (ed.) *The Politics of Risk Society*, Cambridge: Polity.

Beck, U. (1998b) *Democracy without Enemies*, Cambridge: Polity.

Beck, U. (2000) 'Risk society revisited: Theory, politics and research programmes', in Adam, B., Beck, U. and van Loon, J. (eds) *The Risk Society and Beyond: Critical Issues for Social Theory*, London: Sage.

Beck, U., Giddens, A. and Lash, S. (1994) *Reflexive Modernisation: Politics, Tradition and Aesthetics in the Modern Social Order*, Cambridge: Polity.

Becker, H. S. (1967) 'Whose side are we on?', *Social Problems* 14, 3: 239–47.

Beder, S. (1997) *Global Spin: The Corporate Assault on Environmentalism*, Totnes, Devon: Green Books and White River Junction, VT: Chelsea Green.

Bell, A. (1989) 'Hot news: Media reporting and public understanding of the climate change issue in New Zealand' (project report to the Department of Scientific and Industrial Research and Ministry for the Environment), Wellington, Vic.: Department of Linguistics, Victoria University.

Bell, A. (1991) 'Hot air: Media, miscommunication and the climate change issue', in Coupland, N., Giles, H. and Wiemann, J. (eds) *'Miscommunication' and Problematic Talk*, Newbury Park, CA: Sage.

Bell, A. (1994a) 'Climate of opinion: Public and media discourse on the global environment', *Discourse and Society* 5, 1: 33–64.

Bell, A. (1994b) 'Media (mis)communication on the science of climate change', *Public Understanding of Science* 3, 4: 259–75.

Bell, A. (1995) 'News time', *Time and Society* 4, 3: 305–64.

Belsham, M. (1991) 'Cancer, control and causality: Talking about cancer in a working-class community', *American Ethnologist* 18: 152–72.

Benedict, H. (1992) *Virgin or Vamp: How the Press Covers Sex Crimes*, New York and Oxford: Oxford University Press.

Bennett, D., Glasner, P. and Travis, D. (1986) *The Politics of Uncertainty: Regulating Recombinant DNA Research in Britain*, London: Routledge and Kegan Paul.

BEPCAG (Biotechnology and the European Public Concerted Action Group) (1997) 'Europe ambivalent on biotechnology', *Science* 387, 26 June: 845–7.

Beresford, P. (1979) 'The public presentation of vagrancy', in T. Cook (ed.) *Vagrancy: Some New Perspectives*, London: Academic Press.

Berger, A. A. (1997) *Narratives in Popular Culture, Media and Everyday Life*, Newbury Park, CA: Sage.

Berger, J. (1973) *Ways of Seeing*, London: Fontana.

Berland, J. (1993) 'Weathering the north: Climate, colonialism, and the mediated body', in Blundell, V., Shepherd, J. and Taylor, I. (eds) *Relocating Cultural Studies*, London: Routledge.

Beynon, H., Hudson, R. and Sadler, D. (1994) *A Place called Teesside: A Locality in a Global Economy*, Edinburgh: Edinburgh University Press.

Bhopal, R., Moffatt, S., Pless-Mulloli, T., Phillimore, P., Foy, C., Dunn, C. and Tate, J. (1998) 'Does living near a constellation of petrochemical, steel and other industries impair health?', *Occupational and Environmental Medicine* 55: 812–22.

Bishop, J. and Waldholz, M. (1990) *Genome*, New York: Simon and Schuster.

Bloomfield, B. P. and Verdubakis, T. (1995) 'Disrupted boundaries: New reproductive technologies and the language of anxiety and expectation', *Social Studies of Science* 25, 3: 533–51.

Boorstin, D. (1971) 'From news gathering to news making: A flood of pseudoevents', in Schramm, W. and Roberts, D. (eds) *The Process and Effects of Mass Communication*, 2nd edn, Urbana, IL: University of Illinois Press.

Bousé, D. (1998) 'Are wildlife films really "nature documentaries"?', *Critical Studies in Mass Communication* 15: 116–40.

Boyd-Bowman, S. (1984) 'The day after', *Screen* 25: 4–5, 71–97.

Boyer, P. (1985) *By the Bomb's Early Light: American Thought and Culture at the Dawn of the Atomic Age*, New York: Pantheon.

Brandon, D. *et al.* (1980) *The Survivors: A Study of Homeless Young Newcomers to London and the Responses Made to Them*, London: Routledge and Kegan Paul.

Brenner, S. (1991) 'Old ethics for new issues', *Science and Public Affairs* August: 35–8.

Briggs, A. (1963) *Victorian Cities*, Harmondsworth: Penguin.

Brookes, H. J. (1995) '"Suit, tie and a touch of juju" – the ideological construction of Africa: A critical discourse analysis of news on Africa in the British press', *Discourse and Society* 6, 4: 461–94.

Brookes, R. and Holbrook, B. (1998) '"Mad cows and Englishmen": Gender implications of news reporting on the British beef crisis', in Carter, C., Branston, G. and Allan, S. (eds) *News, Gender and Power*, London: Routledge.

Brunsdon, C. and Morley, D. (1978) *Everyday Television: 'Nationwide'*, London: British Film Institute.

Brynin, M. (1987) 'Young homeless: Pressure groups, politics and the press', *Youth and Policy* 20: 24–34.

Bunyard, P. (1988) 'Nuclear energy after Chernobyl', in Goldsmith, E. and Hildyard, N. (eds) *The Earth Report: Monitoring the Battle for our Environment*, London: Beasley.

Burgess, J. (1990) 'The production and consumption of environmental meanings in the mass media: A research agenda for the 1990s', *Transactions: Institute of British Geographers* 15: 139–61.

Burgess, J. and Harrison, C. (1993) 'The circulation of claims in the cultural politics of environmental change', in Hansen, A. (ed.) *The Mass Media and Environmental Issues*, Leicester: Leicester University Press.

Burrows, W. (1980) 'Science meets the press: Bad chemistry', *Sciences* April: 15–19.

Calhoun, C. (ed.) (1992) *Habermas and the Public Sphere*, Cambridge, MA: MIT Press.

Cameron, D. and Frazer, E. (1987) *The Lust to Kill*, Oxford: Polity.

Cameron, D. and Frazer, E. (1994) 'Cultural difference and the lust to kill', in Harvey, P. and Gow, P. (eds) *Sex and Violence: Issues in Representation and Experience*, London: Routledge.

Campbell, C. (1987) *The Romantic Ethic and the Spirit of Modern Consumerism*, Oxford: Blackwell.

Caputi, J. (1987) *The Age of Sex Crime*, Bowling Green, Ohio: Bowling Green State University Press and London: Women's Press.

Carey, J. (1989) *Communication as Culture: Essays on Media and Society*, London: Unwin Hyman.

Carey, J. (1998) 'The story of *Squall* magazine', in McKay, G. (ed.) *DiY Culture: Party and Protest in Nineties Britain*, London: Verso.

Carter, C. (1995) 'Nuclear family fall-out: Postmodern family culture and media studies', in Adam, B. and Allan, S. (eds) *Theorizing Culture: An Interdisciplinary Critique after Postmodernism*, London: UCL Press.

Carter, C. (1998a) 'When the "extraordinary" becomes "ordinary": Everyday news of sexual violence', in Carter, C., Branston, G. and Allan, S. (eds.) *News, Gender and Power*, London: Routledge.

Carter, C. (1998b) 'News of sexual violence against women and girls in the British daily national press', unpublished Ph.D. dissertation, Cardiff University.

Carter, C. and Thompson, A. (1997) 'Negotiating the "crisis" around masculinity: An historical analysis of discourses of patriarchal violence in the *Western Mail*, 1896', in O'Malley, T. and Bromley, M. (eds) *A Journalism Reader*, London: Routledge.

Carter, C., Branston, G. and Allan, S. (eds) (1998) *News, Gender and Power*, London: Routledge.

Carter, S. (1995) 'Boundaries of danger and uncertainty: An analysis of the technological culture of risk assessment', in Gabe, J. (ed.) *Medicine, Health and Risk: Sociological Approaches*, Oxford: Blackwell.

Castells, M. (1996) *The Rise of the Network Society: The Information Age: Volume I*, Oxford: Blackwell.

Castells, M. (1997) *The Power of Identity: The Information Age: Volume II*, Oxford: Blackwell.

Castells, M. (1998) *End of Millennium: The Information Age: Volume III*, Oxford: Blackwell.

Chapman, G., Kumar, K., Fraser, C. and Gaber, I. (1997) *Environmentalism and the Mass Media: The North–South Divide*, London: Routledge.

Chibnall, S. (1978) *Law and Order News*, London: Tavistock.

Chomsky, N. (1989) *Necessary Illusions*, London: Pluto.

Clark, K. (1992) 'The linguistics of blame: Representations of women in *The Sun*'s reporting of crimes of sexual violence', in Toolan, M. (ed.) *Language, Text and Context: Essays in Stylistics*, London: Routledge.

Clark, N. (1997) 'Panic ecology: Nature in the age of superconductivity', *Theory, Culture and Society* 14, 1: 77–96.

Cleveland County Council (1982–3) Pollution Control Group, Notes.

Cohen, B. (1963) *The Press and Foreign Policy*, Princeton, NJ: Princeton University Press.

Cohen, J. L. and Arato, A. (1992) *Civil Society and Political Theory*, Cambridge, MA: MIT Press.

Cohen, S. and Young, J. (eds) ([1973] 1981) *The Manufacture of News: Social Problems, Deviance and the Mass Media*, revised edn, London: Constable.

Cohn, C. (1987) 'Sex and death in the rational world of defense intellectuals', *Signs* 12, 4: 687–718.

Coleman, C. L. (1995) 'Science, technology and risk coverage of community conflict', *Media, Culture and Society* 17, 1: 65–79.

Committee for Interdisciplinary Environmental Studies (CIES) (1997) *Reporting Sustainable Development: The Challenge to the Media*, Cambridge: CIES, University of Cambridge.

Cook-Degan, R. (1994) *The Gene Wars: Science, Politics and the Human Genome*, New York: Norton.

Corner, J., Richardson, K. and Fenten, N. (1990) *Nuclear Reactions: Form and Response in 'Public Issue' Television*, London: John Libbey.

Cosgrove, D. (1994) 'Contested global visions: One-world, whole-earth, and the Apollo space photographs', *Annals of the Association of American Geographers* 84: 270–94.

Cottle, S. (1990) 'Television coverage of the inner city', PhD thesis, Leicester University.

Cottle, S. (1993a) *TV News, Urban Conflict and the Inner City*, Leicester: Leicester University Press.

Cottle, S. (1993b) 'Mediating the environment: Modalities of TV news', in Hansen, A. (ed.) *The Mass Media and Environmental Issues*, Leicester: Leicester University Press.

Cottle, S. (1994) 'Stigmatizing Handsworth: Notes on reporting spoiled space', *Critical Studies in Mass Communication* 11, 4: 231–56.

Cottle, S. (1998a) 'Ulrich Beck, "risk society" and the media: A catastrophic view?', *European Journal of Communication* 13, 1: 5–32.

Cottle, S. (1998b) 'Analysing visuals: Still and moving images', in Hansen, A., Cottle, S., Negrine, R. and Newbold, C. (eds) *Mass Communication Research Methods*, London: Macmillan.

Cottle, S. (2000) 'Rethinking theories of news access', *Journalism Studies* 1 (3).

Coupland, J., Holmes, J. and Coupland, N. (1998) Negotiating sun use: Constructing consistency and managing inconsistency', *Journal of Pragmatics* 30: 699–721.

Coupland, N. and Coupland, J. (1997) 'Bodies, beaches and burntimes: "Environmentalism" and its discursive competitors', *Discourse and Society* 8: 7–25.

Coupland, N., Coupland, J. and Giles, H. (1991) *Language, Society and the Elderly: Discourse, Identity and Ageing*, Oxford: Blackwell.

Croteau, D. and Hoynes, W. (1992) 'Men and the news media: The male presence and its effects', in Craig, S. (ed.) *Men, Masculinity and the Media*, London: Sage.

Cuklanz, L. M. (1996) *Rape on Trial: How the Mass Media Construct Legal Reform and Social Change*, Philadelphia, PA: University of Pennsylvania Press.

Cunningham, A. M. (1986) 'Not just another day in the newsroom: The accident at TMI', in Friedman, S. M., Dunwoody, S. and Rogers, C. L. (eds) *Scientists and Journalists: Reporting Science as News*, New York and London: Free Press.

Curran, J., Douglas, A. and Whannel, G. (1980) 'The political economy of the human interest story', in Smith, A. (ed.) *Newspapers and Democracy: International Essays on a Changing Medium*, Cambridge, MA: MIT Press.

Dahlgren, P. (1995) *Television and the Public Sphere*, London: Sage.

Daley, P. and O'Neill, D. (1991) '"Sad is too mild a word": Press coverage of the *Exxon Valdez* oil spill', *Journal of Communication* 41, 4: 42–57.

Darier, E. (ed.) (1999) *Discourses of the Environment*, Oxford: Blackwell.

Das, V. (1995) *Critical Events: An Anthropological Perspective on Contemporary India*, Oxford: Oxford University Press.

Davis, J. (1995) 'The effects of message framing on response to environmental issues', *Journalism and Mass Communication Quarterly* 67, 4: 723–31.

Dayan, D. and Katz, E. (1992) *Media Events: The Live Broadcasting of History*, Cambridge, MA: Harvard University Press.

Deacon, D. and Golding, P. (1994) *Taxation and Representation*, London: John Libbey.

Dealler, S. F. (1998) 'Can the spread of BSE and CJD be predicted?', in Ratzan, S. C. (ed.) *The Mad Cow Crisis: Health and the Public Good*, London: UCL Press.

Dealler, S. F. and Lacey, R. W. (1990) 'Transmissible spongiform encephalopathies: The threat of BSE to man', *Food Microbiology* 7: 253–79.

Dean, G. and Lee, P. (1977) *Report on a Second Retrospective Mortality Study in North-East England*, London: Tobacco Research Council.

Dearing, J. and Rogers, E. (1996) *Agenda-Setting*, Communication Concepts 6, London and Thousand Oaks, CA: Sage.

Deleuze, G. (1992) 'Postscript on the societies of control', *October* 59: 3–7.

Deleuze, G. and Guattari, F. (1988) *A Thousand Plateaus: Capitalism and Schizophrenia*, trans. Massumi, B., London: Athlone.

Demko, V. (1998) 'An analysis of media coverage of the BSE crisis in the United States', in Ratzan, S. C. (ed.) *The Mad Cow Crisis: Health and the Public Good*, London: UCL Press.

Derrida, J. ([1968] 1992) 'From differance', in Easthope, A. and Mcgowan, K. (eds) *A Critical and Cultural Theory Reader*, Buckingham: Open University Press.

Derrida, J. (1981) *Dissemination*, trans, Johnson, B., Chicago: University of Chicago Press.

Derrida, J. (1982) *Margins of Philosophy*, trans. A. Bass, Chicago: University of Chicago Press.

Detjen, J. (1991) 'Enviromental reporters come under fire by employers' *SEJ* [Society of Enviromental Journalists] *Journal* 1, 2: 2.

Detjen, J. (1997) 'TV's declining enviromental vision', *Enviromental Journalism News* 1, 2: 2.

Diani, M. (1995) *Green Networks: A Structural Analysis of the Italian Enviromental Movement*, Edinburgh: Edinburgh University Press.

Dobash, R. E. and Dobash, R. P. (1979) *Violence Against Wives*, London: Open Books.

Doel, M. and Clarke, D. (1998) 'Transpolitical urbanism: Suburban anomaly and ambient dear', *Space and Culture* 2: 13–36.

Douglas, M. (1985) *Risk Acceptability According to the Social Sciences*, London: Routledge and Kegan Paul.

Douglas, M. (1992) *Risk and Blame: Essays in Cultural Theory*, London: Routledge.

Douglas, M. and Isherwood, B. (1979) *The World of Goods: Towards an Anthropology of Consumption*, London: Allen Lane.

Dovey, J. (1996a) 'The revelation of unguessed worlds', in Dovey, J. (ed.) *Fractal Dreams: New Media in Social Context*, London: Lawrence and Wishart.

Dovey, J. (ed) (1996b) *Fractal Dreams: New Media in Social Context*, London: Lawrence and Wishart.

Downs, A. (1972) 'Up and down with ecology: the "issue-attention cycle"', *The Public Interest* 28: 38–50.

Dryzek, J. S. (1990) *Discursive Democracy: Politics, Policy, and Political Science*, Cambridge: Cambridge University Press.

Dryzek, J. S. (1992) 'Ecology and discursive democracy: Beyond liberal capitalism and the administrative state', *Capitalism, Nature, Socialism* 3, 2: 18–42.

Dunkerley, D. and Glasner, P. (1998) 'Empowering the public? Citizen's juries and the new genetic technologies', *Critical Public Health* 8, 3: 181–92.

Dunwoody, S. (1986a) 'The science writing inner club: a communication link between science and the lay public', in Dunwoody, S., Friedman, S. and Rogers, C. (eds) *Scientists and Journalists*, New York: Free Press.

Dunwoody, S. (1986b) 'The scientist as source', in Dunwoody, S., Friedman, S. and Rogers, C. (eds) *Scientists and Journalists*, New York: Free Press.

Dunwoody, S. and Griffin, R. J. (1993) 'Journalistic strategies for reporting long-term environmental issues: A case study of three superfund sites', in Hansen, A. (ed.) *The Mass Media and Environmental Issues*, Leicester: Leicester University Press.

Dunwoody, S. and Peters, H. P. (1992) 'Mass media coverage of technological and environmental risks', *Public Understanding of Science* 1, 2: 199–230.

Dunwoody, S. and Scott, B. T. (1982) 'Scientists as mass media sources', *Journalism Quarterly* 59, 1: 52–9.

Durant, J., Hansen, A. and Bauer, M. (1996) 'Public understanding of the new genetics', in Marteau, T. and Richards, M. (eds) *The Troubled Helix: Social and Psychological Implications of the New Genetics*, Cambridge: Cambridge University Press.

Dyer, S., Miller, M. and Boone, J. (1991) 'Wire service coverage of the Exxon Valdez Crisis', *Public Relations Review* 17, 1: 27–36.

Eco, U. (1977) *A Theory of Semiotics*, London: Macmillan.

Eden, S. (1996) 'Public participation in environmental policy: Considering scientific, counter-scientific and non-scientific contributions', *Public Understanding of Science* 5: 183–204.

Eder, K. (1996) 'The institutionalisation of enviromentalism: Ecological discourse and the second transformation of the public sphere', in Lash, S., Szerszynski, B. and Wynne, B. (eds) *Risk, Environment and Modernity: Towards a New Ecology*, London: Sage.

Eliot, T. S. (1968) 'East Coker', in *The Four Quartets*, London: Faber and Faber.

ENDS (1995) *ENDS (Enviromental Data Services) Report* (London), 251.

Entman, R. (1991) 'Framing U.S. coverage of international news: Contrasts in narratives of the KAL and Iran air incidents', *Journal of Communication* 41, 4: 6–29.

Entman, R. (1993) 'Framing: Toward clarification of a fractured paradigm', *Journal of Communication* 43, 4: 51–58.

Evans, A. (1996) *We Don't Choose to be Homeless: A Report for the National Inquiry into Homelessness*, London: CHAR (Campaign for Homeless People).

Evans, G. and Durant, J. (1989) 'Understanding science in Britain and America', in Jowell, R. *et al.* (eds) *British Social Attitudes: Special International Report*, Aldershot: Gower.

Evans, K. (1998) *Copse: The Cartoon Book of Tree Protesting*, Biddestone, UK: Orange Dog.

Eyerman, R. and Jamison, A. (1989) 'Environmental knowledge as an organizational weapon: the case of Greenpeace', *Social Science Information* 28, 1: 99–119.

Fairclough, N. (1989) *Language and Power*, London: Longman.

Fairclough, N. (1992) 'Discourse and text: Linguistic inter-textual analysis within discourse analysis', *Discourse and Society* 3, 2: 193–217.

Fairclough, N. (1995) *Media Discourse*, London: Edward Arnold.

Featherstone, M. (1991) 'The body in consumer culture', in Featherstone, M., Hepworth, M. and Turner, B. (eds) *The Body: Social Process and Cultural Theory*, London: Sage.

Featherstone, M. (1993) 'Global and local cultures', in Bird, J., Curtis, B., Putnam, T., Robertson, R. and Tuckner, L. (eds) *Mapping the Future: Local Cultures and Global Change*, London: Routledge.

Fillmore, C. (1968) 'The case for case', in Bach, E. and Harms, R. T. (eds) *Universals in Linguistic Theory*, New York: Holt, Rinehart and Winston.

Fine, T. (1992) 'The impact of issue framing on public opinion toward affirmative action programs', *Social Science Journal* 29, 3: 323–34.

Finn, G. (1989–90) 'Taking gender into account in the "theatre of terror": Violence, media, and the maintenance of male dominance', *Canadian Journal of Women and the Law* 3, 2: 375–94.

Fiorino, D. J. (1990) 'Citizen participation and environmental risk: A survey of institutional mechanisms', *Science, Technology and Human Values* 15, 2: 226–43.

Fisher, K. and Collins, J. (1993) *Homelessness, Health Care and Welfare Provision*, London: Routledge.

Fiske, J. (1987) *Television Culture*, London: Methuen.

Fitzpatrick, S. and Clapham, D. (1999) 'Homelessness and young people', in Hutson, S. and Clapham, D. (eds) *Homelessness: Public Policies and Private Troubles*, London: Cassell.

Ford, B. J. (1996) *BSE – The Facts: Mad Cow Disease and the Risk to Mankind*, London: Corgi.

Foucault, M. (1970) *The Order of Things: An Archaeology of the Human Sciences*, New York: Vintage.

Foucault, M. (1979) *The History of Sexuality*, vol. 1, Harmondsworth: Penguin.

Fowler, R. (1991) *Language in the News*, London: Routledge.

Franklin, B. (1997) *Newzak and Newspapers*, London: Arnold.

Franklin, J. (ed.) (1998) *The Politics of Risk Society*, Cambridge: Polity.

Fraser, N. (1992) 'Rethinking the public sphere', in Calhoun, C. (ed.) *Habermas and the Public Sphere*, Cambridge, MA: MIT Press.

Freudenburg, W. R., Coleman, C., Gonzales, J. and Helgeland, C. (1996) 'Media coverage of hazard events: Analyzing the assumptions', *Risk Analysis* 16, 1: 31–42.

Friedman, S. (1981) 'Blueprint for breakdown: Three Mile Island and the media before the accident', *Journal of Communication* 31, 2: 116–28.

Friedman, S. M., Gorney, C. M. and Egold, B. P. (1987) 'Reporting on radiation: A content analysis of Chernobyl coverage', *Journal of Communication* 37, 3: 58–78.

Funtowicz, S. O. and Ravetz, J. (1993) 'Science for the post-normal age', *Futures* 25, 7: 739–55.

Gaddy, G. D. and Tanjong, E. (1986) 'Earthquake coverage by the Western press', *Journal of Communication* 26, 2: 105–12.

Galtung, J. and Ruge, M. (1965) 'The structure of foreign news', *International Journal of Peace Research* 1: 64–90.

Galtung, J. and Ruge, M. (1982) 'Structuring and selecting news', in Cohen, S. and Young, J. (eds) *The Manufacture of News: Deviance, Social Problems and the Mass Media*, London: Constable.

Gamson, W. (1989) 'News as framing: Comments on Graber', *American Behavioral Scientist* 33: 157–61.

Gamson, W. A. and Modigliani, A. (1989) 'Media discourse and public opinion on nuclear power: A constructionist approach', *American Journal of Sociology* 95, 1: 1–37.

Gamson, W. and Wolfsfeld, G. (1993) 'Movements and media as interacting systems', in Dalton, R. (ed.) *Citizens, Protest and Democracy, Annals of the American Academy of Political and Social Science*, 528, July, 114–25.

Gandy, Jr, O. (1982) *Beyond Agenda Setting: Information Subsidies and Public Policy*, Norwood, NJ: Ablex.

Gardner, C. B. (1988) 'Access information', *Social Problems* 35, 1: 384–97.

Gardner, C. B. (1995) *Passing by: Gender and Public Harassment*, Berkeley, CA: University of California Press.

Garnham, N. (1992) 'The media and the public sphere', in Calhoun, C. (ed.) *Habermas and the Public Sphere*, Cambridge, MA: MIT Press.

Gauntlett, D. (1996) *Video Critical: Children, the Environment and Media Power*, Luton: University of Luton Press/John Libbey.

Giddens, A. (1990) *The Consequences of Modernity*, Cambridge: Polity.

Giddens, A. (1991) *Modernity and Self-Identity: Self and Society in the Late Modern Age*, Cambridge: Polity.

Giddens, A. (1998) 'Risk society: The context of British politics', in J. Franklin (ed.) *The Politics of Risk Society*, Cambridge: Polity.

Gieryn, T. F. (1994) 'Boundaries of science', in Jasanoff, S. *et al.* (eds) *Handbook of Science and Technology Studies*, London: Sage.

Gilroy, P. (1987) *There Ain't no Black in the Union Jack*, London: Hutchinson.

Gitlin, T. (1980) *The Whole World is Watching: Mass Media and the Making and Unmaking of the New Left*, Berkeley, CA: University of California Press.

Glasner, P. (1993) 'Programming nature and public participation in decision-making: A European perspective', in Durant, J. and Gregory, J. (eds) *Science and Culture in Europe*, London: Science Museum.

Glasner, P. (1996) 'From community to collaboratory? The human genome mapping project and the changing culture of science', *Science and Public Policy* 23, 2: 109–16.

Glasner, P. and Rothman, H. (1998) 'Patents, ownership and sovereignty', *Nature* 392, 26: 325.

Goffman, E. (1959) *The Presentation of Self in Everyday Life*, London: Doubleday.

Goffman, E. (1974) *Frame Analysis: An Essay on the Organization of Experience*, Cambridge, MA: Harvard University Press.

Goldblatt, D. (1996) *Social Theory and the Environment*, Cambridge: Polity.

Goodey, J. (1994) 'Fear of crime: What can children tell us?', *International Review of Victimology*, 3: 195–210.

Gordon, M. and Riger, A. (1988) *The Female Fear,* New York: Free Press.

Graddol, D. (1994) 'The visual accomplishment of factuality', in Graddol, D. and Boyd-Barrett, O. (eds) *Media Texts: Authors and Readers*, Clevedon: Multilingual Matters in association with The Open University.

Greenberg, M. R., Sachsman, D. B., Sandman, P. M. and Salomone, K. L. (1989a) 'Risk, drama and geography in coverage of environmental risk by network TV', *Journalism Quarterly* 66, 2: 267–76.

Greenberg, M. R., Sachsman, D. B., Sandman, P. M. and Salomone, K L. (1989b) 'Network evening news coverage of environmental risk', *Risk Analysis* 9, 1: 119–26.

Griffin, C. (1993) *Representations of Youth: The Study of Youth and Adolescence in Britain and America*, Cambridge: Polity.

Grossberg, L. (1986) 'The deconstruction of youth', in Corner, J. (ed.) (1994) *Cultural Theory and Popular Culture*, London: Harvester.

Grove-White, R. (1998) 'Risk society, politics and BSE', in Franklin, J. (ed.) *The Politics of Risk Society,* Oxford: Polity.

Habermas, J. (1989) *The Structural Transformation of the Public Sphere: An Inquiry into a Category of Bourgeois Society*, Oxford: Polity.

Hall, S. (ed.) (1997) *Representations: Cultural Representations and Signifying Practices*, London: Sage.

Hall, S., Critcher, C., Jefferson, T., Clarke, J. and Roberts, B. (1978) *Policing the Crisis*, London: Macmillan.

Halliday, M. A. K. (1985) *An Introduction to Functional Grammar,* London: Edward Arnold.

Halliday, M. A. K. (1990) 'New ways of meaning: A challenge to applied linguistics', *Journal of Applied Linguistics* 6: 7–36.

Hallin, D. (1986) *The Uncensored War*, Berkeley, CA: University of California Press.

Hallin, D. (1987) 'Hegemony: The American news media from Vietnam to El Salvador: A study in ideological changes and its limits', in Paletz, D. (ed.) *Political Communication Research: Approaches, Studies, Assessments*, Norwood, NJ: Ablex.

Hannigan, J. A (1995) *Environmental Sociology: A Social Constructionist Perspective*, London: Routledge.

Hansen, A. (1991) 'The media and the social construction of the environment', *Media, Culture and Society* 13: 443–58.

Hansen, A. (1993a) 'Greenpeace and press coverage of environmental issues', in Hansen, A. (ed.) *The Mass Media and Environmental Issues,* Leicester: Leicester University Press.

Hansen, A. (ed.) (1993b) *The Mass Media and Environmental Issues,* Leicester: Leicester University Press.

Hansen, J. and Takahashi, T. (1984) *Climate Sensitivity: Analysis of Feedback Mechanisms in Climate Processes and Climate Sensitivity*, Washington, DC: American Geophysical Union.

Haraway, D. (1990) 'A manifesto for Cyborgs: Science, technology and socialist feminism in the 1980s', in Nicholson, L. J. (ed.) *Feminism/Postmodernism,* New York: Chapman and Hall.

Haraway,D.(1997)*Modest_Witness@Second_Millennium.FemaleMan©_Meets_Oncomouse™*, London: Routledge.

Harding, T. (1998) 'Viva camcordistas! Video activism and the protest movement', in McKay, G. (ed.) (1998) *DiY Culture: Party and Protest in Nineties Britain*, London: Verso.

Harré, R., Brockmeier, J. and Mühlhäusler, P. (1999) *Greenspeak: A Study of Environmental Discourse*, London: Sage.

Hartley, J. (1992) *Teleology: Studies in Television*, London: Routledge.

Hartley, J. (1996) *Popular Reality: Journalism, Modernity, Popular Culture*, London: Edward Arnold.

Hay, I. (1995) 'The strange case of Dr Jekyll in Hyde Park: Fear, media, and the conduct of an emancipatory geography', *Australian Geographical Studies* 33, 2: 257–71.

Hegedus, Z. (1990) 'Social movements and social change in self-creative society: new civil initiatives in the international arena', in Albrow, M. and King, E. (eds) *Globalization, Knowledge and I*, London: Sage.

Heidegger, M. (1977) *The Question Concerning Technology and Other Essays*, New York: Harper and Row.

Henderson-Sellers, A. (1989) *Opinions about the Greenhouse in Australia*, Kensington, NSW: New South Wales Press.

Hendrickson, L. (1994) 'Media framing of child maltreatment: Conceptualizing framing as a continuous variable', unpublished doctoral dissertation, University of Texas at Austin.

Herman, E. and Chomsky, N. (1988) *Manufacturing Consent*, New York: Pantheon.

Hertsgaard, M. (1990) 'Covering the world: ignoring the earth', *Greenpeace* 15: 14–18.

Hilgartner, S. (1990) 'The dominant view of popularization: conceptual problems, political uses', *Social Studies of Science* 20: 519–39.

Hilgartner, S. and Bosk, C. (1998) 'The rise and fall of social problems: A public arenas model', *American Journal of Sociology* 94, 1: 53–78.

Hillis, K. (1996) 'A geography of the eye: The technologies of virtual reality', in Shields, R. (ed.) *Cultures of Internet: Virtual Spaces, Real Histories, Living Bodies*, London: Sage.

Hobart, M. (1993) 'Introduction', in Hobart, M. (ed.) *An Anthropological Critique of Development: The Growth of Ignorance*, London: Routledge.

Hoff, L. A. (1990) *Battered Women as Survivors*, London: Routledge.

Holland, P. (1987) 'When a woman reads the news', in Baehr, H. and Dyer, G. (eds) *Boxed In: Women and Television*, London: Pandora.

Hollingsworth, M. (1986) *The Press and Political Dissent*, London: Pluto.

Home Office (1996) *Criminal Statistics, England and Wales*, 1995, London: HMSO.

Home Office (1998) *Criminal Statistics, England and Wales*, 1997, London: HMSO.

Honig, B. (1992) 'Towards an agonistic feminism', in Butler, J. and Scott, J. W. (eds) *Feminists Theorize the Political*, London: Routledge.

Hornig, S. (1990) 'Television's NOVA and the construction of scientific truth', *Critical Studies in Mass Communication* 7, 1: 11–23.

Hornig, S. (1992) 'Framing risk: Audience and reader factors', *Journalism Quarterly* 69, 3: 679–90.

Howenstine, E. (1987) 'Environmental reporting: Shift from 1970 to 1982', *Journalism Quarterly* 64, 4: 842–6.

Hudson, E., Downey, D., Moffatt, S. and Phillimore, P. (1998) *Putting the Air Pollution*

Debate to Sleep? The Impact of a Health Study Teesside, Joint Working Paper no.1, Departments of Social Policy and Epidemiology and Public Health, University of Newcastle upon Tyne.

Hudson, R. (1989) *Wrecking a Region*, London: Pion.

Hurford, J. R. and Heasley, B. (1983) *Semantics: A Coursebook*, Cambridge: Cambridge University Press.

Hutson, S. and Jones, S. (1997) *Rough Sleeping and Homelessness and Rhondda Cynon Taff*, Pontypridd: University of Glamorgan.

Hutson, S. and Liddiard, M. (1994) *Youth Homelessness: The Construction of a Social Issue*, London: Macmillan.

Hutson, S., Sutton, M. and Thomas, J. (1995) *The Housing and Support Needs of Young Single Homeless People in Merthyr Tydfil*, Swansea: University of Swansea.

Intergovernmental Panel on Climate Change (IPCC) (1992) *Climate Change: Policymakers Summary of the Scientific Assessment of Climate Change*, New York: Cambridge University Press.

Intergovernmental Panel on Climate Change (IPCC) (1995) *Climate Change 1995: The Science of Climate Change. Contribution of Working Group I to the Second Assessment of the IPCC*, New York: Cambridge University Press.

Irwin, A. (1995) *Citizen Science*, London: Routledge.

Irwin, A. (2000) 'Risk, technology and modernity: Re-positioning the sociological analysis of nuclear power', in Adam, B., Beck, U. and van Loon, J. (eds) *The Risk Society and Beyond: Critical Issues for Social Theory*, London: Sage.

Irwin, A. and Wynne, B. (eds) (1996) *Misunderstanding Science? The Public Reconstruction of Science and Technology*, Cambridge: Cambridge University Press.

Jagtenberg, T. and McKie, D. (1997) *Eco-Impacts and the Greening of Postmodernity*, London: Sage.

Jamison, A. (1996) 'The shaping of the global environmental agenda: the role of non-governmental organisations', in Lash, S., Szerszynski, B. and Wynne, B. (eds) *Risk, Environment and Modernity: Towards a New Ecology*, London: Sage.

Jones, G. (1995) *Family Support for Young People,* London: Family Policy Studies Centre.

Jones, G. W. (1997) 'Challenges and reward: BSE and beyond', in Bristow, G. (ed.) *BSE: The Welsh Dimension*, Aberystwyth: Institute of Welsh Affairs.

Jones, S. G. (1995) *CyberSociety: Computer-Mediated Communication and Community*, London: Sage.

Joss, S. and Durant, J. (1995) *Public Participation in Science: The Role of Consensus Conferences in Europe*, London: Science Museum.

Keane, J. (1991) *The Media and Democracy*, Cambridge: Polity.

Kelling, G. (1995) *Fixing 'Broken Windows': Order and Individualism in American Cities*, New York: Praeger.

Kellogg, W. (1988) 'Human impact on climate: the evolution of an awareness', in Glantz, M. (ed.) *Societal Response to Regional Climate Change: Forecasting by Analogy*, Boulder, CO: Westview Press.

Kellogg, W. (1991) 'Response to skeptics of global warming', *Bulletin of the American Meteorological Society* 74, 4: 499–511.

Kempton, W. (1990) 'Lay perspectives on global climate change', *PU/CEES report 251*, Princeton, NJ: Center for Energy and Environmental Studies, Princeton University.

Kerr, A., Cunningham-Burley, S. and Amos, A. (1997) 'The new genetics: professionals' discursive boundaries', *Sociological Review* 45, 2: 279–303.

Kielbowicz, R. B. and Scherer, C. (1986) 'The role of the press in the dynamics of social movements', in Lang, G. and Lang, K. (eds) *Research in Social Movements, Conflicts and Change*, Greenwich, CT: JAI Press.

Kitzinger, J. (1998) 'Silent voices and the risks of "False Memory"', in Carter, C., Branston, G. and Allan, S. (eds) *News, Gender and Power*, London: Routledge.

Kitzinger, J. and Reilly, J. (1997) 'The rise and fall of risk reporting: Media coverage of human genetics research, "False Memory Syndrome" and "mad cow disease"', *European Journal of Communication* 12,3: 319–50.

Krimsky, S. (1982) *Genetic Alchemy: The Social History of the Recombinant DNA Controversy*, Cambridge, MA: MIT Press.

Krug, G. J. (1993) 'The day the earth stood still: Media messages and local life in a predicted Arkansas earthquake', *Critical Studies in Mass Communication* 10: 273–85.

Kutzbach, J. and Guetter, J. P. (1986) 'The influence of changing orbital parameters and surface boundary conditions on climate simulations for the past 18,000 years', *Journal of Atmospheric Science* 43: 1726–59.

Lacan, J. (1976) *The Language of the Self*, Baltimore, MD: Johns Hopkins University Press.

Lacey, C. and Longman, C. (1993) 'The press and public access to the environment and development debate', *Sociological Review* 41, 2: 207–43.

Lacey, C. and Longman, D. (1997) *The Press as Public Educator*, Luton: University of Luton Press/John Libbey.

Lacey, R. W. (1994) *Mad Cow Disease: The History of BSE in Britain*, Jersey: Gypsela.

Lacey, R. W. (1998) *Poisons on a Plate*, London: Metro.

Lakoff, G. and Johnson, M. (1980) *Metaphors We Live By*, London: University of Chicago Press.

LaMay, C. and Dennis, E. (eds) (1991) *Media and the Environment*, Washington, DC: Island Press.

Lander, E. (1992) 'DNA fingerprinting: Science, law and the ultimate identifier', in Kevles, D. J. and Hood, L. (eds) *The Code of Codes: Scientific and Social Issues in the Human Genome Project*, Cambridge, MA: Harvard University Press.

Lang, T. (1998) 'BSE and CJD: Recent developments', in Ratzan, S. C. (ed.) *The Mad Cow Crisis: Health and the Public Good*, London: UCL Press.

Langer, J. (1998) *Tabloid Television: Popular Journalism and the 'Other' News*, London: Routledge.

Lash, S. and Urry, J. (1994) *Economies of Signs and Space*, London: Sage.

Lash, S. and Wynne, B. (1992) 'Introduction', in Beck, U. (ed.) *Risk Society: Towards a New Modernity*, London: Sage.

Lash, S., Szerszynski, B. and Wynne, B. (eds) (1996) *Risk, Environment and Modernity: Towards a New Ecology*, London: Sage.

Lashoff, D. (1990) *Concern about Global Warming: Panic or Prudence?*, Washington, DC: National Resources Defense Council.

Lay, S. and Payne, C. (1998) *World Out of Focus: British Terrestrial Television and Global Affairs*, London: Third World and Environment Broadcasting Project.

Leach, J. (1998) 'Madness, metaphors and miscommunication: The rhetorical life of mad cow disease', in Ratzan, S. C. (ed.) *The Mad Cow Crisis: Health and the Public Good*, London: UCL Press.

Leiss, W. and Chociolko, C. (1994) *Risk and Responsibility*, Montreal and Kingston: McGill-Queen's University Press.

Lévi-Strauss, C. ([1958] 1972) *Structural Anthropology*, Harmondsworth: Penguin.

Lewontin, R. C. (1993) *The Doctrine of DNA: Biology as Ideology*, Harmondsworth: Penguin.

Liddiard, M. (1999) 'Homelessness: The media, public attitudes and policy-making', in Hutson, S. and Clapham, D. (eds) *Homelessness: Public Policies and Private Troubles*, London: Cassell.

Liddiard, M. and Hutson, S. (1991) 'Homeless young people and runaways – agency definitions and processes', *Journal of Social Policy* 20, 3: 365–88.

Liebes, T. and Curran, J. (eds) (1998) *Media, Ritual and Identity*, London: Routledge.

Liebler, C. M. and Bendix, J. (1996) 'Old-growth forests on network news: News sources and the framing of an environmental controversy', *Journalism and Mass Communication Quarterly* 73, 1: 53–65.

Limoges, C. (1993) 'Expert knowledge and decision-making in controversy contexts', *Public Understanding of Science* 2: 417–26.

Lindzen, R. (1989) 'Some coolness concerning global warming', *Bulletin of the American Meteorological Society* 71: 288–99.

Linné, O. (1991) 'Journalistic practices and news coverage of environmental issues', *Nordicom Review of Nordic Mass Communication Research* 1: 1–7.

Lippman, W. (1922) *Public Opinion*, New York: Harcourt Brace.

Long, M. (1995) 'Scientific explanation in US newspaper science stories', *Public Understanding of Science* 4, 2: 119–30.

Lowe, P. and Morrison, D. (1984) 'Bad news or good news: Environmental politics and the mass media', *Sociological Review* 32, 1: 75–90.

Lowe, P., Clark, J., Seymour, S. and Ward, N. (1997) *Moralizing the Environment: Countryside Change, Farming and Pollution*, London: UCL Press.

Lucas, C. and Schmitz, C. (1988) 'Communications media and current-events knowledge among college students', *Higher Education* 17: 139–49.

Luhmann, N. (1982) *The Differentiation of Society*, trans. Holmes, S. and Larmore, C., New York: Columbia University Press.

Luhmann, N. (1995) *Die Soziologie des Riskos*, Berlin: De Gruyter.

Luke, T. W. (1987) 'Chernobyl: The packaging of transnational ecological disaster', *Critical Studies in Mass Communication* 4: 351–75.

Lundell, A. (1989) *Virus*, Chicago: Contemporary Books.

Lury, C. (1998) *Prosthetic Culture: Photography, Memory and Identity*, London: Routledge.

Lyons, J. (1977) *Semantics*, vol. 2, London: Cambridge University Press.

Lyons, W., Scheb III, J. and Richardson, L. (1995) *American Government: Politics and Political Culture*, Minneapolis, MN: West.

Lyotard, J. F. (1991) *The Inhuman: Reflections on Time*, trans. Bennington, G. and Bowlby, R., Cambridge: Polity.

McCoombs, M. (1981) 'Setting the agenda for agenda setting research', in Wilhoit, G. and de Bock, H. (eds) *Mass Communication Review Yearbook*, vol. 2, London: Sage.

McCoombs, M. and Shaw, D. (1972) 'The agenda-setting function of the mass media', *Public Opinion Quarterly* 36: 176–87.

McCormick, C. (1995) 'Domestic terrorism: The news as an incomplete record of violence against women', *Constructing Danger: The Mis/representation of Crime in the News*, Halifax, NS: Fernwood.

MacDonald, G. (1989) 'Scientific basis for the greenhouse effect', in Abrahamson, D. E. (ed.) *The Challenge of Global Warming*, Washington, DC: Island Press.

MacDougal, C. (1982) *Interpretative Reporting*, 8th edn, New York: Macmillan.

Macedo, S. (1990) *Liberal Virtues: Citizenship, Virtue, and Community in Liberal Constitutionalism*, Oxford: Clarendon.

MacGill, S. (1987) *Sellafield's Cancer-Link Controversy: The Politics of Anxiety*, London: Pion.

McKay, G. (ed.) (1998) *DiY Culture: Party and Protest in Nineties Britain*, London: Verso.

McLuhan, M. (1962) *The Gutenberg Galaxy: The Making of Typographic Man*, London: Routledge and Kegan Paul.

McLuhan, M. (1964) *Understanding Media: The Extensions of Man*, Harmondsworth: Penguin.

Macnaghten, P. and Urry, J. (1995) 'Towards a sociology of nature', *Sociology* 29: 203–20.

Macnaghten, P. and Urry, J. (1998) *Contested Natures*, London: Sage.

McNair, B. (1988) *Images of the Enemy*, London: Routledge.

McNair, B. (1994) *News and Journalism in the UK*, London: Routledge.

McNeish, W. (1999) 'Resisting Colonisation: the politics of anti-roads protesting', in Bagguley, P. and Hearn, J. (eds) *Transforming Politics: Power and Resistance*, London: Macmillan.

Madriz, E. (1997) *Nothing Bad Happens to Good Girls*, Berkeley, CA: University of California Press.

Maher, M. (1994) 'How news media frame the populations–environment connection', paper presented to the Media and Environment Conference of the Association for Education in Journalism and Mass Communication, Reno, NV, April.

Major, A. M. and Atwood, L. E. (1997) 'Changes in media credibility when a predicted disaster doesn't happen', *Journalism and Mass Communication Quarterly* 74, 4: 797–813.

Manabe, S. and Weatherald, R. (1967) 'Reduction in summer soil wetness induced by an increase in atmospheric carbon dioxide', *Science* 232: 626–8.

Marlier, E. (1992) 'Eurobarometer 35.1: opinions of Europeans on Biotechnology', in Durant, J. (ed.) *Biotechnology in Public: A Review of Recent Research*, London: Science Museum.

Massey, D. (1994) *Space, Place and Gender*, Cambridge: Polity.

Mazur, A. (1981) 'Media coverage and public opinion on scientific controversies', *Journal of Communication* 31, 2: 106–15.

Medical Officer of Health (1964a) *Annual Report*, Eston Urban District.

Medical Officer of Health (1964b) *Annual Report*, Stockton Borough.

Meijer, I. C. (1998) 'Advertising citizenship: An essay on the performative power of consumer culture', *Media, Culture and Society* 20: 235–49.

Melucci, A. (1994) 'A strange kind of newness: what's new in new social movements', in Larana, E. (ed.) *New Social Movements*, Philadelphia, PA: Temple University Press.

Melucci, A. (1996) *Challenging Codes: Collective Action in the Information Age*, Cambridge: Cambridge University Press

Meyers, M. (1995) 'News of battering', *Journal of Communication* 44, 2: 47–63.

Meyers, M. (1997) *News Coverage of Violence Against Women: Engendering Blame*, London: Sage.

Meyerson, G. and Rydin, Y. (1996) *The Language of Environment: A New Rhetoric*, London: UCL Press.

Meyrowitz, J. (1985) *No Sense of Place: The Impact of Electronic Media on Social Behavior*, New York: Oxford University Press.

Michaels, P. (1997) 'Top 10 global warming myths', *World Climate Report* 1, 5: 1.

Miller, D. (1993) 'Official sources and "primary definition": The case of Northern Ireland', *Media, Culture and Society* 15, 3: 385–406.

Miller, D. and Reilly, J. (1995) 'Marking and issue of food safety: The media, pressure groups, and the public sphere', in Maurer, D. and Sobal, J. (eds) *Eating Agendas: Food and Nutrition as Social Problems*, New York: Aldine de Gruyter.

Miller, M. (1997) 'Frame mapping and analysis of news coverage of contentious issues', *Social Science Computing Review* 15, 4: 367–78.

Miller, M. and Riechert, B. (1994) 'Identifying themes via concept mapping: A new method of content analysis', paper presented to the Association for Education in Journalism and Mass Communication, Atlanta, GA, August.

Miller, M. and Riechert, B. (1997) 'The interaction of interest group strategies and journalistic norms on news media framing of environmental issues', paper presented to the Media, Risk, and the Environment Conference, Cardiff University, July.

Miller, M. and Riechert, B. (forthcoming) 'Frame mapping: a quantitative method for investigating issues in the public sphere', in West, M. (ed.) *Computer Content Analysis: Theory, Methods, Applications*, Norwood, NJ: Ablex.

Miller, M., Boone, J. and Fowler, D. (1992) 'The emergence of greenhouse effect on the issue agenda: a news stream analysis', *News Computing Journal* 7, 4: 25–38.

Miller, M., Andsager, J. and Riechert, B. (1998) 'Framing the candidates in presidential primaries: Issues and images in press releases and news coverage', *Journalism and Mass Communication Quarterly* 75, 2: 312–24.

Mills, C. W. (1970) *The Sociological Imagination*, Harmondsworth: Penguin.

Milton, K. (1996) *Environmentalism and Cultural Theory: Exploring the Role of Anthropology in Environmental Discourse*, London: Routledge.

Mirrlees-Black, C., Mayhew, P. and Percy, A. (1996) *The 1996 British Crime Survey*, London: Stationery Office.

Moeller, S.D. (1999) *Compassion Fatigue*, New York: Routledge.

Moffatt, S., Phillimore, P., Bhopal, R. and Foy, C. (1995) '"If this is what it's doing to our washing, what is it doing to our lungs?" Industrial pollution and public understanding in North-East England', *Social Science and Medicine* 41: 883–91.

Moffatt, S., Bush, J., Prince, H., Dunn, C. and Howel, D. (1998) 'Community views on ill-health, air quality and expert information; the effects of proximity to heavy industry and poverty', *Epidemiology* 9: S142.

Molotch, H. and Lester, M. (1974) 'News as purposive behavior: On the strategic use of routine events, accidents and scandals', *American Sociological Review* 39, 1: 101–12.

Moore, B. and Singletary, M. (1985) 'Scientific sources' perceptions of network news accuracy', *Journalism Quarterly* 62, 4: 816–23.

Moorti, S. (1991) *Newspaper Coverage of Global Climate Change by Five Papers*, College Park, MD: Center for Global Change, University of Maryland.

Morley, D. and Robins, K. (1995) *Spaces of Identity: Global Media, Electronic Landscapes and Cultural Boundaries*, London: Routledge.

Mormont, M. and Dasnoy, C. (1995) 'Source strategies and the mediatization of climate change', *Media, Culture and Society* 17, 1: 49–64.

Murdoch, I. (1970) *The Sovereignty of Good*, London: Routledge and Kegan Paul.

Murdock, G. (1993) 'Communications and the constitution of modernity', *Media, Cuture and Society* 15, 4: 521–39.

Myers, G. (1994) *Words in Ads*, London: Edward Arnold.

Myerson, G. and Rydin, Y. (1996) *The Language of Enviroment: A New Rhetoric*, London: UCL Press.

Nas, M. and Dekker, P. (1995) 'Environmental attitudes and collective action in Europe: a comparative analysis of patterns of involvement in four countries', paper presented to the Second European Sociological Conference, Budapest, August.

Nash, J. and Kirsch, M. (1988) 'The discourse of medical science in the construction of consensus between corporation and community', *Medical Anthropology Quarterly* 14: 158–71.

National Safety Council and Enviromental Health Center (1994) *Reporting on Climate Change: Understanding the Science*, Washington, DC: National Safety Council.

Nature (1997) 'Caught napping by clones', *Nature* 385, 27 February: 753.

Nelkin, D. (1985) *Controversy: The Politics of Technical Decisions*, 2nd edn, London: Sage.

Nelkin, D. (1987) *Selling Science: How the Press Covers Science and Technology*, New York: W. H. Freeman.

Nelkin, D. (1995) *Selling Science: How the Press Covers Science and Technology*, revised edn, New York: W. H. Freeman

Nelkin, D. and Lindee, S. (1995) *The DNA Mystique: The Gene as a Cultural Icon*, New York: W. H. Freeman.

Nelkin, D. and Tancredi, L. (1994) *Dangerous Diagnostics: The Social Power of Biological Information*, 2nd edn, Chicago: University of Chicago Press.

Neuzil, M. and Kovarik, W. (1996) *Mass Media and Environmental Conflict: America's Green Crusades*, Thousand Oaks, CA: Sage.

Newcomb, H. M. and Hirsch, P. M. (1984) 'Television as a cultural forum: Implications for research', in Rowland, Jr, W. D. and Watkins, B. (eds) *Interpreting Television: Current Research Perspectives*, Beverly Hills: Sage.

Nimmo, D. (1985) *Nightly Horrors: Crisis Coverage by Television Network News*, Knoxville, TN: University of Tennessee Press.

Noelle-Neumann, E. (1984) *Spiral of Silence: Our Social Skin*, Chicago: University of Chicago Press.

Nohrstedt, S. (1993) 'Communicative action in the risk-society: Public relations strategies, the media and nuclear power', in Hansen, A. (ed.) *The Mass Media and Environmental Issues*, Leicester: Leicester University Press.

North, R. D. (1998) 'Reporting the environment: Single issue groups and the press', *Contemporary Issues in British Journalism*, The 1998 Vauxhall Lectures, Cardiff: Centre for Journalism Studies, Cardiff University.

Osborne, R. (1995) 'Crime and the media: From media studies to postmodernism', in Kidd-Hewitt, D. and Osbourne, R. (eds) *Crime and the Media: The Postmodern Spectacle*, London: Pluto.

Ostman, R. E. and Parker, J. L. (1986) 'A public's environmental information sources and evaluations of mass media', *Journal of Environmental Education* 18: 9–17.

Owen, J. B. (1997) 'Bovine Spongiform Encephalopathy: A review of causes and state of present knowledge', in Bristow, G. (ed.) *BSE: The Welsh Dimension*, Aberystwyth: Institute of Welsh Affairs.

Pain, R. (1991) 'Space, sexual violence and social control: Integrating geographical and feminist analyses of women's fear of crime', *Progress in Human Geography* 15, 4: 415–32.

Pain, R. (1993) 'Crime, social control and spatial constraint', unpublished PhD thesis, University of Edinburgh.

Pain, R. (1997) '"Old age" and ageism in urban research: The case of fear of crime', *International Journal of Urban and Regional Research* 21,1: 117–28.

Pain, S. (1990) 'BSE: What madness is this?', *New Scientist* 9 June: 32–4.

Parlour, J. W. and Schatzow, S. (1978) 'The mass media and public concern for environmental problems in Canada, 1960–1972', *International Journal of Environmental Studies* 13: 9–17.

Pêcheux, M. (1982) *Language, Semiotics and Ideology*, trans. Nagpal, H., London: Macmillan.

Phillimore, P. (1998) 'Uncertainty, reassurance and pollution: the politics of epidemiology in Teesside', *Health and Place* 4, 3: 203–12.

Phillimore, P. and Moffatt, S. (1994) 'Discounted knowledge: local experience, environmental pollution and health', in Popay, J. and Williams, G. (eds) *Researching the People's Health*, London: Routledge.

Phillimore, P. and Moffatt, S. (1999) 'Narratives of insecurity in Teesside: environmental politics and health risks', in Vail, J., Wheelock, J. and Hill, M. (eds) *Insecure Times: Living with Insecurity in Modern Society*, London: Routledge.

Phillimore, P. and Morris, D. (1991) 'Discrepant legacies: premature mortality in two industrial towns', *Social Science and Medicine* 33: 139–52.

Pless-Mulloli, T., Phillimore, P., Moffatt, S., Bhopal, R., Foy, C., Dunn, C. and Tate, J. (1998) 'Lung cancer, proximity to industry and poverty in northeast England', *Environmental Health Perspectives* 106, 4: 189–96.

Porritt, J. and Winner, D. (1988) *The Coming of the Greens*, London: Fontana.

Poster, M. (1995) 'Postmodern virtualities', *Body and Society* 1, 3/4: 79–95.

Powell, D. and Leiss, W. (1997) *Mad Cows and Mother's Milk: The Perils of Poor Risk Communication*, Montreal and Kingston: McGill-Queen's University Press.

President's Science Advisory Committee (PSAC) (1965) 'Restoring the quality of our environment', *Report of the Environmental Pollution Panel*, Washington, DC: PSAC.

Price, D. de Solla (1963) *Little Science, Big Science*, New York: Columbia University Press.

Propp, V. (1958) *Morphology of the Folk-Tale*, trans. Scott, L., Bloomington, IN: Indiana University Press.

Purdue, D. (1995) 'Whose knowledge counts? "Experts", "counter-experts" and the "lay-public"', *The Ecologist* 25, 5: 170–2.

Quirk, R., Greenbaum, S., Leech, G. and Svartvik, J. (1972) *A Grammar of Contemporary English*, London: Longman.

Rakow, L. and Kranich, K. (1991) 'Woman as sign in television news', *Journal of Communication* 41, 1: 8–23.

Randall, G. (1988) *No Way Home: Homeless Young People in Central London*, London: Centrepoint.

Ratzan, S. C. (ed.) (1998) *The Mad Cow Crisis: Health and the Public Good*, London: UCL Press.

Reese, S. (1997) 'Framing public life: A bridging model for media study', paper presented to Framing and the New Media Landscape, inaugural conference for the Center for Mass Communication Research, College of Journalism and Mass Communication, University of South Carolina, Columbia, SC, October.

Reicher, S. (1984) *The St Paul's Riot*, London: Wiley.

Rheinberger, H. (1995) 'Beyond nature and culture: A note on medicine in the age of molecular biology', *Science in Context* 8: 249–63.

Rheingold, H. (1994) *The Virtual Community: Finding Connection in a Computerised World*, London: Secker and Warburg.

Riechert, B. (1995) 'Science, society and the media: Associated Press coverage of the Human Genome Project', paper presented to the Eighteenth Annual Communications Research Symposium, University of Tennessee College of Communications, March.

Riechert, B. (1996) 'Advocacy group and news media framing of public policy issues: Frame mapping the wetlands debates', unpublished doctoral dissertation, University of Tennessee, Knoxville, TN.

Riechert, B. and Miller, M. (1997a) 'Computerized content analysis: Identifying themes and frames in text on pesticides, wetlands, and forest salvage', in Senecah, S. (ed.) *Proceedings of the Fourth Biennial Conference on Communication and Environment*, Syracuse, NY: State University of New York College of Environmental Science and Forestry.

Riechert, B. and Miller, M. (1997b) 'Swamped in politics: News coverage of wetlands in three presidential administrations', paper presented to the Association for Education in Journalism and Mass Communication, Chicago, August.

Robertson, G., Mash, M., Tiekner, L., Bird, J., Curtis, B. and Putnam, T. (eds) (1996) *FutureNatural: Nature/Science/Culture*, London: Routledge.

Robins, K. (1996) 'Cyberspace and the world we live in', in Dovey, J. (ed.) *Fractal Dreams: New Media in Social Context*, London: Lawrence and Wishart.

Roper, W. B. (1998) *Public Attitudes Toward Television and Other Mass Media*, New York: Roper Organization – Television Information Office.

Rose, H. (1994) *Love, Power and Knowledge*, Cambridge: Polity.

Rose, H. (2000) 'Risk, trust and scepticism in the age of new genetics', in Adam, B., Beck, U. and van Loon, J. (eds) *The Risk Society and Beyond: Critical Issues for Social Theory*, London: Sage.

Rossow, M. D. and Dunwoody, S. (1991) 'Inclusion of "useful" detail in newspaper coverage of a high-level nuclear waste siting controversy', *Journalism Quarterly* 68, 1/2: 87–100.

Rubin, D. M. (1987) 'How the news media reported on Three Mile Island and Chernobyl', *Journal of Communication* 37, 3: 42–57.

Rutherford, P. (1999) 'Ecological modernization and environmental risk', in Darier, E. (ed.) *Discourses of the Environment*, Oxford: Blackwell.

Ruthven, K. (1993) *Nuclear Criticism*, Melbourne, Vic.: Melbourne University Press.

Ryan, C. (1991) *Prime Time Activism: Media Strategies for Grassroots Organizing*, Boston, MA: South End Press.

Ryan, F. (1996) *Virus X: Understanding the Real Threat of the New Pandemic Plagues*, London: HarperCollins.

Sachsman, D. (1993) 'Communication between scientists and the media: Introducing the concepts of risk, risk analysis, and risk communication to journalists', paper presented to the International Congress on Health Effects of Hazardous Waste, Atlanta, GA, May.

Sachsman, D. B. (1976) 'Public relations influence on coverage of environment in San Francisco area', *Journalism Quarterly* 53, 1: 54–60.

Salomone, K. L., Greenberg, M. R., Sandman, P. M. and Sachsman, D. B. (1990) 'A question of quality: How journalists and news sources evaluate coverage of environmental risk', *Journal of Communication* 40, 4: 117–30.

Sandman, P. M. and Paden, M. (1979) 'At Three Mile Island', *Columbia Journalism Review* 18, 2: 43–58.

Sandman, P. M., Weinstein, N. D. and Klotz, M. L. (1987) 'Public response to risk from geological radon', *Journal of Communication* 37, 3: 93–108.

Sasson, T. (1995) *Crime Talk*, New York: Aldine du Gruyter.

Schlesinger, M. and Mitchell, J. F. B. (1985) 'Climate model simulations of the equilibrium climatic response to increased carbon dioxide', *Review of Geophysics* 25: 760–98.

Schlesinger, P. (1990) 'Rethinking the sociology of journalism: Source strategies and the limits of media centrism', in Ferguson, M. (ed.) *Public Communication: The New Imperatives*, London: Sage.

Schlesinger, P. , Dobash, R. E., Dobash, R. P. and Weaver, C. K. (1992) *Women Viewing Violence*, London: British Film Institute.

Schneider, S. (1989) *Global Warming: Are We Entering the Greenhouse Century?*, San Francisco: Sierra Club Books.

Schneider, S. (1990a) 'Cooling it: the global warming debate has gotten out of hand', *World Monitor*, July: 30–8.

Schneider, S. (1990b) 'The global warming debate heats up: an analysis and perspective', *Bulletin of American Meteorological Society*, 71, 9: 1292–304.

Schoenfeld, A. C. (1980) 'Newspersons and the environment today', *Journalism Quarterly* 57, 3: 456–62.

Schoenfeld, A. C., Meier, R. F. and Griffin, R. J. (1979) 'Constructing a social problem: The press and the environment', *Social Problems* 27, 1: 38–61.

Schon, D. A. and Rien, M. (1994) *Frame Reflection: Toward the Resolution of Intractable Policy Controversies*, New York: Basic Books.

Schramm, W. (1949) 'The nature of news', in W. Schramm (ed.) *Mass Communications*, Urbana, IL: University of Illinois Press.

Segal, L. (1994) *Straight Sex: The Politics of Pleasure*, London: Virago.

Senecah, S. (ed.) (1997) *Proceedings of the Fourth Biennial Conference on Communication and Environment*, Syracuse, NY: State University of New York College of Environmental Science and Forestry.

Shanahan, J. (1993) 'Television and the cultivation of environmental concern: 1988–92', in Hansen, A. (ed.) *The Mass Media and Environmental Issues*, Leicester: Leicester University Press.

Shanahan, J. and McComas, K. (1997) 'Television's portrayal of the environment: 1991–1995', *Journalism and Mass Communication Quarterly* 74, 1: 147–59.

Shaw, D. L. (1967) 'News bias and the telegraph: A study in historical change', *Journalism Quarterly* 44: 3–12, 31.

Shields, R. (1991) *Places on the Margin: Alternative Geographies of Modernity*, London: Routledge.

Shilling, C. (1993) *The Body and Social Theory*, London: Sage.

Shoemaker, P. and Reese, S. (1996) *Mediating the Message: Theories of Influence on Mass Media Content*, 2nd edn, White Plains, NY: Longman.

Sibbison, J. (1988) 'Dead fish and red herrings: How the EPA pollutes the news', *Columbia Journalism Review* November/December: 25–8.

Sigal, L. V. (1973) *Reporters and Officials*, Lexington, MA: Lexington Books.

Simon, A. F. (1997) 'Television news and international earthquake relief', *Journal of Communication* 47, 3: 82–93.

Singer, E. and Endreny, P. (1987) 'Reporting hazards: Their benefits and costs', *Journal of Communication* 37, 3: 10–26.

Singer, E. and Endreny, P. (1993) *Reporting on Risk: How the Mass Media Portray Accidents, Diseases, Disasters, and Other Hazards*, New York: Russell Sage Foundation.

Skidmore, P. (1998) 'Gender and the agenda: Reporting of child sexual abuse in the UK', in Carter, C., Branston, G. and Allan, S. (eds) *News, Gender and Power*, London: Routledge.

Slovic, P. (1992) 'Perceptions of enviromental hazards: psychological perspectives', *Advances in Psychology* 96: 223–48.

Smith, C. (1992) *Media and Apocalypse: News Coverage of the Yellowstone Forest Fires, Exxon Valdez Oil Spill, and Loma Prieta Earthquake*, Westport, CT: Greenwood.

Smith, J., Guilford, S. and O'Sullivan, A. (1998) *The Family Background of Homeless Young People*, London: Policy Studies Centre.

Solesbury, W. (1976) 'The environmental agenda', *Public Administration* 54: 379–97.

Sood, R., Stockdale, G. and Rogers, E. M. (1987) 'How the news media operate in natural disasters', *Journal of Communication* 37, 3: 27–41.

Soothill, K. and Walby, S. (1991) *Sex Crime in the News*, London: Routledge.

Soper, K. (1995) *What is Nature?*, Oxford: Blackwell.

Sparks, R. (1992a) *Television and the Drama of Crime: Moral Tales and the Place of Crime in Public Life*, Buckingham: Open University Press.

Sparks, R. (1992b) 'Reason and unreason in Left Realism: Some problems in the constitution of the fear of crime', in. Matthews, R. and Young, J. (eds) *Issues in Realist Criminology*, London: Sage.

Spector, M. and Kitsuse, J. I. (1987) *Constructing Social Problems*, New York: Aldine de Gruyter.

Spinardi, G. (1997) 'Aldermaston and British nuclear weapons development: Testing the "Zuckerman Thesis"', *Social Studies of Science* 27: 547–82.

Spranger, M. (1989) 'Role of education in policies and programmes dealing with global climate change', paper presented to the international conference on Adaptive Options and Policy Implications of Global Climate Change, Miami, FL, December.

Stacey, M. (1992) *Changing Human Reproduction: Social Science Perspectives*, London: Sage.

Stanko, E. (1990) *Everyday Violence*, London: Pandora.

Stanko, E. (1996) 'Warnings to women: Police advice and women's safety in Britain', *Violence Against Women* 2: 5–24.

Stanko, E. (1997) 'Safety talk: Conceptualizing women's risk assessment as a "technology of the soul"', *Theoretical Criminology* 1, 4: 479–501.

Stanko, E. (1998) 'Taking stock: What do we know about violence?', Uxbridge: ESRC Violence Research Programme.

Stanko, E., Crisp, D., Hale, C. and Lucraft, H. (1998) *Counting the Costs*, Swindon: Crime Concern.

Steiner, L. (1998) 'Power at work: Accounting for discrimination in the newsroom', in Carter, C., Branston, G. and Allan, S. (eds) *News, Gender and Power*, London: Routledge.

Stephens, M. and Edison, B. G. (1982) 'News media coverage of issues during the accident at Three Mile Island', *Journalism Quarterly* 59, 2: 199–204.

Stevenson, N. (1995) *Understanding Media Cultures: Social Theory and Mass Communication*, London: Sage.

Stocking, H. and Leonard, J. P. (1990) 'The greening of the media', *Columbia Journalism Review* December: 37–44.

Sudnow, D. (1967) *Passing On: The Social Organization of Dying*, Englewood Cliffs, NJ: Prentice Hall.

Sullivan, K. (1998) 'Nuclear monsters', unpublished PhD thesis, Lancaster University.

Swisher, K. and Reese, S. (1992) 'The smoking and health issue in newspapers: Influence of regional economies, the tobacco institute, and news objectivity', *Journalism Quarterly* 69: 987–1000.

Szerszynski, B., Lash, S. and Wynne, B. (1996) 'Introduction: ecology, realism and the social sciences', in Lash, S., Szerszynski, B. and Wynne, B. (eds) *Risk, Environment and Modernity: Towards a New Ecology*, London: Sage.

Tankard, J. and Ryan, M. (1974) 'News source perception of accuracy of science coverage', *Journalism Quarterly* 51: 219–334.

Tankard, J., Hendrickson, L., Silverman, J., Bliss, K. and Ghanem, S. (1991) 'Media frames: Approaches to conceptualization and measurement', paper presented to the Association for Education in Journalism and Mass Communication, Communication Theory and Methodology Division, Boston, MA.

Taubes, G. (1995) 'Epidemiology faces its limits', *Science* 269, 14 July.

Taylor, C. (1989) *Sources of the Self: The Making of the Modern Identity*, Cambridge: Cambridge University Press.

Teesside Environmental Epidemiology Study (TEES) (1995) *Health, Illness and the Environment in Teesside and Sunderland: A Report*, University of Newcastle upon Tyne.

Terragni, F. (1992) *Bioethics in Europe: The Final Report*, Luxembourg: European Parliament, Directorate General for Research.

Thompson, J. B. (1995) *The Media and Modernity: A Social Theory of the Media*, Cambridge: Polity.

Thompson, L. (1994) 'The breast cancer gene: A woman's dilemma', *Time* 17 January: 38.

Thrift, N. (1996) *Spatial Formations*, London: Sage.

Tichener, P. (1970) 'Communication accuracy in science reporting', *Journalism Quarterly* 47: 673–83.

Toogood, M. and Myers, G. (1998) 'Banal globalism: Images, actions and frames in a survey of broadcast output', unpublished paper, Centre for the Study of Environmental Change and Department of Linguistics, Lancaster University.

Trumbo, C. (1996) 'Constructing climate change: claims and frames in US news coverage of an environmental issue', *Public Understanding of Science* 5, 3: 269–83.

Tuchman, G. (1976) 'The news' manufacture of sociological data (Comment on Danzger, ASR [American Sociological Review] October 1975)', *American Sociological Review* 41: 1065–7.

Tuchman, G. (1978) *Making News: A Study in the Construction of Reality*, New York: Free Press.

Tulloch, J. (1993) 'Policing the public sphere: The British machinery of news management', *Media, Culture and Society* 15, 3: 363–84.

Tulloch, J., Lupton, D., Blood, W., Tulloch, M., Jennett, C. and Enders, M. (1998) *Fear of Crime,* (2 vols), Canberra: National Campaign Against Violence and Crime Unit, Attorney General's Department.

Tunstall, J. (1996) *Newspaper Power*, Oxford: Clarendon.

Turk, J. (1986) 'Information subsidies and media content: A study of public relations influence on the news', *Journalism Monographs* 100.

Turk, J. (1988) 'Public relations' influence on the news', in Hiebert, R. E. (ed.) *Precision Public Relations*, White Plains, NY: Longman.

Turner, B. S. (1995) *Medical Power and Social Knowledge*, 2nd edn, London: Sage.

Turney, J. (1998) *Frankenstein's Footsteps: Science, Genetics and Popular Culture*, New Haven, CT: Yale University Press.

Urry, J. (1990) *The Tourist Gaze*, London: Sage.

Urry, J. (1992) 'The tourist gaze and the "environment"', *Theory, Culture and Society* 9: 1–26.

Urry, J. (1999) *Sociology Beyond Societies*, London: Routledge.

Valentine, H. (1989) 'The geography of women's fear', *Area* 21, 4: 385–90.

van Loon, J. (2000) 'Virtual risks in an age of cybernetic reproduction', in Adam, B., Beck. U. and van Loon, J. (eds) *The Risk Society and Beyond: Critical Issues for Social Theory*, London: Sage.

van Loon, J. and Sabelis, I. (1997) 'Recycling time: The temporal complexity of waste management', *Time and Society* 6, 2/3: 287–306.

van Zoonen, L. (1994) *Feminist Media Studies*, London: Sage.

van Zoonen, L. (1998) '"One of the girls?" The changing gender of journalism', in Carter, C., Branston G. and Allan, S. (eds) *News, Gender and Power*, London: Routledge.

Vincent, R., Crow, B. and Davis, D. (1989) 'When technology fails: The drama of airline crashes in network television news', *Journalism Monographs* 117.

Viscusi, K. (1992) *Smoking: Making the Risky Decision*, New York: Oxford University Press.

Voumvakis, S. and Ericson, R. (1984) 'News accounts of attacks on women: A comparison of three Toronto newspapers', Research Report of the Centre of Criminology, Toronto: University of Toronto.

Waddington, D., Wykes, M. and Critcher, C. (1991) *Split at the Seams*, Buckingham: Open University Press.

Walklate, S. (1997) 'Risk and criminal victimisation: A modernist dilemma?', *British Journal of Criminology* 37, 1: 35–46.

Wall, D. (1999) *Earth First! and the Anti-Roads Movement: Radical Environmentalism and Comparative Social Movements*, London: Routledge

Wardhaugh, J. (1996) '"Homeless in Chinatown: Deviance and social control in cardboard city', *Sociology* 30, 4: 701–16.

Weart, S. R. (1988) *Nuclear Fear: A History of Images*, Cambridge, MA: Harvard University Press.

Weaver, C. K. (1995) 'Representations of men's violence against women: Audio-visual texts and their reception', unpublished DPhil dissertation, University of Stirling.

Weaver, C. K. (1998) '*Crimewatch UK*: Keeping women off the streets', in Carter, C., Branston, G. and Allan, S. (eds) *News, Gender and Power*, London: Routledge.

Weedon, C. (1987) *Feminist Practice and Poststructuralist Theory*, Oxford: Blackwell.

Weedon, C. (1994) 'Feminism and the principles of post-structuralism', in Corner, J. (ed) *Cultural Theory and Popular Culture*, London: Harvester.

Welsh, I. (2000) 'Desiring risk: Nuclear myths and the social selection of risk', in Adam, B., Beck, U. and van Loon, J. (eds) *The Risk Society and Beyond: Critical Issues for Social Theory*, London: Sage.

Wheale, P. and McNally, R. (1995) *Animal Genetic Engineering: Of Genes, Oncomice and Men*, London: Pluto.

Wicken, A. and Buck, S. (1964) *Report on a Study of Environmental Factors associated with Lung Cancer and Bronchitis Mortality in Areas of North-East England*, London: Tobacco Research Council.

Wiegman, O., Gutteling, J. M., Boer, H. and Houwen, R. J. (1989) 'Newspaper coverage of hazards and the reactions of readers', *Journalism Quarterly* 66, 4: 846–52.

Wilkins, L. (1990) 'Taking the future seriously', *Journal of Mass Media Ethics* 5: 88–101.

Wilkins, L. (1993) 'Between facts and values: Print media coverage of the greenhouse effect, 1987–1990', *Public Understanding of Science* 2, 2: 71–84.

Wilkins, L. and Patterson, P. (1987) 'Risk analysis and the construction of news', *Journal of Communication* 37, 3: 80–92.

Wilkins, L. and Patterson, P. (1990) 'Risky business: Covering slow-onset hazards as rapidly developing news', *Political Communication and Persuasion* 7, 1: 11–23.

Wilkins, L. and Patterson, P. (1991) 'Science as symbol: the media chills the greenhouse effect', in Wilkins, L. and Patterson, P. (eds) *Risky Business: Communicating Issues of Science, Risk and Public Policy*, Westport, CT: Greenwood.

Williams, R. (1961) *The Long Revolution*, London: Pelican.

Williams, R. (1974) *Television: Technology and Cultural Form*, London: Fontana.

Williams, R. (1977) *Marxism and Literature*, Oxford: Oxford University Press.

Wilson, A. (1992) *The Culture of Nature: North American Landscape from Disney to the Exxon Valdez*, Cambridge, MA: Blackwell.

Wilson, D. (1984) *Pressure: The A–Z of Campaigning in Britain*, London: Heinemann.

Wilson, K. (1995) 'Mass media as sources of global warming knowledge', *Mass Communication Review* 22, 1: 75–89.

Wilson, K. (1999) 'Drought, debate, and uncertainty: Reporters' misconceptions about climate change', *Public Understanding of Science* 8, 3.

Wober, M. and Gunter, B. (1990) *Crime Reconstruction Programmes: Viewing Experiences in Three Regions, Linked with Perceptions of and Reactions to Crime*, London: Independent Broadcasting Authority (IBA) Research Paper.

Woodward, K. (1991) 'Aging and its discontents: Freud and other fictions', Bloomington, IN: Indiana University Press.

Woolacott, M. (1997) 'The future is behind us', *Guardian* 26 February.

Wykes, M. (1995) 'Passion, marriage and murder: Analysing the press discourse', in Dobash, R. E., Dobash, R. P. and Noaks, L. (eds) *Gender and Crime*, Cardiff: University of Wales Press.

Wykes, M. (1998) 'A family affair: The press, sex and the Wests', in Carter, C., Branston, G. and Allan, S. (eds) *News, Gender and Power*, London: Routledge.

Wynne, B. (1992) 'Misunderstood misunderstanding; social identities and public uptake of science', *Public Understanding of Science* 1, 3: 281–304.

Wynne, B. (1996a) 'May the sheep safely graze? A reflexive view of the expert–lay knowledge divide', in Lash, S., Szerszynski, B. and Wynne, B. (eds) *Risk, Environment and Modernity: Towards a New Ecology*, London: Sage.

Wynne, B. (1996b) 'Patronising Joe Public', *The Times Higher* 12 April: 13.

Yearley, S. (1994) 'Social movements and environmental change', in Redclift, M. and Benton, T. (eds) *Social Theory and the Global Environment*, London: Routledge.

Young, A. (1991) *Femininity in Dissent*, London: Routledge.

Zechendorf, B. (1994) 'What the public thinks about biotechnology', *Bio/technology* 12, September: 870–5.

Index